# Pluralism in Economics

# Pluralism in Economics

## New Perspectives in History and Methodology

*Edited by*

Andrea Salanti

*Professor of Economics, University of Bergamo, Italy*

*and*

Ernesto Screpanti

*Professor of Economics, University of Siena, Italy*

**Edward Elgar**

Cheltenham, UK • Brookfield, US

Published by
Edward Elgar Publishing Limited
8 Lansdown Place
Cheltenham
Glos GL50 2HU
UK

Edward Elgar Publishing Company
Old Post Road
Brookfield
Vermont 05036
US



A catalogue record for this book is available from the British Library

**Library of Congress Cataloguing in Publication Data**
Pluralism in economics : new perspectives in history and methodology
/Andrea Salanti and Ernesto Screpanti.
Includes bibliographical references.
1. Economics—Congresses. 2. Economics—Methodology—Congresses.
3. Economics—Philosophy—Congresses. 4. Economics—History—Congresses. I. Salanti, Andrea, 1950– . II. Screpanti, Ernesto 1948– .
HB21.P55 1997
330—dc20 96–15996
CIP



ISBN 1 85898 140 9

Printed and bound in Great Britain by
Hartnolls Limited, Bodmin, Cornwall

Typeset by Manton Typesetters, 5–7 Eastfield Road, Louth, Lincolnshire LN11 7AJ, UK.

# Contents

# Contributors

**Riccardo Bellofiore**, University of Bergamo, Italy
**Eugenio Benedetti**, University of Padua, Italy
**Marina Bianchi**, University of Cassino, Italy
**Bruce Caldwell**, University of North Carolina, Greensboro, USA
**John B. Davis**, Marquette University, USA
**Robert Delorme**, University of Versailles and CEPREMAP, France
**Sheila C. Dow**, University of Stirling, UK
**Carlo A. Favero**, Bocconi University, Italy
**D. Wade Hands**, University of Puget Sound, USA
**Shaun P. Hargreaves Heap**, University of East Anglia, UK
**Geoffrey M. Hodgson**, University of Cambridge, UK
**Bruna Ingrao**, University of Rome 'La Sapienza', Italy
**Heinz D. Kurz**, University of Graz, Austria
**Maurice Lagueux**, University of Montreal, Canada
**Tony Lawson**, University of Cambridge, UK
**Uskali Mäki**, Erasmus University Rotterdam, The Netherlands
**Neil De Marchi**, Duke University, USA
**Maria Cristina Marcuzzo**, University of Rome 'La Sapienza', Italy
**Philip Mirowski**, University of Notre Dame, USA
**Robert Nadeau**, University of Québec, Montreal, Canada
**Andrea Salanti**, University of Bergamo, Italy
**Neri Salvadori**, University of Pisa, Italy
**Warren J. Samuels**, Michigan State University, East Lansing, USA
**Roberto Scazzieri**, University of Bologna, Italy and Claire Hall, Cambridge
**Augusto Schianchi**, University of Parma, Italy
**Ernesto Screpanti**, University of Siena, Italy
**Stefano Solari**, University of Padua, Italy
**E. Roy Weintraub**, Duke University, USA

# Acknowledgements

Essays and comments collected in this volume were originally presented at the conference on 'Pluralism in Economics: Theory, History and Methodology', held in Bergamo in May 1994 and jointly organized by EAEPE and the Department of Economics of the University of Bergamo.

The editors would like to thank the other members of the organizing committee as well as all the participants for their valuable contributions,[1] and, last but not least, Ms Laura Capelli of the secretarial staff of the Department of Economics for her invaluable help.

Financial support from CNR (the Italian National Research Council), EAEPE (the European Association for Evolutionary Political Economy), MURST (the Italian Ministry for University and Scientific Research) and the Department of Economics of the University of Bergamo is also gratefully acknowledged.

## NOTE

1. At the same conference we had a round table on 'Pluralism in Editing Economic Journals'. Papers by Duccio Cavalieri and Riccardo Faucci, Daniel Hausman, Roger Backhouse and John Davis, originally prepared for that meeting, are now published in *History of Economic Ideas*, **2** (3), 1994, pp. 61–128.

# Introduction

## Andrea Salanti

The origins of the recent renewal of interest in economic methodology may be variously explained. However, it is unquestionable that a significant characteristic of the huge amount of literature on economic methodology that has appeared in the last two decades[1] is the recurrent plea for a kind of methodological inquiry that pays much more attention to what economists really practise or practised concerning methodology (as opposed to what they are or were merely preaching). As I have pointed out on a previous occasion (cf. Salanti, 1989) and as Boylan and O'Gorman (1995, pp. 27–35) have perceptively noted more recently, strictly connected with such a proposal we find the typical post-positivistic consciousness of the impossibility of solving demarcation and justification problems (and, consequently, of the inexistence of an ultimate criterion for the choice between competing theories) together with a strong sense of disillusionment about the possibility of applying to economics (and to other disciplines, for that matter) Popperian falsificationism or any other prescriptive methodology suggested during the 'growth of knowledge' debate.

Such a dissatisfaction has prompted a number of attempts to develop alternative approaches to economic methodology. According to Boylan and O'Gorman (1995, p. 29),

> These current developments have propelled us into what Caldwell has called 'a more pluralistic age' (Caldwell 1989: 14). This is for him very good news, but as he also perceptively notes the bad news is that a pluralistic environment is very unsettling. As he succinctly states: 'Everyone agrees that we are better off without the Puritanical rigidity of positivism, but is a methodology of free love much better?' (ibid.: 14). The central question on the economic methodologist's agenda is: what lies beyond positivism, more particularly where are current developments of the post-positivist era taking us?

The various essays and comments in this collection deal precisely with this central question, focusing on the various meanings and consequences of pluralist approaches to the history and methodology of economics.

In this respect it must be noted from the outset that the locution 'methodological pluralism' was originally proposed by Bruce Caldwell (1982, ch. 13

and 1988) as a label for his own preferred approach to economic methodology, while the term 'pluralism' is here used in a broader sense. In this way I hope to overcome the confusion of terminology applied to approaches in many ways similar to Caldwell's but variously christened by their authors,[2] and hope also to catch a common pluralist attitude shared by scholars adopting widely different perspectives.

In the following sections, commenting upon the essays in this collection, we will see that pluralism in history and methodology can be advocated on the basis of at least two different perspectives. One is offered by those who, conscious of the difficulties encountered by all traditional empiricist methodologies as well as by recent attempts to reconstruct an epistemological framework in the same tradition, are nevertheless not prepared to abandon any hope of obtaining fruitful advances in that direction: this is because they are not prepared to withdraw from the belief that the world 'out there' must be, after all, a determining factor of our scientific knowledge. They are not prepared, in other words, to embrace the view that what comes to be scientific knowledge can be ultimately reduced to (and explained uniquely by means of) the sociological aspects of the scientific enterprise[3] and/or the most successful rhetorical devices employed in scientific literature.

Another perspective on pluralism is supported by those who endorse, to use the title of a paper by Roger Backhouse (1992), the 'constructivist critique of economic methodology'. Among economists this approach is mainly known through the works of Donald McCloskey (1983, 1985 and, more recently, 1994), who publicized it under the heading of 'the rhetoric of economics', even if – as pointed out by Roy Weintraub (1992, p. 53) – it would be better thought of as 'the set theoretic union of philosophical pragmatism, post-modernist literary theory, post-modern historiography and rhetoric'.

In spite of the many points of disagreement between the adherents of these two different perspectives (and among these adherents themselves, for that matter), disagreement that has given rise to a number of intense debates over the last decade,[4] the issue of pluralism seems capable of fostering some convergence between them. Perhaps this is due, as Caldwell has properly pointed out, to the fact that

> The pluralist believes that the primary goal of methodological work is to reveal the strengths and weaknesses of various research programs in economics. Many tools of criticism are employed, and the focus is on the practice of economists. … The goals of pluralism *are* modest. Methodologists are not set up as experts offering advice to economists on how to do their science. Methodologists do not try to solve the demarcation problem, or the theory choice problem, or the problem of truth. Rather, methodologists try, together with their colleagues in history, sociology, and rhetoric of science, to enable us to reach a better understanding of

> the science of economics. This is a modest goal. But it is also an achievable one. And it finally provides an answer to the question that has gone too long unanswered among methodologists: What is the purpose of our work? (Caldwell, 1988, p. 243, italics in the original)

Whether the various contributions to this collection help to answer this last question posed by Caldwell is left to the judgement of the reader, but at the first blush I would doubt it, because the implicit answers appear to me to be still too diverse to provide the basis for a general consensus. As organizer of the conference from which the present volume comes forth, I would be content if we succeed in prompting some clarification as well as in pointing out the necessity of further reflection on the meaning and content of methodological pluralism

## DOES METAPHYSICS MATTER?

The first part opens with three chapters dealing with the possible ontological foundations of pluralist approaches to methodology. Tony Lawson reproposes his own preference for a 'transcendental realist metaphysics of science' derived from Bhaskar's views and advocates a normative role for philosophy when applied to the study of scientific practice. At a methodological level, however, he limits himself to the rejection of methodological monism, suggesting the necessity of approaching the objects of social sciences in different ways to those of natural science. He ends up, therefore, by advocating methodological pluralism in the traditional sense of the term.

Uskali Mäki tries to set to rights the different meanings of pluralism. In particular, he is concerned with the possibility of advocating pluralism about theories while rejecting ontological and veristic pluralism and identifying different degrees of theoretical pluralism. Through a number of definitions, he comes to the conclusion that theoretical pluralism should be always endorsed with some qualifications about the particular epistemic situation that can justify it.

In contrast with Lawson and Mäki (who, despite some differences, both start from a realist perspective), Eugenio Benedetti and Stefano Solari claim from the outset that in their opinion 'no metaphysical realism is acceptable' and then sketch their own plea for 'a hermeneutical approach based on the analysis of the cognitive substrate of economic theory' which, in its turn, determines different levels of description. Such different levels of description, according to the authors, carry with them different theories originating from, among other things, ontological discrepancies. Consequently, their main conclusion is that 'pluralism is not only possible but necessary in economics'.

Even such a very brief account of the content of these chapters suffices to show how different conclusions about the desirable degree of pluralism emerge from different ontological (or, if you prefer, metaphysical) perspectives. This is precisely the result that I thought might emerge when I invited the above-mentioned authors to the conference.

Somewhat surprisingly, commenting upon these chapters, Robert Nadeau maintains that economics has nothing to gain from metaphysics and hermeneutics. In a sense he may be right, but then – if the underlying reason is simply that philosophy 'cannot itself produce any new economic knowledge' – I suspect that one could equally maintain that economics has nothing to gain from economic methodology either. It may well be that economists' (inevitably approximate) discussions about ontology and metaphysics have upset a learned philosopher, but on closer scrutiny it appears that the real bone of contention between Nadeau and economists engaged in ontological analyses lies with what the three chapters, according to Nadeau himself, share in common, that is 'that they explicitly suggest that we forego traditional economic methodology, or they at least leave aside momentarily this traditional approach to science to do something other than methodology'.[5]

Arguments for and against hermeneutic approaches will reappear here and there in a number of other chapters and comments in this collection (including the Afterword by my co-editor), so I think that it would be out of place to add here further comments of mine, so that the final judgement, at this point, is left to the reader. My only two observations on the exchange between Lawson, Mäki, Benedetti & Solari and Nadeau are that it confirms: (1) what I pointed out in the first edition, namely that the disenchantment about the possibility of solving traditional methodological problems such as demarcation and theory choice is one of the primary sources of pleas for methodological pluralism, and (2) the apparent correlation between the preferred metaphysics and the degree of methodological pluralism that is argued for.[6]

My impression is reinforced by the content of the following two chapters by Warren Samuels and Sheila Dow. They address the issue at stake in a more direct and explicit way, but nevertheless ontological considerations play a significant role in reaching their respective conclusions. Samuels's chapter is a real summa of all the arguments which can be produced in support of methodological pluralism from a 'relativist' stance (as Riccardo Bellofiore does not fail to note in his comment), whereas Dow is prepared to adhere to methodological pluralism only on the basis of an 'open-system epistemology'. No wonder, therefore, that the most ardent and unreserved advocacy of pluralism is made by Warren Samuels, while I must confess to have been somewhat surprised by the accommodating attitude displayed by Caldwell in his comment.[7]

## METHODOLOGICAL PLURALISM AS A RESPONSE TO THE COMPLEXITY OF ECONOMIC SYSTEMS

The notion of an open system employed by Dow (who, as pointed out by Bruce Caldwell, takes it from Lawson's views on the nature of the subject-matter of social sciences) introduces the idea of methodological pluralism as a proper device for dealing with the complexity of the object(s) of economic analysis. This idea is shared by the authors of the last three chapters in the first part of the volume, even if they differ in their identification of the specific reasons of such a complexity.

Robert Delorme, drawing his reflections 'from the standpoint of research practice in the economic discipline', identifies pluralism as a consequence of radical uncertainty as well as a by-product of procedural rationality and complexity. Geoffrey Hodgson grounds his confidence in 'theoretical' pluralism on his preference for biological (instead of mechanistic) metaphors in economics and finds the internal lack of consensus within biology quite refreshing in comparison with the increasing 'standardization of thought' typical of current economics. Finally, Roberto Scazzieri argues that (some) economists try to make economic processes suitable to theoretical investigations by devising 'economic structures', that is abstract representations of 'virtual processes' which constitute the immediate counterpart of any analytical representation, so that the necessity of theoretical pluralism emerges quite straightforwardly as a consequence of the plurality of possible representations of this kind.

All the discussants (Schianchi, Mirowski and Hands) dissent, more or less strongly, from the arguments set forth by the authors of the chapters they are commenting upon, so that one might well think that these exchanges simply show how complex it is to deal with complexity. In my opinion, however, such criticisms (though different in each particular case) signal the existence of a real and serious problem, that I would summarize as follows: those who advocate (theoretical) pluralism on the basis of the complexity of the phenomena to be explained are eventually forced to endorse, in one way or another, the view of scientific theories as 'mirrors of nature'. In doing so, apart from having to defend themselves from the usual postmodernist critiques, they have to deal with the requests (by possibly more sympathetic readers) for clearer definitions of their conceptions of 'correspondence', 'explanation', 'meaning', 'representation', 'truth' (among other things). This would be a Herculean task for any professional philosopher, so we can just imagine the daunting prospect for the mere economist, trying to deal with all these issues at the same time.

## CASE STUDIES

The second part of the collection includes six case studies which deal with quite diverse issues but have in common the pluralist attitude endorsed by their authors in one way or another among those detected in the previous part of the collection.

Marina Bianchi and Neil De Marchi provide a critique of Stigler and Becker's (1977) reductionist attempt to explain apparently irrational choices, seemingly due to changes in tastes, by means of a special version of the standard consumer's theory based on a modified utility function. They argue that the process of a consumer's choice involves his confrontation with novelty and changes, i.e. factors that can be better dealt with through a more sensitive analysis of consumer's attitudes and goals.

Wade Hands reconstructs Frank Knight's philosophical positions, pointing out a number of elements (his opposition to positivism and scientism, together with his recognition of the theory-ladenness of empirical observations and of the importance of the social aspect of human knowledge) that appear to be consistent with some more recent contextualist perspectives. Nonetheless Knight never endorsed theoretical pluralism and this, according to Hands, shows the necessity for further reflection about the common presumption of the inevitability of theoretical pluralism for those who are sympathetic to contemporary forms of contextualism.

In recent years Roy Weintraub has been one of the most effective and enthusiastic supporters of a contextualist approach to the history of economics. His chapter in this volume is meant to show that, precisely because economists continuously recreate the past history of their discipline for a number of contingent reasons (and not only when they are explicitly engaged in studying the history of economics, but also when they appeal to the past in order to justify their current research), the judgement 'is a precursor of' can by no means be interpreted as a transitive relation.

Heinz Kurz and Neri Salvadori, on the contrary, are not particularly interested in more contextualized histories of economics. They take the 'Cambridge controversy' on capital theory in the 1960s and 1970s as an example of economic debates arising from the possibility of having a plurality of theory within economics. Their interest in theoretical pluralism seems to emerge mainly from their disappointment in finding that propositions (about the neoclassical relationship between the quantity of an input used in production and its own price) that have been conclusively shown to be false are nevertheless still assumed by so many economists.

Another contribution arising from a clearly expressed dissatisfaction with the usual mainstream approach to the problem of testing the validity of theoretical propositions is provided by Philip Mirowski. The target of his criticism is the absence of any effort within the economic profession to estimate the quantitative errors involved in repeated econometric estimations of the same 'constant'. Mirowski attempts to lay on some meta-analysis of applied econometrics, using Birge's ratios[8] to evaluate the consistency of different estimations of the same parameter in a number of relevant cases, and finds that comparison with other disciplines (like physics or behavioural psychology) is quite disappointing.

The last chapter in the second part is by Shaun Hargreaves Heap. Differently from the other authors in this volume, he does not deal with theoretical, methodological, epistemological or even ontological pluralism, but with a possible justification of political commitment to pluralism. He is interested in singling out a universalizable principle of justice (or, if you prefer, of fairness) to be applied even to a society where people 'agree only to disagree' and therefore cannot rely on free market mechanisms. Such a principle, according to the author, is provided by a rule of 'equal relative concessions'. It is not clear to me (nor to the discussant, for that matter) if such a rule could really avoid any interpersonal comparison of utility and I guess that Hargreaves Heap's analysis needs to be further refined. In any case he succeeds in showing that under the heading of 'pluralism' we may put a set of questions even wider than the already large enough set that we are accustomed to consider (of which the above-mentioned case studies represent nothing but a very incomplete and disordered, albeit hopefully interesting, sample).

## FINAL REMARKS

As we have seen, all people interested in economic methodology seem to be, in a broad sense, ready to endorse one kind or another of 'pluralism', but as soon as we ask them to specify what they mean by this term, we discover a puzzling array of quite different answers. The sole discernible distinction seems to be between those authors who are sympathetic to sociological, hermeneutical and/or other post-modernist approaches and those who (in spite of the well-known and by no means negligible difficulties of traditional methodologies in dealing with – among other things – justification, demarcation and theory choice) are unwilling to completely abandon any concern with some of the most respectable and fascinating issues in the history of western philosophy and, I would dare say, civilization.

Ernesto Screpanti, the other co-editor of this collection who decidedly belongs to the former group, concludes his Afterword by claiming that 'Methodological pluralism is not a methodological canon; it is only an ethical precept.'[9]

In this respect, as an unrepentant member of the latter group, I cannot abstain from noting that appeal to ethics is by no means new in economic methodology. Take, for instance, Terence Hutchison. What has characterized for decades his reiterated quest for falsificationism has always been his strong and explicit agrement with Popper's ethical and political concerns. In Hutchison (1988, p. 169) he openly states that 'Any significant case for adopting, or "striving after", a methodological principle must rely ultimately on some ethical, moral, or political argument (as Popper emphasized in the debate with Habermas and elsewhere).'[10] Coherently, he also notes that

> [A] kind of superhuman utopianism seems to prevail, even regarding economists themselves, who are urged to disregard all rules except 'honesty, clarity and tolerance' (McCloskey, 1983, p. 482). Of course, if we were all intellectually superhuman ... there might well be no role for critical codes of discipline, demarcation, and adequacy. For we would be living in an intellectual utopia. But for those of us concerned with the discussion of economic processes and policies in the real world, within a reasonably free democratic framework, a vital role may always remain for critical principles and criteria of adequacy, such as the falsifiability principle. (pp. 180–81)

As I argued in Salanti (1994), the problem with such a way of approaching the question is that it is far from clear who is more utopian, whether McCloskey, who takes somewhat for granted scientists' 'honesty, clarity and tolerance', or Popper, who invites us to adopt critical rationalism as a safeguard against violence.

Let me end, therefore, by saying that one of the very few firm conclusions we have reached after so much discussion on 'pluralism' is perhaps that it represents not so much a generally accepted methodological stance as an ethical precept. Another one, as previously observed, is that one's attitude towards methodological pluralism largely depends upon one's ontological beliefs and epistemological premises. But ethical precepts and ontological beliefs, by their very nature, are undecidable and potentially contradictory. If all this is true, therefore, the plurality of possible and equally respectable ethical perspectives will continue to foster this discussion for a long time to come.

## NOTES

1. For a comprehensive account of such a literature, see the various essays in the collection recently edited by Roger Backhouse (1994), which delineate a really impressive picture of what has been discussed in this field of study in the last twenty years or so.
2. I am referring to, for instance, Lawrence Boland (1982, pp. 188–96) who advocates a 'problem-dependent' methodology and Daniel Hausman (1981, pp. 215–26) who prefers to speak of an 'empirical' approach to the philosophy of (economic) science.

3. For recent and balanced surveys of the sociology of scientific knowledge as seen from an economist's perspective, see Mäki (1992) and Hands (1994).
4. The concerned literature is too extensive to be quoted here in detail. The interested reader may identify a number of such discussions starting from the recent replies to his critics in McCloskey (1994).
5. Cf. p. 59 in this volume. The somewhat harsh conclusion drawn by Nadeau is that 'If metaphysics is about finding very abstract principles and hermeneutics about denying that there is objective truth, I dare say that these new approaches actually lead us nowhere' (ibid., p. 65).
6. While Lawson, starting from a strictly realist perspective, seems to be prepared to embrace 'pluralism' only in a very narrow sense, and Mäki openly discloses his own preference for a 'relative pluralism' (that is, subject to certain conditions), Benedetti and Solari, following a hermeneutic approach, applaud pluralism much more enthusiastically (and with fewer reservations) than the other two.
7. Caldwell (1982, ch. 13, and 1988), explicitly based his proposal on the inexistence of universally applicable and logically compelling methods of theory appraisal, and therefore – as noted by Wade Hands in his chapter in this volume – endorsed theoretical pluralism but retained a kind of methodological monism based on the Popperian conception of critical rationalism. Otherwise, commenting on Samuels's and Dow's contributions to this volume, he now seems to concede that different ontological perspectives do not necessarily conflict and, in a sense, do not necessarily entail different forms of pluralism.
8. For the formal definition of this index, see pp. 268–9.
9. To a similar conclusion comes Geoffrey Hodgson at the end of his chapter. He seems to advocate 'pluralism' as a code of ethical behaviour in order to avoid detestable discriminations against unorthodox economists with the profession.
10. The indirect reference is to Popper (1976), who went so far as to claim that, differently from other species, 'Man has achieved the possibility of being *critical of his own tentative trials, of his own theories*. These theories ... can be critically discussed, and shown to be erroneous, without killing any authors or burning any books ... . If the method of rational critical discussion should establish itself, then this should make use of violence obsolete: *critical reason is the only alternative to violence so far discovered.* It seems to me clear that it is the obvious duty of all intellectuals to work for *this* revolution for the replacement of the eliminative function of rational criticism' (p. 292, italics in the original). Popper repeatedly expressed similar concerns in many of his writings: the most explicit discussions may be found in Popper (1950 and 1957).

## REFERENCES

Backhouse, Roger E. (ed.) (1992), 'The constructivist critique of economic methodology', *Methodus*, **4** (1), June, pp. 65–82.

Backhouse, Roger E. (ed.) (1994), *New Directions in Economic Methodology*, London: Routledge.

Boland, Lawrence A. (1982), *The Foundations of Economic Method*, London: Allen & Unwin.

Boylan, Thomas A. and O'Gorman, Paschal F. (1995), *Beyond Rhetoric and Realism in Economics. Towards a Reformulation of Economic Methodology*, London: Routledge.

Caldwell, Bruce J. (1982), *Beyond Positivism. Economic Methodology in the Twentieth Century*, London: Allen & Unwin.

Caldwell, Bruce J. (1988), 'The case for pluralism', in Neil De Marchi (ed.), *Popperian Legacy in Economics*, Cambridge: Cambridge University Press.

Caldwell, Bruce J. (1989), 'The trend of methodological thinking', *Ricerche Economiche*, **43** (1–2), June, pp. 8–20.
Hands, D. Wade (1994), 'The sociology of scientific knowledge: some thoughts on the possibilities', in Roger E. Backhouse (ed.), *New Directions in Economic Methodology*, London: Routledge.
Hausman, Daniel M. (1981), *Capital, Profits and Prices. An Essay in the Philosophy of Economics*, New York: Columbia University Press.
Hutchison, Terence (1988), 'The case for falsification', in Neil De Marchi (ed.), *The Popperian Legacy in Economics*, Cambridge: Cambridge University Press.
McCloskey, Donald M. (1983), 'The rhetoric of economics', *Journal of Economic Literature*, **31** (2), June.
McCloskey, Donald M. (1985), *The Rhetoric of Economics*, Madison: University of Wisconsin Press.
McCloskey, Donald M. (1994), *Knowledge and Persuasion in Economics*, Cambridge: Cambridge University Press.
Mäki, Uskali (1992), 'Social conditioning of economics', in Neil De Marchi (ed.), *Post-Popperian Methodology of Economics*, Boston: Kluwer.
Popper, Karl (1950), *The Open Society and Its Enemies*, London: Routledge & Kegan Paul.
Popper, Karl (1957), *The Poverty of Historicism*, London: Routledge & Kegan Paul.
Popper, Karl (1976), 'Reason or revolution?', in Theodor W. Adorno *et al.*, *The Positivist Dispute in German Sociology*, London: Heinemann.
Salanti, Andrea (1989), 'Recent work in economic methodology: much ado about what?', *Ricerche Economiche*, **43** (1–2), June, pp. 21–39.
Salanti, Andrea (1994), 'Popper, Lakatos and economics: are we begging the questions?', in Karen I. Vaughn (ed.), *Perspectives on the History of Economic Thought. Volume X*, Aldershot: Edward Elgar.
Stigler, George J. and Becker, Gary S. (1977), 'De gustibus non est disputandum', *American Economic Review*, **67** (2), March, pp. 76–90.
Weintraub, E. Roy (1992), 'Roger Backhouse's straw herring', *Methodus*, **4** (2), December, pp. 53–7.

# PART I

# Philosophical and Methodological Issues

# 1. On criticizing the practices of economists: a case for interventionist methodology

**Tony Lawson**

## 1. INTRODUCTION

A feature of recent writing of a methodological kind in economics is a reluctance to criticize the actual practices of contemporary economists. Certainly there is a relative paucity of any such criticism.[1] At the level of meta-methodology, moreover, some recent contributors have actively opposed any explicitly normative methodological intervention into economics, suggesting that a critical input from methodology is either unhelpfully imposing,[2] or even impossible.[3] Instead, it seems to be reckoned that methodology should be reduced to, or replaced by, something like an endeavour to describe the practices, rhetorics, or contexts merely, of contemporary economists. This situation, no doubt, has come about partly in (over-) reaction to the influence of those who would impose upon economics a philosophy of natural science which begs the question of the degree of similarity, or comparability, of the natural and social domains at the outset. But, while such errors or pitfalls are to be avoided it is equally a mistake to suppose that the only (or even sustainable) alternative is a kind of meta-sociological empiricism. It is erroneous, in other words, to suppose that the only fall-back position is a sort of naive or simple-minded describing of the practices of economists which (in intent at least) altogether evades the question of their epistemic worth, including their qualifying for the ascription of 'scientific'. Indeed, any injunction to avoid critically evaluating economic practices seems particularly perverse at a time when, in the view even of many of its most prominent practitioners, the discipline of economics is, one way or another, in a state of some significant disarray.[4]

Of course, I do not want to suggest that *all* recent methodology, or meta-methodology, aspires, or boils down, to one or other of these extremes. Indeed, methodological pluralism, an aspect of the theme of the conference, does, in the writings of Caldwell anyway, expressly state the goal of achieving a 'critical' position somewhere in between. However, Caldwell, along with many others, seems to want to reject, or anyway – in refusing to deal with the 'demarcation problem' – abandon, the idea of achieving an evaluative stance through examining what it means to be scientific. My own view, in contrast, is that foreclosing this line of pursuit is not only without good reason, but succeeds in fencing off a path that, in the light of recent developments in the philosophy of science, appears particularly likely to bear fruit.

In what follows, then, I diverge radically with recent trends. Specifically I want to suggest that not only is methodology always capable of having a critical impact upon the practices of economists, but also it is legitimate and (given recent developments in the philosophy of science) actually feasible to proceed by questioning explicitly whether economics does, or can, achieve the status of (social) science.

## 2. THE CASE AGAINST NORMATIVE METHODOLOGY

Why, first of all, is it supposed by some meta-methodologists that methodology *could not* have a critical input into the doing of economics? In stark terms the argument runs roughly as follows. If methodologists presume to take as premises arguments from 'outside' or 'above' the discipline in question, their input must necessarily be irrelevant – or, equivalently, if not irrelevant then not external after all.[5] If however, methodologists take, as premises, arguments, aspects or claims which are internal to the discipline, then they are necessarily taking sides with, or at least (and probably arbitrarily) making judgements on, some substantive contribution and can have nothing extra to add.[6]

When they are stated in this way it is easy enough to see that both strands of the argument must be wrong. In regard to the first strand, methodological suggestion of consequence for economics can certainly derive from an investigation of determinate, historically specific, social forms including practices and yet emanate from outside of economics.[7] However, it is essential in this to recognize the modal status of external results, criteria and comparisons. It is this that tends to be missed by those who deny any role for methodology which draws on 'external' results. Certainly, there is no basis for supposing that results or orientations of one domain can be automatically and unthinkingly applied in another. But there can still be a role for such results in framing the questions which are put, in pointing to the sorts of practices, etc., whose possibility may be worth investigating. We reason by analogy from one sphere to others all the time. In science ideas and insights are continually abducted from one field to another. Where, for example, a new symptom of physiological disorder is identified it is not unusual for medical researchers to hypothesize a virus to be the cause on the basis of previous experiences in different domains. But to do so marks the initiation of an investigation, not its conclusion. It indicates one possible direction of research, one that has proven successful in other contexts. The same can be as true of scientific practices as it is of theories. If certain actual practices judged as scientific – say experimental practices – have been found to be illuminating in one sphere, it makes sense to investigate the *possibility* of similar successes with such practices is some *prima facie* different sphere. Assuming, then, that there is a role for philosophy in any domain at all (a contested point to be considered below) there is no reason *a priori* to suppose that any results that are established in one sphere could not be useful in framing possibilities for another no *a priori* reason, that is, to accept Weintraub's (1989, p. 486) assertion that 'there *is* no position totally apart from the doing of economics which can inform the consideration of the doing of economics'. In short, the rejection of normative methodologism, that is, of merely asserting the value to one realm of a methodology that is (assumed to be) of widespread relevance to another, does not entail the impossibility of any legitimate and fruitful philosophical influence across scientific domains.

In regard to the second strand of the argument against normative methodology, the question here is how can methodology or philosophy go to work from premises internal to a discipline or subject area? Specifically, how can it avoid merely siding with one or other theoretical position, with nothing of its own to add? Now an essential point to acknowledge here is that the alternative to an explicit philosophy of science is not an absence of philosophy. Rather, it is an implicit and often bad philosophy. And, whatever may be the theoretical or substantive orientations of contemporary economists (whether econometricians, axiomatic-deductive theorists, hermeneuticists, and so on) their practices are all underpinned, or informed, by (competing) science-orientated philosophies of some sort. Of course, much of this is often tacit or unacknowledged, and it may be in contradiction with other beliefs. But it is precisely because of this that philosophical analysis can go to work. There is always the possibility that explicit methodological investigation of scientific practice, or other social forms, can make a contribution by rendering explicit some knowledge that is already implicit but unrecognized and, perhaps, in the reporting of economists (or whoever), openly contradicted. As Kant argued it is a function of philosophy to analyse concepts which are already given but confused. Notice that philosophy here is not merely going to work to satisfy idle curiosity. Rather it takes the form of immanent critique. Philosophy can expose internal incoherences in beliefs implicit in practices, or it can demonstrate how certain beliefs that are held cannot in fact accommodate something which, through practice, is actually being done, and so on. In short, philosophy as a critical rational activity is always a real possibility.

## 3. A QUESTION OF SCIENCE

If the potential for philosophy to contribute to scientific practice is something that cannot reasonably be denied, the question arises whether it is possible to go further and use philosophy to question the possibility of economics as social science. Specifically, is it possible to elaborate an adequate conception of science, or scientific method, and then to use it to assess the scientific possibilities for, or scientificity of actual, economic practice? In pursuing this line of questioning I am persuaded not only that the current crisis in economics warrants a reconsideration of the question of *naturalism* – i.e., whether social, including economic, phenomena are susceptible to explanation in essentially the same sense as are natural phenomena, that is scientifically – but also that recent developments in the philosophy of science allow it.

It appears to be precisely at this point, in pursuing this question, that I part company with many, and perhaps even a majority of, methodologists, including those who otherwise are prepared to advocate an evaluative stance towards economic practice. This is even the case with regard to such avowedly broad-minded approaches as Caldwell's methodological, or critical, pluralism. The focus of Caldwell's (1989) 'critical pluralism' is the 'methodological writings of economists' (p. 43) and the task at hand includes the 'evaluation of the positions contained in these writings' (p. 43). However, Caldwell is rather uncommitted about how the evaluations might be carried out: 'There is a variety of criteria of assessment; there are many ways to evaluate methodologies' (p. 45). A few lines on he adds: 'The "pluralism" in critical pluralism shows up, then, in the plurality of methodologies that are evaluated and in the plurality of criteria that are used to asses them' (p. 45). Now, if this appears to be a bit on the open-ended side, there is one strategy that does appear to be ruled out in all this. And it is precisely the one that I am interested in pursuing: of elaborating a conception of science, and using it to inform, or to assess the scientific possibilities for, economics. Indeed, it is just because of the historical failure, as Caldwell see it, of attempts to distinguish science from non-science that his particular position is put forward – 'Had [such attempts] been successful, there would be no need for critical pluralism' (p. 44).

On the face of it at least, Caldwell's 'pluralism' might be interpreted as an attempt to steer a path between, on the one hand, the absurdity of either denying that science exists or abandoning methodology altogether as irrelevant to science and, on the other, the apparent foolhardiness of claiming some insight as to what scientific practice and/or method entail. Caldwell, indeed, is explicit in identifying these 'opponents' of critical pluralism: 'On the one hand, there are those who claim to know what the scientific method is…', while the 'other group … either denies that science exists, or denies that methodology has any important connection to science' (p. 46). But upon reading his various asides it is not altogether clear that Caldwell totally rejects the idea of attempting to elaborate a conception of scientific method.[8] If, however, he does reject the idea then an obvious dilemma arises (as it does for McCloskey[9], Weintraub and other meta-methodologists who talk regularly of science and the scientific community). For either there are real differences between the practices of scientists on the one hand, and those of TV watchers, sun-bathers and those who chew gum, by virtue of which the label scientific is applicable to the former and not (typically) to the latter, or there are no grounds for *consistently* using the term scientist to designate one rather than another group of people. To persist with talk of science, but to reject the slide of nominalism, is to concede the case for a real definition. The latter, I suggest, is ultimately what Caldwell (and most others) must do.

In short, it is no more the case that the usefulness of methodological analysis can be ruled out *a priori* than that it can be inferred that pursuing an account of science is necessarily doomed to failure. If previous attempts at either endeavour have proved to be unsuccessful or even debilitating so far, the only compelling conclusion is that we should attempt to learn from such failures; not that we should abandon the respective enterprises involved entirely. Certainly, I know of no *argument* to the contrary that can be found in the writings of those in disagreement with this conclusion. Rather the supposition, sometimes stated but usually implicit, is that failure and/or misapplication so far, entails failure and/or misapplication in all cases. This, I want to demonstrate, is not a conclusion that follows in practice, any more than it does in logic.

## 4. REALISM AND SCIENCE

Once the case for a real definition of science is conceded and the task of pursuing it is accepted, the problem arises of deciding how to proceed. Many routes, or approaches, of course, may be ventured. The account of science that I find most compelling, however, and wish to argue for below is a realist one. Now a scientific realism is a theory that the ultimate objects of scientific enquiry exist and act (mostly) quite independently of scientists and their practices. And the particular conception that, following Bhaskar's work, I am arguing for is a metaphysical realism, consisting in an account of what the world must be like before it is investigated by science, and for scientific activities to be possible. Such a realism, it will be seen, neither turns on, nor endorses, a realistic interpretation of any substantive theory. But once obtained it does provide insight as to how science can be done.

Now clearly the possibility of such a metaphysical realism introduces explicitly the issue of a philosophical ontology – theories or questions about the nature of being and existence explicitly enter the picture. But, of course, questions or issues of (philosophical) ontology arise with every commentary upon science. Every philosophy presupposes a reality. Anyone who seeks to deny, or to banish, ontology only succeeds in smuggling it in illicitly. Those such as Hume who maintain that all we can have are experiences or impressions presuppose a (knowable) world of atomistic events given in experience. Those who would reduce science to conversation presuppose objects of that conversation. Even if they claim that conversation is only about conversation they thereby introduce a distinction between conversation as an (intransitive) object of knowledge, and conversation as a (transitive) form or medium of knowledge. Similarly, the attempted reduction of methodology to (or its attempted replacement by) history of thought or naive descriptivism, presupposes a reality of economic thought, practices, conversations, or whatever it is that is being re-told or simply described.

Realism, then, is inexorable: all theories of knowledge, science-orientated philosophies, social practices, etc., presuppose an ontology, i.e., some conception of the nature of reality. Equally, though, contending theories of ontology can sponsor quite different conceptions of science. The question, then, is how best to proceed in elaborating a sustainable ontology for, or metaphysics of, science? In pursuing this question I have been significantly influenced by Bhaskar's (1978) elaboration of his 'transcendental realist' position. Starting from premises concerning experimental practices in science Bhaskar – in a manner to be elaborated below – derives an account of a metaphysics of science, referred to as transcendental realism, by investigating their intelligibility, that is by enquiring what the world must be like for such scientific practices to be possible. Before running through Bhaskar's specific derivation of his results, however, I want to trace out various essential steps in the type, or mode, of argument involved. Recently Bhaskar's contribution appears to have been gaining some attention in economics. But if this is so it is equally clear (especially in its negative reception in some quarters) that the nature of 'transcendental enquiry' upon which Bhaskar's derivations rest, along with the *status* of the results established, are frequently misunderstood. Let me then, if briefly, indicate essential aspects of the relevant mode of argumentation, as well as the standing of results obtained.

## 5. TRANSCENDENTAL ANALYSIS

The case for a transcendental realist metaphysics of science constitutes a particular example of a general mode or method of argument that takes the form of an enquiry into the conditions of the possibility of some central, especially significant, or pervasive, feature of our experience. In Bhaskar's example he essentially asks what the world 'must'[10] be like for experimental practices, as conceptualized in experience, to be possible. His results follow from investigating this question. But if such a mode of enquiry, following Kant, is appropriately identified as 'transcendental' it is important to acknowledge that there is nothing inherent in it which forces us to accept the individualist and/or idealist mode in which Kant framed his own enquiries. Specifically, if the form of analysis at issue is a general investigation into the necessary conditions of certain conceptualized activities, then several essential points must be acknowledged. First, the social activity in question and the way in which it is philosophically conceptualized (i.e. the premises for the transcendental inference) may each be corrigible, contested, historically transient and spatially highly restricted. Second, the activity in question may, and will usually, depend on an array of powers that people possess as physical, biological and social agents, and not merely those most directly implicated in thinking and perceiving. Third, and, as already indicated, the analysis itself, which in the manner of its premises may be normatively corrigible and contested, may give rise to transcendental realist, not idealist, and so epistemically relativist, not absolutist, results – and to conclusions which may only be domain-specific.

On this account of transcendental analysis, then, both premises and conclusions of philosophical argument necessarily constitute contingent claims. If in the manner suggested it turns out that philosophy can so establish synthetic *a priori* knowledge (of the sort we are hoping to achieve) it can only be in the relative or conditional sense noted. That is philosophy (in the form of transcendental analysis) can get going on the basis *only* of prior conceptualizations of determinate social forms, and any results must be interpreted as conditional and expressed in hypothetical form. On this conception, transcendental enquiry (as is the case for science orientated philosophy generally) does not exist independently of the various sciences and other social practices and nor is it used to investigate a different world: philosophy treats the very same world as science. And on Bhaskar's conception, and perhaps generally, philosophy investigates that world transcendentally – it aims to reveal what our conceptions of certain practices of interest presuppose about that world. It represents, in short, an investigation that necessarily takes contingent historical premises and specific social conditions, and aims to produce hypothetical and conditional conclusions; an investigation which can never be foreclosed, it is always open to elaboration and transformation. On this conception, there is no philosophy in general, only philosophy of particular, geo-historically determinate, social forms.

How though are the premises for a transcendental enquiry to be selected? In particular how are the premises to be selected without implying an arbitrary, 'external', unjustified, or otherwise unpersuasive and/or unwarranted, commitment to the epistemic (or other) worth of the practices described? Science, or research activity, never takes place in a philosophical vacuum. All science-related practices are informed by one or more prevailing philosophies of science. Transcendental enquiry, then, as must be the case with philosophy generally, takes the form of immanent critique. That is, the premises chosen for transcendental analysis should be not only acceptable to the investigator (if conditional synthetic *a priori* knowledge of possibilities for science is the aim) but also, and fundamentally, acceptable to, if possible of paramount importance to, doubtful conceptions of philosophy currently dominant, or at least in contention. In other words, the premises of transcendental arguments will be descriptions of practices which are given prominence by influential, or potentially influential, science-orientated philosophies. In this way successful transcendental arguments will constitute transcendental refutations (or confirmations) of pre-existing accounts of science. Thus conceived, transcendental analysis is ultimately a process of *determinate negation*. The target will be a (dubious but influential) science-orientated philosophy which focuses on some more or less inadequately analysed activity. And the aim is first to render explicit the ontological, sociological and other presuppositions of the science-orientated philosophy, and hence set it in the form of a science-orientated realism, sociology, and so on. And the project is completed through demonstrating how, when the activity in question is adequately analysed, it is seen to presuppose a transcendental realist conception incompatible with that of the science-orientated philosophy thus critiqued.

## 6. EXPERIMENT ACTIVITY AND A THEORY OF ONTOLOGY

With this overview of transcendental enquiry in mind, let me briefly run through Bhaskar's derivation of his transcendental realist metaphysics. As already reported, the basic question that Bhaskar poses is: how are experiments possible? Now this question in itself needs some elaboration. The philosophical context is that experimentation is heavily sponsored by Kantians and empiricists. For such traditions, regularities of the form 'whenever event x then event y' are at least necessary (transcendent idealism) and perhaps sufficient (empiricism) conditions for causal laws (and other features of knowledge). And these traditions have seized upon the experimental establishment, knowledge and practical application of such 'laws' as being of fundamental epistemic significance in science. Bhaskar's initial input is to point out that, outside of astronomy at least, most of the constant conjunctions of events that are held by these traditional philosophies to be significant in science, in fact *only* occur under restricted conditions of experimental control – they are not typically spontaneously occurring but a product of human intervention. The second observation is that results and insights obtained through experimental activity are, along with other forms of knowledge, nevertheless successfully applied outside the experimental situation. Put differently, constant conjunctions of events are in fact extremely rare, spatio-temporally restricted, and usually artificially produced, while law-like knowledge appears to be generally available and useful, and some (but only some) of it experimentally corroborated.

We can see immediately that these observations raise fundamental problems for those traditional philosophies which tie laws, or 'significant results' in science, to constant conjunctions of events. For, if scientific laws, or significant results, only occur in such restricted conditions as experimental set-ups this bears the (rather inhibiting) implication that science and its results, far from being universal, are effectively fenced off from most of the goings-on in the world. In other words, most of the accepted results of science are not of the form 'whenever event x the event y always follows' after all, but are of the form 'whenever event x then event y always follows, as long as conditions e hold', where conditions e typically amount to a specification of the experimental situation. This also bears the rather counter-intuitive implication that any actual regularity of events that a law of nature supposedly denotes generally does not occur independently of human intervention. But in addition to such problems and at least as seriously, the constant-conjunctions view of laws leaves unaddressed the question of what governs events outside of the experimental situation. And, in doing so it also leaves the observation that experimentally obtained results *are* successfully applied outside of experimental situations without any valid explanation.

What then is the alternative? How are experiments, or those features of them just noted, possible? Specifically, how is it possible that scientists, in their experimental activities, (frequently) co-determine a particular pattern of events, approximating to regularities of the form 'whenever event x then event y', which would not have come about but for their intervention? What must the world be like for experimental practices and results, in the manner just conceptualized, to be possible?

In order to provide an answer to such a question, one which renders the situation described intelligible, it is necessary to abandon the view that the generalizations of nature consist of event regularities, and to accept instead (something like) an account of the objects of the world, including of science, as *structured*, i.e. irreducible to the events of experience, and *intransitive*, i.e.

existing and acting independently of their being identified. From this (transcendental realist) perspective the world is constituted not only by events and states of affairs, and our experiences or perceptions of those actualities, but also by structures, mechanisms, powers and tendencies that, although perhaps not directly observable, nevertheless exist, whether or not detected, and govern the actual events, etc., that we do experience. Thus not only does the autumn leaf pass to the ground, and not only do we experience it as falling, but, according to this perspective, underlying such movement and governing it are real mechanisms such as gravity (or curved space or whatever). In the UK at present not only are cows prematurely dying, or showing signs of losing control of their bodily functions, and not only is their behaviour interpreted as 'madness'[11] but, according to scientists implicitly acting on the perspective in question, this phenomenon is governed by some, albeit as yet incompletely understood, agent or causal mechanism, and the search is on to find out more about it. In short, three overlapping, but ontologically distinct domains of reality are, from this perspective, distinguished – namely the *empirical* (experience and impression), the *actual* (actual events and states of affairs in addition to the empirical) and the *real* (structures, mechanisms, powers, and tendencies, in addition to actual events and experiences).

Now according to the perspective here being put forward not only is it the case that the three domains identified are ontologically distinct, but, and crucially, they are unsynchronized, or out of phase with one another. Thus while experiences are out of phase with events, allowing the possibility of contrasting, as well as revisions to, experiences of a given event, so events are typically unsynchronized or out of phase with the mechanisms that govern them. On the latter structure/event non correspondence, for example, autumn leaves are not in phase with the action of gravity for the reason that they are also subject to aerodynamic, thermal and other causes or tendencies.

From the perspective of the theory of reality in question, then, one which, following Bhaskar, I shall refer to simply as transcendental realism, it is easy enough to see that, or how, the experimental situation elaborated above can be rendered intelligible. For experimental activity can now be recognized as an attempt to intervene in order to insulate a particular mechanism of interest by holding off all other potentially counteracting mechanisms. The aim is to engineer a system in which a one-to-one correspondence can obtain between the way a mechanism acts and the events which eventually ensue. In other words, on this view, experimental activity is rendered intelligible *not* as the production of a rare situation in which an empirical law is put into effect but as an intervention designed to bring about those special circumstances under which a non-empirical law, a power, a tendency, or mechanism, etc., can be empirically identified. If the triggering conditions are activated the mechanism in question is operative whatever else is going on. On this transcendental realist view, for example, a leaf is subject to the gravitation tendency even as it lies on the ground or 'flies' off over roof tops and chimneys.

In short, although the traditional conception of science is the seeking of constant conjunctions of events, in practice such event regularities as have been elaborated have been restricted to situations of experimental control. The transcendental realist theory of metaphysics, and derivatively of science, unlike that currently dominant empiricist or transcendental idealist conceptions of science, can render this situation intelligible. For this reason, the transcendental realist account in question, I submit, emerges as the most adequate, indeed uniquely sustainable, analysis that is available.[12] And it follows that the traditional event-regularity account of science rests upon an inadequate analysis and illegitimate generalization of a situation which emerges as a special case: wherein a single and stable (set of) aspect(s) or mechanism(s) is physically isolated and thereby empirically identified.

## 7. THE NATURE OF KNOWLEDGE AND SCIENCE

A condition of the intelligibility of the experimental generation and practical application of scientific knowledge, then, is that its objects are real structures which exist and act independently of the patterns of events they govern. But if this is so, if knowledge has structured and intransitive objects, how does the knowledge of them that we acquire come about? Where does it come from? If the transcendental realist ontology just defended entails that knowledge is not merely given in experience it is hardly intelligible that it is created out of nothing as it were. It must, then, come about through the transformation of pre-existing knowledge-like material. In other words it is necessary to acknowledge a *transitive* dimension to knowledge, or epistemology, to compliment the intransitive dimension, or ontology, already established. That is, it is necessary to recognize a dimension of transitive objects of knowledge, including facts, observations, theories, hypotheses, guesses, hunches, intuitions, speculations, anomalies, etc., which facilitate, and come to be (actively) transformed through the (laborious) social practice of science. Knowledge, in other words, is produced by means of production (of further knowledge) while science must be recognized as an ongoing transformative social activity. Knowledge is a social product, actively produced by means of antecedent social products – albeit on the basis of a continual engagement, or interaction, with its intransitive object.

In the light of all this a rational account of scientific development quickly follows. The aim is the production of knowledge of mechanisms that, singularly or in combination, produce the phenomena that we are interested in.

Usually (in natural science), this will involve employing antecedently existing cognitive resources and operating on the basis of something like a logic of analogy and metaphor, in constructing a hypothesis, or 'model', of a mechanism which, if it were to exist and act in the postulated manner, would account for the phenomenon in question. The reality of the postulated mechanism (and usually there will be several hypotheses) must then be empirically assessed of course. Once this is achieved any explanation accepted must itself in principle be explained; and its explanation in turn explained; and so on. On this conception then, science is distinguished by its *retroductive* mode of inference: the move from knowledge of some phenomenon existing at any one level of reality, to the knowledge of mechanisms (at a deeper level or strata of reality) by which the original phenomenon of interest was generated. As Bhaskar (1989) formulates it: 'On the transcendental realist view of science, its essence lies in the *movement* at any one level from knowledge of manifest phenomena to knowledge, produced by means of antecedent knowledge, of the structures that generate them' (p. 20).

With these results to hand it is easy enough to see how philosophy of science has the potential to provide a directional input into the practices of science. For although it follows, on accepting Bhaskar's analysis, that when scientists are practising science they are implicitly acting upon transcendental realism, there is nothing in what is being said that supposes, or necessitates, that transcendental realism, or any other philosophy, is always or consistently acted upon, or dominant, or even acknowledged. It is for that reason that Bhaskar (1979) is able to conclude that 'one is … qua philosopher of science, at perfect liberty to criticise the practice of any science for its lack of scientificity' (p. 15). Of course, nothing in the foregoing should be taken to imply that philosophy can do the actual work of science for it. If the elaboration of a transcendental realist perspective provides grounds for supposing that science both can, practically and fruitfully, and should aim to, uncover structures and mechanisms that govern some identified phenomenon of interest, philosophy cannot do the work of uncovering. This is the task of science alone. Philosophy, however, is able to make a difference to science in the manner noted: by, amongst other things, affecting the questions put to reality, and the manner in which this is done. Given, moreover, the disarray, confusion, and uncertainty that abounds in the area of economic research, any critical rational philosophical groundwork or prompting of this sort always seemed likely to bear fruit.

## 8. THE POSSIBILITY OF ECONOMICS AS SCIENCE

How does the foregoing realist analysis of natural science bear upon the possibilities for a social science including perhaps economics? The central insight is that if the essence of science is acknowledged to lie in the move, at any one level, from manifest phenomenon to the structures which generate it, a questioning of the possibility of naturalism boils down to investigating the feasibility of making a comparable move in illuminating the objects of the social realm.

From this perspective we can see immediately that not only has the question of naturalism been erroneously begged at the outset in previous (positivist) injunctions from the philosophy of natural sciences, but just as significantly (natural) scientific methods have been inadequately, or misleadingly, expressed. For the conception, or goal of science explicitly or implicitly underpinning naturalistically inclined contemporary orthodox economics, and reacted against in the explicitly anti-naturalistic alternative, is, or turns upon, the popular constant event conjunctions, i.e. formulations of the form 'whenever event x then event y'. However, it has been found that the intelligibility of the experimental establishment, and application, of scientific knowledge presupposes that its objects are real structures, and mechanisms which exist and act independently of the events they co-determine – so that causal laws must be analysed as tendencies, which are only manifest as event regularities (including probabilistic ones) under relatively unusual, typically intentionally engineered, conditions. Thus, contrary to specific claims of Popper, Hempel, Blaug, Hutchison, etc., and the tacit presuppositions of Hayek, Shackle and Winch, deducibility from event regularities is neither sufficient *nor* even necessary for natural scientific explanation. There is an ontological gap between a causal law and its empirical grounds. In short recent (positivist) methodological injunctions into economics are not only unwarranted but false, just as the most familiar subjectivist or hermeneutical contrasts stand in need of reorientation and perhaps rejection.

Now all this being the case it does not (yet) follow that the popular constant conjunctions of events are not a viable or legitimate goal for those investigating the objects of the social realm. If it is a mistake to impose *a priori* a conception of natural science as necessarily relevant to investigating social objects, it must also be a mistake to suppose that a conception that is only of limited relevance to natural science is, by that reason alone, necessarily of minor, or even without, relevance to an investigation of the social realm. Such questions can only be addressed through exploring the possibilities for social investigation directly. The noted results do immediately signal, however, that where positivist incursions into the social realm have been accepted precisely for the reason that they are interpreted as displaying proper (natural) scientific method, then their adoption has been based on mistaken criteria. And as this is, by all accounts, a dominant factor in explaining the desires of many economists to conform to the injunctions of Popper and Lakatos, etc., the results in question are not without significance. In any case, the 'whenever event x then event y' conception of natural science stands discredited. Certainly there are grounds for supposing that the transcendental realist conception of natural science now established facilitates a fairer comparison or standard when exploring links between the putative sciences of society and of nature. But that, if to repeat, is essentially all that it achieves. To determine whether a social science, including economics, is possible it is necessary to look to the social realm directly.

Notice, though, that the situation which Bhaskar focuses upon in determining an account of (natural) science is quite different to the one that must be faced up to in the social realm. In his analysis of the experimental situation, Bhaskar starts from the insight that science exists and that it includes experimental activities amongst its practices. He then questions what the world must be like for such scientific practices to be possible. Here, in contrast, the actuality of a social science cannot be taken as given or uncontentious. The continued failure of economics over the last 50 years or so is such that the existence of a social science of economics cannot be accepted as a premise. Instead, we must identify some more or less universally recognized feature of substantive social life to initiate the analysis – and question whether a science of economics is possible. In other words, the situation facing us is that we now have a conception of (natural) science at hand (obtained through reflection on natural scientific practices) and the question we must address is: are there objects of a particular domain of interest (here specifically the social domain) with features or properties which facilitate (or place limits upon) the possibility of (or which prohibit) those objects (where they exist) being studied scientifically?

## 9. HUMAN INTENTIONAL AGENCY

The most obvious entry point here is the phenomenon of human intentional agency. Indeed, it would seem to be (relatively) uncontentious to take human intentional agency, including the capacity for choice which is analytic to it, as criterial for the social sphere, as well as content for premises to initiate an inquiry into the possibility of social science. Certainly the intuition that, in their activities, human individuals exercise the powers of reason and choice is, I think, explicitly sponsored by all contending traditions in economic thought. Orthodox or mainstream economists often even stylize their project (or at least a prominent strand of it) as 'choice theory', while the capacity of human beings to exercise some control over their lives has always been central to the anti-orthodox reaction, whether formally anti-naturalist or not.[13]

An interesting question here, then, is what does the reality of people making choices presuppose? What must the world be like for human choice to be possible? Now if choice is real any agent could always have acted otherwise, any agent could always have acted differently than he or she in fact did. Keynes, for example, insists that 'A decision to consume or not to consume truly lies within the power of the individual; so does a decision to invest or not to invest' (*CW* VII, p. 65). And a necessary condition for this clearly, is that the world, social as well as natural, is open in the sense that events, and specifically actions, could always, under the conditions prevailing, have been different.

Immediately, we see that the familiar positivist injunctions into the social realm – to adopt, universally, methods or modes of explanation that take the event-regularity conception as at least a necessary component of science – are invalid. If there are any event regularities at all in the social realm – and complementing the above derivation from the phenomenon of choice, of course, is the *ex posteriori* experience of a complete absence of any scientifically significant ones (see e.g. Lucas, 1976) – they will most likely be intentional products like the regular re-occurrence of annual holidays, or of shopping hours, etc. It is the case, of course, that positivistically inspired projects in economics (e.g. econometrics, deductivist 'theorizing') have often felt a tension here. But they have coped with it only by trivializing or posing dilemmas.[14] Economic orthodoxy, which is a barely disguised manifestation of positivist philosophy at work in economics (Lawson, 1994a, 1994b, 1995), cannot coherently sustain the reality of people exercising their power of choice even though the latter is an aspect of human behaviour that it claims explicitly to sponsor.

Of course, subjectivists or hermeneuticists (such as the Austrians, including Hayek) have recognized this all along. However, their acceptance of the positivist 'whenever event x then event y' conception as nevertheless constitutive of, or necessary for, science has tended to encourage, in reaction, an essentially voluntarist conception of human agency and an almost non-existent role for social science. That is, by erroneously ceding science to positivism, and recognizing the inapplicability of that conception to the social realm, the tendency has been to abandon the idea of *explaining* social phenomena at all.[15]

An obvious additional question to address, in this light, is whether it follows that, because the social world is open (in the sense that, under conditions which prevailed, events, including actions, could always have been otherwise), a social science is necessarily impossible? Specifically, the interesting question facilitated by the preceding elaboration of a non-positivistic, more adequate, transcendental realist account of science is, are there nevertheless *social* structures of some kind operative in the social realm that can be identified? Once more, at this point, it is necessary to look to substantive social investigations themselves for the answer. We can acknowledge, as a criterion for differentiating any social structures from purely natural ones, the property that, should they exist and endure, it is only by virtue of human agency. Thus conceived any specific social structure, if it exists, is something which, if the human race were to disappear tomorrow, would 'vanish' along with it. But it must be left to the work of social research including economics, not philosophy, to uncover such social structures, etc., as there are.

Turning to social investigations the obvious candidates for social structure are rules, relationships, positions and the like, as components, and perhaps constitutive, of societies. Existing studies of all identified putative societies, whether industrial or not, couch their explanations in such terms. Not only are such 'societies' *rule* governed (in language use, games, modes of exchange, etc.) but also they are typically structured along hierarchical lines – with *positions* (kingships, tribal leaderships, teachers, studentships) occupied by specific individuals who may, and do often, exit (some of) their positions – where such positions are always defined in *relation* to others (teachers to students, tribal leaders to other tribal members, landlords to tenants); and so on. Notice that even self-styled 'methodological individualists', or at least the more reflective ones, do not flinch from making reference to (or at least from using the language of) social structures such as these in their contributions (see Hodgson, 1988, for an assessment). Rather the latter group seems to feel the needs, primarily, to distance itself from others (whoever they may be) who apparently attribute emergent human properties – such as intentions and purposes – to some or other 'aggregate' or 'collectivity'.

Social structures such as rules and relationships, then, figure widely in explanatory contexts. This recognition, however, is not sufficient to establish their autonomy or reality. For it may yet be suggested that such items are not real but merely scientific constructs used to organize our interpretations and understandings – of, say, the (routine) patterns of everyday life. It is necessary, then, if a case is to be made for the possibility of naturalism, to establish that such putative objects of scientific investigation are both irreducible and real.

The essential point here is that science employs not only a perceptual but also a causal criterion for the ascription of reality to a posited object. The latter turns on the ability of an entity whose existence is in doubt to bring about changes in material things. It is the causal criterion, and not perceivability, that is satisfied by magnetic and gravitational fields, and which is grounded in Bhaskar's analysis of experimental situations outlined earlier.

The task here, then, is to demonstrate that, but for society, or at least for various social structures, certain physical conditions, including actions, would not be performed. To the extent that this proves possible then, employing the causal criterion, we are justified in accepting such structures as real.

Now it was noted above that a necessary condition for the possibility of choice is that the world is open – in the sense that under the conditions which prevail any agent could always have acted otherwise. How about intentional agency more generally? What are its preconditions? Notice, first, that intentional human agency is necessarily transformative in that it is agency, and reasoned, purposeful, knowledgeable and skilled in that it is intentional. What in particular, then, do such aspects presuppose about reality?

An essential point here is that any (transformative) agency, including that of human intentional causality, would be impossible in the sense of being unable to go to work without material causes which preceeded it. Just as acids cannot corrode without materials to break down, nor bees produce honey without plants to harvest, so human activity cannot take place without means, media or resources of some kind – conditions which, through human agency, come to be (in part intentionally) transformed.

And, of course, amongst these necessary conditions are *social* material causes of the sort just identified. The human (intentional) activities of speaking, writing, driving on public roadways, cashing cheques, playing games, giving lectures, etc., would be impossible without rules of language, highway codes, banking systems, rules of play, teacher–student relationships, etc., – all are structures that exist prior to activities they facilitate and make a difference to, constrain as well as enable, the sort of activities which takes place.[16]

In effect, then, the possibility of social science has been established – societies, or social structures more generally, are both real and irreducible to human agency. This conclusion has been arrived at via a transcendental argument from intentional agency as dependent upon social material causes (so establishing the latter's existence) which are available to be drawn upon prior to any individual act (so establishing their relative autonomy and rendering them susceptible to social investigation). In other words, a transcendental argument from intentional agency (a premise accepted by the supernaturalist and anti-naturalist traditions in economics alike) establishes the *sui generis* reality and the temporal pre-existence of forms of social structure, as its necessary conditions and means.

It warrants emphasis, finally, that although the possibility of social science is sustained, the investigations of social objects may require very different methods, techniques and criteria to those employed in the natural sciences. If knowledgability presupposes that the social structures acted upon are enduring to a degree, the fact that they are dependent upon inherently transformative agency means that they will be only relatively so, being faster, or more temporal-spatially restricted, than (most of) the objects of natural science. Economics, then, is necessarily historical-geographical. If, in addition, social structures must, for the same reason, be continually reproduced it follows that economics is concerned with intrinsically dynamic processes. Thus a market, for example, is not a static object where change is (merely) something external that happens to it; change is essential to what a market is. The market is a process. Social science, then, must be alert to this condition, and its methods tailored to it. Moreover the dependence of social structure on intentional human agency entails an inescapable hermeneutic moment in social science. In addition the impossibility of engineering, and the absence of spontaneously occurring closed systems, or constant conjunctions of social events or actions, necessitates a reliance upon non-predictive, purely explanatory criteria of theory development and assessment; and so on.

All such considerations, to repeat, indicate that social objects may need to be studied using procedures that are different to those of natural sciences. Nevertheless, the (knowable) structured and open conditions of the social realm allow the possibility of a project of investigating social forms that can be scientific in the sense of natural science. I submit, then, that the quest for a successful social science should not be abandoned, whether in the name of pluralism or anything else. Indeed, it is perhaps the case that a pluralist orientation should *before all others* facilitate approaches such as defended here: for which grounds can be established, and yet to which opposition is likely because of the challenge provided to the contemporary mainstream.

Whether or not, or the degree to which, a successful social science is achieved, of course, is down to the local conditions and the activities of those investigating substantive social issues, including economists. However, the preceding argument indicates how, in any such endeavours, philosophy of some kind will always be conditioning. Indeed, given the current state of the discipline, it seems beyond serious dispute that if progress is to be achieved, then a more explicit and critical intervention from philosophy is required. Any methodological pluralism that does not encompass such a critical orientation can only serve as a device to make, and so to preserve, the state of incoherence and disarray that constitutes the *status quo*.

## NOTES

1. This point has been well made in C. Lawson *et al.* (1996) where a position similar to the one developed below is taken in the context of 'underlabouring for an economics with institutions'. The current chapter is a shortened version of an argument found in Lawson (1997).
2. McCloskey (1986) for example writes of 'methodological authoritarians' (p. 36) and

asserts that 'Methodology is Bourgeois' (p. 24), suggesting that 'If it were not so damaging to the sense, Methodology, strutting around issuing orders to working scientists, would only be funny' (p. 24).

3. According to Weintraub (1989) 'any normative role for Methodology rests upon a profound misconception, and thus Methodology cannot possibly have consequences for the way economics is done. Methodology ... cannot have any impact on the manner of practice' (p. 478).
4. Thus Hendry (1980) questions whether econometrics is 'Alchemy or Science', and Leamer (1983) implores others: 'Lets take the con out of Econometrics', etc. In the latter contribution Leamer observes that 'after three decades of churning out estimates, the econometrics club finds itself under critical scrutiny and faces incredulity as never before' (p. 42). He even suggests that 'hardly anyone takes anyone else's data analyses seriously' (p. 37). Within so called 'theory' the failure and disarray of the project is manifest, for example, in Kirman's (1984) paper, 'The Intrinsic Limits of Modern Economic Theory', which is appropriately subtitled 'The Emperor Has No Clothes'; and so on. Of course, non-orthodox economists have been emphasizing this desperate state of affairs for quite a while (see e.g. Phelps Brown, 1972; Worswick, 1972; Wiles and Routh, 1984; Posner, 1986; Hodgson, 1988, 1993). Donaldson (1985) sums the situation up with his observation that the 'charge against economists is, above all, that of irrelevance' (p. 13).
5. Thus Weintraub (1989) drawing upon Fish's (external?) injunctions from Literary Criticism concludes that 'there *is* no position totally apart from the doing of economics which can inform the consideration of the doing of economics' (p. 486). In supporting this result Weintraub reproduces the following passage by Fish, inviting us to insert the term 'Methodology' where Fish uses 'Theory':

   > Theory can be seen as an effort to guide practice in two senses: (1) it is an attempt to *guide* practice from a position above or outside it ... and (2) it is an attempt to *reform* practice by neutralizing interest, by substituting for the parochial perspective of some local or partisan point of view the perspective of a general rationality to which the individual subordinates his contextually conditioned opinions and beliefs. ... The argument *against* theory is simply that this substitution of the general for the local has never been and will never be achieved. Theory is an impossible project which will never succeed. It will never succeed simply because the primary data and formal laws necessary to its success will always be spied or picked out from within the contextual circumstances of which they are supposedly independent. The objective facts and rules of calculation that are to ground interpretation and render it principled are themselves interpretative products: they are, therefore, always and already contaminated by the interested judgements they claim to transcend (Fish, 1985, p. 110).

6. Weintraub (1989, p. 486) seems to takes this position too. Relying of Fish's conclusions once more, and again allowing us to insert 'Methodology' where Fish uses 'Theory', Weintraub reproduces the following passage with approval:

   > Theory cannot guide practice because its rules and procedures are no more than generalizations from practice's history (and from only a small piece of that history), and theory cannot reform practice because, rather than neutralizing interest, it begins and ends in interest and raises the imperatives of interest – of some local, particular, partisan project – to the status of universals (Fish, 1985, pp. 111–12).

   For Weintraub, on accepting Fish's conclusions that local interests are always involved, it then seems to follow unproblematically that such interests are necessarily theoretical so that methodology must be inconsequential:

   > The differences [between the various competing groups in economics – Post Keynesian, neoclassical, Marxian, Austrian] are theoretical, not epistemological, and certainly cannot be resolved through Methodological argumentation (Weintraub, 1989, p. 487).

He adds, just a few lines on, 'And if the Methodological agenda, of providing a sure basis of judging whether one theory is better than another from considerations that stand apart from the two theories, cannot be begun, cannot succeed, then Methodology has no consequences for practice' (p. 487).

7. That is it may result from reflections upon such matters as, for example, natural scientific practices. Certainly it is erroneous to suppose that philosophy has access (and misleading to represent all philosophy as supposing itself to have access) to some autonomous realm of generalizations, or being, etc.
8. In fact, given the basic anti-dogmatic connotations of any such pluralism there is ultimately no reason why pluralists should do other than welcome the project that I am suggesting. For any account of science elaborated will clearly be contingent, and if, as I have urged, any such account that is derived from reflection within the natural sciences is used mainly to frame questions about possibilities, to set fair contrast with the natural sciences, then such an approach must surely be recognized as in keeping with an open-minded, albeit critical or evaluative, orientation. In any case, it should be clear that a rejection of normative methodologism does not actually render the posing of the question of the possibility of naturalism as illegitimate, necessarily inconsequential, or debilitating, while a foreclosing of any questioning of the *possibility* of naturalism sits uneasily with a declared attitude of pluralism.
9. McCloskey captures well the negative connotations that many contemporary meta-methodologists in economics clearly associate with any (apparently necessarily positivist or 'modernist') attempts to derive (or, apparently, impose or assert) a sustainable conception of science:

   > In practice methodology serves chiefly to demarcate Us from Them, demarcating science from nonscience. Once the modernists have founded a Bantustan for nonsciences such as astrology, psychoanalysis, acupuncture, nutritional medicine, Marxist economics, spoonbending, or anything else they do not wish to discuss, they can get on with the business at hand with a clear head. Methodology and its corollary, the Demarcation Problem (What is Science? How is It to be distinguished from nonscience?), are ways of stopping conversation by limiting conversation to people on our side of the demarcation line.
   >
   > The replies to such scepticism about the uses of methodology and epistemology have been unpersuasive. Indeed, it has not usually been thought necessary to stoop so low as persuasion (McCloskey, 1986, p. 26).

10. The word 'must' is used here because it figures in the transcendental question as originally posed. But of course, and as emphasized below, the question being asked is really what is the most explanatorily adequate, albeit fallible, account that we can come up with which renders intelligible the phenomenon of interest – here experimental practices as conceptualized in experience.
11. The illness is widely known in the UK as 'mad cows disease'.
12. The use of the term transcendental to describe the theory of ontology, etc., so inferred is, in this light, both comprehensible and yet, I think, questionable. It is comprehensible, of course, and as noted, precisely because the theory of ontology, the realist perspective in question, derives support from transcendental argument from experience. It is questionable because it is at least conceivable that other conceptions might (eventually) similarly derive support via transcendental argument from (the same or alternative) accepted features of experience – facilitating different, perhaps competing, accounts equally qualifying for the ascription of 'transcendental realism'. A better label then would be one that captured the structured, intransitive, nature of the ontology elaborated above – perhaps 'structural realism' or 'transfactual realism'. However, I persist with the transcendental realism label here because it is now so ingrained in the (fast growing) literature and because, for the time being at least, there is no comparably viable alternative theory of ontology on the scene. But this usage may have to be temporary. Of course, if competing 'transcendental realist' accounts are so derived they will have to be selected amongst on

the basis of their relative explanatory powers, according to their relative capabilities to illuminate a range of generalized features of experience, and so on.

13. Since drafting this chapter I have come across Nadeau (1995) who emphasizes, in similar fashion to the position taken here, the centrality of human intentionality to any putative discipline of economics. Thus Nadeau argues that 'neoclassical economics is a theoretical framework thoroughly based on intentional concepts' (p. 3); that 'the phenomenon of intentionality … [is a] reality [which] is *constitutive* of the domain of economic theory …' (p. 7); 'that all economic concepts are thoroughly intentional' (p. 9); that 'intentionality should be acknowledged as the trademark of all important economic concepts since the marginalist revolution' (p. 13); suggesting that it was the 'subjectivist approach to economic value that seems to have made it necessary to recognise the intentionality of economic phenomena' (p. 9); and so on. While our contributions are in many ways mutually supportive, Nadeau, however, does seem to suggest that, in assessing the possibilities for economics, any approach must be either external *or* internal:

> Now, there are at least two radically different ways of looking at this situation. One can start with some preconception concerning what a 'legitimate empirical science' must look like and try to see whether neoclassical theory passes the test, or one can choose to deal somewhat more directly with the epistemological specificity of economic reality as captured by neoclassical theory (p. 3).

My own intention in this chapter is to try to convince the reader that these 'two radically different ways' of proceeding (appropriately interpreted) can actually be two mutually supportive aspects or strands of a single endeavour.

14. An example arises with the partitioning of postulated econometric relationships into endogenous and exogenous components, with only the latter being regarded as subject to choice, albeit in the exercise solely of a privileged policy-making elite. Of course, this latter assignment of the possibility of choice is, in turn, no sooner made than undermined by the remorseless tendency of that some project to endogenize ever more variables. A recent prominent example of this lies in the attempts of proponents of the rational expectations hypothesis to convince us all to accept, and to produce models consistent with, the claim that all agents' beliefs are (in the sense of the hypothesis) rational. A version of the dilemma of 'conundrum' which thereby arises is noted by Sargent and Wallace (1976, p. 183):

> The conundrum facing the economist can be put as follows. In order for a model to have normative implications, it must contain some parameters whose values can be chosen by the policy maker. But if these can be chosen, rational agents will not view them as fixed and will make use of schemes for predicting their values. If the economist models the economy taking these schemes into account, then those parameters become endogenous variables and no longer appear in the reduced form equations for the other endogenous variables. If he models the economy without taking the schemes into account, he is not imposing rationality.

This 'conundrum' for orthodox economics is put more generally (or accurately) by Reder (1982, pp. 34–35).

> Successfully to endogenize a new variable is to enhance the explanatory power of economics, and there is much interest in such achievements. However, it must be noted that where variables are made 'endogenous', they can no longer serve as objects of social choice.
>
> To the extent that variables are endogenized – choice is explained – 'society's' freedom of choice is seen as illusory. Freedom appears to consist not in power of choice, but (*pace* Hegel) in recognition of necessity. This is not a likely conclusion for followers of Adam Smith, and surely not one they desire, but one from which they can be saved only by the failure of this direction of research.

15. Or rather to abandon it, in effect, to some more basic science such as physics, biology or psychology. Hayek (1942–4), for example, suggests that 'What is relevant in the study of society is not whether ... laws of nature are true in any objective sense, but solely whether they are believed and acted upon by the people' (p. 51); and concludes 'It is a mistake, to which careless expressions by social scientists often give countenance, to believe that their aim is to *explain* conscious action. This, if it can be done at all, is a different task, the task of psychology' (p. 68). See also Hayek (1943). (For a further elaboration of this reaction see Lawson, 1994b, c).
16. Commons (1934) captures this property of social structures as follows:

> The business man who declines to use the banking system which has grown up in the past, the labourer who refuses to come to work when others come, may be industrious, but he cannot live in industrial society. This is familiar enough. ... But when customs change, or when judges and arbitrators enforce a custom by deciding a dispute, or when labourers or farmers strike in order to modify a custom of business, or when a revolution confiscates slaves or other property of capitalists, or when a statute prohibits a customary mode of living, or when a holding company extends an old custom into new fields – then it is realised that the compulsion of custom has been there all along, but unquestioned and undisturbed (1934, p. 701).

## REFERENCES

Bhaskar, R. (1978), *A Realist Theory of Science*, Hemel Hempstead: Harvester Wheatsheaf, 2nd edition (1st edition, Leeds, 1975).

Bhaskar, R. (1979), *The Possibility of Naturalism*, Hemel Hempstead: Harvester Wheatsheaf.

Bhaskar, R. (1987), *Scientific Realism and Human Emancipation*, London: Verso.

Bhaskar, R. (1989), *Reclaiming Reality*, London: Verso.

Caldwell, B.J. (1982), *Beyond Positivism: Economic Methodology in the Twentieth Century*, London: George Allen and Unwin.

Caldwell, B.J. (1988), 'The Case for Pluralism', in N. De Marchi (ed.), *The Popperian Legacy in Economics*, Cambridge: Cambridge University Press, pp. 231–44.

Caldwell, B.J. (1989), 'Post-Keynesian Methodology: An Assessment', *Review of Political Economy*, **1** (1), March, pp. 43–64.

Commons, J.R. (1934), *Institutional Economics*, London: Macmillan.

Donaldson, P. (1985), *Economics of the Real World*, Harmondsworth: Penguin Books.

Fish, S. (1985), 'Consequences', in W.J.T. Mitchell (ed.), *Against Theory*, Chicago: University of Chicago Press, pp. 106–31.

Giddens, A. (1984), *The Constitution of Society*, Oxford: Polity Press in association with Basil Blackwell.

Hayek, F.A. (1942–4), 'Scientism and the Study of Society', *Economica* (various issues). Reprinted in *The Counter-Revolution of Science*, London: Routledge (page references are to the latter).

Hayek, F.A. (1943), 'The Facts of the Social Sciences', *Ethics*, **LIV** (1), pp. 1–33.

Hendry, D.F. (1980), 'Econometrics – Alchemy or Science?', *Economica*, **47**, pp. 387–406.

Hodgson, G.M. (1988), *Economics and Institutions: A Manifesto for a Modern Institutionalist Economics*, Cambridge: Polity Press.

Hodgson, G.M. (1993), *Economics and Evolution: Bringing Life Back into Economics*, Cambridge: Polity Press.

Keynes, J.M. (1973), *The Collected Writings of John Maynard Keynes, Vol II, The General Theory*, London: Royal Economic Society.

Kirman, A. (1989), 'The Intrinsic Limits of Modern Economic Theory: The Emperor Has No Clothes', *Economic Journal*, **99** (395), Supplement.

Lawson, C., Peacock, M. and Pratten, S. (1996), 'Realism, Underlabouring and Institutions', *Cambridge Journal of Economics*, **20** (1), January, pp. 137–51.

Lawson, T. (1989a), 'Abstraction, Tendencies and Stylised Facts: A Realist Approach to Economic Analysis', *Cambridge Journal of Economics*, **13** (1), March, pp. 59–78. Reprinted in T. Lawson, G. Palma and J. Sender (eds), *Kaldor's Political Economy*, London and San Diego: Academic Press. Also reprinted in P. Ekins and M. MaxNeef (eds), *Real Life Economics: Understanding Wealth Creation*, London: Routledge, 1992.

Lawson, T. (1989b), 'Realism and Instrumentalism in the Development of Econometrics', *Oxford Economic Papers*, **41** (1), pp. 236–58. Reprinted in N. De Marchi and C. Gilbert (eds), 1990, *History and Methodology of Econometrics*, Oxford University Press.

Lawson, T. (1994a), 'Why Are So Many Economists So Opposed To Methodology?', *Journal of Methodology*, **1** (1), June, pp. 105–33.

Lawson, T. (1994b), 'Critical Realism and the Analysis of Choice Explanation and Change', *Advances in Austrian Economics*, **1** (1), pp. 3–30.

Lawson, T. (1994c), 'Realism and Hayek: A Case of Continuous Transformation', in M. Colonna, H. Hagemann and O.F. Hamouda (eds), *Capitalism, Socialism and Knowledge: The Economics of A. Hayek, Vol II*. Aldershot: Edward Elgar, pp. 131–59.

Lawson, T. (1995), 'A Realist Perspective on Contemporary "Economic Theory"', *Journal of Economic Issues*, **XXIX** (1), March, pp. 1–32.

Lawson, T. (1997), *Economics and Reality*, London: Routledge.

Leamer, E.E. (1983), 'Lets Take the Con Out of Econometrics', *American Economic Review*, **73** (1), March pp. 31–4.

Lucas, R.R. (1976), 'Econometric Policy Evaluation: A critique', in *The Philips Curve and Labour Markets*, K. Brunner and A.H. Meltzer (eds), *Journal of Monetary Economics*, Supplement, pp. 19–46.

McCloskey, D. (1986), *The Rhetoric of Economics*, Brighton: Wheatsheaf Books Ltd.

Mäki, U. (1989), 'On the Problem of Realism in Economics', *Richerche Economiche*, **43**, pp. 176–98.

Mäki, U. (1990), 'Scientific Realism and Austrian Explanation', *Review of Political Economy*, **2** (3), November, pp. 310–44.

Mäki, U. (1993), 'Methodology might matter, but Weintraub's Meta-Methodology Shouldn't', mimeo, Helsinki.

Nadeau, R. (1995), 'Economics and Intentionality', in M. Marion and R.S. Cohen (eds), *Quebec Studies in the Philosophy of Science*, Dordrecht/Boston/London: Kluwer Academic Publishers, Boston Studies in the Philosophy of Science. (Page references to a mimeo: Université du Québec à Montréal.

Posner, M. (1986), 'The State of the Economy', *Scottish Journal of Political Economy*, **33** (4), pp. 305–16.

Phelps Brown, E.H. (1972), 'The Underdevelopment of Economics', *Economic Journal*, **82**, March, pp. 1–10.

Reder, M. (1982), 'Chicago Economics', *Journal of Economic Literature*, **20**, March, pp. 1–38.

Sargent, T.J. and Wallace, N. (1976), 'Rational Expectations and the Theory of Economic Policy', *Journal of Monetary Economics*, **2**.
Weintraub, E.R. (1989), 'Methodology Doesn't Matter, But the History of Thought Might', *Scandinavian Journal of Economics*, **91**, pp. 477–93.
Wiles, P. and Routh, E. (1984), *Economics in Disarray*, Oxford: Basil Blackwell.
Worswick, G.D.N. (1972), 'Is Progress in Economic Science Possible?', *Economic Journal*, **82**, pp. 73–86.

# 2. The one world and the many theories

**Uskali Mäki**

## 1. INTRODUCTION

'Pluralism' has become a popular label amongst those who are not entirely comfortable with what they see as the prevailing situation in economics. As is so typical of many other similar labels, it is not at all clear what is behind it. It is not clear what people mean when they say they advocate pluralism in economics. Not only is it seldom recognized that pluralism proper comes in different kinds and different degrees, it is also easily conflated with the simpler notion of plurality. The following remarks are intended to provide a sketch of two endeavours: first, a partial clarification of the very concept of pluralism; second, a defence of pluralism about theories.

My title hints at a principle – let us call it the 'one world principle' – which I take as imposing a constraint upon the sorts of pluralisms I am willing to espouse. Provided there is only one world – or only one way the world is – pluralism about the world is not acceptable. On the other hand, the actually and potentially obtaining plurality of theories – also referred to in my title – can be justified, hence pluralism about theories is acceptable. This paper is an attempt to outline a systematic justification for theoretical plurality in economics without succumbing to ontological pluralism.

## 2. PLURALITIES AND PLURALISMS

When considering the issue of pluralism, the proper place to begin is the more primitive notion of plurality, since the notion of pluralism presupposes that of plurality. We can say that the *plurality of Xs* is a situation where *X* exists in the plural; there is (where 'is' can take on the meaning of 'is actually', 'is potentially', 'is hopefully') more than one (actual, potential or desired) value for *X*. Let us look at some of the typical items which may be claimed or required to exist in the plural. In the expression 'plurality of *Xs*', *X* may be specified in a number of ways, which gives us pluralities such as the following:

- Ontological plurality - world
- Veristic plurality - truth
- Intensional plurality - meaning
- Theoretical plurality - theory
- Linguistic plurality - language of formulating theories
- Epistemological plurality - way of rationally justifying theories or beliefs in them
- Pragmatic plurality - aim, question, problem
- Methodological plurality - method, criterion, standard
- Meta-methodological plurality - methodology
- Axiological plurality - value
- Ethical plurality - moral value
- Ideological plurality - ideology

The list of pluralities can easily be extended beyond those cited above, but it would be unnecessary for the purposes of our discussion. The important next step is to consider the nature of the distinction between the plurality of *X*s and *pluralism about X*. An obvious way of characterizing the difference between the two is to say that pluralism is a theory or principle that justifies or legitimizes or prescribes the plurality of items of some sort. Whenever the plurality of *X*s constitutes an issue, pluralism about *X*s or its denial is an attempt to settle the issue.

A list of pluralisms can be created in the same way as the list of pluralities was constructed above. Thus, we have ontological, veristic, intensional, theoretical, linguistic, epistemological, pragmatic, methodological, meta-methodological, and axiological pluralisms about world, truth, meaning, theory, language, knowledge acquisition, problem and goal, method and standard, methodology, value, etc.

A statement about plurality is descriptive in character, while pluralism has a normative connotation. It is one thing to say that a plurality of items obtains or does not obtain in fact, and quite another to argue that it is fine that such a plurality obtains or that such a plurality should obtain.[1]

We have above implied a further distinction between *actual plurality* and *non-actual plurality*. In the former case, the relationship between plurality and pluralism is this: a plurality of *X*s (which actually obtains) is *justified* by pluralism about *X*. For example, one may argue that the actually prevailing multiplicity of approaches in business studies is an applaudable state of affairs. In the latter case, the relationship is as follows: a plurality of *X*s (which does not actually obtain) is *prescribed* by pluralism about *X*. For instance, one may argue that there is little or no plurality of fundamental theories exhibited in mainstream economics journals, and that there should be more of it.

Pluralism involves arguments or reasons for plurality. This adds a further element to the picture: pluralism about *X* is based on *reasons Y.* The reasons for which a given type of pluralism and hence plurality, can be defended may be of various kinds, from ontological or epistemological to aesthetic or moral.

Combining the various values of *X* and *Y* we then get a number of different pluralisms which either justify actually obtaining pluralities or require actually non-obtaining pluralities for different reasons. Let us gather these elements together in the following definition:

> *Pluralism.* P is an instance of pluralism about *X* if and only if it is a theory or principle which either justifies an actually obtaining plurality of *X*s or prescribes an actually non-obtaining plurality of *X*s by appealing to reasons *Y*.

It is obvious that one may have reasons such that they neither justify an actually obtaining plurality of *X*s (because such a plurality does not actually obtain) nor prescribe that such a plurality should obtain (since it cannot obtain). As an example, hard-boiled realists claim to have reasons that preclude ontological and veristic pluralism: a plurality of worlds and truths does not and cannot obtain (to avoid misunderstandings, this idea will be qualified in the next section).

Now that we have come some way to clarifying the basic conceptual setting of the general issue of pluralism, we can specify the particular issue that will concern us in the following. Our *X* will be theory, and our reasons *Y* will be mainly ontological and epistemological reasons. In other words, we will be concerned with theoretical pluralism. Whenever a plurality of theories actually obtains, we will ask whether there are good ontological or epistemological reasons which would justify this situation; whenever a plurality of theories does not obtain, we ask whether there are good ontological or epistemological reasons requiring that a plurality of theories should obtain.

## 3. ONTOLOGICAL AND SEMANTIC PRELIMINARIES

Before entering the issue of theoretical pluralism it is very important that we understand what is implied by a denial of pluralism about the world and of pluralism about truth. Indeed, our reasons involve the kind of realism that implies the denial of both ontological and veristic pluralism and hence a plurality of worlds and truths.

In a sense, it is trivially true that the world is plural in that it has many facets. The world is constituted by an infinite number of things and their properties, including their behavioural features. Yet it seems possible to say that the world is one in a sense that the many theories we hold do not each create worlds of their own; plurality of theories does not imply plurality of worlds, but rather the many theories are about the one world. This is consistent with saying that the one and only world consists of a huge number of things and properties and processes and potentialities, and also that the world appears in a vast number of ways to an observer or a set of observers viewing it from different perspectives. The one world principle is consistent with a plurality of theories. The denial of ontological pluralism implies that the many facets of the world are discovered rather than created by means of the many theories and perspectives. For example, fixprice theories and flexprice theories do not create fixprice and flexprice worlds, but at most help to illuminate features of the one and only world.[2]

It is also trivially the case that truth is plural in the sense that there is or can be an infinite number of true sentences (or propositions, utterances, beliefs) about the world, each illuminating one aspect or feature of the world and its constituents. However, this does not imply veristic pluralism. To put it in a manner that requires careful qualifications, the denial of veristic pluralism implies that for each question, pragmatically and semantically so circumscribed that it amounts to one unambiguous question, there is only one correct answer. For instance, the denial of veristic pluralism implies that there is only one correct answer to questions such as 'Did Adam Smith write *Foundations of Economic Analysis*?' or 'Do economic agents have perfect information?'

## 4. THEORIES AS SUBSTITUTES AND COMPLEMENTS

Let us then try to clarify some sorts of theoretical plurality and some reasons that we might have for justifying or recommending the plurality of theories in economics. The plurality of theories actually obtains, but not all economists are happy about its extent and nature. How should the actually obtaining plurality and the desired plurality be characterized? What are the related forms of pluralism and their presuppositions?

We begin with two intuitively simple ideas. The first is the distinction between *nothing but the truth* and *the whole truth.* Economists have a habit of occasionally conflating these two notions, but it is important to keep them separate. The second is the idea that theories can be *substitutes* or *complements* with respect to one another. It is typical of economists to conflate these two cases, too. These two ideas can then be combined in a formulation of two different cases of theoretical plurality. First, a multitude of theories may be based on their being substitutes, being *rival claims to nothing but the truth.* Second, a multitude of theories may be based on their being complements, being *complementary claims to parts of the whole truth.* These simple ideas have to be developed further to see what kinds of reasons there may be for theoretical pluralism.

Let us then note the obvious idea that the apparent claims of a given theory or model are not all equally important or central to the description the theory gives of the world; some claims are more central than others. This idea suggests a simple distinction between two kinds of claims; let us call them the *core claims* of a theory and the *peripheral claims* of a theory. Intuitively, this distinction would seem to be exemplified by claims about gravity as opposed to claims about a vacuum in an account of the behaviour of a falling body; and claims about maximization as opposed to claims about the perfect divisibility of goods in an account of the behaviour of economic agents and markets (granting that such classifications are often very contestable).

The distinction between core claims and peripheral claims can be based on pragmatic or ontological considerations or both: the distinction may be due to a methodological decision to treat certain components of theory differently from others, or it may be due to beliefs concerning the objective constitution of the domain of reality being studied. Let us consider the distinction as ontologically grounded.

We may say that in some cases at least, the core claims and peripheral claims of a theory are supposed to have ontological correlates: the core claims purport to be about the *ontic core,* while the peripheral claims are purportedly about the *ontic periphery* of the domain of the theory. One specific version of the distinction between the ontic core and the ontic periphery is the one between major causes and minor causes that we find in J.S. Mill.

We can now develop the idea of theories being substitutes and complements by giving the following definitions:

- *Strong substitute.* Two or more theories are strong substitutes if and only if they contain rival core claims to nothing but the truth about the ontic core.
- *Weak substitute.* Two or more theories are weak substitutes if and only if they contain rival peripheral claims to nothing but the truth about the ontic periphery.
- *Strong complement.* Two or more theories are strong complements if and only if they contain complementary core claims to parts of the whole truth about the ontic core.
- *Weak complement.* Two or more theories are weak complements if and only if they contain complementary peripheral claims to parts of the whole truth about the ontic periphery.

Keeping to the one world principle, we may now say that there are good *ontological* and *veristic* reasons for a plurality of theories if these theories are strong or weak complements. Such theories do not make conflicting claims about the world, on the contrary, they are supposed to supplement one another. On the other hand, it is less obvious that theoretical plurality can be defended on ontological and veristic grounds if the many theories are strong or weak substitutes. If there is only one way the world is, two or more theories making mutually inconsistent claims about the world cannot all be true at the same time. There is genuine conflict between such theories.

The situation is different in regard to *epistemological* considerations. Given the radical epistemic uncertainty that characterizes economics, there seem to be good epistemological reasons for plurality of theories in all four cases above, including the cases of strong and weak substitutes. Familiar problems related to the availability of relevant evidence and the reliability of testing constitute an example of why the exclusion of rival claims to nothing but the truth involves major risks. There is the further consideration that for similar reasons of epistemic uncertainty it is often difficult to tell theory complements from theory substitutes so as to sort them out for differential treatment from the point of view of pluralism.

## 5. ABSOLUTE AND RELATIVE PLURALISM

In economics as well as elsewhere, theories seem to be regarded much more often as strong or weak substitutes or as weak complements than as strong complements. A synthesis of strong complements often constitutes a major breakthrough in scientific progress. So does the replacement of a dominant theory by its strong substitute. The replacement of a theory by its weak substitute or weak complement constitutes a less significant episode in the development of a discipline. Indeed, the adjustment of weak complements seems to constitute a major activity in normal research in conventional economics.

These dynamic considerations are important since they are related to differences between kinds of pluralism. One can be a *temporary pluralist* with respect to a specific historical situation without being a *permanent pluralist* irrespective of the historical situation at hand. For example, Thomas Kuhn's theory of the structure of scientific revolutions can be interpreted as involving temporary pluralism about strong substitutes; it involves pluralism about extraordinary research but not about normal research (this has to be taken with the proviso that Kuhn's theory does not easily lend itself to the sort of ontologically inspired account that we have attempted above).

Temporary pluralism is a temporal version of *relative pluralism*, while permanent pluralism is a temporal version of *absolute pluralism*. Someone may endorse absolute pluralism, that is, pluralism irrespective of anything else. Some others, such as myself, hold relative pluralism, that is, pluralism relative to certain conditions. For example, I am willing to accept pluralism relative to a certain epistemic situation in economics; it may be that at some point in time, such as now, the epistemic standing of economic theories is such that we had better tolerate a number of strong substitutes at the same time; it may be that our epistemological and methodological understanding of how to find out the best way of theorizing about the economy falls short of the demands that economists are expected to fulfill. Pluralism may be a wise strategy in such a situation. Let us summarize these notions in the form of the following definitions:

- *Relative pluralism.* P is an instance of relative pluralism if and only if P is pluralism relative to a limited set of conditions.
- *Absolute pluralism.* P is an instance of absolute pluralism if and only if P is pluralism relative to all possible conditions.
- *Temporary pluralism.* P is an instance of temporary pluralism if and only if P is pluralism relative to a limited set of time periods.
- *Permanent pluralism.* P is an instance of permanent pluralism if and only if P is pluralism relative to all times.

## 6. STRATEGIES WITH RESPECT TO THEORETICAL PLURALITY

The scientific process is characterized by two partly opposing tendencies. On the one hand, scientists, among them economists, do their best to invent new theories and get them accepted by their fellow scientists. This often leads to a tendency towards greater plurality of theories. The reasons for this tendency are several, including the fact that novelty is often valued for its own sake. There are always constraints on theoretical novelty, but the character and strength of such constraints vary from discipline to discipline and from one phase of development to another. An aspect of this is that the nature of novelty which is valued varies similarly. However, there are reasons for the first tendency which are in some cases related to the second tendency, that of scientists persistently trying to reduce theoretical plurality. Let us briefly consider conditions under which these tendencies obtain.

Obviously, when two or more theories are identified as rival *substitutes,* scientists tend to defend the ones they endorse and, depending on the structure of the field, either to ignore other theories or to try to eliminate them by arguing that they are mistaken. These two approaches to rival theories have consequences for theoretical plurality. *The strategy of negligence* gives support to whatever plurality of theories prevails, while *the strategy of elimination* aims at reducing the number of theories, with or without success.

- *Strategy of negligence.* Practitioners follow the strategy of negligence if and only if they ignore rival theory substitutes, thus supporting the prevailing plurality of theories.
- *Strategy of elimination.* Practitioners follow the strategy of elimination if and only if they try to get rival theory substitutes rejected, thus reducing the plurality of theories.

We may then conjecture that in fields or subfields where the number of theory substitutes is large, practitioners tend to adopt the strategy of negligence, that is, they ignore theories that conflict with those they endorse, *ceteris paribus.* On the other hand, in fields or subfields where the number of theory substitutes is small, practitioners tend to adopt the strategy of elimination, that is, theory substitutes tend to be taken more seriously and attempts tend to be made to eliminate them, *ceteris paribus*. It seems that both cases can be found in economics.

When two or more theories are identified as *complements,* there are again several alternative responses to the situation. The first is to accept the situation as it is and to employ the theories for whatever purpose they seem to serve best, based on the principle of *division of labour*. This strategy tends to retain the plurality of complementary theories. The second strategy is to try to integrate the complementary theories by following the principle of *vector addition* or something similar. The idea is that each complementary theory is taken to identify a separate force or factor that has an impact on the phenomenon under study, and the total effect can be calculated by adding up the separate effects. The third strategy is to pursue integration of the complementary theories by attempting to unify the theories and their subject matters within a more fundamental theoretical framework. This is the principle of *unification.* The unifying theory is taken to be more fundamental in the sense that the objects of the complementary theories are believed to be moments or phases or manifestations of the objects of the more fundamental theory. These two latter strategies involve assigning a subordinate status to some theories. Let us summarize:

- *Strategy of division of labour.* According to the principle of division of labour, practitioners use each theory complement for whatever purpose it seems to serve best, thus supporting the prevailing plurality of theories.
- *Strategy of vector addition.* According to the principle of vector addition, practitioners integrate theory complements by adding up the components they represent, thus supporting the prevailing plurality of theories while subordinating them to the total representation.
- *Strategy of unification.* According to the principle of unification, prac-

titioners integrate theory complements by unifying them in terms of a more fundamental framework, thus reducing the plurality of theories or assigning a subordinate status to some of them.

It is also notable that the implementation of the strategies of vector addition and unification, if at all permitted by the attendant difficulties, typically presupposes revision of component theories.

## 7. DEGREES OF PLURALISM

In the foregoing, we have discussed plurality and pluralism as if they were simple dichotomous notions; either one has them or one hasn't. In fact, it often seems important to think of them in terms of degrees; one may have more or less of them. The notion of degree of plurality and pluralism appears to be a useful one. This notion appears in several forms which define different dimensions or scales on which the degree varies.

To begin, we have already encountered the ontologically based idea of theories being substitutes or complements. We may now say that there is a scale on which the degree of pluralism is higher in the case of substitutes than in the case of complements. In other words, toleration of rival claims to nothing but the truth is more demanding than toleration of complementary claims to parts of the whole truth. Furthermore, the strong cases of substitutionality and compementarity generate higher degrees of pluralism than the weak cases, because the risks related to the core claims of a theory are higher than those involved in its peripheral claims. Let us formulate the idea in the case of these two dimensions:

- *Degree of pluralism 1.* The degree of pluralism about theory is higher if the two or more theories in question are substitutes than if they are complements.
- *Degree of pluralism 2.* The degree of pluralism about theory is higher if the two or more theories in question are strong substitutes or complements than if they are weak substitutes or complements.

There are other dimensions related to the number of theories and the distribution of their endorsement. First, one may say that the larger the number of theories, each endorsed by at least one economist, the higher the degree of plurality and pluralism. At one extreme, were all economists to endorse one and the same theory, the degree of pluralism would be at its minimum. Note that there is no clearly defined other extreme, such as there being as many theories endorsed as there are economists; this is because each economist may endorse a very large number of theories, to the extent that his or her capacity allows.

Second, one may say that the more even the distribution of endorsement of theories within economics, the higher the degree of plurality and pluralism. At one extreme, all economists except one lonely heretic endorse one theory, while this remaining dissenter alone endorses a different theory. The distribution of endorsement is maximally uneven and the degree of pluralism is at its smallest. At the other extreme, all theories – which are two or more in number – are each endorsed by the same number of economists. The distribution of endorsement is maximally even and the degree of pluralism is at is greatest. Let us summarize:

- *Degree of pluralism 3.* The larger the favoured number of theories endorsed, the higher the degree of pluralism about theory.
- *Degree of pluralism 4.* The greater the favoured evenness of the distribution of endorsement between theories, the higher the degree of pluralism about theory

With these definitions, it should be obvious that it would be difficult to defend the idea that the higher the degree of pluralism, the better. It may be the case that there is an optimum degree of plurality well below the maximum degree; an adequate form of pluralism has to be able to justify or prescribe this optimum degree. It is likely that there is a limit to a functional number of theories, and that some unevenness of the distribution of endorsement is functional for the advancement of economics.

In any case, I think we are now approaching some of the key issues which explain why the idea of pluralism is nowadays found to be so important by economists who do not identify themselves as mainstream economists. To see this, at least one more step has to be taken. It seems that those who speak in favour of pluralism do not mean to imply that they necessarily prefer the maximum degree of pluralism 3 or the maximum degree of pluralism 4. They are not only concerned about the number of theories endorsed or the evenness of the distribution of endorsement, but also, and emphatically, about the distribution of what may be called the academic power attached to theories. By 'academic power' I mean the amount of relevant resources (relating to publishing, promotion, prestige, etc.) controlled by the endorsers of particular theories. The idea of the degree of pluralism can now be linked to the variation in the evenness of the distribution of academic power. We may state the following.

- *Degree of pluralism 5.* The greater the favoured evenness of the distribution of academic power attached to the endorsement of theories, the higher the degree of pluralism about theory.

Again, one may well accept that there are limits to a reasonable degree of pluralism in this sense, and yet insist that the economics profession should advocate a higher degree of pluralism 5 than currently seems to be the case.

## 8. CONCLUSION

The foregoing exercise has attempted to serve two purposes. First, it has sought conceptual clarity about some aspects of the issue of pluralism in economics. More specifically, I have suggested that pluralism and plurality have to be kept separate and that the concept of pluralism has to be defined in terms of plurality; pluralism is a theory or statement about plurality. I have suggested distinctions between pluralisms about different things; between absolute and relative (and permanent and temporary) pluralism; and between degrees of pluralism on various dimensions.

The second purpose has been to outline a defence of pluralism about theory in ontological and epistemological terms, constrained by the One World Principle. This defence was sketched in terms of theory substitutes and theory complements. The defence was further qualified in terms of relative and absolute pluralism; different strategies that can be followed with respect to theory substitutes and complements; and degrees of pluralism.

My focus has been on pluralism about theory while rejecting pluralism about the world and truth; hence 'the one world and the many theories'. These and other forms of pluralism (such as epistemological and linguistic pluralism) need to be clarified and scrutinized carefully before any justified positions for or against them comes forth in conversations among the Econ.

## NOTES

1. However, in the ontological and veristic cases, plurality and pluralism seem to be more closely connected. If one states that there are multiple realities and multiple truths, one commits oneself to a pluralism about reality and truth. On the other hand, if one says that a multitude of theories and methods obtains, this does not yet imply pluralism about theories and methods.
2. For some purposes, it may be useful to employ the notion of thought world or model world, and keep it separate from the real world. Thought worlds are indeed created by means of theories, which means that they exist in a different sense from the real world which exists unconstituted by acts of theorizing. Of course, those aspects of the real world that are of interest to a social scientist, are often subjectively and even theoretically constituted by the agents of social processes. This, however, is consistent with their being irreducible to the thought worlds of an economist. Importantly, pluralism about thought worlds is consistent with the denial of pluralism about the real world.

# 3. Levels of description in the hermeneutics of economic theory

**Eugenio Benedetti and Stefano Solari**

## 1. INTRODUCTION

When considering the problem of pluralism in economic theory the analysis of its relations with cognition makes an interesting contribution. The evolution of some other disciplines reveals the emergence of a new disposition towards pluralism. Scientific research in economics should find a convergence with other social sciences and all related studies. This approach goes beyond the adoption of similar methodologies as in the case of neoclassical economics and the neopositivistic interpretation of Newtonian physics.

We think it opportune to shift from a search for objective foundations and laws of economics towards a hermeneutical approach based on analysis of the cognitive substrate of economic theory. A plurality of points of view corresponding to different levels of description could improve our understanding of the economy. Pluralism in economics will necessarily follow when we adopt a hermeneutical approach that reveals the possibility of a plurality of levels of description.

## 2. THE EPISTEMOLOGICAL CONTRIBUTIONS OF OTHER DISCIPLINES

The most relevant aspect of the evolution in contemporary philosophy is the diminishing interest in metaphysics, and the increasing interest in the subject and problems of cognition and knowledge. The most interesting positions are the philosophy of language, pragmatism (recently neo-pragmatism), practical philosophy and existentialism. Among the problems raised by these currents of thought phenomenology and hermeneutics are relevant to our analysis. In fact, both have many points of convergence with cognitive sciences such as linguistics, neuro-sciences, cognitive psychology and artificial intelligence. There are many similarities between the works of

Rorty or Merleau-Ponty and those of Piaget, Maturana, Varela and Watzlawick.

As economists we are not interested in detailed analysis of the similarities and contrasts between these currents of thought. However, it is relevant that economics finds a convincing philosophical and scientific background as an alternative to the neopositivistic approach. The most important innovation of this new *Weltanschauung* is that the subject, the observer, is inseparable from the world he projects. This perspective allows us to go beyond object–subject dualism, an unsatisfactory approach to cognition. A further step is to abandon realism and absolute objectivity.

The network of relations composing an economic system is characterized by its complex evolutionary nature. These relations depend on the context in which they are defined. The context changes spatially, from region to region, and historically with the flow of time and the evolution of society. These are problems common to all sciences because they depend on the role of the observer and not on the characteristics of the object studied.[1] Objectivity in analysis is normally seen as a prerequisite for scientific studies. From our point of view, since the object of research is not clearly defined and is unstable, the question of observer objectivity is inseparable from that of object definition. We prefer not to raise the question of the existence of a real world.

These arguments should shift the theorist's attention away from the problem of the correct methodology towards a hermeneutical[2] approach which includes the role of subject cognition. The problem of the difference between *realism* and *realisticness* follows this line of reasoning (Mäki, 1989), but we stress here that no metaphysical realism is acceptable.[3]

Some theorists have rightly underlined the fact that economic reality is a social construction (Samuels, 1991). In this way, a theory is valid because of its predictive potential, however it is also a kind of language. It is a formalized and synthetic standard by which theorists communicate and can minimize the incomparability of their thoughts. However, since it is a construction and not a representation of reality, this language is not simply a means of communication but contributes to form the mind itself. Therefore, theories are not only means but a constituent part of our cognitive possibilities in economics. Knowledge depends on the language in which it is expressed and thus influences perception and definition of the issues. A simple probabilistic view of knowledge in itself is of no help (Lawson, 1988). The economist, therefore, should be aware of psychological and sociological mechanisms that mediate our knowledge.

## 3. COGNITION AND CONSTRUCTIVISM

From a constructivist point of view, what are normally considered as the ontological foundations of the physical domain of existence are determined by the limitations of our cognitive domain (Maturana, 1990). For this reason we should try to understand how our cognition works.

As Maturana and Varela hold, cognition is the process of the production of a world. It consists of making distinctions, which in turn constitute existence. There are as many domains of existence as there are different kinds of distinctions made by the observer (Maturana, 1990; Varela, 1979). A non-realist, constructivist approach implies the existence of many worlds and the existence of as many domains of truth as there are domains of existence.

There are several models for the study of cognition. However, we are not interested in simulations here, and prefer to conduct a pragmatic analysis of the mechanisms of the construction of our knowledge.

There are three main problems in cognition that are relevant to economic epistemology.[4] The first is *spatial perception* (or *selective perception*). In economics this is not always three dimensional as normally perceived but the space determined by the variables chosen to study the object. The second is *flow of time* (or *definition of the object*). We define as objects things that in reality are processes. Everything is a process because it changes with time, in a more or less stable way. Everything we select should be relative to historical time. The third is *inference*, that is to say making sense of or finding a direction of causation.

As Lorenz affirmed (Lorenz, 1973), all our knowledge of the real world is derived from information mechanisms of a philogenetic origin. Space, time and causality links are functions of a neurosensorial organization developed for the conservation of our species. For this reason we suppose the perception of the 'real world' to be relatively objective. At the same time we think that there is only an indirect and non-objective knowledge of abstract things that have no direct relations with our perceiving apparatus. In this sense the Kantian view that there is no relation between an economic system and our perception of it is also misleading. In fact, we are interested in the fitness of our knowledge and not in unreachable truth.

As Maturana affirmed, scientific statements are consensual statements valid only within the community of standard observers that generate them. Science, as the domain of scientific statements, does not need an independent objective reality, nor does it reveal one (Maturana, 1990). This means that, as radical constructivism affirms, there is no direct relation between reality and the knowledge we have of it.[5]

This fits the concept of hermeneutics as 'making sense from a background of knowledge'. Economics, like any other science, cannot be directly objective. It should therefore pay particular attention to the model–reality link with respect to our cognitive potential. This also implies the possibility of a plurality of models describing the same object and that a plurality of viewpoints is better than a single one.

## 4. ECONOMIC MODELS AND COGNITION

A basic problem in economics, and particularly in the models concerning aggregates, is the definition of the object of study. The properties of the system studied are a function of the observer. This fact was affirmed in a most formal and precise way by Maturana and Varela. We cannot have absolute objectivity but only objectivity relative to the ontological foundations of the observation, that is to say what Maturana called 'objectivity between parentheses' (Maturana and Varela, 1980; Varela, 1979). The set of ontological foundations define what we call *levels of description*. Only at single levels of description can we have a certain 'objectivity'.

We cannot scientifically define a system referring only to common sense. The difficulty in defining dynamic systems (processes) is underlined in pre-Socratic thought where the problem of change was very important (Vercelli, 1991). The problem is finding a point of reference from which to assess the identity of an evolutionary system in time and on which to base the description of change. A precondition for the observability and intelligibility of a system is that of a fixed point in its transformation used as a parameter for the observation (Benedetti and Solari, 1992). Contemporary cognitive scientists (constructivists) solve this problem in the same way as ancient philosophers. They divide the definition of the system into two levels: a concrete level, called *structure*, that changes with time, and a 'meta-level', called *organization*, which is perceived as invariant and defines the identity of the system.[6] Since organization, as a property of a system, is dependent on the observer, we see that the object observed is inseparable from the subject observer. The difficult task of the economist is to find a fixed point, the invariant characteristic of a system, that permits definition through time. It should be noted how this definition is always socially conditioned. In this case we can go beyond the object–subject duality which, as many philosophers affirm, is a bad approximation of cognition.

A further problem is the definition of conditions of observation to produce a reference for establishing relative objectivity. The economist needs an 'ontology of observing' to help define the levels of description when studying arbitrary aggregates and abstract relations.

These kinds of problems are particularly evident in macroeconomics where the object of study is large aggregates that are rarely defined uncontroversially.

Macroeconomics thus involves a preliminary definition of facts and boundaries of systems that are the object of study. Since facts and boundaries cannot be objectively set, the theorist has to chose an appropriate perspective for them.

Bateson clearly synthesized this, affirming that a model furnishes a stylized language through which we can examine the internal relations of the system studied by means of comparison with the internal relations of the model itself (Bateson and Bateson, 1987). Hermeneutics in economics is the analysis of these relations.

At this point we need a set of principles to help the hermeneutical analysis to characterize the different possible points of view relative to our cognitive standpoints. The difference is that we do not propose any foundations of the object, the economic system, as in textbooks, but we propose a foundation of the observation of an economic system.

## 5. ONTOLOGY OF OBSERVING IN ECONOMICS

In economics there are some basic assumptions made implicitly and necessarily within every observation of an economic fact. A similar approach was used by Kant in the *Kritik der reinen Vernunft*, where he argued that the conditions of possible experience coincide with the conditions of the possibilities of the objects of experience.[7] This fact is strictly related to the cognitive problems listed above.

The indeterminacy of cognition constitutes a field of variability of pre-theoretic knowledge that determines the orientation of effective knowledge. These foundations differ from the hypotheses of theories. Hypotheses are already based on these foundations. The foundations of cognition normally remain hidden and implicit, are not normally assumed consciously and are part of the preconceptual world view. Despite this, they determine the development and explicative potential of a model or theory. We pointed out three basic dimensions of cognition in economics related to the main cognitive problems:

1. *Space*. It is not simple physical space, but the space defined by the variables considered. We normally give our knowledge geometric form when representing it and when elaborating it. Some possible descriptions of space are continuity, aggregation and uniformity of the variables. The description of phenomena occurs at different levels corresponding to different logical types.[8] These are at times disconnected[9] and thus complementary.

A further problem is the theorist's point of view with respect to the system studied. There are two basic possibilities of observation: the first is the observer in the environment $E_i$, outside the observed system $S_i$. The second is the observer inside $S_i$. In both cases the boundaries of $S_i$ are defined by the observer, while $E_i$ is undefined. The former is a common case of observation, the latter is the case of an 'observing system'.[10] In the first case the information about $S_i$ is a function of $E_i$, $S_i = f(E_i)$. In the second, $S_i = f(S_i)$, while $E_i$ is exogenous; that is to say there is a problem of cognitive self-referentiality. Things become more complicated when we introduce subsystems because complex self-referentiality of problems.

2. *The time dimension*. The perspective can be static or dynamic and the latter 'diachronic' or 'synchronic'.[11] The diachronic view, in economics, represents the undetermined unfolding of processes. The synchronic represents long term constraints and equilibrium. From a thermodynamic point of view, the first represents the possibility of locally reducing entropy, the latter the general law of increasing entropy. The theorist's task is to decide which of the two is more appropriate to an economic analysis. When in doubt, he may consider both. While the diachronic point of view is difficult to formalize, the synchronic is normally simpler because it is relative to some equilibrium. On the contrary, if the first can be described precisely by the available data, the second implies deep uncertainty concerning the equilibrium of reference. Most economic laws are based on synchronic time which has contributed to the confusion in studying evolution.

In economics the possibility of increasing welfare, far from equilibrium, depends on the efficacy of our investments. Wrong investments lead us closer to long-run equilibrium (entropic death). This point leads directly to the problem of time representation. One current of thought considers the correct representation of time as physical (in coordinates). Another prefers to keep time implicit by assuming the irreversibility of processes (Vercelli, 1991). These are simply forms of time representation; the first being more deterministic. The only sure fact for economics is that if a synchronic interpretation of time is correct and helpful, theories with reversible time are incorrect and can be seriously misleading whatever they attempt to explain.

3. *Inference*. The causal structure is the most important aspect of inference, and in fact causality is quite controversial in economic theory. As Hicks affirmed, the structure of causality is an important ontological feature of a theory (Hicks, 1979). As we have already explained, causal relations are strictly dependent on level of description and at the same time affect the determination of levels. We do not believe causal relationships to be objective and real. From the constructivist point of view, causality belongs to the cognitive domain of the observer, not to the observed system. This is not the same as saying that causality is subjective, but that it is dependent on context.

From a point of view within the observed system the uncertainty of information grows and the structure of causation becomes vague. In this case the theorist must 'put forward' the relevant relations occurring in a system and make some hypotheses about their effective functioning. In particular, the most arbitrary task of the economist is to decide the direction of causation, and not which variables to connect. The choice of these variables is a less controversial fact. The task of the theorist is to 'put forward' and analyse what are, in his opinion, the relevant relations. In fact, even simple lineal causation does not diminish the relevance of the analysis.[12]

A relevant part of inference is given by assumptions about *rationality*, *learning* and *information*. These refer to individuals, aggregates of individuals, or to economic systems in general. The form of rationality is the main hypothesis when studying decisional processes in microeconomics and expectations in macroeconomics. Generally perfect rationality is considered as opposed to learning. Information has always been considered an independent variable of the system, whether perfect or scarce, but seldom studied in detail as an endogenous economic good.

We do not include the concept of equilibrium as a foundation of economics as some have done. This is because equilibrium is given by a particular combination of time and space levels. Moreover, equilibrium is often assumed as an operational hypothesis, which is quite different from a foundation. Finally, it seems that equilibrium has many different meanings, with economists often not referring to the same thing.

As a result the economist should abandon the ambition of explaining everything with a single theory, but instead chose appropriate theories applicable to limited levels of description. Objectivity in this case is given only by weighting results from the given points of view.

## 6. HERMENEUTICS AND LEVELS OF DESCRIPTION

With reference to the studies of Gregory Bateson and the cognitive sciences, we propose that the hermeneutical analysis of economic theories should be based on the 'epistemology' of cognition in economics. Bateson stressed the need for a double description of object and context (Bateson, 1972, 1979). It is the self-referentiality of the cognitive process that involves an ontological investigation into thought (von Glasersfeld in Watzlawick, 1988; von Foester, 1982; Maturana and Varela, 1984).

The assumption of particular solutions about space, time and the determinants of inference decides the level of description of a theory. In this way there could be several different levels of description. They cannot be simply defined in a single-dimension hierarchy from micro to macro, such as consumer, firm, industry, nation, world. A classic example used in epistemology is the dualism between *holism* and *methodological individualism*. These, however, are only two relative perspectives. In economics only a few different spatial perspectives are acknowledged. Levels of description are best defined in complex multidimensional networks and can only be ordered by logical types.

Some of these levels fit the object studied, some are misleading. We cannot exclude the possibility of several different points of view fitting the same object. In this case a plurality of models will increase our information about the economic system studied. If we analyse existing economic theories we will find that at the core of the different views there are different ontological assumptions. The assumption of synchronic time in neoclassical economics versus the diachronic time of Keynesians is a straightforward example. The latter also assume a point of view within the system studied while monetarists assume an external point of view influencing their concept of the government role in fiscal policies.

'Everything that is said is said by an observer' at a certain level of description (Maturana, 1990)[13] and extending the results of a description from one level to another is a source of error, a typical *abstraktive Fehlschluss*. The hermeneutical approach should also develop a criterion by which inappropriate approaches are questioned to reach a certain appropriateness of the cognitive process in economics. An explicit set of ontological foundations of observing would help.

In macroeconomics a lack of familiarity with the principles of logical types seems to cause an unnecessary need to justify certain operational hypotheses of models. This is seen in the case of disaggregate models in the theory of growth and capital, where authors sometimes make the hypothesis of an economy composed of one, two or three industries. A disaggregate macroeconomic analysis does not need to refer to industry to legitimate its assumptions. A macroeconomic analysis can be legitimated only by itself, that is to say by the possibility of disaggregating the whole economy by some self-identifying relation proposed by the theorist himself. A good example of a self-identifying relation is the representation of the economy in tradables and non-tradables. In this case we do not refer to objects defined by objects of another level of description, but to self-justifying macroeconomic relations.

There are two main implications of our interpretation. The first is that we cannot say that a theory is absolutely inadequate, irrelevant or misleading. A theory is strictly related to what we wish to analyse, so it can only be said to be inadequate relative to a particular aspect of reality studied. This is the same as saying the theory gives an unsatisfactory explanation of that part of economic phenomena.[14] The second is that theories are not only alternatives but also complementary in explaining complex facts. This is a substantial change from the traditional approach oriented to the demonstration of a thesis, to an approach based on searching for where a theory works.

The need for compatibility between epistemology[15] of the theory used and the fact to be explained should be underlined. There must be compatibility between the object studied and the approach used to explain it. We must choose the epistemological bases of theories properly, and this is at least as important as methodological questions.

## 7. CONCLUSIONS

We have seen that a hermeneutical approach needs to refer to the cognitive bases of economics that determine levels of description. A theory is a stylized language, and as a language it needs to refer to objects (otherwise normally called symbols). The process of objectivizing what is not an object determines some ontological differences among theories. These ontological discrepancies are due to the limitations of our cognitive domain. The result is a non-comparability and the complex complementary nature of different theories. Further, theories have a limited field of application and one of the main roles of the theorist is to make explicit and account for these intrinsic limits. Static and evolutionary theories are not distinguished by a simple question of methodology. The ontological foundations of observing are the key differences and, therefore, we should consider the two theories as having two different objects. For this reason pluralism is not only possible but necessary in economics.

Therefore, the kind of pluralism proposed does not comprise a plurality of schools of thought composed of a clearly defined hierarchy of models. Rather we propose a plurality of models organized in complex networks corresponding to the plurality of levels of reality naturally originating in the cognitive process.

## ACKNOWLEDGEMENTS

The present work has been elaborated in strict collaboration between the authors, however the first two paragraphs are attributable to Prof. Eugenio Benedetti, the remaining to Stefano Solari. We are indebted to R. Tamborini for comments on an earlier draft of this chapter. We wish also to thank M. Egidi, A. Graziani, A. Salanti, A. Vercelli and S. Zamagni for their encouragement.

## NOTES

1. With reference to Hausman (1992), we can say that economics is inexact but not a separate science.
2. We refer to the meaning of hermeneutics as proposed by Rorty (1979). Neo-pragmatism

acknowledges the incommensurability of theoretical perspectives, and leads to a critical-interpretative approach, instead of the critical-normative one of methodology.

3. Metaphysical realism is when we affirm the possibility of discovering a truth corresponding to an independent objective reality. See also Feyerabend (1978).
4. Normally epistemology and hermeneutics are considered as incompatible or opposed. Since we adopt a broader sense of what epistemology is (a Batesonian evolutionary epistemology), the only remaining contrast is between hermeneutics and methodology.
5. Constructivism in its radical forms affirms that knowledge is constructed to order the flow of experience in repeatable experiences and certain relations. The problem is not finding a true theory but analysing the fit between knowledge and experience and pre-existing knowledge. Verificationism confuses a test conducted in the space of thought with an effective test made in the real world. See the work of von Glasersfeld in Watzlawick (1988), and Berger and Luckmann (1966).
6. It is the theory of autopoiesis.
7. This is a rather free interpretation of Kantian theories that were developed in a different context. In particular, our approach does not refer to neo-Kantism but rather to constructivism, neo-pragmatism and also to the practical philosophy of Gadamer that is partially in contrast with original Kantian thought.
8. The theory of logical types was formulated by Bertrand Russell in Whitehead and Russell (1913).
9. Reductionism considers the 'whole' as a simple sum of parts. Disconnected levels of description mean a 'boot-strapping' view and give to the 'whole' a certain autonomy with respect to what composes it.
10. We refer to the 'observing systems' as described by von Foester (1982).
11. A synchronic perspective is a point of view external to the temporal dimension of the system where things happen. Its feature is the eternal present where every moment of passing time could be seen at once. It is deterministic. For example, the product cycle theory could be considered dynamic and synchronic.

    A diachronic perspective is a point of view oriented to the process and flow of events in the evolution of the system considered. From this perspective events are possible but not determined.
12. That is obviously true in the short run, while in the long run some kind of circularity should be necessarily considered if we do not want to risk dangerous extrapolations.
13. With the concept of objectivity in parenthesis, he wants to go further with the subjectivist point of view by introducing an objectivity limited to the level of description determined by the point of view of the observer, then a plurality of objective views is possible.
14. For this reason, with reference to Hodgson (1992), we think that there could still be room for some neoclassical models, but not for the entire theory.
15. In the Batesonian sense, that is to say the ontological foundations.

## REFERENCES

Bateson, G. (1972), *Steps to an Ecology of Mind*, New York: Ballantine.

Bateson, G. (1979), *Mind and Nature*, New York: Dutton.

Bateson, G. and M.C. Bateson (1987), *Angels Fear*, New York.

Benedetti, E. and S. Solari (1992), *Economics and Evolutionary Systems*, Quaderni del Dipartimento di Economia no. 14, University of Padua.

Benedetti, E. and S. Solari (1993), *Ontology and Hermeneutics of Economic Theory*, Quaderni del Dipartimento di Economia no. 27, University of Padua.

Berger, P.L. and T. Luckmann (1966), *The Social Construction of Reality*, New York: Doubleday.

de Marchi, N. (ed.) (1988), *The Popperian Legacy in Economics*, Cambridge: Cambridge University Press.
Feyerabend, P.K. (1978), *Der wissenschaftstheoretische Realismus und die Autorität der Wissenschaften*, Braunschweig: Vieweg & Sohn.
Gadamer, H.G. (1972), *Wahrheit und Methode*, Tübingen: J.C.B. Mohr.
Hausman, D.M. (1992), *The Inexact and Separate Science of Economics*, Cambridge: Cambridge University Press.
Habermas, J. (1981), *Theorie des kommunikativen Handelns*, 2 vols, Frankfurt am M.: Suhrkamp.
Hicks, J.R. (1979), *Causality in Economics*, Oxford: Blackwell.
Hodgson, G.M. (1992), 'The Reconstruction of Economics: Is there still a Place for Neoclassical Theory?', *Journal of Economic Issues*, **26** (3), pp. 749–83.
Lavoie, D. (ed.) (1990), *Economics and Hermeneutics*, London: Routledge.
Lawson, A. (1987), 'The Relative/Absolute Nature of Knowledge and Economic Analysis', *Economic Journal*, **97** (4), December, pp. 951–70.
Lawson, A. (1988), 'Probability and Uncertainty in Economic Analysis', *Journal of Post Keynesian Economics*, **11** (1), Fall, pp. 38–65.
Lorenz, K. (1973), *Die Rückseite des Spiegeles. Versuch einer Naturgeschichte menschlichen Erkennes*, Münich: R. Piper & Co.
Mäki, U. (1989), 'On the Problem of Realism in Economics', *Ricerche Economiche*, **43** (1–2), pp. 176–98.
Maturana, H.R. (1990), *The Biological Foundations of Self Consciousness and the Physical Domain of Existence* (Italian transl. [1993], *Autocoscienza e Realtà*, Milan: Raffaello Cortina Editore).
Maturana, H.R. and F.J. Varela (1980), *Autopoiesis and Cognition. The Realization of the Living*, Dordrecht, NL: Reidel.
Maturana, H.R. and F.J. Varela (1984), *El Arbol do Conocimiento* (Italian transl. [1987], *L'Albero della Conoscenza*, Milan: Garzanti).
Mirowsky, P. (1988), *Against Mechanism: Protecting Economics from Science*, Totowa, NJ: Rowman & Littlefield.
Rorty, R. (1979), *Philosophy and the Mirror of Nature*, Princeton: Princeton University Press.
Rorty, R. (1989), *Contingency, Irony and Solidarity*, London: Cambridge University Press.
Samuels, W.J. (1991), 'Truth and Discourse in the Social Construction of Economic Reality: An Essay on the Relation of Knowledge to Socioeconomic Policy', *Journal of Post Keynesian Economics*, **18**, pp. 511–24.
Varela, F.J. (1979), *Principles of Biological Autonomy*, New York: Elsvier North-Holland.
Varela, F.J., E. Thompson and E. Rosch (1991), *The Embodied Mind. Cognitive Science and Human Experience*, Cambridge, Mass.: The MIT Press.
Vercelli, A. (1991), *Methodological Foundations of Macroeconomics*, Cambridge: Cambridge University Press.
von Foester, H. (1982), *Observing Systems*, Seaside, Calif.: Intersystems Publications.
Watzlawick, P. (1988), *Die Erfundene Wirklichkeit*, Münich: R. Piper & Co.
Whitehead, A.N. and B. Russell (1913), *Principia Mathematica*, Cambridge: Cambridge University Press.
Zamagni, S. (1980), 'Causalità ed Economia: A Proposito di un Saggio di Hicks', *Note Economiche*, **3**, pp. 3–26.

# COMMENT: HAS ECONOMICS ANYTHING TO GAIN FROM METAPHYSICS AND HERMENEUTICS?

**Robert Nadeau**

Simultaneous appraisal of Uskali Mäki's, Tony Lawson's, and Eugenio Benedetti and Stefano Solari's chapters is possible only if one sees that, different as they may be and legitimate as the problems addressed by each one may appear, these three chapters have something in common which allies their authors and gives them a shared purpose. In these chapters the authors can appear to have their interests bound up together in the sense that they either move away from traditional methodology (in the cases of Lawson, and Benedetti and Solari) or at least keep it at a distance (in the case of Mäki).

Indeed, all three chapters reject what traditionally has been the main purpose of philosophical analysis when applied to scientific knowledge. This goal can be easily identified: the work of the philosopher is to assess what Kant termed the *Geltungsanspruch* of all theoretical knowledge, in other words the 'claim to validity' of those conceptual structures constructed to account for the phenomena we observe in various realms or domains of reality. Traditionally, notwithstanding radical divergences between different schools of thought (for example: transcendental idealism, pragmatism, conventionalism, logical positivism, critical rationalism, antirealism, constructive empiricism, etc.), this general goal has been pursued until now through, largely speaking, logical, epistemological and methodological analysis. What the three chapters I will speak about share in common, it seems to me, is that they explicitly suggest that we forego traditional economic methodology, or they at least leave aside momentarily this traditional approach to science to do something other than methodology. Each one presents something which pretends of course to be worthwhile and fruitful, if not immediately at least in the long run. Directly or indirectly they all plead against tradition in philosophy of economics and in favour of new approaches to economics.

Metaphysics and hermeneutics are the new approaches favoured here. Of course I will not pretend that the three chapters are identical on every point or that they convey the same message to us. To the contrary, it must be noted that when the time comes for each to select its path of attack, slight, if not large, differences appear. Moreover, there certainly are dividing lines between the chapters and we could even say that they contradict each other. On the one hand, Uskali Mäki and Tony Lawson, who can be said to have something in common, purport bluntly to assume a metaphysical stand instead of an epistemological one. They both adopt metaphysical realism, though they do it differently. Eugenio Benedetti and Stefano Solari, on the other hand, would rather have us accept the general thesis that contemporary philosophy is no longer interested in metaphysics and has switched interest to 'problems of cognition and knowledge' (see p. 48 of their chapter). But they would also promptly urge us to understand that to act in accordance with this statement, economists should take what has been called elsewhere 'the interpretive turn'. The two perspectives are quite different and we need to examine each of them more carefully.

To begin with, however, I would like to stress that there can be no greater reassurance that the context is pluralist than when divergent views can be seen at work or when tough incompatibilities in theoretical perspective can be observed. The views expressed in these chapters are more than merely discrepant, of course, but I am not sure that, if we consider all sides of each philosophical position, we will find the divergence to be as great as it first seems. Let us throw a rapid glance at these three chapters and try to understand their aims and where they lead.

First, let me ask whether economics has anything to gain from metaphysical analysis in general. This question presupposes, of course, that we may legitimately entertain some doubts in this respect, and I will shamelessly express my personal scepticism about the whole enterprise. Is there something about metaphysics that economists have always wanted to know but were afraid to ask? Perhaps, perhaps not: I will not speak for them. However, from my own philosophical standpoint, it makes sense to ask whether there is something in traditional metaphysics that could prove useful to economists. Could metaphysics, added to the mathematics, sociology, history, psychology that, *ex hypothesi*, economists already know and work with, help them to do a better job? This will be, quite obviously, my central preoccupation throughout my commentary.

I really do not think that, for economists *qua* economists, there is a lot to be learned from Uskali Mäki's 'One World Principle' (OWP). In fact, to reveal my deepest thoughts on this subject, I must say that I do not even know whether economists should accept or challenge this metaphysical principle. My reason is rather simple: I see no difference it could make. So, at this point, my concern can be put in straightforward terms: I cannot think of any observable consequence that the adoption or the rejection of the OWP would or could make. I can, of course, easily imagine logical consequences philosophers could infer from it in the framework of a general epistemology or of a general metaphysics. This is not what I challenge. What I mean is that I cannot see what the economist is to do with so broad a commitment.

I do not say that I cannot understand why metaphysical questions should be addressed. I fully grant that *inside a systematically articulated philosophical system* one has to be as radical and exhaustive as one can be. Great philosophers from the past – pre-Socratic and medieval thinkers, for example, but also philosophers of modern times from Descartes, Leibniz and Hume to Heidegger, Sartre and Quine just to name a few – have raised metaphysical questions. For instance, they have asked radical questions about 'what there is' and how it should be depicted and classified. A systematic philosopher cannot help but be concerned, *qua* systematic thinker, by metaphysical queries.

Metaphysics seems to give way to the most radical and also the most abstract kind of questioning, and stimulation of this kind of questioning is probably the hallmark of philosophy as an intellectual enterprise. So, metaphysical puzzlement is real and legitimate, for philosophers at least. Philosophers like to see themselves as endowed with an unlimited interrogative faculty. As a matter of principle, they do not believe in the possibility of finding the last word on any human concern, be it cognitive or moral. Even after more than two thousand years, philosophers still seek answers about everything there is to be puzzled about, but they are increasingly aware, with the passing of time and with the growth in knowledge brought by scientific progress, that almost every time a question is addressed it must be kept in mind that it could manifest epistemological or methodological peculiarities.

As exotic as it may seem to economists, there is nothing strange about philosophers asking what it means to say that 'something exists'. As the history of philosophy shows, there is something like a continuum from Aristotle's explanation that 'to exist' can be interpreted in accordance with ten different categories, Kant's addition of two more categories to this list, Heidegger's demarcation of the question of the 'ontic field' (the questions about all kinds of existing things as such) from the 'ontological question' (the question about the fact that there is something in general as opposed to the fact that there could have been nothing), and Quine's statement that 'to be' means 'to be the value of a quantified variable'. All this regards general philosophy and is part of what philosophers train themselves to do as specialists. I do not mean by this that only philosophers should be concerned with this particular kind of intellectual game, for it should interest everyone, but of course everybody cannot devote time to it. I just mean that even if I found an algebraist, an astrophysicist or an econometrician interested in these topics, I would be quite surprised if any one of them could show me a relevant application of this line of questioning *inside his or her own discipline.* What would be really strange for a philosopher would be to open a book in topology or in quantum electro-dynamics, for example, and discover that the scientist's operational starting point is a very broad commitment to a particular metaphysical point of view, such as that found in Mäki's and Lawson's chapters.

This is the kind of feeling I get when I read Tony Lawson's chapter in particular. I cannot really say the same for Uskali Mäki's chapter, for it is mostly an exercise in definition which seeks to clarify certain terms revolving around and connected with the topic of pluralism in general. Apart from the OWP, Mäki strives for almost no philosophical theses in his chapter. Thus there is nothing to be really challenged from my point of view. However, the situation is not the same in Lawson's case for, appearing to accept Donald McCloskey's deterring argument that 'methodology is bourgeois' and that there is no fact of the matter in methodology because methodology is nothing but misleadingly 'issuing orders to working scientists', Tony Lawson argues that, in view of the disaster produced by this philosophical discipline, one can choose to do something other than sociology ('meta-sociological empiricism'). This means that one can choose to continue doing critical analysis of economics, but this time by asking very broad metaphysical questions instead of narrow methodological ones. This is the only way I can interpret his adoption of Roy Bhaskar's transcendental realism.

It is not clear what *economists* can gain in switching from 'normative methodology' to this brand of metaphysics. For example, asking in a Kantian mood what are the conditions of economic knowledge or economic experience will not deliver, it seems to me, the results Tony Lawson still appears to be seeking: a new approach to economics which leaves aside the question of demarcation but still tries to answer the question of what makes economics scientific knowledge. The endorsement of a brand of metaphysical realism cannot do by itself precisely what only an epistemological or methodological type of analysis can do, in other words reveal to us the epistemic characteristics of economics as a kind of theoretical practice.

It is no wonder then that, even when he does what he takes to be metaphysics, Tony Lawson articulates broadly the same kind of viewpoint as that to which we became accustomed in reading traditional epistemology and methodology. For, if we recognize with Lawson that economic phenomena reveal underlying structures (as in physics) and if we grant that, as Lawson writes, 'causal laws must be analysed as tendencies, which are only manifest as event regularities (including probabilistic ones) under relatively unusual, typically intentionally engineered, closed conditions' (see his chapter, p. 13), then we are back to precisely the kind of considerations we specifically wanted to avoid from the start when we decided to dismiss normative methodology in favour of descriptive metaphysics.

It seems that nothing important has changed and this journey into metaphysics appears to have been a useless detour. Indeed, metaphysics *à la Bhaskar* notwithstanding, we still have to cope with the epistemological hard fact, constantly referred to by twentieth-century methodologists, that there are apparently no *causal laws* in economics because, as Robbins said more than 60 years ago, there seems to be no 'constant regularities' in this domain of reality (see his 1932 *Essay on the Nature and Significance of Economic Science.* 2nd Edn, London, Macmillan, 1935). So, if I am right, even if we follow Uskali Mäki and Tony Lawson down the meandering path of metaphysics, we find ourselves – albeit after a long and perhaps philosophically interesting walk through the metaphysical forest – exactly back at the point we started from. We find ourselves back in town, smack in the middle of traffic. We are back where economics is pursued as a scientific endeavour and we are still trying to make sense of it.

Would we be better off if we were to take the interpretive turn and do hermeneutics instead of metaphysics? To my mind, absolutely not. Certainly, Eugenio Benedetti and Stefano Solari are right in contrasting phenomenology and hermeneutics with neopositivism by alluding to the fact that what characterizes the phenomenological and hermeneutic approach to knowledge is that it centres attention on the *subject* rather than the object of knowledge. However, contrary to Mäki's and Lawson's metaphysical confessions, the central tenet of the Benedetti and Solari doctrine amounts to the general claim that 'no metaphysical realism is acceptable'. By this they mean to challenge the very 'possibility to discover truth corresponding to an independent objective reality' (their chapter, p. 48). Here again I must say that I do not concur, but apart from the fact that I see no interest in challenging this philosophical creed, the point I wish to make now concerns Benedetti and Solari's interpretation of 'subjectivism' and 'objectivism'. And to make this point, I will base myself on Uskali Mäki's and Tony Lawson's chapters.

As Tony Lawson himself points out in his chapter, Hayek was the first to insist on the fact that the only 'reality' which is of interest to economists is the 'subjective reality' of economic agents. By this, Hayek meant to emphasize the fact that the exclusive reality economists should be interested in explaining is thoroughly constituted by the beliefs of all economic agents when they try to coordinate their personal plans and when, for that reason, they interact with one another. As Hayek says, it does not matter to the economist whether the laws of Nature are objectively true or not: what matters is whether people *believe* them to be true because they act accordingly and because the course of action they take is precisely what the economist should try to understand, theorize and explain.

For the sake of argument, let us suppose that this situation is an epistemological hard fact and regard it as indisputable as such. What is nonetheless disputable is the methodological consequence we often see economists inferring from this. It is indeed often asserted that, because economic reality is thoroughly subjective, objectivity cannot be achieved in economics. Following the same line of reasoning, some social scientists even go as far as pretending that it can never be achieved in social science in general, but this argument is plainly mistaken. Surely we should not infer from the epistemological fact of the subjectivity of all economic reality the epistemological and methodological consequence that this reality cannot be objectively investigated and known. Those who, like Benedetti and Solari, take that step commit a fallacy probably due to a category mistake: they take a characteristic of the object of economics (subjective value, individual action and economic institutions supervening on those individual valuations and actions) for a limitation of the method of economic inquiry. However, as Mäki himself writes, 'those aspects of the real world which are of interest to a social scientist are often subjectively and even theoretically constituted by the agents of social processes. This, however, is consistent with their being irreducible to the thought worlds of an economist' (chapter 2, n. 2).

More importantly, the 'interpretive turn' in economics cannot be presented, as it is in Benedetti and Solari's chapter, as a necessary consequence of having to take serious account of the bare fact of subjectivity. 'Subjectivism' in economics should only mean that economists start from the subjective facts of economic life, and it should not mean that economists themselves cannot help but being 'subjective' rather than 'objective' about those subjective facts. We have to take for granted that, in economics as in all other social sciences, theoreticians deal with human intentionality. This means that economists have to cope with purposefulness, beliefs, preferences, subjectively held information, individual expectations and subjective utility. So much for that. Nothing in this supports the idea that economic inquiry cannot be *objective* if we mean by this that every explanatory hypothesis advanced in economics must be intersubjectively criticized and, if possible, empirically controlled. Certainly, taking the interpretative turn cannot imply that in economics theoreticians, themselves part of the domain they intend to investigate, must assume a methodological stance different in nature from that they would take if they were doing physics or, more generally, natural science instead of social science.

In particular, taking this turn absolutely cannot mean that we can put aside 'normative methodology'. Yet Eugenio Benedetti and Stefano Solari oppose, right from the beginning, a 'critical-interpretative approach' to the 'critical-normative' approach to which methodology is supposed to lead (their chapter, note 1). Thus, following Rorty, they urge us to switch from an 'ascriptivist' to a 'descriptivist' brand of philosophical analysis. But is it truly possible, when articulating a philosophical analysis of economics or of any other scientific discipline, to avoid all evaluations and normative arguments? I really do not think so. Normative judgements made by phenomenologists or hermeneuticists will perhaps escape notice for a time, but sooner or later they will be made manifest. It is no wonder, then, that Eugenio Benedetti and Stefano Solari, while explicitly embracing pluralism, come to the conclusion that 'the economist *should* abandon the ambition to explain everything with a single theory, but *must* choose appropriate theories applicable to limited levels of description' (their chapter, p. 48; my emphasis). This assertion is plainly, undeniably, normative. I hold this as evidence, only a small piece of proof of course, but empirical evidence nonetheless, that, interestingly enough, the adoption of phenomenology and hermeneutics will not in itself naturally exempt us from speculating about standards, criteria and norms. Even if hermeneuticists and phenomenologists explicitly chose not to entertain such normative questions, it surely should be possible to discover in their analyses implicit norms which they use at least unconsciously.

In conclusion let me ask where this leads us. If metaphysics is about finding very abstract principles and hermeneutics about denying that there can be objective truth, I dare say that these new approaches actually lead us nowhere. The real problem here is that none of the three chapters I have discussed ends up with something specific to say about economics. In my opinion, the brand of metaphysical or hermeneutic analysis favoured here is not 'analytical' enough to be of any use to those economists still interested in articulating a metascientific reflection on their discipline.

Of course I do not hold anything against metaphysics and hermeneutics *per se,* if only because it would be foolish not to accept the kind of conceptual clarifications ontological analysis can provide when applied to the theoretical commitments of economists. But this is the only kind of metaphysics I myself would promote. I in no way challenge the fact that metaphysical and hermeneutic analysis could give rise to new approaches to economics. Moreover, as a general matter of principle, economists should agree that they have to support all elucidations that philosophy can possibly produce. Considering the epistemological mess economics is often said to be in, economists should grant that, in science, nobody can afford to ignore any approach that could produce interesting results, but I still entertain doubts concerning metaphysics and hermeneutics. Certainly pluralism, at least the pluralism I am praising here at the philosophical level, is not to be seen as the symptom of an intellectual disease or, as Kuhn would perhaps want us to think, as the chief sign of an epistemic deficiency. It should simply be promoted as a research strategy for a discipline in need of better results.

A tree should be judged by the fruit it bears. This should also apply to the tree of knowledge. In order to be fruitful, the metaphysics and hermeneutics of economics should be more to the point, much more specific than they are in Mäki's, Lawson's and Benedetti and Solari's chapters. They should give rise to new understandings *of economics* as a kind of epistemic enterprise, and not content themselves with providing new general definitions or disclosing new philosophical ideas about reality in general. But neither should they, by the same token, give rise to new misunderstandings about the kind of benefits philosophy can bring to economics.

Philosophy can surely help to clarify concepts and arguments that are already proposed by economists, especially if those arguments are only loosely structured and articulated, but it cannot itself produce any new *economic knowledge.* For that matter, metaphysics, phenomenology, and hermeneutics cannot replace mathematical and empirical research. They cannot replace epistemological and methodological analysis either because, as I have tried to show, in the best cases, they converge on it. Philosophy can only provide a new context of discussion and justification in which to situate the practical ways of conducting inquiry in economics and the theoretical findings to which those ways lead. This is all economics should try to find there.

# 4. The case for methodological pluralism

**Warren J. Samuels**

## 1. INTRODUCTION

The objective of this chapter is to present a brief summary statement of the case for methodological (epistemological) pluralism. The subject is so vast, so complex and so laden with nuance that the most I can hope to provide here is a version of what Martin Bronfenbrenner once called a 'middlebrow' treatment.

The case for methodological pluralism ultimately rests on the necessity of choice in the absence of a single conclusive final methodological or epistemological principle. We have to choose between alternative methodologies each of which has its own internal limitations and there is no single unequivocal, conclusive meta-principle on which to make that choice. Methodological pluralism is admittedly uncomfortable for those who assume the existence of (1) a given reality, (2) one correct theory and/or (3) one correct methodology and who further assume (4) that our task to is find those singular things; that is, for those who seek determinacy and closure and are uncomfortable with open-endedness and ambiguity. But even if we all believed these assumptions we would still likely disagree as to their substantive content, with a resulting inexorable necessity of choice. The fact of the matter is that, whatever the status of those four assumptions, our definition of the economy ('economic reality'), economic theory and methodology are all socially constructed, *made* not found. This situation is complicated by the fact that the object of study, the economy itself, is a matter of social construction – although social constructivism and methodological pluralism are two different matters. The situation is further complicated by that fact that epistemological (methodological), ontological and theoretical considerations are not mutually exclusive in practice. Although one can define each independent of the others, in practice, positions on one of them are frequently extended to the other. This is perhaps especially the case with the ontological assumptions and/or implications of epistemology. Moreover, complications arise from the inexorable operation of selective perceptions of 'order' and 'anarchy' in epistemological and ontological matters. Finally, not all the elements of the version of methodological pluralism presented here need be accepted; different versions would have different formulations – a situation consistent with methodological pluralism itself.

The task of prescriptivist epistemology has been to generate *the* principles of knowledge acquisition which permit accurate identification, description and explanation of the subject. The problems are that the object of study cannot be known directly, independent of the operation of the human mind; that there are multiple possible principles of knowledge acquisition, with no single unequivocal meta-principle on which to choose between them; and that the identification of everything relevant – the problem under study, the domain of study, the methodological principles, and so on – is not given but is socially constructed. In perhaps literally every respect, therefore, there is a fundamental tautological relationship between the assumed principles of knowledge acquisition and the knowledge that is produced: the knowledge that is produced is a function of and gives effect to the assumed principles of knowledge. We face both multiplicity and the hermeneutic circle: insofar as choice among methodological alternatives rests on choice of meta-principle, there is no single meta-principle on which to make a conclusive choice, and choice of meta-principle is tantamount to choice of methodological alternative. Moreover, neither the principles of knowledge nor the knowledge produced bears any necessary relationship to the object of study.

In recent years, scepticism has developed regarding the prescriptivist logical positivist/logical empiricist methodology. Prescriptivism has been seen to be prematurely and/or presumptuously foreclosing, with no single conclusive metaprinciple on which to ground a particular position, positivist or any other. The social construction of any and all prescriptions has been recognized for what it is: the choice of a position without conclusive grounding plus the deployment of persuasive modes of argument, often involving defining terms in such a way as to produce the desired results, which means defining them so as to give effect to what is assumed by the definitions, therefore amounting to tautology. Instead of rejecting methodology/epistemology because prescriptivism is flawed, as Donald (Deirdre) McCloskey insists, methodological pluralism affirms recognition of alternative methodological credentials, with each scholar having to make his or her own choice as to which set of credentials to accept and within what limits. This stipulated recognized necessity of choice is the answer to the prescriptivist criticism that pluralism amounts to 'anything goes'. Another answer is that already, under the general prescriptivist programme in the absence of a conclusive metaprinciple, 'anything *necessarily* goes'.

My intention in this chapter is not to condemn any particular methodological position. Positivism, if it were to work, possesses the most subtle and sophisticated principles of epistemology involving the combination of induction and deduction. The problems are that deduction, induction and the positivist combinations thereof have internal limitations which render their results much less conclusive and persuasive in practice than it would appear from principle. Indeed, practice seems, inevitably, to be dominated by some version of pragmatism – a statement which I do not intend to be negative. My intention is to substitute credentialist methodological pluralism for prescriptivist methodological monism.

Nor is it my intention to challenge the concept or search for 'truth'. Truth – descriptive accuracy and/or correct explanation – is important and the search for truth is important.[1] Truth is so important, however, that it behooves us not to jump to conclusions about it, even when the jumping-off point appears to be a sophisticated or otherwise attractive methodological position. Truth is not unequivocally produced by any particular prescriptivist methodological position; such truth is relative to and tautological with both the position itself and the use(s) made thereof. Truth is principally a name given to what we accept and privilege as confident knowledge, and it bears no necessary relation to the subject about which statements deemed to be true are made. Truth with a capital T is not necessary for rational analysis and criticism. What is necessary, indeed absolutely necessary, is a recognition of both the particularity of the credentials of that which is taken to be true and the limitations that inexorably define the meaningfulness of each set of credentials.

Section 2 examines the epistemological limitations of induction, deduction and logical empiricism. Section 3 presents several illustrative vignettes concerning multiplicity. Section 4 presents the case for methodological pluralism.

## 2. THE EPISTEMOLOGICAL LIMITATIONS OF INDUCTION AND DEDUCTION AND OF LOGICAL EMPIRICISM

It is neither possible nor necessary to present here a comprehensive analysis and critique of epistemology in general and positivism (logical empiricism) in particular. The following statements, while necessarily conclusionary, represent the situation both from within positivism and from the perspective of its critics:

1. Deduction produces validity, not necessarily truth in the sense of descriptive accuracy, correspondence with reality, and/or correct explanation. Aprioristic deduction is circular and tautological. Deduction has to do with the derivation of conclusions from premises, given the system of logic. The results are driven by and are tautological with the assumptions from which they are derived and to which they give effect. A conclusion properly derived

from premises is not necessarily true. Within the context of deduction alone, a conclusion possesses necessarily only validity, given the system of logic and that the conclusion is properly derived from premises. Conclusions that are empirically false can be derived from premises that are empirically false and yet be validly derived.[2] Deduction is a tool useful in the pursuit of truth but does not itself yield truth.

2. At its most sophisticated, positivism involves the confrontation of a theory with the evidence. It involves the specification of the theory in terms of a particular hypothesis; the specification of the social space to which the hypothesis is said to apply (the data to be used in testing); and the specification of a decision rule by which the hypothesis will be confirmed or refuted. Notice first that none of these three specifications is given by the subject; they are socially constructed by the researcher or community of researchers. Notice next that if confirmation takes place, it applies not to the theory as such but to the particular hypothesis, social space and decision rule. Even if all tests result in confirmation, the theory is still not confirmed because there may be forms of the hypothesis, data, and decision rule by which it may be refuted. Even if all tests result in refutation, the theory is still not disconfirmed because there may be forms of the hypothesis, data, and decision rule by which it may be confirmed. Confirmation and rejection are therefore limited, subjective and probabilistic.

Economists have been criticized for their failure to subject their theories to testing. But the more important point is that even rigorous testing cannot yield conclusive results.

3. General theories/hypotheses are usually employed with auxiliary theories. It is impossible to falsify single hypotheses because they are invariably combined with these supplemental hypotheses and one can never be certain as to the basis of the falsification (the Duhem–Quine thesis). Correlative to this is the Heisenberg principle, the impossibility of complete specification.

4. All observation, data and facts are theory-laden. It is therefore impossible to test a theory by the facts with conclusivity. One faces the circularity in which a theory is tested by facts defined in terms of the theory when the data are theory-generated. Circularity results when theory-based data are used to test a theory as explanation of 'reality' when reality is defined on the basis of theory-based data.

Knowledge of reality is mediated by the human mind (and therefore by the processes of cognition, which are themselves socially influenced, with the comprehension of experience) and embodied in definitions of concepts and data.

5. Universal adherence to a particular philosophical position with epistemological implications – such as realism versus nominalism, absolutism versus relativism, and so on – is inconclusive. Individuals will likely adduce

quite different substantive content to a particular position; for example, even if all people were philosophical (or scientific) realists as to ontology, they likely will disagree as to the content of reality. This is not to be understood (for example) as a rejection of the existence of 'reality' (whatever is meant by the term; another problem is that people mean different things by it), only that there is no warrant to jump to or otherwise support substantive conclusions based on a particular philosophical or ontological position.

6. Prediction of the actual future is not warranted by epistemology. Prediction can take place within the context of a particular model but that is not the same thing as predicting the actual future of the world. Prediction within a model is determinate (assuming the model enables uniquely determinate results) but lacks any necessary relevance to actual events. This inability to predict is due to the limited content of the model on the basis of which prediction is made; to the operation in the actual economy of variables and forces not contained in the model; and to the fact of radical indeterminacy in the actual economy – that the future cannot be known until it exists and it will not exist until it has been made on the basis, in part, of human choice, including choices based on 'predictions'. Prediction therefore can not be a conclusively meaningful objective of social science, although it can be a means by which the results of science can be tested.

7. Economics is comprised of hypotheses and models which by their very nature are unrealistic: they do not include all possibly relevant variables or scenarios. This is a necessity and a limitation of empirical and deductive work. This means that all schools of economic thought consist of sets of stories and are, in a non-pejorative sense, grand compilations of economic science fiction.

8. Economics is conducted in terms of language, an artifact, not given by physical or social reality. Language is the means in terms of which we approach, understand and analyse 'the economy' – or what we take to be the economy. Language is both cause and consequence of general culture and selective perception. It defines economic reality and organizes experience for us, encapsulating our interpretation of past experience and speculations.

Economics is constituted by and gives effect to some mode of discourse, consisting of signs. On the one hand, each mode of discourse imposes it own structure on the material with which it is used; on the other, each sign has meaning only in terms of the system in which it operates. There is no necessary relationship between language and the object of discussion. Data and concepts – for example, those, like 'market', comprised of metaphors – are interpretive constructions. The putative subjects of economics are matters of human construction and have meanings given them by human beings. They may only have the meaning that is attributed to them and then acted upon, and bear no necessary relation to some given, independent and transcendent reality.

Perception, thought and analysis in economics are channelled, typically non-cognitively, by deep discursive structures. These are socially constructed and bear no necessary relation to reality.

9. Economic reality seems to be heterogeneous and kaleidoscopic; it is both complex and multifaceted and it changes in material ways. Economic reality can be perceived and interpreted in different ways, depending upon which putative element of the economy is identified and how it is identified, that is, depending upon differences in perspective. Inasmuch as different analysts do in fact differ in the perspective or standpoint from which they approach the economy, it is not surprising that the same economy can give rise to or have applied to it quite different descriptions and explanations, to have associated with it a variety of different schools of economic thought, each of which is also heterogeneous in material ways.

Different social sciences and schools of thought within each science privilege different methodologies and different representations and meanings of the reality each deems to be relevant. It therefore seems obvious that no case for a singular, absolutist prescriptive methodology can be maintained. This situation cannot and indeed does not prevent individual scholars from choosing, on some basis acceptable to them, some set of methodological credentials. Nor does it prevent a scholar from accepting substantive conclusions based on various alternative sets of methodological credentials and using that narrowly defined knowledge in a manner acceptable to the scholar.

Epistemology is a branch of rhetoric, concerned with producing persuasive epistemological principles, *and* rhetoric is a branch of epistemology, concerned with the discursive limits of knowledge.

## 3. SEVERAL ILLUSTRATIVE VIGNETTES: MULTIPLICITY

1. The parable of the blind men and the elephant: Different blind men are led to an elephant and each touches a different part of the animal. One, having touched a leg, concludes that it is shaped like a tree trunk; another, having touched its nose, concludes that it is shaped like a snake; and a third, having touched its massive side, thinks that it is shaped liked a wall. Clearly a heterogeneous object is capable of being selectively perceived quite differently by individuals approaching it from different substantive and methodological standpoints. All are 'true' but incomplete.

2. A person knocks a table with his fist, concluding, because it is unyielding to the hit and causes some pain, that the table is 'hard'. A physicist

examines the atoms of the materials with which the table is constructed and concludes, because of the fluidity identified at the subatomic level, that the table is 'soft'. Clearly the same object is capable of being perceived differently because different operational and methodological modes of perception are employed. Both are 'true' but incomplete.

3. Immanuel Kant informed us of our inability to know reality directly and that our knowledge of reality is not of a reality unmediated by our minds. Ludwig Wittgenstein adds to this that there is no necessary connection between our language and the reality which it is putatively used to describe and/or explain. Benjamin Whorf (and numerous other linguists) tells us that language itself imposes a particular structure on reality, for example, that a different specification of reality is given by a language in which subjects operate upon predicates and by a language in which events simply happen. Claude Lévi-Strauss and Michel Foucault tell us that both our languages and our philosophical and scientific structures contain deep structural features which help to form our comprehensions of reality and problems and to channel analysis.

4. The history of any country can be told in quite different, often mutually contradictory terms, and specific provisions of its constitution can be given different interpretations. This neither should nor does keep individuals from pursuing a 'true' history or interpretation, but it does militate against considering any of them to be necessarily and conclusively true. The same is true of the economy.

The conclusions are that multiplicity characterizes all relevant human activities and that reality does not impose itself upon us in any singular way – unless it is to say that there is no singular specification of reality, which would obviously establish an interesting conundrum, much as does the liar who admits to lying.

Economics is laden with both methodological and theoretical, or substantive, multiplicity. Apropos thereof is a wonderfully insightful statement by John R. Hicks in which Hicks affirmed *theoretical* pluralism, emphasizing the necessity, inevitability and gains to be derived from complementary economic theories:

> Our theories, regarded as tools of analysis, are blinkers .... Or it may be politer to say that they are rays of light, which illuminate a part of the target, leaving the rest in the dark. As we use them, we avert our eyes from things that may be relevant, in order that we should see more clearly what we do see. It is entirely proper that we should do this, since otherwise we should see very little. But it is obvious that a theory which is to perform this function satisfactorily must be well chosen; otherwise it will illumine the wrong things. Further, since it is a changing world that we are studying, a theory which illumines the right things now may illumine the wrong things another time. This may happen because of changes in the world

> (the things neglected may have grown relatively to the things considered) or because of changes in our sources of information (the sorts of facts that are readily accessible to us may have changed) or because of changes in ourselves (the things in which we are interested may have changed). *There is, there can be, no economic theory which will do for us everything we want all the time.* (Hicks, 1983, pp. 4-5; emphasis added)

Economists encounter multiple *methodological* positions, each with its limitations, no one of which can do for us everything we might want all the time. Theoretical and methodological multiplicity and pluralism go hand in hand. The same is true of ontological pluralism. Absolutism and monism are not solely the last refuge of the scoundrel, but they may be attractive to the myopic; more important, however, we cannot solely rely on any singular methodology, because all of them have their internal and external limits.

Economics is therefore replete with multiplicity. This multiplicity can be ignored but doing so will deplete and impoverish one's economics. As Frank Hahn has written,

> we are encompassed by passionately held beliefs ... . In fact all these 'certainties' and all the 'schools' which they spawn are a sure sign of our ignorance ... we do not possess much certain knowledge about the economic world and ... our best chance of gaining more is to try in all sorts of directions and by all sorts of means. This will not be furthered by strident commitments of faith. (Hahn, 1984, pp. 7-8)

## 4. METHODOLOGICAL PLURALISM

Methodological pluralism affirms either that there are no methodological/epistemological absolutes or that no such absolutes have been demonstrated unequivocally. It also affirms that there are no meta-criteria by which to choose between alternative methodologies. The position, therefore, affirms the existence *and legitimacy* of multiple methodological positions.

Induction and deduction, rationalism and empiricism, realism and nominalism, and similar antinomies are understood to be meaningful on their own terms. But each is seen to have fundamental limits and to present no conclusive demonstration of the error of the other, such that no position is conclusively dispositive of the issues on which it takes a position. Logic may yield valid inferences (conclusions) given the premises and system of reasoning but a valid inference is not necessarily true. Neither can empirical testing yield a singular and conclusive Truth. Methodological pluralism does not deny the usefulness of the several positions constituting these antinomies. It does maintain that no position can be summarily disregarded, for example, on *a priori* grounds. It further affirms that substantial insight can be achieved on the basis of the matrix formed by knowledge generated, potentially using each position in all antinomies, whatever individual preferences may be.

Methodological pluralism rejects any exclusivist prescriptivism that seeks to establish one approach to methodology as supreme or to give it a privileged position. It favours a credentialist approach which attempts to establish the specific bases on which particular claims to knowledge rest, without affirming that one set of credentials is necessarily *a priori* prescriptively superior to another.

The rationale of methodological pluralism is that in the absence of meta-criteria by which one methodology can be shown unequivocally to be superior to all others, analyses should not be rejected solely on the basis of methodological considerations. On the other hand, methodological anarchy is avoided by emphasizing, first, the identification of the precise nature, grounds and limits of particular methodologies; second, the importance of the *process* by which knowledge and the credentials of knowledge are pursued and knowledge worked out; third, the burden on each researcher to make studied determinations of credentials for him or her self; and fourth, the process of *criticism* itself.

Methodological pluralism stresses the inconclusivity of the various methodologies. It also emphasizes that the object of study likely has many different facets to it, that it can be approached from different standpoints or perspectives, and that in fact different approaches coupled with different facets yield quite different theories and understanding. The possibility that the world is not heterogeneous, and that the multiplicity of facets may be illusory, is not denied. But methodological pluralism argues that conclusive decisions about such subjects cannot properly be made *a priori* on either methodological or substantive grounds without foreclosing the process of intelligent inquiry.

Methodological pluralism, with particular views about the status of individual methodologies and the putative character of the objects of study, also draws on the philosophy of language and the sociology of science. From the philosophy of language derives the view that established linguistic usage is insufficient to ground conclusively statements of putative fact and epistemological procedure. Substantive statements tend to have both epistemological and discursive meaning, with the latter seemingly tending to predominate. From the sociology of science derives the view that prescriptivist methodology tends to be conventional in character and to arise from the more or less temporary hegemony of particular sociological groups, including scientists and philosophers. Discursive meaning tends to be a matter of sociological situation and context. With regard to both the philosophy of language and the sociology of science, emphasis is on social constructivism.

Apropos of the conduct of science, methodological pluralism affirms that science is not a singular, homogeneous enterprise, e.g., science is measurement. Science, along with the logical empiricism or logical positivism which tends to be its epistemological rationalization, is comprised of several different methodological positions, so the concept or claim of 'science' does not obviate the case for methodological pluralism.

Methodological pluralism affirms that there are at least three kinds of work in which an economist can be engaged. As specified by the agricultural economist, Glenn Johnson (1986), they are: (1) Disciplinary work, pursuing the agenda of a particular paradigm or research programme – in economics, predominantly that of neoclassical economics. (2) Subject-matter work and (3) problem-solving, or policy, work, pursuing knowledge of particular subjects and/or bringing that knowledge to bear on policy questions and seeking that knowledge from all relevant disciplines. Methodological pluralism also affirms that an economist may properly do *a priori* theory, quantitative and/or non-quantitative empiricism, history, and so on. Methodological pluralism affirms, too, that an economist may properly do static partial and/or general equilibrium theory or evolutionary economics. Within each of these modes of work there can be, and indeed are, varying methodological approaches – and there certainly are varying methodological approaches among them. It is also the case that no methodological procedure is or can be conducted in practice in absolute isolation from all others (for example, the choice is not between pure induction and pure deduction but between various procedural combinations of the two).

Methodological pluralism acknowledges that theory can perform several roles, and that different modes of practising economics do not perform all roles. These roles include (with variations within each category): explanation; description; prediction; hypothesis; confirmed hypothesis; definition of reality; providing a sense of economic order; understanding; tool of analysis; mode of discourse (systematization of ideas, framework of discussion, organizing principle, mode of concentrating attention); facilitating manageability; element in a logical-epistemological structure; prescription; basis of social construction of reality; basis of legitimation/criticism; vehicle of ideology, wishful thinking, paradigm; means of projection; social control; psychic balm; telling a story; giving economics the status of a science; and to refer to neoclassical economics.

Methodological pluralism, so far from affirming a particular conception of economic truth and identifying same with a particular practice of school of economics, holds that economics as a discipline is an organon of inquiry comprising a vast set of tools, instruments used in probing and telling stories about the economy. These tools include concepts, models, theories, assumptions, and so on. They do not in and of themselves necessarily, if at all, define economic reality; rather they are so many instruments available for use by economic analysts. Moreover, because no one theory can answer every question, and no one theory need give a comprehensive, complete answer to any particular question, tools are available for the selective use and modification of economists to suit their perceived needs, or preferred modes, of analysing the economy.

Methodological pluralism, in addition to denying hierarchical superiority to any particular methodology, emphasizes (1) the establishment of diverse, rather than the invidious ranking of, credentials; (2) the comprehension and recognition of methodological limits to substantive research; and (3) the *process* of inquiry, which is always laden with and channelled by metaphysical, discursive and sociological presuppositions. Methodological pluralism will tend to appeal to those who are comfortable with indeterminacy, ambiguity (e.g., plurality of meanings) and openness; and not to those who emphasize or seek determinacy and closure.

Methodological pluralism should also appeal to those who see any particular conception of 'science' as socially constructed and open to challenge – and therefore to those who are prepared to accept science and methodology not as finite givens but as matters of process – a process in which studied identification, juxtaposition and criticism of alternatives figure prominently.

Two issues remain to be discussed: the question of the need for some conventional rule and the problem of (in)commensurability. The need for some conventional rule is a response to the perceived danger of 'anything goes', and is predicated upon a belief that in the absence of some rule nothing can be determined; a vacuum would exist. This concern misapprehends the problem: There is no need for a *discipline-wide* conventional rule. What is needed is clear identification of the varying epistemological credentials of each statement or theory, and to let *each scholar* make up his or her mind what to accept. That is pretty much what we do now, but seem hesitant to say so explicitly.

As for the problem or incommensurability, theories and paradigms, etc., can be compared. They may be distinct (though each usually has enormous elements of ambiguity) and self-contained (in the sense that each poses and answers questions on its own terms), but they can be compared. There is a matrix of specifications of each formed by the views of adherents and of critics, no one of which need be privileged. Conversation can centre on comparing and contrasting (1) the different objectives, (2) the different paradigmatic structures, (3) the different variables, and, *inter alia,* (4) the different chains of reasoning which advocates and critics have advanced; thereby both forming a matrix of differences of specification and interpretation and allowing for changes of specification and interpretation. If by incommensurability is meant solipsistic isolation and independence, such is not embraced by methodological pluralism.

## NOTES

1. Vilfredo Pareto argued, with both accuracy and cynicism, the empirical relevance of the principle of the social utility of falsity, but that is largely a matter for the policy realm (in which he believed that hypocrisy reigned). In any case I will abstract from it here.
2. Consider the syllogism, 'All men are immortal' (in the conventional sense of 'immortality') and 'Socrates is a man', yielding the inference or conclusion that 'Socrates is immortal', a statement which is empirically false albeit valid.

## REFERENCES

Caldwell, Bruce (1982), *Beyond Positivism: Economic Methodology in the Twentieth* Century. New York: George Allen & Unwin,

Dancy, Jonathan (1985), *Introduction* to *Contemporary Epistemology.* Cambridge, MA: Basil Blackwell.

De Marchi, Neil and Mark Blaug (eds) (1991), *Appraising Economic Theories: Studies in the Methodology of Research Programs.* Aldershot,: Edward Elgar.

Diesing, Paul (1971), *Patterns of Discovery in the Social Sciences.* Chicago, IL: Aldine-Atherton.

Diesing, Paul (1991), *How Does Social Science Work?: Reflections on Practice.* Pittsburgh: University of Pittsburgh Press.

Eisenberg, John A. (1992), *The Limits of Reason: Indeterminacy in Law, Education, and Morality.* New Brunswick, NJ: Transaction.

Hahn, Frank (1984), *Equilibrium and Macroeconomics.* Boston: Basil Blackwell.

Hicks, John R. (1983), *Classics and Moderns.* Cambridge, MA: Harvard University Press.

Hutchison, Terence (1992), *Changing Aims in Economics.* Cambridge, MA: Basil Blackwell.

Johnson, Glenn L. (1986), *Research Methodology for Economists.* New York: Macmillan.

Laudan, Larry (1990), *Science and Relativism: Some Key Controversies in the Philosophy of Science.* Chicago, IL: University of Chicago Press.

Raven, Diederick; Lieteke Van Vucht Tijssen; and Jan de Wolf (eds) (1992), *Cognitive Relativism and Social Science.* New Brunswick, NJ: Transaction.

Rescher, Nicholas (1987), *Scientific Realism: A Critical Reappraisal.* Boston, MA: Reidel.

Rosenberg, Alexander (1992), *Economics – Mathematical Politics or Science of Diminishing Returns?* Chicago, IL: University of Chicago Press.

Roth, Paul (1987), *Meaning and Method in the Social Sciences: A Case for Methodological Pluralism.* Ithaca, NY: Cornell University Press.

Samuels, Warren J. (1993), 'John R. Hicks and the History of Economics', in Warren J. Samuels, Jeff Biddle, and Thomas W. Patchak-Schuster, *Economic Thought and Discourse in the 20th Century.* Aldershot: Edward Elgar.

Samuels, Warren J. (1994), 'The Roles of Theory in Economics', in Philip Klein (ed.), *The Role of Theory in Economics,* Boston, MA: Kluwer Academic Publishing.

Weintraub, E. Roy (1991), *Stabilizing Dynamics: Constructing Economic Knowledge.* New York: Cambridge University Press.

# COMMENT

**Riccardo Bellofiore**

Sic veritas norma sui et falsi
(Spinoza)

## 1. Prologue

The chapter by Warren J. Samuels is composed of two connected, but still different, arguments. The first argument (mainly represented by section 2 of the chapter) is a sophisticated critique of positivist methodological positions – or, as Samuels puts it, of 'prescriptivist methodological monism'. Positivism is not rejected because it is 'false', but because of its internal limitations, and because of its lacking in persuasive power. Practising economists are not following its principles. The second argument (mainly represented by section 4 of the chapter) is a plea for 'methodological pluralism'. Knowledge is here depicted as a social and linguistic construction which has no outside. It is, then, impossible to find an ultimate ground, a final epistemological principle. We have to choose 'which set of [alternative methodological] credentials to accept and within what limits' (p. 68); and we need thereafter to deploy rhetorical modes of argument. Conclusive demonstrations are substituted by persuasion.

In the following, I will accept most of Samuels's critique of traditional absolutist methodology. I shall also find something worthwhile in his effort to embrace a credentialist (and conventionalist) approach without falling into the *non-sequitur* of methodological anarchy. Nevertheless, I think Samuels has been – so to speak – trapped by his anti-absolutist argument. It drives him to delineate methodological pluralism at a too abstract level. Samuels's positive stance looks, in fact, like a photographic negative of methodological monism. On the contrary, I am persuaded that what is needed is a more radical break with the problematic of 'epistemology' in both its (seemingly opposed, but internally related) variants – 'positivism' and 'post-positivism'; 'absolutism' and 'relativism'; 'prescriptivism' and 'rhetoric'. Method is *so* linked to substantive inquiry, that we can speak of the former only *after* and *within* the perspective of the latter – which means that we must abandon altogether the terrain of *any* kind of general philosophy of science, and gain access to concrete, specific knowledge enterprises with their concrete, specific methods. According to this outlook, once a peculiar object of knowledge has been framed, it leaves no 'choice' to researchers investigating it; it rather 'compels' them on the way to local, but all the same necessary, truths.

In the short space of a comment I can only give some hints of the reasons justifying this proposed 'dissolution' of epistemology. In the following section, I shall briefly show how a rhetorical approach replicates the traditional questions of positivist methodologies, and then sketch a different route going beyond epistemology. In the last part of this comment, I will recall some very plural voices (Bakhtin, Bachelard, Hacking) to show in what sense a dialogical, anti-foundationalist, local stance may not entail any relativist rejection of the objectivity of knowledge.

## 2. Epistemology as a Trap

The unifying feature of logical empiricism and of falsificationism is the quest for *guarantees* of knowledge – see the criteria grounding the logical empiricists's demarcation between science and methaphisics, or Popper's demarcation between science and non-science. All Popperian qualifications notwithstanding, the search for a universal, prescriptive method is still there – the correct methodological principle guaranteeing the scientific nature of the theory, as it confronts the given, independent reality.

Samuels rightly recalls the host of difficulties this train of thought has found on its way: deduction does not itself yield truth; rigorous testing cannot yield conclusive results; falsification never applies to single hypotheses, because they are combined with auxiliary ones; complete specification is impossible; all observation, data and facts are theory-laden; and so on. Following this critique, one has to recognize that truth (whatever it may mean) can be ascertained only within a textual representation of some constructed object of knowledge. Therefore, looking at the 'justification' of knowledge, the coherence account of truth is the correct one, as far as it underlines that logical accuracy and correspondence with 'facts' are wholly internal features of a peculiar system of thought.

This does not mean, however, either that the knowledge situation exhausts itself in a discursive matter or, as Samuels affirms, that 'there is a fundamental tautological relationship between the assumed principles of knowledge acquisition and the knowledge that is produced' (p. 68). If science is mere discourse, there is no 'outside' to the conversation – *about* what, then, are the conversants talking? And from this viewpoint can the conversation really be seen as a *dialogue?* Method – Samuels says – amounts to the 'stipulated recognized necessity' to argue and persuade in one's own peers' community. In the subjectivist reduction of knowledge to story-telling I am not able to see how the conventional nature of scientific inquiry can avoid slipping into arbitrariness. Along this path, one is forced to follow McCloskey, and before him his philosophical mentor Richard Rorty, to the extreme conclusion that researchers, while they do not offer 'legitimations', still give each other the legitimacy in doing their own job. As Zygmunt Bauman (1987, p. 198) noted some years ago, this move seems to fit very well with intellectuals' (and academicians') concern with their own self-reproduction. But I suggest it is ill suited to account for what is the concrete practice of knowledge-gathering.

Before going on, let me set down a curious feature of Samuels' critique of positivism. Samuels is right when he observes that in the knowledge situation there is no direct access to the 'real' object; accordingly, the object of knowledge should not be identified with the world 'out there'. But then it is rather odd to adduce as a damaging statement against traditional epistemology that 'prediction ... within the context of a particular model ... is not the same thing as predicting the actual future of the world' (p. 71). To say that 'prediction within a model is determinate ... but lacks any necessary relevance to actual events' (ibid.) means precisely to forget that 'actual' world and 'actual' events *never* enter science *as discourse.* Here we find conspicuous evidence of the trap in which one finds oneself if one remains within the boundaries defined by the epistemological alternative – the question whether science is a sort of 'seeing', where truth must ultimately be seen as a correspondence with a given outside reality, or if it is a story-telling, where only coherence and persuasion matter.

Sure, there is no privileged outside viewpoint giving us a principle to discriminate the correct theory and the correct methodology. At the same time, knowledge should not be reduced to rhetoric. What is lost by both sides of the current *Methodenstreit* is that though the justification of knowledge is entirely discursive, the production of knowledge entails by its essence a practical *intervention* on some 'outside' realm. Let me put it this way: knowledge, rather than a 'picture' or a 'discourse' is rather a (specific) kind of 'action'. From this point of view, paraphrasing what the same Samuels has written elsewhere, the pursuit of knowledge amounts to a 'discipline'. This discipline has nothing to do with 'choice'. Once in place, and put to work, a putative 'science' has to accept the feedbacks on it as a system of representation coming from the power it shows or the failures it meets when it is applied in its outside realm – and from the ability or the lack of it in answering the problems generated in the process – in accordance with its own aims and following its own standards.

Economics is a good place to test this way out of the epistemological question. In economics, the outside realm is mainly made by social relations and human motives. In this domain it is crystal clear that the adequacy of theories cannot be divorced from their policy side, that knowledge cannot be divorced from action. Here we have a mutual dependence of knowledge seen as discourse (and hence persuasion) from knowledge seen as intervention (and hence change). *Objective* knowledge no longer means the static 'reflection' of an external object, but the dynamic process of 'construction' both of theory and of reality – theory *making* itself objective; reality *constraining* how this same process is going on.[1]

Looked at from this angle, the case for pluralism acquires a different content. Within a particular theoretical approach there is no place for methodological pluralism; there is rather a necessary relationship between that approach and its method. Among different approaches, pluralism may simply mean the irreducible split of human conversation in different traditions, because there is no final, 'external', methodological point of view, and therefore the only meaningful task is the hermeneutical one. But I suggest there is a more interesting kind of pluralism to endorse: pluralism as *dialogue* among competing theories. This variety of pluralism *presupposes* that there is *no absolute incommensurability* among theories. More than that, people engaged in conversation must take for granted that, at least in a minimal sense, they are talking about the *same* world. To have disagreement, you must have some point of contact. What is distinctive of this activity is that no side – the subject and the object of knowledge; the competing theories – will remain unaffected by the relation with 'the other'. *Change* is a constitutive feature of the knowledge situation.

To summarize the argument so far. The 'objectivity' of knowledge I advocate in this 'dissolution' of both methodology and anti-methodology is not meant to revive the traditional idea of a given reality which the epistemological subject must passively describe and explain. On the contrary, knowledge is objective in these two very different senses: (1) that it entails an activity, a practical intervention, an interaction with some outside realm, though the outcomes of this interaction are always assessed (justified) within the boundaries of language; (2) that the conversation among plural theories cannot be reduced either to solipsism, which leaves theories unaffected by the interaction, or to identification, which means an impossible immediate capability to understand the other (again leaving the conversants as they were at the beginning), but must reach the stage of a true dialogue. In both senses, which are in fact complementary, the knowledge situation compels to an 'exit from the self' foreign both to the dogmatism of positivist methodologies and to the scepticism of most post-positivist methodologies.

## 3. Dialogue, Objective Knowledge, and Styles of Scientific Reasoning

The preceding discussion leads us to a negative conclusion – i.e., to understand the practical undertaking of objective knowledge we must leave altogether the epistemological debate. The other side of the coin is a positive suggestion: the only legitimate way to continue the 'discourse on method' is to address the concrete, specific, research programmes. From this perspective, the dilemma 'absolutism vs. relativism' is shown to be an empty one, because each side of the coin is right in what it denies and wrong in what it affirms. The posing and solving of specific problems is the site where appropriate methods are detected and refined.

In this last section of the comment I will not try any 'demonstration' of this point of view. I shall rather limit myself to quoting some authors I find useful in 'displacing' our questions, throwing in doubt any kind of passive epistemology and replacing it with the view of 'science' as active, objective knowledge. The pluralism appropriate to this form of life will prove to be incompatible with any strong version of either absolutism or relativism.

Let me start with the Russian thinker Mikhail Bakhtin, and his 'dialogical principle'.[2] According to Bakhtin, in the human sciences 'we are interested towards the thoughts, the meanings, the significations that come from the other and become accessible to the scholar only *sub specie* of the text'. Where there are not voiceless things but persons that contemplate and speak, think and act, 'there is no knowledge of the subject but dialogical' (quoted in Todorov, 1984, p. 17). Dialogue 'is the encounter of two texts: the already given text and the reading text being created' (in ibid. p. 18). Bakhtin rejects both absolute objectivism and individualistic subjectivism. Translating his train of thought from linguistics to the philosophy of science, his critique may be restated in this way: positivism and rhetoric see the epistemological subject as the individual, either confronting an external 'independent' world or constituting 'freely' that same world. Bakhtin tries instead a third way, seeing the individual himself as the product of social interrelations.

The dialogical situation shows this very well: the two texts are to be put in a *common context,* where alone they can be understood, and they produce an *intertext,* where each text is described by the other and replies to it. The speaker and the listener, in their changing roles, do not exist as such before the dialogue – just as in the knowledge situation the knowing subject and the object to be known are neither pre-constituted poles nor independent from each other, but are jointly defined only in that same practical relation. To understand *the* dialogue, and to understand *in* the dialogue, the primacy of the social background and horizon, the plurality of the voices, the reality of the other, ought to be recognized, both by the conversants and by whoever is studying the dynamics of the conversation. Discourse cannot be seen as self-enclosed: it has an 'outside' in which it is framed and with which it interacts. Not in the form of passive reflection or of mere persuasion: rather, in the form of an active encounter with the other:

> *Creative understanding* – writes Bakhtin – does not renounce itself, its place in time, its culture; it does not forget anything. The chief matter of understanding is the *exotopy* of the one who does the understanding – in time, space, and culture – in relation to that which he wants to understanding creatively. Even his own external aspect is not really accessible to man, and he cannot interpret it as a whole; mirrors and photographs prove of no help; a man's real external aspect can be seen and understood only by other persons, thanks to their spatial exotopy, and thanks to the fact that they are *other*. (Quoted in ibid., p. 109)

Bakhtin forces us to recognize the crucial role of exotopy and context to conversation seen as true dialogue, and not as a plurality of monologues. We are invited to read the encounter with the other – in a sense, we are invited to look *beyond* the individual text – *through* the textual dimension itself. It is possible to refer discourse to the material conditions and social relations in which it is inscribed, exploiting the tensions revealed by the polyphonic nature of the concrete use of language.

The French Gaston Bachelard emphasizes a similar dialectic within scientific knowledge, this time between theory and experiment.[3] Bachelard is quite clear in stating that there is no neutral standpoint from which to evaluate and make theories commensurable. Nevertheless, he does not see in the discursive nature of theory, in the absence of a permanent foundation, and in the discontinuities marking the history of sciences, a threat to rationality and objectivity. As an interpreter of Bachelard, Mary Tiles has aptly written, for him scientific thought is 'a structured constructive *activity*, manifest in the *discourse of* scientists ... the phenomena of contemporary science are products of experimental techniques and methods of preparation' (Tiles, 1984, p. 205; emphasis added). In the interference between theory and experiment, the one is constrained by the other as (partly) 'external' to it. Knowledge, then, is *rational* insofar as it is a planned, justifiable practice; and it is *objective* knowledge, because 'it has to recognize the nature of the constraints on and obstacles to successful action' (ibid.).

If we follow the reading of the late Wittgenstein put forward by Doyal and Harris (1986, pp. 147–8), we may further say that the theoretical representations 'materialized' in instrumentation come from an understanding of (external and human) nature which has a non-discursive grounding in constitutive activities appraised *prior* to the development of linguistic competence. Thus knowledge is not only applied rationalism; it is also rational *materialism.* Materialism intended as the centrality of material practice *before* and *outside* the discursive domain, however, can never be 'justified' at the epistemic level; it is rather 'a *Weltanschaaung* – a "view" or "outlook" on the whole world', a 'line' or 'policy' leading the inquiry (Suchting, 1986, p. 60 and p. 66).

From this standpoint, 'truth' has no guarantee other than itself – i.e. that of being the temporary, open-ended result of critically reflective knowledge:

> The scientific spirit is essentially a rectification of knowledge ... . Scientifically, one thinks of the truth as historical rectification of an initial common illusion. The whole of the intellectual life of science plays dialectically on this differential of knowledge, at the frontier of the unknown. The very essence of reflection is to understand what one has not understood. (Quoted in Tiles, 1984, p. 208)

According to Bachelard's 'new scientific mind', knowledge is again dialogue, this time in the form of contradiction and critique relative both to common-sense thought and to 'mainstream' anterior theories. Often old ways of scientific thinking are (translated and) incorporated in a more general one. The price to be paid to this kind of practice is that the 'new' approach will become itself subject to future revision and criticism. Epistemology can here consist only in the portrait of the concrete, plural, ways in which actual, plural, sciences have historically evolved and produced their results. The philosophy of science derives from science itself. The former is inevitably spelled out with 'local' pretences, as 'local' is the domain of inquiry of the latter. And it is set forth systematically only *a posteriori* ; it can never be identified with the *a priori,* general, positivist or Popperian method.

Ian Hacking has recently proposed the concept of 'style of scientific reasoning', which is very close to the position I am here trying to sketch:[4]

> A style of scientific reasoning is put in place in a network of people, answering to the needs, interests, ideology or curiosity of its members, defended by bluster or insidious patience. But when it becomes fixed as a new way to truth, it needs no support or rhetoric, for as it assumes self-confidence it generates its own standard of objectivity and its own ideology. It starts by being pushed and shaped by social vectors of every sort; we end with a self-sustaining mode of knowledge. It becomes less something moulded by interest, and more an unquestioned resource upon which any interest must draw, if it ever hopes for the accolade of objectivity. And it further determines how people conceive of themselves and their world, opening new horizons, but also constraining the possible forms of knowledge. (Hacking, 1990, pp. 3–4)

In this outlook, while *what* is true does not depend on how we think, the truth *conditions* depend on the style of reasoning. 'There is no truth-or-falsehood in the matter, independent of the style of reasoning', says Hacking. However, this does not lead to a relativist position because, recalling Wittgenstein's *On Certainty,* 'a style of reasoning, once in place, is not relative to anything. It does not determine the standard of objective truth. It *is* the standard' (pp. 7–8).

## 4. Coda

On this account, pluralism is mainly to be intended as dialogue, and struggle, among competing 'styles'. Dialogue and struggle need, if they ever can be conceived as possible, some implicit reference – call it, if you wish, a metaphysics, or a philosophical *pris de position* – to a common natural and social world of material, and to some common understanding (though the more precise nature of this reference and of this understanding is, of course, controversial). 'Absolute', sceptical relativism is a sort of monologue, just as is dogmatic absolutism.

Samuels's case for methodological pluralism seems to me to be too much concerned with the problematic and the language of traditional epistemology. Maybe this is the reason for its 'relativist' flavour. As an instance, I may quote this phrase from page 69: 'Truth is principally the name given to *what we accept and privilege* as confident knowledge, and it bears *no necessary relation* to the subject about which statements deemed to be true are made.' However, a few lines later I find a position I am quite comfortable with: 'What is necessary, indeed *absolutely* necessary, is a recognition of both the particularity of the credentials of that which is taken to be true and the limitations that *inexorably* define the meaningfulness of each set of credentials.' Is the difference between Samuels's excessive concern with the subjectivity of 'scientific' theories against my stress on making knowledge objective only a difference in rhetorical attitude? No small difference, after all.

## Acknowledgement

Financial aid from MURST 40% and 60% grants are gratefully acknowledged.

## Notes

1. For a more extended critique of positivism and rhetoric *à la* McCloskey see my 'The Poverty of Rhetoric: Keynes vs. McCloskey', in Marzola and Silva (1994). I have found useful in developing my own position Lecourt (1981) and Suchting (1986), but see also the references in 'The Poverty of Rhetoric' and section 3 of this comment.
2. The writings of Bakhtin I am referring to are not, to my knowledge, easily accessible in English. In the following I shall use the very valuable study of Tzvetan Todorov, and the translations there included. On Bakhtin, see also Eagleton (1983).
3. The reference here is mainly to *Le nouvel esprit scientifique, Le materialisme rationnel, Le rationalisme appliqué, La philosophie du non.* As for Bakhtin, also in this case, for convenience, I shall refer to an interpreter: this time the first-class study by Mary Tiles. See also, on Bachelard, Lecourt (1975).
4. I borrow some arguments from Bellofiore (1994). Following this train of thought one would rescue some valuable insights by Neurath and Fleck, on one side, and Lakatos, on the other.

## References

Bauman, Z. (1987), *Legislators and Interpreters. On Modernity, Post-Modernity and Intellectuals,* Cambridge: Polity Press.

Bellofiore, R. (1994), 'History of Economic Thought as a Problem', *History of Economic Ideas,* **II** (2), pp. 124–46.

Doyal, L. and Harris, R. (1986), *Empiricism, Explanation and Rationality. An Introduction to the Philosophy of Social Sciences,* London: Routledge & Kegan Paul.

Eagleton, T. (1983), *Literary Theory. An Introduction,* Oxford: Blackwell.

Hacking, I. (1990), 'The Metaphysics of Styles of Scientific Reasoning', mimeo (Italian translation published in *Iride,* n. 4–5).

Lecourt, D. (1975), *Marxism and Epistemology. Bachelard, Canguilhem and Foucault,* London: New Left Books.

Lecourt, D. (1981), *L'ordre et les jeux. Le positivisme logique en question*, Paris: Grasset.

Marzola, A. and Silva, F. (1994), *John Maynard Keynes: Language and Method*, Aldershot: Edward Elgar.

Suchting, W. A. (1986), *Marx and Philosophy. Three Studies,* London: Macmillan.

Todorov, T. (1984), *Mikhail Bakhtin. The Dialogical Principle*, Manchester: Manchester University Press.

Tiles, M. (1984), *Bachelard: Science and Objectivity,* Cambridge: Cambridge University Press.

# 5. Methodological pluralism and pluralism of method

**Sheila C. Dow**

## 1. INTRODUCTION

Pluralism is the philosophical position that the ultimate reality of the universe consists of a plurality of entities; it is an ontological position. But the concept of pluralism can be applied at a variety of levels: to the (epistemological) understanding of reality (whether its ultimate nature is a plurality or not), to the methods employed to theorize about that understanding of reality, to the methodology which sets the criteria for theory choice, and to the study of methodologies themselves. Pluralism has been advocated at all of these levels in economics discourse. But an understanding of what is entailed by methodological pluralism and pluralism of method has been hampered by lack of reference to epistemological and ontological foundations. In particular, pluralism takes on a different meaning in a closed-system mode of thought (as in mainstream economics) from its meaning in an open-system mode of thought (as in post-Keynesian economics). The former can be thought of as 'pure pluralism', as the dual of a monist position, while the latter involves a more limited, although crucial, pluralism.

It is the purpose of this chapter to attempt to distinguish pluralism at the different levels, and according to different ontological and epistemological positions, and to assess whether the validity of the pluralist position differs as between these different levels. It is concluded that a pure pluralist position is untenable at any level, but that a modified methodological pluralism is to be welcomed if grounded in an appropriate ontological and epistemic position, i.e. that reality and knowledge of it are understood as open systems.

## 2. OPEN AND CLOSED SYSTEMS

Much of the following argument rests on the distinction between open and closed systems. Therefore, before considering pluralism as such, we consider first the nature of that distinction. An open system is one whose boundaries are not predetermined. Further, the nature and range of its constituent variables and the structure of their interrelationships are not predetermined. This is not a matter of stochastic variation. In contrast, the boundaries of a closed system are predetermined, as are the full range of constituent variables and the structure of their interrelationships. This does not preclude the possibility of stochastic variation. While closed systems are the province of classical logic, open systems are the province of a broader system of logic – ordinary logic, or human logic, as exemplified by Keynes (1973). While including classical logic as a special case for application under conditions of certainty, ordinary logic can also be applied to conditions of uncertainty, as pertain in open systems.

At the ontological level, the system is a system of real processes and phenomena. An understanding of reality as conforming to an open system may involve notions of human creativity and freedom of choice, for example. A closed-system understanding of reality may involve the notion of a grand plan on the part of the deity, and the absence of free will. Knowledge systems applied to this reality may be open or closed in either case. On the face of it, it might seem that an open-system ontology would entail an open-system epistemology, and similarly for a closed-system ontology. But, even if reality is an open system, it can be argued that knowledge can only be acquired by proceeding as if reality were a closed system. Alternatively, even if reality is a closed system, it can be argued that human knowledge inevitably cannot encompass the full system, so that it must itself conform to an open system.

General equilibrium theorizing is a fine example of a closed-system theoretical structure. Variables are clearly defined with fixed meaning, and the boundaries of the system are well defined according to which variables are endogenous and which exogenous. The aim is to reach agreement on the best representation of the structural relationships between variables, for universal application. This entails conformity of representation through formalism. The appraisal criterion of conformity to the principles of classical logic reflects a closed-system epistemology; where the additional criterion is applied of goodness of fit in econometric testing, a closed-system ontology is evident.

If reality is an open system, then any closed theoretical system can only have partial application. Formal systems are necessarily closed, since it is necessary to give variables fixed meaning, and to specify structural relationships and the exogenous variables. Other methods, however, can themselves be open; verbal analysis in particular allows for shades of meaning.

Once we move away from a closed-system ontology and/or a closed-system epistemology, the question of pluralism – its meaning and role – becomes interesting. If reality is an open system, how do we specify open systems of knowledge, and what role can closed subsystems of knowledge play? If knowledge is open (even if reality is closed), how do we choose the forms of (inevitably partial) knowledge to aim for? In what follows, we attempt to unravel the different possible senses of pluralism, and how they relate to different ontological and epistemological positions.

## 3. ONTOLOGICAL PLURALISM

Pluralism at the ontological level involves the belief that reality constitutes a plurality of entities. If this position is to be non-trivial, it involves a rejection of the notion of the unity of nature. In its pure form, ontological pluralism denies the existence of unifying forces in nature; if nature is pluralistic, then there is no scope for general theorizing. In economics, this position is most closely associated with postmodernism; postmodernism emphasizes fragmentation, even of the self (see Amariglio, 1988). Ontological pluralism entails epistemic pluralism (understanding is fragmented). Together these pluralisms deny any scope for theory (see Amariglio, 1990); indeed some postmodernists embrace the term 'nihilism' (see Amariglio and Ruccio, 1995), the term with which Gordon (1991) chooses to characterize pluralism. Similarly, they deny any role for methodology.

Yet the content of postmodernism belies these implications; general statements are made about reality, theories are put forward, and methodological statements made. In other words, pure ontological pluralism and its implications are untenable; any theoretical statement requires the belief in some regularity in understanding and/or in nature. The only possibilities then, if discourse is to occur at all, are a modified pluralism (partial regularities), or the belief in universal regularities. Many non-mainstream economists, other than postmodernists, hold a modified pluralist position, based on an organicist ontology (see for example Carabelli's (1995) account of Keynes's organicism). This position holds that there are regularities in nature which science should aim to identify, but that these regularities are of process rather than events (see Lawson, 1989, 1995); they cannot be isolated from evolutionary or other irregularities. The economy, like knowledge, is therefore best understood as an open system.

Mainstream economics on the other hand has traditionally seen its scope as being defined by universal regularities which can be separated dualistically from irregularities and are best understood within a closed theoretical system (see Dow, 1990a). Most mainstream economists, notably deductivists, are not explicit about their ontological position. But Lawson (1994) demonstrates that the view of science on which deductivism is based entails a Humean ontology in terms of event regularities.

How far regularities can be perceived, if they exist, is an epistemic issue. We shall see in the next section that epistemic pluralism is not the sole preserve of ontological pluralists.

## 4. EPISTEMIC PLURALISM

Epistemic pluralism entails a plurality of understandings of reality; there is no known way of establishing what constitutes true knowledge. Logical positivism requires that theory be appraised with reference to an independent set of facts, implying that there is only one way in which (correctly) to know facts. Logical positivism came under serious threat in the 1960s, a period in which the notion that authority had sole access to the truth was fundamentally questioned. In the philosophy of science, Popper's (1959) fallibilism had laid the groundwork, but it was Kuhn (1962) who captured the imagination with his argument that understanding is paradigm-specific; what appears to be contrary evidence may not be perceived as such if it threatens the power of the dominant paradigm.

Out of this change developed a distinctive perspective on understanding; this perspective is evident both in the rhetoric/hermeneutic approach as well as in postmodernism. Both take a pluralist position on understanding. The postmodernist epistemic pluralism follows directly from the postmodern pluralist ontology; even the individual has the potential for a plurality of understanding. The rhetoric/hermeneutic approach is inspired by Rorty's (1979) view that philosophy cannot mirror nature; no position is taken on whether ultimate reality is a plurality or not. (See the exchange between Mäki's (1988) attempt to tease out a rhetoric ontology, and McCloskey's (1988) reply.) Rather, understanding of reality is expressed by means of a plurality of narratives. Thus not only is reality discussed by means of a plurality of narratives, but that reality itself is to be read as a plurality of narratives (see Lavoie, 1990, Introduction, and Brown, 1994). There is no basis for choosing one narrative over another.

The logical positivist belief in a unitary objective understanding of facts nevertheless persists in much of economics (see Boland, 1991 and Lawson, 1994). The difficulty of devising definitive empirical tests has thrown increasing doubt on the truth-value of theory (see Boland, 1989, p. 88), but in general the truth-value of the facts themselves is not questioned among mainstream economists. For the increasingly dominant deductivists, the truth-value of facts is seen as having relevance only regarding axioms, and these are asserted to be self-evident. A significant exception is the explicitly pluralist epistemic position taken by Weintraub (1989); his position has shifted from being Lakatosian (which as a basis for theory appraisal requires a unitary set of facts) to denying the scope for theory appraisal on the grounds that facts are theory-laden, i.e. there is a plurality of understanding of reality.

Epistemologically, there should be a direct parallel between a pluralist understanding (possibly of a pluralist reality) among economic agents and economists alike. This is the case for postmodernists and the rhetoric approach; there is no basis for choosing between understandings among agents or among economists. In contrast, the logical positivist position entails a unitary understanding of facts by agents and a corresponding unitary understanding by economists (though both may be expressed probabilistically). Curiously no such parallel is evident in Weintraub's work; if facts are theory-laden for economists, surely they must also be theory-laden for agents. An acceptance of this point would have profound implications for general equilibrium theorizing. It is the plurality of understanding by economic agents, in the postmodern view, which undermines theorizing in general.

Non-mainstream economists other than employers of postmodernism and the rhetoric approach (post-Keynesians for example) employ an open-system epistemology which allows for a range of understandings but also for theorizing. Following directly from an organicist ontology, or from the view that human understanding of reality (whether ultimately organicist or not) is necessarily limited, it is argued that we can only understand reality as an open, organic system. Keynes's (1973) philosophy provides an epistemology for open organic systems; since knowledge in general is based on imperfect knowledge, it is inevitable that there will be a range of understandings of reality, among agents as well as economists. But this epistemology differs from pure pluralism in that there are regularities in the knowledge-generation process of agents and economists which limit the range of rational benefits; the choice of belief (among agents and economists) is a matter for rational debate.

We now see how these different epistemologies feed through into positions on method, and then on methodology.

## 5. PLURALISM OF METHOD

Pluralism of method is the methodological position that there are no decisive criteria for selecting one best method of analysis (for example the deductivist method, or the experimental method); economists should therefore employ a plurality of methods. The major influence is Popper (1959) who saw a role for situational logic in the social sciences, given the difficulties with falsificationism; the choice of method should then be problem-dependent (see Caldwell, 1991, who also appears supportive of pluralism of method). This version of pluralism (also known as eclecticism) has been advocated by

Hutchison (1988), Boland (1982) and Solow (1988) without any hint of pluralism at the epistemic or ontological levels; all three subscribe to a unitary epistemology and ontology. But if there is unitary understanding of such regularities as can be perceived (i.e. the epistemology and ontology conform to those of logical positivism) then pluralism of method can only be explained in terms of the failure of traditional methodology to produce satisfactory criteria for choosing methods. Practising economists must choose methods by some criteria; on what grounds are these criteria to be selected? In principle, it should be possible to construct a taxonomy of problem-types and advocate methods accordingly, given the starting point that economics aims to identify regularities that are presumed to exist. Boland (1989) takes case studies to illustrate the process of method choice. Mayer (1993) advocates a particular set of criteria based on the distinction between pure and applied theory. He advocates internal, formalist criteria for deductive theory and client satisfaction for empirical theory. But without any epistemological explanation for the need for a range of methods, given a unitary ontology and epistemology, a body of thought made up of pure theory and applied theory, with no explicit connection between the two, appears simply incoherent.

It might seem that pluralism of method could be justified by a pluralist epistemology. Since reality may be understood in a variety of ways, and there are no grounds for preferring one understanding over another, there are no grounds for choosing one method of acquiring knowledge over another. The rhetoric/hermeneutic approach takes an agnostic position (different methods are taken on their own merits but there is no advocacy of pluralism, indeed there is a denial of methodology in general). The postmodernist approach might be interpreted as advocating a plurality of methods; one of its most notable features is the denial of general theories. But, as has been suggested above, any postmodern position on method is self-contradictory; the essence of postmodernism is to eschew normative statements, and indeed theory in general.

The advocacy of a range of methods is entailed by the open-system epistemology of post-Keynesian economics. But this is not pluralism of method in the eclecticism sense, although it is commonly misunderstood by others as such. It is entailed by an open-system epistemology that knowledge is acquired by gathering evidence and constructing arguments in order to build up rational belief. These contributions to knowledge are incommensurate in the sense that they do not build up to a single probability statistic, i.e. they do not fit into closed-system theorizing. Certainly the choice of a range of methods depends on the nature of the problem and the context. But the choice is guided (and thus limited) by reason, by convention and by vision; it is differences in these that account for different schools of thought which have in common open-system theorizing (see Dow, 1990b). To distinguish this approach from that of the eclecticists, it must be emphasized that reason, conventions and vision all take on a particular meaning and play an explicit part in open-system epistemology (terms do not have unitary meaning). Closed-system reason is only a subset of open-system reason (see Carabelli, 1988). Conventions are a necessity in building up knowledge in Keynesian logic (see Hodgson, 1988), while in mainstream epistemology they lack logical foundation, as Boland (1982) has tirelessly pointed out. Finally, vision (or ontology) determines how problems are identified and interpreted (see Dow, 1990b). Given an open-system ontology, there is a range of possibilities; given a closed-system, unitary ontology, there is only one.

## 6. METHODOLOGICAL PLURALISM

Methodological pluralism is a meta-methodological position; it advocates that methodologists study a range of methodologies (by means of rational reconstruction). Critical pluralism involves the criticism of this range of methodologies by means of a range of criteria. This position has been advocated most notably by Caldwell (1982, 1986, 1988). The underlying reasoning is that there is no basis for deciding on one methodology. Rather than devoting fruitless efforts to finding the best methodology, methodologists should devote their efforts to promoting methodological understanding among economists by clarifying the nature of the different possibilities and demonstrating their strengths and weaknesses according to different criteria. (Boland (1982, 1991) at times also seems to be a methodological pluralist as well as a pluralist of method. Redman (1991) advocates a critical rationalist version of methodological pluralism.)

Although this positive role for methodology counters the anti-methodology position of the rhetoric/hermeneutic approach, Caldwell (1990) embraces the hermeneutic idea of taking each approach on its own merits to promote a better understanding among practitioners of different approaches. The critical element is additional, however, and represents the fundamental meta-methodological difference from the hermeneutic approach. The rhetoric/hermeneutic approach accepts plurality of understanding and plurality of method as a description of reality, but refuses to make any normative judgement about the nature or extent of those pluralities; postmodernists positively welcome plurality of understanding and method (the more the better, as a reflection of a fundamentally fragmented reality). Caldwell, rather (from his Popperian starting point) appears to regard a wide plurality of methodologies as a regrettable necessity, and looks forward to the outcome of methodological pluralism as being a narrowing-down of possibilities (see Caldwell, 1989).

But, as was pointed out in the discussion of Caldwell's (1988) paper (see de Marchi, 1988, pp. 53-6), Caldwell does not spell out the epistemological foundations of his methodological pluralism (nor its ontological foundations). What is the reason for a range of methodologies in the first place? Is it in the nature of knowledge (and reality) that it be so, as the open-system approach suggests? Or is it a temporary limitation on our understanding, as the eclecticist approach suggests? Or is it pure folly that methodologies and methodologists persist at all in spite of the fragmentation of knowledge (and possibly reality) as the rhetoric approach and postmodernists suggest?

Critical methodological pluralism explicitly aims to go beyond description. But as with eclecticist pluralists, the question arises as to the criteria for criticism. Caldwell advocates particularly criticism in a methodology's own terms as a way of promoting greater understanding of a particular methodology. Such an effort is clearly preferable to the all-too-common criticism of one methodology by the criteria of another (see Caldwell, 1986). But it is only feasible up to a point. If the justification of methodological pluralism is epistemic, then, just as facts are theory-laden and theories are methodology-laden, so must the knowledge of methodologists be coloured by their own vision of reality and of how knowledge is constructed; epistemic pluralism, after all, is a recognition that there are different understandings of reality, but in general any one economist or methodologist only has one understanding. I can attest from personal experience of trying to present a range of schools of thought in their own terms (Dow, 1985) that it is not possible to switch fully satisfactorily in a detached fashion from one ontology-plus-epistemology to another. But without a pluralist epistemology, what is the justification for methodological pluralism?

While I share Caldwell's view that trying to understand different methodologies in their own terms is a worthwhile exercise and should serve to promote more constructive debate among economists, the scope for that understanding is always conditional on the methodologist's own ontological and epistemological position. This applies even more strongly to the application of external criteria, which must be chosen according to some further criteria if the exercise is to have meaning.

Caldwell's statements of methodological pluralism have tremendous appeal in their advocacy of civilized, reasoned, non-self-serving behaviour. But methodological pluralism, as presented so far, lacks force because of its lack of epistemic and ontological foundations. In traditional epistemic (i.e. dualist) terms, methodological pluralism can be interpreted as non-methodology because it does not establish standards. Understood as the dual of traditional methodology, methodological pluralism may be understood as according with the rhetoric approach, which denies methodology any role. But understood as a means of improving knowledge, where knowledge is understood as an open system, methodological pluralism is fully justified. Methodologists cannot escape their own preconceptions any more than anyone else. But an ontological and epistemic awareness can enhance awareness of these preconceptions, which in turn can enhance awareness among economists at large of their preconceptions.

## 7. CONCLUSION

I conclude therefore that methodological pluralism in a pure form, like pluralism of method, pluralist epistemology and pluralist ontology, is untenable as a basis for knowledge. Pure pluralism is taken here to be the dual of the traditional unitary position of mainstream economics. Further, the justification of methodological pluralism or pluralism of method is not at all clear when either is combined with a unitary, closed-system epistemology and/or ontology. On the other hand, the recognition of the inevitability of a range of methodologies and the advocacy of the employment of a particular range of methods is the logical outcome of an open-system epistemology and ontology.

This chapter is offered as an exercise in open-system meta-methodology. It offers an attempt at a rational reconstruction of a range of positions with respect to pluralism, in the full knowledge that these reconstructions may be flawed, not least because of my own preconceptions. But this is how knowledge progresses: offering arguments provides scope for feedback to correct misunderstandings and to direct modifications in thinking. Within an open-system approach there is no contradiction involved in arguing for one's own viewpoint while respecting and being open to the viewpoints of others.

## REFERENCES

Amariglio, J.L. (1988), 'The Body, Economic Discourse, and Power: An Economist's Introduction to Foucault', *History of Political Economy*, **20** (4), pp. 583–613.

Amariglio, J.L. (1990), Economics as a Postmodern Discourse. In W.J. Samuels (ed.), *Economics as Discourse*, Boston: Kluwer.

Amariglio, J.L. and Ruccio, D.F. (1995), 'Keynes, Postmodernism and Uncertainty', in S.C. Dow and J. Hillard (eds), *Keynes, Knowledge and Uncertainty*, Aldershot: Edward Elgar.

Backhouse, R.E. (1988), 'The Value of Post Keynesian Economics: A Neo-Classical Response to Harcourt and Hamouda', *Bulletin of Economic Research*, **40** (1), pp. 35–41.

Boland, L.A. (1982), *The Foundations of Economic Method*, London: Allen & Unwin.

Boland, L.A. (1989), *The Methodology of Economic Model Building: Methodology After Samuelson*, London: Routledge.
Boland, L.A. (1991), 'The Theory and Practice of Economic Methodology', *Methodus*, **3** (2), pp. 6–17.
Brown, V. (1994), 'The Economy as Text', in R.E. Backhouse (ed.), *New Directions in Economic Methodology*, London: Routledge.
Caldwell, B.J. (1982), *Beyond Positivism: Economic Methodology in the Twentieth Century*, London: Allen & Unwin.
Caldwell, B.J. (1986), 'Towards a Broader Conception of Criticism', *History of Political Economy*, **18**, pp. 675–81.
Caldwell, B.J. (1988), 'The Case for Pluralism', in N. De Marchi (ed.), *The Popperian Legacy in Economics*, Cambridge: Cambridge University Press.
Caldwell, B.J. (1989), 'Post-Keynesian Methodology: An Assessment', *Review of Political Economy*, **1** (1), pp. 43–64.
Caldwell, B.J. (1990), 'Does Methodology Matter? How Should it be Practiced?', *Finnish Economic Papers*, **3** (1), pp. 64–71.
Caldwell, B.J. (1991), 'Clarifying Popper', *Journal of Economic Literature*, **29** (1), pp. 1–33.
Carabelli, A. (1988), *On Keynes's Method*, London: Macmillan.
Carabelli, A. (1995), 'Uncertainty and Measurement in Keynes: Probability and Organicness', in S.C. Dow and J. Hillard (eds), *Keynes, Knowledge and Uncertainty*, Aldershot: Edward Elgar.
de Marchi, N. (ed.) (1988), *The Popperian Legacy in Economics*, Cambridge: Cambridge University Press.
Dow, S.C. (1985), *Macroeconomic Thought: A Methodological Approach*, Oxford: Blackwell.
Dow, S.C. (1990a), 'Beyond Dualism', *Cambridge Journal of Economics*, **14** (2), pp. 143–58.
Dow, S.C. (1990b), 'Post Keynesianism as Political Economy: A Methodological Discussion', *Review of Political Economy*, **2** (3), pp. 345–58.
Gordon, S. (1991), *The History and Philosophy of Social Science*, London: Routledge.
Hodgson, G. (1988), *Economics and Institutions*, Cambridge: Polity Press.
Hutchison, T.W. (1988), 'The Case for Falsification', in N. De Marchi (ed.), *The Popperian Legacy in Economics*, Cambridge: Cambridge University Press.
Keynes, J.M. (1973), *The Treatise on Probability. Collected Writings*, vol. VIII, London: Macmillan for the Royal Economic Society.
Kuhn, T.S. (1962), *The Structure of Scientific Revolutions*, Chicago: Chicago University Press.
Lavoie, D. (ed.) (1990), *Economics and Hermeneutics*, London: Routledge.
Lawson, T. (1989), 'Abstractions, Tendencies and Stylised Facts: A Realist Approach to Economic Analysis', *Cambridge Journal of Economics*, **13** (1), pp. 59–78.
Lawson, T. (1994), 'Why Are So Many Economists Opposed to Methodology?', *Journal of Economic Methodology*, **1** (1), pp. 105–34.
Lawson, T. (1995), 'Economics and Expectations', in S.C. Dow and J. Hillard (eds), *Keynes, Knowledge and Uncertainty*, Aldershot: Edward Elgar.
McCloskey, D.N. (1983), 'The Rhetoric of Economics', *Journal of Economic Literature*, **21**, pp. 481–517.
McCloskey, D.N. (1988), 'Two Replies and a Dialogue on the Rhetoric of Economics: Mäki, Rappoport, Rosenberg', *Economics and Philosophy* **4** (1), pp. 150–66.

Mäki, U. (1988), 'How to Combine Rhetoric and Realism in the Methodology of Economics', *Economics and Philosophy*, **4** (1), pp. 89–109.
Mayer, T. (1993), *Truth Versus Precision in Economics*, Aldershot: Edward Elgar.
Mehta, J. (1993), 'Meaning in the Context of Bargaining Games – Narratives in Opposition', in W. Henderson, T. Dudley Evans and R. Backhouse (eds), *Economics and Language*, London: Routledge.
Popper, K. (1959), *The Logic of Scientific Discovery*, London: Harper & Row.
Redman, D.A. (1991), *Economics and the Philosophy of Science*, Oxford: Oxford University Press.
Rorty, R. (1979), *Philosophy and the Mirror of Nature*, Princeton: Princeton University Press.
Solow, R.M. (1988), 'Comments from Inside Economics', in A. Klamer, D. McCloskey and R.M. Solow (eds), *The Consequences of Economic Rhetoric*, Cambridge: Cambridge University Press.
Weintraub, E.R. (1989), 'Methodology Doesn't Matter, But the History of Economic Thought Might', *Scandinavian Journal of Economics*, **91**, pp. 477–93.

# COMMENT: VARIETIES OF PLURALISM

**Bruce Caldwell**

There are many types of pluralism, as the chapters by Sheila Dow and Warren Samuels demonstrate. In this comment their positions are compared and contrasted, both with one another and with my own. My goal is not to advocate one variant over the others, but to clarify some of the meanings of the term 'pluralism' as it has been used by methodologists.

There are a variety of paths to pluralism. Though it is not emphasized in her current chapter, Sheila Dow came to pluralism as an advocate of post-Keynesian economics. For her, the position provided a means of reconciling the (particular) plurality of methods entailed by the methodology and 'shared vision' of post-Keynesianism. Warren Samuels does not discuss the origins of his views, but anyone familiar with the eclecticism and tolerance for new ideas that he has exhibited in his long career as an editor will know the fruits of his beliefs. For example, there was a period not too long ago when the *Journal of Economic Issues*, edited by Samuels, was virtually the only outlet for the publication of articles on methodology. Indeed, it is no exaggeration to say that many of the younger members of the audience at the conference (I among them) owe their start in academia to Warren Samuels's pluralist sympathies as an editor. My own path to methodological pluralism was prompted by the dual discovery of, first, disarray within the philosophy of science (where I had gone in search of the philosophical underpinnings of current economic practice), and second, an equally strange situation in economics, where it appeared that a dominant paradigm prevailed, but one which had very little in common with any accounts within the philosophy of science, a possible exception being Popper's situational logic, which was then being ignored.

The fact that there are many roads to pluralism may simply mean that we are all talking about different things. One of the goals of this conference surely must be to clarify our linguistic usage. But it also seems true that the advocacy of pluralism is typically linked with the perception that there exists a dominant practice within economics, a practice that is either unjustified, or perhaps even unjustifiable, or at best simply wrong-headed, yet which nonetheless retains its dominance and, further, which is itself intolerant of alternative modes of investigation.

An important question facing advocates of pluralism is whether it should somehow be constrained, or controlled, or grounded. Here there appears to be a difference between Samuels and Dow. The notion that pluralism must be constrained receives much less emphasis from Samuels.[1] Starting from two ideas, that all knowledge is socially constructed and that there is no conclusive meta-methodological principle by which to choose among methods, he ends up with a global advocacy of pluralism at the theoretical, methodological, epistemological, and ontological levels. In Samuels's pithy phrasing, 'anything *necessarily* goes' (p. 68).

Dow prefers to ground her advocacy of methodological pluralism. In an early work she claimed that post-Keynesians rightly employ a 'Babylonian mode of thought' in which a structured plurality of methods is used to understand a complex social reality (Dow, 1985). She takes these notions further in the current chapter by attempting to specify more carefully in epistemic and ontological terms the nature of reality. The constraint that emerges is a specific ontological commitment, that of the social universe as being best characterized as an 'open system'. This commitment leads her to criticize ontological pluralists, whom she associates principally with the postmodernist movement in economics. She is also critical of my refusal to discuss the ontological and epistemological foundations that might underlie my own espousal of pluralism.

Dow is right that I avoided epistemological and ontological issues completely in *Beyond Positivism*, and that I essentially ducked them in a later paper where I claimed to be an agnostic when it came to choosing among theories of truth (Caldwell, 1988, pp. 241–3). But I have always believed that pluralism requires constraints, and even changed the name of my position (from 'methodological pluralism' to 'critical pluralism') to emphasize the nature of one of the most important of the constraints: criticism. Reflecting the influence of the critical rationalist Karl Popper, mine was a broad endorsement of criticism, with no attempt made to specify the exact form that it might take until a particular problem-situation was also specified.[2] My position was (and remains) that pluralism constrained by criticism holds the best hope for 'progress' within 'science', though I do not claim to be able to offer convincing definitions of such terms. On the question of whether pluralism requires constraints, then, my views are closer to Dow's than to those of Warren Samuels.

But what of the particular ontological commitments that Dow endorses, that of an open system universe? Dow appears to be drawing in part on Tony Lawson's work here, and in particular on his advocacy of transcendental realism (e.g., Lawson, 1994, and citations therein). Lawson draws a distinction between a closed-system universe, which has as a distinguishing characteristic the existence of 'event regularities', and an open-system universe, which is distinguished by the absence of such regularities. Lawson endorses the open-universe view, and from this ontological premise he develops a critical argument. His bedrock critical claim is that the ontological commitment underlying 'positivist' or 'neoclassical' economic science is that of a closed-system universe. Positivist methods aim to discover the event regularities that are presumed to exist. But if in reality the world is an open system, such a search is chimerical. Theoretical and empirical techniques of increasing sophistication are continually developed by contemporary mainstream economists, but little in the way of progress results.

I studied with Tony Lawson at Cambridge in the Spring of 1994, and I found many areas where I disagreed with him, particularly over the definitions of such terms as 'event regularity', 'positivism,' and 'neoclassical economics.' But I share his view that when we look at economics we see little in the way of empirical progress. I think further that this claim is broadly 'testable' by reference to the intellectual and economic history of the discipline, and that such testing can and should be initiated. And I think finally that the reason that we see so little progress has something to do with the nature of the subject that we study; that is to say, with the nature of social reality; that is to say, with social ontology.

Warren Samuels, I suspect, will have none of this. For him, pluralism at all levels is the key. I do not agree with Samuels, but I think that I understand what might be motivating him. His problem is the same one facing any advocate of tolerance: What is the proper response to intolerance? Many advocates of tolerance answer: Tolerate everything except the intolerant. As a pluralist, Samuels is tolerant of any beliefs except those that explicitly deny pluralism at some level. This might be why he has no truck with the recent claims of realists like Lawson or Uskali Mäki, who are ontological monists. There may be another reason: it may be simply that Samuels is enough of a pragmatist that he does not see what difference a commitment to realism makes. And indeed, the advocates of realism have still not demonstrated this. As the saying goes, much work remains to be done.

As for me, I feel closer to the realists than I do to those who emphasize the 'social constructedness' of knowledge. (I should quickly add that I do not think that the two positions, appropriately qualified, necessarily conflict; and both Mäki (1992) and Lawson (1994) apparently share this view.) My preference is dictated by my belief that there has been precious little 'empirical progress' in economics, and that this belief may well be 'testable' by reference to history. I think that both of these ideas fit better into an ontologically grounded, rather than a socially constructed, framework.

As to the specifics of my commitments, I am now prepared to come clean. Using the categorization scheme provided by Mäki (this volume, p. 38), I believe in ontological monism, am moving towards veristic monism (though I feel that we do not yet have an adequately formulated theory of truth; thus my previous claim of agnosticism still should be considered operative), and endorse theoretical, methodological, and meta-methodological pluralism because of the existence of radical epistemic uncertainty in economics. The endorsement of realism I owe to the persistent hammering (gentle persuasion, actually) I have received from the likes of Uskali Mäki and Tony Lawson. But the last and most specific of my commitments, that of radical epistemic uncertainty, comes from studying the writings of the Austrian economist F.A. Hayek. Hayek did not use terms like 'social ontology' in his writings, and we cannot blame him for this; he was writing, after all, at a time when 'metaphysics' was considered to be a very bad word indeed. But in the 'Scientism' essay (Hayek, 1952a) and in his book *The Sensory Order* (1952b) he clearly was making some ontological claims about the nature of what he called 'complex phenomena', claims that have affinities with Lawson's notion of an open-system universe, and claims that, to me at least, seem to make a good deal of sense.

## Notes

1. See chapter 4 of this volume. On page 67, Samuels discusses ways of avoiding methodological anarchy, and 'the process of criticism' is included among them. The topic is again broached in his penultimate paragraph. But it does not seem to me that constraints play as important a role in his system as they do in those of Dow and Caldwell.
2. For example, it was the specific problem-situation of assessing the methodological positions of heterodox groups in economics (e.g., Ludwig von Mises's apriorist variant of praxeology) that led me to endorse 'internal criticism', an approach in which the general methodological principles of a group are criticized from within. It seemed to me that internal criticism would be both more interesting and more effective than simply pointing out, for example, that praxeology does not meet the strictures of falsificationism, or that it does not employ the sorts of mathematical models favoured by mainstream economists. This does not mean, of course, that internal criticism is the only or always the best form of criticism; the problem situation will determine in each case what the preferred forms of criticism(s) may be.

## References

Caldwell, B. (1982), *Beyond Positivism: Economic Methodology in the Twentieth Century*, London: Allen & Unwin.

Caldwell, B. (1988), 'The Case for Pluralism', in N. De Marchi (ed.), *The Popperian Legacy in Economics*, Cambridge: Cambridge University Press, pp. 231–44.

Dow, S.C. (1985), *Macroeconomic Thought: A Methodological Approach*, Oxford: Blackwell.

Hayek, F.A. (1952a), 'Scientism and the Study of Society', in *The Counter-Revolution of Science: Studies in the Abuse of Reason*, Indianapolis: Liberty Press, pp. 17–182.

Hayek, F.A. (1952b), *The Sensory Order: An Inquiry into the Foundations of Theoretical Psychology*, Chicago: University of Chicago Press.

Lawson, T. (1994), 'A Realist Theory for Economics', in R. Backhouse (ed.), *New Directions in Economic Methodology*, London: Routledge, pp. 257–85.

Mäki, U. (1992), 'Social Conditioning of Knowledge', in N. De Marchi (ed.), *Post-Popperian Methodology of Economics*, Boston: Kluwer, pp. 65–104.

# 6. The case for controlled pluralism: a bottom-up approach

**Robert Delorme**

## INTRODUCTION

This chapter addresses the issue of how to make pluralism compatible with the need for some criteria with which to assess proposed explanations and theories and to guide research practice.

The author is not a philosopher of science nor a methodologist. The issue is tackled from the standpoint of research practice in the economic discipline, i.e. as a research problem to be solved. Consequently, the approach developed here may be termed a bottom-up one instead of an approach emanating from the methodological level and perceived from the practical research level as being top-down.

It is suggested that a key problem arises from the scientist's radical uncertainty about the best method. Incorporating this radical uncertainty into an otherwise scientific framework immediately pushes the approach followed away from mainstream economics.[1] The reflexiveness implied here will be dealt with through decision-making theory based on radical uncertainty and complexity. This is the reason why complexity theory provides the backbone of the reasoning developed in this chapter, a by-product of which will appear as controlled complexity.

But the notion of complexity used here is a restricted one. It pertains to what may be termed reflexive complexity. Its self-referential character and the logical difficulties attached to it may explain why it is still often considered a purely philosophical issue, although it goes well beyond this level in the fields where certain pioneers invented it and showed its relevance in method and in research strategy. These fields are mainly psychology, decision theory and what may be called biophysics. Among the precursors whose names stand out most are Jean Piaget, Gregory Bateson and their followers in psychology; Herbert Simon in decision theory and Heinz von Foerster in biophysics.[2] This chapter is part of research in progress on the application of this kind of complexity in economics.

In the end it will be suggested how the complexity perspective offers an alternative to the analytical perspective currently dominating economic research and may be a means for unifying several separated and still confused socio-economic perspectives.

This chapter is structured as follows. The way pluralism imposed itself on a case study is explained in section 2. The problem it produces is presented in section 3. The principles of the search for a solution are exposed in section 4. A solution is developed in section 5. The scope for an extension of the complexity perspective is briefly sketched out in section 6.

## 2. A CASE IN POINT

For the sake of clarity, I take the liberty of saying a few words on how I came to pluralism. I discovered the need for pluralism while doing research on the long-run determinants of public expenditure growth in France, and while extending this research to state–economy interactions. Hence my path to pluralism is not top-down as is the case when the standpoint is methodological. My starting point originated in research practice and led to the search for a foundation at a higher, more general level. It is thus a bottom-up procedure.

This research developed in a pragmatic manner. It started with building observations and statistical data and with testing the available theoretical explanations concerning the determinants of public spending (Delorme and André, 1983; Delorme 1984). Several hypotheses were tested. It was found that most of them had some relevance. But it was a kind of relevance valid for particular, local matters, under precise and sometimes very constrained conditions. An example is the theme of the productivity lag in the public sector. It may be viewed as a cause of the growth of public expenditure relative to overall economic activity. It was demonstrated that the empirical evidence for this thesis is difficult to establish, even in the cases most suited for it, such as the provision of services in health, hospital and education. Still more problematic, it leaves wide open the issue of the rationale for projecting this kind of assumption to public expenditure taken as a whole.

Extending this research to international comparisons of the role of the state in market-led economic systems (Delorme, 1992) reinforced the discrepancy between what could be reasonably derived from the available theories and what appeared as features of the subject matter which were robust enough to be considered as stylized facts in the Kaldorian, not the ad hoc sense (Boland, 1988; Lawson, 1989). The notion of a strong diversity, not amenable to the one-sided character of available theories, summarizes the main finding. It gives support to the idea that a challenging theoretical issue on this subject is to capture difference and sameness in an articulated, unified, theoretical framework. The notion of characteristic *modes of interaction between the state and the economy* (MISE) was elaborated as an answer to this question. MISEs are plural, since they differ over time and across countries. This is a conjecture. It could be stated only because the decision was taken at some point in the research programme to go ahead without obeying any of the methodological lines associated with the available theoretical systems since none of them appeared satisfactory.[3] Consequently, the approach followed was and still is pluralist.

## 3. THE PROBLEM

Pluralism has advantages and disadvantages. The former have been thoroughly studied (Caldwell, 1982). The challenge comes from its disadvantages. A first problem with pluralism is its ambiguity. Considering the various styles of doing economics associated with the names who signed the announcement on 'A plea for a pluralistic and rigorous economics' in the May 1992 issue of the *American Economic Review* (**82** (2) p. XXV), it seems highly doubtful that they share a homogeneous conception of what it means to have pluralistic economics. This may be the result of talking about pluralism without having established the compatibility of the ingredients composing it. This drawback is similar to pure eclecticism. Some leading thread seems to be required. At the methodological level, anarchism, scepticism, relativism or nihilism may be viewed as other drawbacks of pluralism giving support to the need to put limits on it, through criticism (Caldwell, 1988, 1989a). According to another approach, the world view associated with a given conception of the economic process provides this constraining factor (Dow, 1990, 1992). An instance is the post-Keynesian world view.

A still different way is to refer to empirical evidence as an arbiter and have some conception of the realism of a theory. The difficulties are that everybody pretends to be realist in theorizing and that in economics it is difficult to find a final arbiter for empirical evidence on most issues. The reason is due to the absence of a controlled observation and experimentation of the type one finds in natural science. There, the debate on pluralism in doing research appears of secondary relevance since the results can in most cases be rigorously evaluated against empirical reality. Such a specified rule is almost totally absent in economics apart from a few instances. As a consequence it renders problematic in economics the idea that the lack of a binding factor can be compensated for by the pretence of the empirical fruitfulness of theory.

All in all methodological pluralism is useful when there is a reason to free oneself from the constraints of monism. But it is a defensive and interim stance. At the practical level of research, the case evoked in the previous section suggests that pluralism arises from uncertainty on what the best method is or, equivalently, from the lack of an adequate method for the problem at hand. Uncertainty is taken here in its strong sense of a non probabilistic event. It is synonymous with ignorance. Yet, from this standpoint, there remains the question: How do we know that diverse methods are compatible? In the following sections an attempt is made to answer this question. It is based on the idea that a specified rule is required and that the available ways of dealing with this issue do not provide a rule adequate to the problem at hand.

## 4. IN SEARCH OF A SOLUTION

### 4.1. Pluralism as a Consequence of Radical Uncertainty

Pluralism is warranted when there is no certainty over what is the correct method. It could be objected that stating this is having already a method in mind. This is true, but it need not contradict the very definition of pluralism once one differentiates the object level and the meta level of any statement. The developments of the next paragraphs are precisely based on this kind of hierarchical connection. It is not contradictory to have several methods at the object level whose link is a single method at the meta level.

Radical uncertainty and ignorance play the same roles here. A quasi similar situation applied to future scientific knowledge is evoked by Popper (Popper, 1984, pp. 54–7). These notions create a kind of trauma in economics. They are rejected by the analytical mainstream because they would make reasoning based on prediction irrelevant as a general foundation. But they are more or less key notions to non-orthodox traditions such as the Keynesian, post-Keynesian, Austrian and institutionalist views. Yet these theoretical perspectives do not help solve the problem beyond the point mentioned earlier. They simply provide world views based on what they consider economics to be composed of. While they may make the concern about pluralism appear as a simple matter of initial choice between diverse world views, our perspective is to treat it as a problem to be solved. Thus, almost none of the available theoretical perspectives embodying radical uncertainty do help. The reason why it is so will hopefully be clear when we reach the end of this chapter. However, two theoretical systems are exceptions. One is Simon's theory of decision-making. The other is a particular development in complexity theory. They both make pluralism appear as a by-product. This idea is developed in the next paragraphs.

## 4.2. Pluralism as a By-product of Procedural Rationality

Uncertainty, imperfect knowledge and complexity form the roots of Simon's theory of decision making. Simon's theory rests on the distinction between substantive rationality and procedural rationality: 'Behavior is substantively rational when it is appropriate to the achievement of given goals within the limits imposed by given conditions and constraints ... . Behavior is procedurally rational when it is the outcome of appropriate deliberation. Its procedural rationality depends on the process that generated it' (Simon, 1976, pp. 130–31). Procedural rationality may be expected in situations that are not 'sufficiently simple as to be transparent to [the] mind'. Then 'we must expect that the mind will use such imperfect information as it has, will simplify and represent the situation as it can, and will make such calculations as are within its powers' (ibid., p. 144). Using the correct available algorithm is the usual way to operate in substantive rationality. There is no interference between the decision-maker and the way to solve a problem.

No such thing is by definition available when uncertainty prevails. In this case, decision embodies deliberation, search, and the personal forms of representation the decision-maker prefers. A solution is then constructed through a heuristic process in which it is reasonable to choose 'an alternative that meets or exceeds specified criteria, but that is not guaranteed to be either unique or in any sense the best', which defines 'satisficing' (Simon, 1988). A situation is 'satisficing' when it is adequate to some aspiration level.

Simon's theory subverts conventional economics since it makes the case for seriously considering the formation of human preferences as part of the problem of decision-making. It says that it is no longer possible to get rid of deliberation when there is uncertainty. Decision-making gets contaminated, so to speak, by the decision-maker's mind: 'A body of theory for procedural rationality is consistent with a world in which human beings continue to think and continue to invent; a theory of substantive rationality is not' (Simon, 1976, p. 146).

This view accords with the problematic developed here. We have no available algorithm for solving the problem at hand. Our situation is a Simonian decision-maker's one. We make an attempt at satisficing. However, we are still far from achieving a solution as the next paragraph will show.

## 4.3. Pluralism as a By-product of Complexity

The notion of complexity used here denotes the impossibility of reducing a 'complex' phenomenon to a unique causal, analytical explanation. It is equivalent to unpredictability. Uncertainty is one of its consequences. When complexity is evoked in economics, it is still most often done with reference to non-linear dynamic models, to chaos theory, and to the ultra-high complication and multidimensional character of some given system. A common feature of these views is that complexity is considered as a property intrinsic to the outside world. The notion of complexity relevant here is different. It is *perceived* complexity. To paraphrase Simon on uncertainty (Simon, 1976, p. 437), complexity exists in the eye and mind of the beholder. The complexity of an object for an observer depends on the way he/she interacts with it (Klir, 1985; Morin, 1985, 1992; Le Moigne 1990a, 1991; Segal, 1990; Watzlawick, 1988).

A consequence of this is the fundamental importance of interaction. It is primarily the interaction between a human being and what is perceived or, to refer to more general categories, between a generating principle and what is generated. It is secondarily the multifaceted interaction between parts of a 'complex' entity. Complexity denotes the unpredictability of what is generated. Without going into details, it has become usual to symbolize by a recursive loop this property and the kind of autonomy of the system formed by the generating principle and its product (Le Moigne, 1990b). The recursive loop differs from feedback. In the feedback, a part of the output is picked up as information. It is used as the input of a command or controlling system whose orders are directed to the input of the regulated phenomenon. In the recursive loop the product is producing what produces it. The process is not directed from the outside although it is not separated from it and can be influenced by it. But the recursive loop is to itself its own programme (Dupuy,

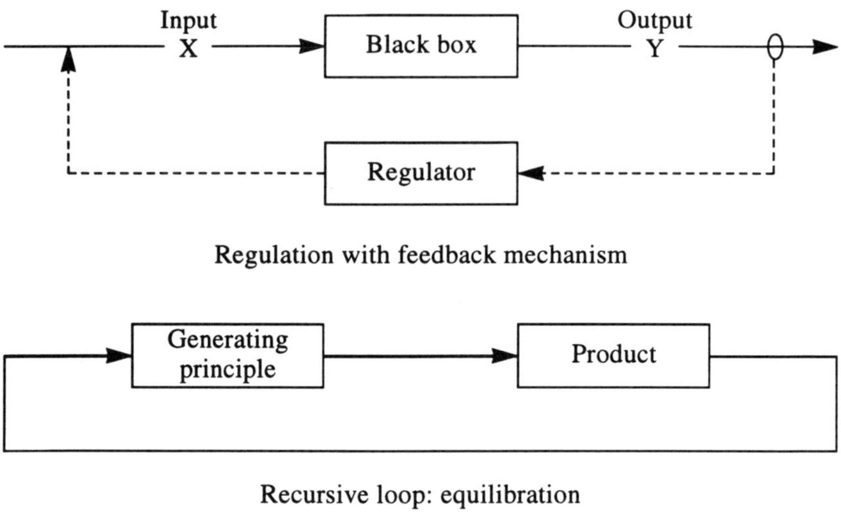


*Figure 6.1 Feedback and recursive loop schematized*

1982). The recursive process is better summarized as equilibration whereas the feedback denotes regulation (Figure 6.1).

The problem at hand can be represented as a complex problem. The observer is part of the system. The result is unpredictable. In uncertainty, procedural rationality will prevail. However, a new dimension is introduced when the author-researcher her/himself portrays her/his own reflection as a complex one. This dimension is reflexivity.

Considering the scientist as a Simonian decision-maker leads to reflexivity in case of procedural rationality. It portrays the scientist reflecting upon her/his own reflection. Implied here is the threat of infinite regress and subjectivism. It is noticeable that, to the author's knowledge, Simon never introduced the observer's reflexivity explicitly in his writings although his contribution to the epistemology and method of *de facto* reflexive reasoning is decisive (Simon, 1991).

However, on the whole, we have gained some useful insights. From procedural rationality, a pattern of behaviour has been obtained. Complexity theory provides a logical structure enabling to compare it to the analytical stance. And radical uncertainty has become structured in a theoretical pattern. But a big jump in the mode of reasoning has been necessary. Interaction is substituted for the analytical standpoint. Moreover, the pillar of positivism, namely the separation between the observing unit and the observed object, is replaced by their interdependence.

It remains nevertheless that satisficing has no determined substantive contents and may lead to subjectivism. A way to avoid this is to constrain it by submitting satisficing to an external control. This control cannot but be related to the environment of the search process. Here, the relevant environment is scientific activity. The constraint is: *do science.* And in consideration of the developments above, it is logically complemented by two other constraints: *embody uncertainty* and *be operational.* These three constraints define the task ahead and provide the basis for what may be viewed as an anchoring of complexity to fixed guidelines. Anchoring seems to convey best the idea that on the one hand complexity cannot be controlled, by definition and that on the other hand subjectivism and a kind of floating eclecticism are hardly acceptable. Anchoring is in between and avoids these two extreme cases.

# 5. THREE RULES FOR A LEADING THREAD: ANCHORED COMPLEXITY

## 5.1. Scientific Practice

Viewed from the bottom, practical level, what distinguishes doing science from other cognitive or intellectual operations may be discovered from the dictionary definition of science. There seems to be a wide consensus on the combination of three elements. Doing science is to search for some explanation of some reality and to systematically put it to the test (Granger, 1990). It seems reasonable to consider that this definition is the common reference to all scientific activity. It is the shared vision from which the divide between conceptions of science arises. This divide comes from the various ways of conceiving explanation, reality and testing.

Explanation is taken here, at this stage, in a broad sense. It refers to the operation of producing knowledge. It can be causal explanation in a strict sense, but also prediction, representation or understanding. For the purpose at hand the main differentiation is between the goals of causal explanation and prediction of mainstream economics and the emphasis on representation common to most non-orthodox views.

The next divide occurs over what is considered as reality. The subject matter of science bears on the real world. But here there is a profound separation between two positions. One is ontological realism. It attempts to know the nature of reality, to discover its laws. Viewing reality as objective and independent from the mind, the goal is to produce statements that will be scientific because they depict reality independently from the observer's eye.

According to another conception, one would consider that the true reality is beyond reach and that we know it only through our experience of phenomena. This is phenomenological realism. Instead of being discovered, laws and other statements are invented. Scientific practice aims more at diminishing our ignorance than at establishing truths. It is a fallible standpoint. Complexity fits well with it. It is based on a rich intellectual tradition which has been maintained for a long time in an untaught and ignored status by the overwhelming pressure and dazzling influence of the analytical, positivist scientific doctrine in science. This tradition is known nowadays as constructivism. Its modern revival finds roots in Piaget's genetic epistemology, Simon's design, and the 'construction of reality' perspective offered by Bateson, Morin, von Foerster, von Glasersfeld and Watzlawick, among other names (see the references). Although positivism has been slowly eroded for decades in the natural sciences, it is still pervasive in the discipline of economics. It finds its strength in the ignorance of constructivism as an alternative and in the wide unspoken consensus about immunizing stratagems in economics, a practice which destroys the possibility of identifying when a theory is false or irrelevant and which deprives economic theory of the possibility of learning from its errors and to progress. In this sense, the practical invulnerability of analytical positivist economics is its main weakness.

This brings us to the third feature, testing. This is the key and most difficult question in economic science, for it lacks a final arbiter. The situation is incomparably better in natural science. There, experimentation and controlled observation provide criteria of empirical validity. Insofar as we are interested in empirical-theoretic science and not in formal science, a final arbiter rests in controlled protocols of empirical validation. It is not indulging in catastrophism to acknowledge that standard economics is in a disastrous state concerning this point. Exceptions would be found in simple, transparent enough problems such as those for which substantive rationality is relevant, at a micro level, or those which are simple enough at the macroeconomic level, thus enabling more reliable prediction. This state of affairs is widely admitted in the literature on economic methodology. Until now one must say that its influence has been nil on the way most economists work. It consists mainly in conversation on formal theorizing defined on an immunizing space. As a consequence, such a practice eschews establishing a final arbiter.

There are two other features that are closely linked to scientific practice. They pertain to the manner in which reasoning is conducted and is communicated. It needs a language. As any other language, it is made with signs, symbols and rules.

The first feature has to do with the requirement contained in the triplet of communicability, systematicness and cumulativeness of science. Communication is the basis for diminishing confusion and establishing systematicness thanks to which some progress and cumulative knowledge may be envisaged. These notions point to the second feature – the way scientific knowledge is represented and communicated. Every science embodies its statements and results in signs. Semiotics, the science of signs, comprises three fields of investigating languages, also termed portions of semiotics (Morris, 1971) or levels of communication (Weaver and Shannon, 1975). Syntax, also called syntactics (Morris) or the technical level (Weaver), pertains to the relations of signs to one another independently from the relations of signs to objects or to interpreters. Semantics deals with the signification of signs understood as the relation of signs to the objects they denote. Pragmatics designates the relation of signs to their interpreters, thus dealing with the origin, the uses and the effects of signs. Scientific practice may be expressed as covering necessarily these three fields (Figure 6.2).

Within the economics discipline, perspectives can be differentiated according to the relative weights they give to these levels. The formal orientation focuses on syntax while most dissident perspectives emphasize the two

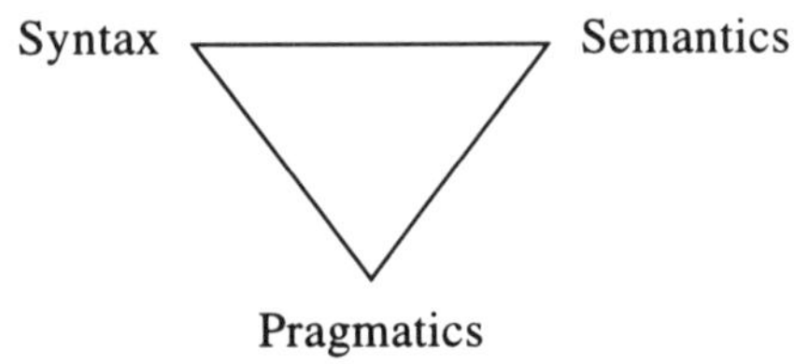


*Figure 6.2 The three levels of communication*

other summits of the triangle. The ideal is a balance. The standard perspective in economics gives a priority to syntax. Then, in case of radical uncertainty, it is no surprise that primacy will be given to the method over the object of inquiry, i.e. to syntax over semantics. Exclusion of radical uncertainty, because it cannot be captured with the analytical toolkit, illustrates this point clearly. The tools are thus taken for granted and applied to situations which are made to adapt to them thanks to ad hoc assumptions. A different approach is to start from problematic situations and empirical facts and try to adjust the method and syntax applied to them, thus putting the bulk of adjustment on the pragmatic and syntaxic levels. Yet this procedure does not mean that facts can be taken *a priori* as granted. They are inevitably arbitrary. However, we would find it difficult to express our experience of reality without relying on facts. Thus it seems reasonable to admit that some adaptation of the facts is inevitable. Of course it does not mean that observation will be modified in order to fit the observer's own preferences! Adjusting facts means making them relevant to the question addressed. In the research reported above, we found that it was impossible to address public spending in the long run independently from public finance. And we discovered in a next step than it would be quite difficult to investigate public finance over time and in international comparisons independently from the other forms, both quantitative and qualitative, of interaction between the state and the economy. Thus the facts investigated were initially public spending, then public finance, then quantitative and qualitative dimensions of the public sector (Delorme, 1984).

One would expect that in any empirical science consistency prevails not only in the manner in which the signs are used, in the way they are relevant and in the way they combine in syntax, but also in the overall consistency of the triangle. It is difficult here not to think of the kind of discrepancy existing in economics between professed and actual method.

It is the price paid to preserve formalism. It illustrates how excessive formalism may constrain scientific practice either by preventing the study of empirical situations that do not fit with syntax or by asking indefinitely the public at large first to accept that economics relies mainly on syntax and to be programmatic for the time being, and second to believe that it will have empirically relevant results in an ever postponed unknown future.

The alternative approach also has its own price: it is the weakness of its syntax, the evasiveness or the absence of a body of founding logical principles. Here we face once again the ongoing debate over the trade-offs of 'well derived' versus 'empirically relevant' theories.

## 5.2. Complexity

The choice made in the divide above is driven by the condition that it be consistent with radical uncertainty. Complexity comes into the picture here. It led to the introduction of recursiveness. How can we ensure that a procedure is consistent with complexity? How does it compare with the analytical perspective? A condensed way to answer these questions consists in concentrating on the logical bases of each perspective. The contention is that complexity may be related to a set of founding principles which have the same status as those of the analytical perspective. This may answer a criticism often made against heterodoxy, namely that heterodoxy has no chain of basic principles ensuring its internal consistency in a way comparable to orthodoxy. Hence the superiority of orthodoxy. That this seems to be no longer true, at least for complexity, can be shown through a comparison of the well-known axioms of classical logic with the progressively emerging axioms of complexity. The latter are naturally much less codified, diffused and known than the former. It may thus make them appear quite abstract and strange. Yet, if we reflect on the rationale of the axioms of classical, bivalent, logic which form the basis of analytical theorizing, we would see that they are not more obvious than the complex ones. It is habituation which makes them look familiar and self-evident to the point where we never refer to them explicitly as if they were the unspoken basic consensus to be protected from questioning.

Moreover, there exists a plurality of logical systems. Each one has its own, inevitably arbitrary, basis. A logic quite relevant to the problem of complexity is the intuitionist logic, developed by Brouwer and Heyting (Heyting, 1980). Indeed, the effort undertaken to put the parts together is recent and borrows from different sources. The number of propositions that may be considered as axiomatic is not stabilized. It is not without hesitation that I introduce these axioms below since limited space does not allow to go into details. The presentation made here is inspired to a large extent by Le Moigne (1991).

**The axioms of analytical modelling**
The reality to be modelled is perceived through three axioms. A and B stand for propositions.

- Identity: A is A.
- Non contradiction: A cannot be simultaneously B and $\overline{B}$ (not-B)
- Excluded middle: A is either B or $\overline{B}$.

**The axioms of complex modelling**
The phenomena to be modelled are perceived through three axioms.

*Operationality and intentionality* Modelling is the conjunction of the modeller's purpose with her/his environment. It differentiates it from the analytical disjunction between causes and effects. Action and interaction, as opposed to 'things', and process, not its result, are the basic categories here.

*Irreversibility* Action and process take place over time. Time is perceived as irreversible.

*Included middle* Operation or action is perceived as generating a product. The generating principle and its product are not separable. The product is producing what produces it. This is a situation of recursiveness.

## 5.3. Operationality

Until now we have remained at the logical and the methodological levels. The next task is to combine what has been stated about scientific practice and about complexity in an operational way, i.e. allowing these results to apply to the case in point and to compare them with alternative theoretical perspectives. Let us recall our goal of taking into account reflexive radical uncertainty, a task which is incorporated in reflexive complexity.

The satisficing principle has thus been fulfilled until now. But we still need to submit complexity to the test of its adequacy to the problem. In this sense complexity will become anchored complexity. We contend that the operational control relies on three rules: consistency, communicability and relevance.

*Consistency is* concerned with avoiding the discrepancy between professed and actual method and avoiding an imbalance between the three elements of the semiotic triangle. Although it is difficult to define substantively a balance between these elements, it can be defined procedurally as mutually adjusting semantics and syntax up to the point where the actually practised pragmatics meets the declared pragmatics – i.e. the professed method.

It may be summarized as 'preach what you can do, do what you preach'. In the study of a phenomenon perceived as complex, for which there exists no available substantive theory or model, empirical investigation comes first together with abduction and the attempt at theorizing. Hence the priority given to the object of study and to the semantics over the syntax in a first step.

It may look trivial to insist on *communicability* as a rule. Yet it is conditioning potential systematicity and cumulativeness. Above all it is the precondition for mutual criticism and a real exercise of control within and outside the scientific community. It implies transparency and voluntary exposure to criticism. It runs opposite to the immunization so often denounced by methodologists in economics (Caldwell, 1991). Even if it may look too idealistic to believe in eliminating immunization, the least that can be done is to eliminate hidden immunization. This requires that when immunization is introduced, it be made explicit. One finds here an illustration that the proof of the pudding might actually be more in the making than in the eating. A way to foster transparency is the comparison between theories for a given problem, in a meliorative strategy. It implies that statements be designed in a way that makes comparison possible.

In line with the fallibilistic stance of the complex perspective, *relevance* amounts to reducing ignorance and arbitrariness in theorizing.

Emphasizing arbitrariness seems fruitful because of its generality and of its capacity to be used as a criterion for comparison and for assessment. We express this in the following proposition:

- There is no non-arbitrary way of reasoning. There is no non-arbitrary ultimate foundation.
- There are degrees of arbitrariness. They can be identified through comparison.
- The aim is to reduce the degree of arbitrariness for a given problem.

These conditions constitute what may be called anchored complexity. It provides a solution to the problem of the unifying principle mentioned above: anchored complexity is a guideline satisfying the conditions enumerated. The plurality of methods is intrinsic to complexity and is bounded by what is admissible for anchored complexity. Moreover, anchored complexity reduces *ipso facto* the degree of arbitrariness in comparison to the analytical approach, since it takes into account radical uncertainty.

Finally, anchored complexity can be considered as a generating principle whose product stimulated its own production. This sentence simply describes the recursive loop (Figure 6.3) between an initial inference (stylized facts) transformed into a stylized conjecture (characteristic configuration of the interaction between the state and the economy) and later into a theoreti-

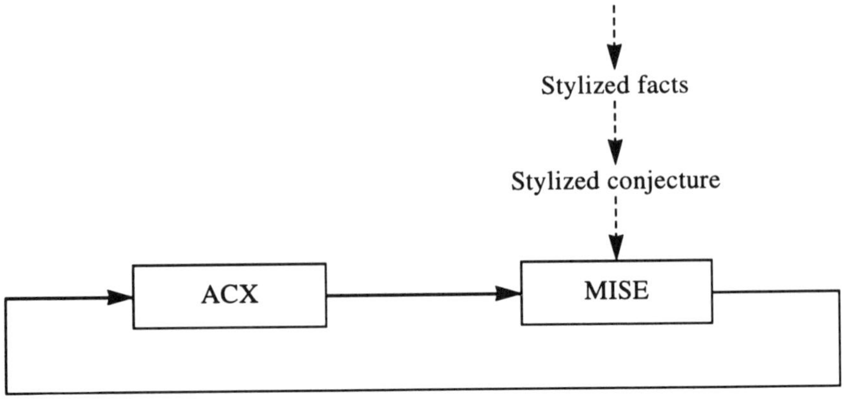


*Figure 6.3 Research on the case in point as a recursive loop*

cal conjecture (mode of interaction between the state and the economy: MISE) after having been informed by anchored complexity (symbolized as ACX).

It seems reasonable to think at this point that the above development is adequate to the purpose at hand and is thus a satisficing solution. But it must be acknowledged that there is no external universal criterion to assess whether it is true or false The only way is to expose it to criticism. But here, what is exposed to criticism is more accurate, more specified, more operational for research strategy than what was available at the beginning. And that was the purpose of our effort.

## 6. CONCLUDING REMARKS

*Pluralism was progressively specified in five steps.* It has thus been shown that pluralism is firstly a consequence of the heterogeneity or diversity perceived in a subject matter; secondly, a consequence of radical uncertainty or ignorance concerning the adequate method; thirdly, a consequence of procedural rationality; fourthly a consequence of complexity, and lastly an attribute intrinsic to anchored complexity, i.e. controlled pluralism.

In this notion the binding factor is not a matter of world view based on a preference for a particular class of economic phenomena. It is instead a matter of world view based on how science is done on average, on a type of cognitive orientation consistent with an explicitly exposed conception of scientific practice. Therefore, although in the absence of another unifying leading thread it may be useful to identify some basic premises of evolutionary perspectives (Delorme, 1994) or of any other theoretical paradigm such as the post-Keynesian or the Austrian varieties, the reasoning developed here suggests that it is not enough and proposes another solution.

*This solution belongs to a hopefully consistent chain of reasoning.* This chain is complete in the sense that it compares with the analytical chain at every stage. Putting together the pieces that have been introduced in the argument of this chapter makes possible a comparison of the analytical (positivist) and the complex (constructivist) perspectives (Table 6.1).

The construction proposed here conforms to a hierarchy covering ten levels. We assume that the dictionary definition of scientific practice is

*Table 6.1 The analytical and the complex scientific perspectives compared*

| | | Analysis | Complexity |
|---|---|---|---|
| 1 | General definition of scientific practice | Common to both perspectives: some kind of explanation of reality, systematically put to the test | |
| 2 | Conception of scientific knowledge | Positivism | Constructivism |
| 3 | Mode of reasoning | Analytical | Complex |
| 4 | Position on reality | Ontological realism<br>Objective character of reality | Phenomenological realism<br>Constructed character of reality |
| 5 | Main purpose of scientific practice | Explanation and prediction | Active representation |
| 6 | Logical core | Axioms of classical logic | Axioms of complex logic |
| 7 | Methodological framework | Deductivism<br>Disjunction<br>Discovery<br>Universal norm of truth | Abduction, investigation<br>Conjunction<br>Design, invention<br>Satisficing |
| 8 | Method | Taken as granted: 'The scientific method' | Adjusted according to anchored complexity: built-in pluralism |
| 9 | Theoretical perspective and theorizing | $x, y, z, \ldots$ | $a, b, c, \ldots$ |
| 10 | End product (statements on the real world, policy prescriptions) | $x', y', z', \ldots$ | $a', b', c', \ldots$ |

considered relevant by proponents of both perspectives. The divide occurs about the conception of scientific knowledge and unfolds downwards until the end product level.

The terms mentioned in each column indicate the primary focus of each perspective at each level. They do not describe all the ingredients. We simply contend that the terms retained here form the respective starting points, on which other features are dependent, in each approach. Considering the previous developments, the items in Table 6.1 do not seem to require further explanation, given the scope of this contribution. A more detailed presentation is in Delorme (1996). The exception to this concerns the main purpose of scientific practice in the complex perspective at level 5. A common trait of complex reasoning is its representation of a reality that is itself perceived primarily through a process of construction. Representation is then active, not passive. In passive representation, knowledge is viewed as reflecting a world with intrinsic predefined properties leaving the scientist with the task of uncovering some hidden truth 'already there'. In active representation, design and invention play an important part.

Let us come back to the world-view issue. Having a world view cannot be abolished. It is commonly understood in the economics discipline as pertaining to a set of basic statements shared by a scientific community on how the economy functions. Neoclassical, Keynesian, post-Keynesian, Austrian, Marxian world views, among others, illustrate this definition. The divide in the discipline is usually thought of in terms of these world views. The conception presented here is different. We have attempted to show that introducing complexity displaces the issue from a matter of substantive preferences shared by respective communities to a matter of cognitive procedure. We introduced the conception of scientific knowledge as a basic criterion of choice independently of any preference on the substance of how the economy performs. Indeed it is only at level 9 that particular theoretical perspectives come into the picture. On the one hand, one may find at this level the theoretical perspectives mentioned in section 2 together with the particular theorizing derived from them ($x, y, z \ldots$) and end statements ($x', y', z' \ldots$). On the other hand, the MISE may appear as $a$, together with other theoretical notions and end statements likely to be developed along complex lines ($b, c, b', c', \ldots$). The end statements will logically differ from one approach to another.

In view of the confusion and of the limitations attached to the substantive world views in case of complexity, there is ground to think that the cognitive conception developed here clarifies the issue and is more general.

The complex and the analytical perspectives are not symmetrical. At first sight, one might think that the analytical perspective is warranted whenever we are in a situation of no uncertainty and that the same goes for complexity in case of uncertainty. However, the analytical approach cannot accommodate uncertainty while the complex approach can accommodate the situations pertaining to the analytical approach. One finds the same asymmetry between substantive and procedural rationality: the former excludes consideration of the latter whereas the inverse is not true since procedural search allows by definition for the possibility of constructing situations locally relevant for substantive rationality (Delorme, 1996).

Thus complexity subsumes analysis. The situations relevant for analysis appear as particular cases. Whereas the trademark of analysis is exclusivism, complexity does not exclude *a priori* the analytical method. It excludes only analytical exclusivism. It subsumes the analytical approach thanks to its greater generality and relevance. It allows for the local relevance of analytical and positivist methods provided their relevance is established on the specific subject matter under consideration.

This asymmetry supports the case for considering that the complex perspective offers a more general methodological stance than the analytical one. However, complexity does not reduce to methodology. We have attempted to show how designing a research strategy and putting it to work as anchored complexity is of utmost importance. The analytical perspective can no longer base its strength on the absence of an alternative perspective which would meet similar standards of consistency and of operationality.

Finally the argument developed here suggests a redistribution among theoretical systems and world views. Instead of opposing neoclassical, Keynesian, post-Keynesian, Austrian, institutionalist and evolutionary paradigms, it suggests that something might be gained in considering the divide between analytical reasoning and complex reasoning, i.e. between *analytical* Keynesian, post-Keynesian, Austrian, institutionalist and evolutionary economics, on the one hand and *complex* Keynesian, post-Keynesian, Austrian, institutionalist and evolutionary economics, on the other hand.

## NOTES

1. This point is discussed in Lawson (1985).
2. See Piaget (1968), Bateson (1972), Simon (1991), von Foerster (1960, 1977, 1988) and Dupuy (1982), Hofstadter (1985), Le Moigne (1990b), Morin (1985, 1992), Segal (1990), UNU (1985), von Glasersfeld (1988), Watzlawick (1988).
3. The theoretical systems referred to have been grouped in four approaches: the determinant models (productivity differential, displacement effect, etc.), the individualistic approach (collective goods theory, public choice), the constraint approach (exogenous state, industrial state, etc.) and the Marxist approaches (Delorme, 1984).

# REFERENCES


Bateson, G. (1972), *Steps to an Ecology of Mind*, New York: Chandler.

Boland, L.A. (1988), 'Stylized facts', *The New Palgrave*, Basingstoke: Macmillan.

Caldwell, B.J. (1982), *Beyond Positivism. Economic Methodology in the Twentieth Century*, London: George Allen & Unwin.

Caldwell, B.J. (1988), 'The case for pluralism', in N. De Marchi (ed.), *The Popperian Legacy in Economics*, Cambridge: Cambridge University Press, pp. 231–44.

Caldwell, B.J. (1989a), 'Post-Keynesian methodology: an assessment', *Review of Political Economy*, **1** (1), pp. 43–64.

Caldwell, B.J. (1989b), 'The trend of methodological thinking', *Ricerche Economiche*, June–July, pp. 8–20.

Caldwell, B.J. (1991), 'Clarifying Popper', *Journal of Economic Literature*, March, pp. 1–33.

Delorme, R. (1984), 'A new view on the economic theory of the state. A case study of France', *Journal of Economic Issues*, September, pp. 715–44. Reprinted in M.R. Tool and W.J. Samuels (eds), 1988, *State, Society and Corporate Power*, New Brunswick: Transaction Publishers.

Delorme, R. (1992), 'Economic intervention in the history of the French and other European states: A comparative study', in A.A. Zini Jr (ed.), *The Market and the State in Economic Development in the 1990s*, Amsterdam: North-Holland, Contributions to Economic Analysis, pp. 23–50.

Delorme, R. (1994), 'Economic diversity as cement and as a challenge to evolutionary perspectives', in R. Delorme and K. Dopfer (eds), *The Political Economy of Diversity. Evolutionary Perspectives on Economic Order and Disorder*, chapter 1, Aldershot: Edward Elgar.

Delorme, R. (1996), 'From first order to second order complexity in economic theory', Paris: CEPREMAP discussion paper.

Delorme, R. and C. André (1983), *L'état et l'économie*, Paris: Seuil.

Dow, S. (1985), *Macroeconomic Thought. A Methodological Approach*, Oxford: Basil Blackwell.

Dow, S. (1990), 'Beyond dualism', *Cambridge Journal of Economics*, **14**, pp. 143–57.

Dow, S. (1992), 'Post-Keynesian methodology: a comment', *Review of Political Economy*, **4** (1), pp. 111–13.

Dupuy, J.P. (1982), *Ordres et désordres. Enquête sur un nouveau paradigme*, Paris: Seuil.

Feynman, R. (1970), *La nature des lois physiques* (The Character of Physical Law), Paris: R. Laffont.

Granger, G.G. (1990), 'Epistémologie', Paris: Encyclopaedia Universalis.

Heyting, A. (1980), *Intuitionism, an Introduction*, Amsterdam: North-Holland.

Hofstadter, D. (1985), *Gödel, Escher, Bach. Les brins d'une guirlande éternelle*, Paris: Inter Editions.

Klir, G.J. (1985), 'The many faces of complexity', in UNU, *The Science and Praxis of Complexity*, Tokyo: The United Nations University, pp. 81–98.

Lawson, T. (1985), 'Uncertainty and economic analysis', *Economic Journal*, December, pp. 909–27.

Lawson, T. (1989), 'Abstraction, tendencies and stylised facts: a realist approach to economic analysis', *Cambridge Journal of Economics*, **13**, pp. 59–78.

Le Moigne, J.L. (1990a), 'Epistémologies constructivisites et sciences de l'organisation', in A.C. Martinet (ed.), *Epistémologie des sciences de gestion*, Paris: Economica, pp. 81–140.
Le Moigne, J.L. (1990b), *La modélisation des systèmes complexes*, Paris: Dunod.
Le Moigne, J.L. (1991), 'Sur les fondements épistémologiques de la science de la cognition: contribution de la systémique aux constructivismes', in E. Andreewsky (ed.), *Systémique et Cognition*, Dunod: Paris, pp. 11–49.
Morin, E. (1985), 'On the definition of complexity', in UNU, *The Science and Praxis of Complexity*, Tokyo: The United Nations University, pp. 62–8.
Morin, E. (1992), 'From the concept of system to the paradigm of complexity', *Journal of Social and Evolutionary Systems*, **15** (4), pp. 371–85.
Morris, C. (1971), *Writings on the General Theory of Signs*, The Hague: Mouton.
Piaget, J. (ed.) (1968), *Logique et connaissance scientifique*, La Pléiade, Paris: Gallimard.
Popper, K. (1984), *L'Univers irrésolu. Plaidoyer pour l'indéterminisme*, Paris: Hermann.
Segal, L. (1990), *Le rêve de la réalité*, Paris: Seuil, Edition in French of *The Dream of Reality*, New York: W.W. Norton.
Simon, H.A. (1976), 'From substantive to procedural rationality', in S. Latsis (ed.), *Method and Appraisal in Economics*, Cambridge: Cambridge University Press, pp. 129–48.
Simon, H.A. (1988), 'Satisficing', *The New Palgrave*, Basingstoke: Macmillan.
Simon, H.A. (1991), *Sciences des systèmes, Sciences de l'artificiel*, Paris: Dunod.
UNU (1985), *The Science and Praxis of Complexity*, Tokyo: The United Nations University.
von Foerster, H. (1960), 'On self-organizing systems and their environments', in M.C. Yovits and S. Cameron (eds), *Self-Organizing Systems*, Oxford: Pergamon Press.
von Foerster, H. (1977), 'Les objets: gages de comportements propres' (Objects: tokens for Eigenbehavior) in B. Inhelder, R. Garcia and J. Vonèche (eds), *Epistémologie génétique et équilibration, Hommage à Jean Piaget*, Actualités pédagogiques et psychologiques, Neuchatel: Delachaux et Niestlé, pp. 76–92.
von Foerster, H. (1988), 'La construction d'une réalité', in P. Watzlawick (ed.), *L'invention de la réalité. Contributions au constructivisme*. Paris: Seuil, pp. 45–69.
von Foerster, H. (1992), 'Ethics and second order cybernetics', *Cybernetics and Human Knowing*, **1** (1), pp. 9–19.
von Glasersfeld, E. (1988), 'Introduction à un constructivisme radical', in P. Watzlawick (ed.), *L'invention de la réalité. Contributions au constructivisme*, Paris: Seuil, pp. 19–43.
Watzlawick, P. (ed.) (1988), *L'invention de la réalité. Contributions au constructivisme*, Paris: Seuil, Edition in French of *Die Erfundene Wirklichkeit. Wie wissen wir, was wir zu wissen glauben? Beiträge zum Konstruktivismus*, München: R. Piper Co. Verlag, 1981.
Weaver, W. and C.E. Shannon (1975), *Théorie mathématique de la communication*, Paris: CEPL.

## COMMENT

**Augusto Schianchi**

In Delorme's bottom-up approach, the need for a new pluralistic view originates from three main issues: radical uncertainty (the reasoning based on prediction is unable to give a general foundation to science, see Popper); procedural rationality (decision-making is contaminated by the decision-maker's mind, see Simon); and perceived complexity (the complexity of an object depends on the way the observer interacts with it, see Morin, Le Moigne).

To solve the operative problems that arise from these interactions, Delorme draws from Le Moigne's recursive loop pattern, that is, a situation in which the product is producing what produces it.

However, making use of this scientific tool implies developing a further analysis concerning new axioms to work with, and consequently a new language to express them.

The need for a new language is well explained by the semiotic triangle (syntax, semantics, pragmatics) as the need for complex axioms is well represented by the following:

a. Operationality and intentionality: actions and interactions are the basic scientific categories;
b. Irreversibility: actions and processes take place over time;
c. Included middle: actions and processes are characterized by recursiveness, that is to say situations in which the product is producing what produces it.

In our reply to Delorme we will concentrate on complexity and the recursive loop issue and we will stress that the recursive loop approach is weak from an epistemological and philosophical point of view.

We agree with Delorme that complexity does not exclude the analytical method. We agree with him that the feature of recursiveness gives us the likely foundations of a pluralistic approach.

But we argue that recursive loop reasoning is widely tautological.

To break this tauto-logical process we need a new sort of logical approach. Without this, even the most genuine ideas are bound to turn into a form of complicated procedures, adding new complications to the existing one.

Therefore, to enlarge the significance of Delorme's view, we stress the need for a more general conception of complexity and complex reasoning. We stress the need for a new radical sort of complex reasoning.

## Complexity is not Complication

To some extent, the concept of complexity has become a sort of magic word. The same has been true for entropy, a fashionable way of describing a situation of increasing disorder. There are also more complicated cases. For example, the concept of incompleteness shows that an undemonstrable proposition exists in every theoretical system. What we name Gödel's Axiom, a generalization of Gödel's Theorem which applies to formal systems only (Gödel, 1990), explains why this is so. According to Gödel's Axiom, every theory (or padigram) is an open theory, i.e. a theoretical system is unable to prove all its propositions within its own cognitive tools.

Gödel's Axiom shows first that knowledge gives rise to ignorance; secondly, that each theoretical system needs to link itself to other theoretical systems so as to prove the undemonstrable proposition it contains, and this linking activity is the soul of science; but thirdly, it says that our scientific tools are unable to control this regress to infinity.

There is a large demand for this sort of fuzzy-definition, especially in the economic field, and historically we have seen a real migration of them from natural sciences to social services. Delorme's approach is certainly part of this positive migration, and his contribution is valuable.

But the problem still remains: unlike other concepts, that of complexity is not well defined.

In fact, we do not have a single definition of complexity, but many. For instance, we can say that a phenomenon is complex when its analysis cannot be reduced to the study of its single parts; when it shows simple behaviour despite an underlying confused (chaotic) activity; when it cannot be analysed by usual linear logic and mathematics; when it is characterized by uncertain and unforeseeable events; and so on.[1]

There is great confusion: the science of complexity, since its origins (Weaver, 1948), has not always been a science of complexity but a science of complicated matters, which is slightly but essentially different. Its early engineering and cybernetic models (Ashby, Shannon, Marcus, Simon) have shown themselves to be a pure description of a hyper-complicated world rather than of its complexity. And complexity is not always synonymous with complication.

Complexity, as we will argue, is a qualitative approach based on historical relations while complication is a quantitative approach based on zero-time algorithms. Delorme's approach does not take into account the difference between complexity and complication.

From a logical point of view our science is the science of numbers. 'All things have a number; if they didn't have, they wouldn't be knowable', Filolao said, and this is still the creed of our science. All that in reality is reducible to a number (to a procedure, a routine, a step) is science, the rest is not. All that can be described by an algorithm is science, the rest is not science, but is a philosophical matter and must be thrown out of the scientific window.[2]

Since its origins philosophy has devoted itself to complex matters, although without explicity adopting this term.[3]

In the history of philosophy there has always been a sort of anarchical subterranean current, from pre-Socratic speculations up to postmodernism. This philosophical view has been a complex view, not an ontological one. It rejected the existence of a generative principle according to which each thing could be identified and known once and for all, in a totality and simplicity which is rationally manifest.

In this sense, postmodernism can be viewed as a natural result of this process, an anarchical 'ontologism', a deconstruction of objective certainty by the assertion of intersubjective plurality.

A single principle does not exist. The sole existing principle is the existence of a plurality of principles, view, histories. The end of modernity, as Gianni Vattimo (1995) says, is the end of metaphysics, thus the end of an objective world.

At a linguistic level this philosophical approach leads to a pluralistic model of description. As in Wittgenstein's linguistic games, we no longer have a single description which is uniquely true, but we have a plurality of views to be joined together in another level of knowledge. 'Our, comprehension is but a sort of blindness with regard to our incomprehension', Wittgenstein said. There is no 'arche' to follow, no universal principles to be discovered, no objective way to describe and understand the world.

In order to understand the world men have to carry out a threefold process:

a. identify a thing (somehow describe it);
b. communicate this identification;
c. put the thing in relation to us.

To carry out this process, men have defined through the ages three general approaches: the first was based on *images* – the iconic approach; the second was based on *language* and its rules (concepts) – the linguistic approach; the third was based on *numbers* and algorithms – the numerical or quantitative approach.

The iconic approach applies to all models of 'knowledge by representation', from prehistoric paintings up to medieval cartography and modern art. It is an approach primarily based on identification, but poor with regard to the need of communication and consequently for the definition of functions. In fact, images identify only specific things and so they always refer to another system of relations and functions. Furthermore, an autonomous iconic grammar does not exist, and images are unable to use a language for speaking to each other.

The linguistic approach had a shorter history, at least until words had been used to identify things rather than concepts. But when an analytical logic was invented (Parmenide) and when a way to identify classes of objects by concepts was defined (Socrates, Plato) and finally when a system of logical relations amongst concepts was brought to perfection (Aristotle), this approach proved to be extremely powerful. However it is an approach essentially based on communication and poor with regard to identification of things and functions. In fact, the linguistic approach, being founded on concepts and conceptual relations, ended up by moving away from the iconic way of knowledge.

The numerical approach (Pythagoras) succeded in quantifying all the functions of real things (their value), in giving, as Filolao wanted, a number to each thing, but now it seems to have reached its boundaries: not everything can be described by numbers and even complicated quantitative models are unable to communicate reciprocally.

While an analytical approach was discovered a long time ago, the opposite logic of the synthesis (postulated by Eraclito but never tested) has not been developed until now. This logic is complex since it consists in formulating the rules which supervise the transformation by combination of things, thus *qualitative* transformations. *What complexity is cannot be described by algorithms.*

## Searching for a New Logic

Our logic is the Aristotelian logic. It is based on three self-consistent principles, as correctly described by Delorme:

- *the identity principle* : A is A;
- *the non-contradiction principle* : A cannot be simultaneously B and not-B;
- *the excluded middle principle* : A is B or not-B.

Aristotelian logic is perfectly consistent with the classical reductionistic approach which tries to isolate the elementary units of a phenomenon. These elementary units correspond to the concept of 'the same thing' in the Aristotelian principles. In this way classical logic reinforced the simplifying features of classical science. We do not argue that these features are wrong. We do argue that they are unsuitable for a complete description of reality. They are partial, inadequate.

Let's take society. We cannot understand the social world only be adding individual experiences. Society goes beyond them. It has overall features. We cannot understand the economic world only be adding our information or theories about single consumers or single agents.

To understand the totality we need a larger logic. Totality is a meta-world made of relations evolving in time, a world in which relations among objects have their own life, their own rules, their own consistency.

Let's take a brick. What is a brick? Our common sense tells us that a brick is something that we join together with other bricks so as to build a house.

What something? Something made of specific materials, because a brick made of whipped cream cannot be joined together with other bricks to form a house. In this case, it wouldn't be a brick.

Together with what? Together with other bricks, because a brick joined together with toy balloons cannot be used to build a house. In this case, it wouldn't be a house.

To build what? To build a house (or something like that) because we cannot build a jacket with bricks. In this case, it wouldn't be a jacket.

So, three conditions must prevail for a brick to be recognized as a brick:

- a certain *material* ;
- a certain *relation* with other things;
- a certain *function* to carry out (with those materials and those relations).

We call it the MRF model, the materials–relations–functions model (Betti, 1995).

A brick does not exist in itself. What we call a brick is an interlacement of conditions – a certain material, a certain network of relations it has, a certain set of functions it carries out. If materials, relations or functions change, we cannot define the same thing as a brick. For example, if we throw a brick at a burglar, the same brick is no longer a brick but a weapon: the material has not changed but its relation has been modified (it is in the air and no more joined together with other bricks to form a house) and consequently its function (to defend ourselves from the burglar).

The conclusion is: the nature of a thing depends on the interlacement of conditions it fulfills, that is, it depends on its placing within a global system of interlacements. We have to study this global system in order to define its constituent parts. Exactly the opposite of the Aristotelian approach.

The MRF model leads us to important conclusions in the scientific-logical field. In a word, it destroys the Aristotelian logical approach giving us the foundations of a new radical approach. In fact:

1. It disrupts the identity principle; the *same thing* A could be B if we place it in another system of interlacements; we define this as the *non-identity principle*.
2. Secondly it disrupts Parmenide's non-contradiction principle, stating that A can be simultaneously B and not-B at the same time, if we change its MRF conditions; the *same thing* (A = brick) can be simultaneously a weapon if we throw it (B = weapon) or not-B if we do not throw it (not-B = not a weapon); the MRF conditions define a thing, not the thing in itself; we call this the *contradiction principle*.
3. Thirdly A can be not only B and not-B but even C; there is not a generating principle, a kind of universal law to be discovered, but a combination-based dynamic among things, that is among MRF conditions of each thing; this is what we define as the *included middle principle*; generally speaking this states that the logic of reality is the logic of combinations, a combination-based logic; accordingly, we cannot say that A produces B and B produces C, under certain conditions; we can say that A is characterized by a spectrum of possibilities and only a few of them are put into action when A conditions come into contact with other MRF conditions; so, A can become B if certain conditions are fulfilled or it can become C if certain others are; the phenomenon A has no natural tendency to become B rather than C; its evolution depends on the dynamics of materials, relations and functions involved.

Thus, the logic of reality is conceived not as generative but as *combination-based*. For example, if our brick (and its MRF pattern) meets the MRF pattern of other bricks, it will become a house; if it meets the MRF pattern of a man's head it will become a weapon. Obviously it will never become a cigarette, because its MRF pattern will never fulfil all the conditions of being a cigarette (material = tobacco; relations = to burn when it comes into contact with fire; function = to give pleasure).

The chain of combinations among MRF conditions is what we call a historical process. A historical process does not concern dates or chronology. It does concern combinations of interlacements. The *temporal persistence* of a thing depends on how stable its MRF conditions are or, rather, how reciprocally compatible they are. Just to give an example, a street has a high temporal persistence because its materials allow the development of many relations so as to carry out its functions (communication, transport, exchange...). Needless to say, when its materials become poor (the asphalt disintegrates) or when its relations fail (a new motorway is built beside the old street) or when its functions fade away (the market previously linked by the street gets closed), its MRF pattern and so its historical persistence collapses.

In general perspective the MRF model tells us that a thing does not exist in itself, that there is not a Nature-in-itself of which we have to discover laws and principles. Nature is a totality of interlacements which we penetrate only within a narrow spectrum, the spectrum of our narrow perceptive and cognitive capabilities (von Foerster, 1984). The task of science is to enlarge this spectrum, and for that science has to go beyond human rationality.

Furthermore, in reality each thing is linked to every other thing. We need new kinds of knowledge, since things have a sense only if we observe them in a sensible way. Each time we observe a phenomenon, we inevitably open the Pandora's box of our world views. Things exist only if we give them a sense, that is to say only when we light up – by our cerebral activity – the totality of interlacements thanks to which things get a meaning. This is undoubtedly a classical philosophical matter, but we can no longer consider science without looking at these questions.

## Notes

1. Compare the different approaches of Morin (1977–91); Prigogine (1984); Prigogine and Nicolis (1987); and finally Simon (1962).
2. We underline the strong analogy existing between the Cherniak's approach to informatics and David Marr's epistemic scheme for cognitive sciences. They both recognize the three following levels: (1) a computational level, (2) an algorithmic level, and (3) an implementation level. See Cherniak (1988) and Marr (1982).
3. This section partially draws from Brivio (1995).

## References


Betti, Francesco (1995), 'Complexity in Economics. An Introduction', Graduation thesis, University of Parma, July.

Brivio, Guido (1995), Manuscript, University of Turin.

Cherniak, C. (1988), 'Undebuggability and cognitive science', *Communications of the Association for Computing Machinery*, n. 31, pp. 402–13.

Gödel, Kurt (1986–90), *Collected Works*, 2 vols, Oxford: Oxford University Press.

Marr, D. (1982), *Vision*, San Francisco: Freeman.

Morin, Edgar (1977–91), *La méthode*, 4 vols, Paris: Editions du Seuil.

Prigogine, Ilya (1984), *From Being to Becoming. Time and Complexity in the Physical Sciences*, New York: Freeman.

Prigogine, I. and Nicolis, G. (1987), *Exploring Complexity. An Introduction*, Monaco: R. Piper.

Simon, H.A. (1962), 'The architecture of complexity', *Proceedings of the American Philosophical Society*, n. 106, pp. 467–82.

Vattimo, Gianni (1995), Notes distributed during A.S.I.A. seminar, Lago di Braies, September.

von Foerster, H. (1984), *Observing Systems*, Intersystem Publications, Seaside, California.

Weaver, W. (1948), 'Science and complexity', *American Scientist*, n. 36, pp. 536–44.

# 7. Metaphor and pluralism in economics: mechanics and biology

**Geoffrey M. Hodgson**

'Complexity' is the word of the moment. Books about a new 'emerging science' based on a recognition of complexity have now made their way into the best-seller lists (e.g. Lewin, 1993; Waldrop, 1992). Such populist outcomes should make us cautious. Nevertheless, there is some substance in the claims made by those who see an emergent paradigm in the making. There are several methodological implications of this shift. One of central importance is the breakdown of the reductionist project in sciences addressing complex systems, such as economics and biology.[1] Two further implications follow immediately: first, the necessity for a much more self-conscious and open use of metaphor in the analysis of complex systems, and second, the recognition that there can be no complete and final explanation and that we shall always be faced by a plurality of competing theories.

The first section of this chapter discusses the breakdown of reductionism, with particular attention to economics and biology. The second section asserts the need for the self-conscious use of metaphor in science and argues that metaphor has always, in fact, been constitutive for science and has a subterranean presence in economic theory. The third section discusses the implications for theoretical pluralism and concludes the essay.

## 1. THE LIMITS TO REDUCTIONISM

Inspired in particular by classical physics and its apparent analytical and practical successes, orthodox economists have long been labouring under a reductionist research programme. The complexities of economic systems have been addressed by attempting to build up a composite picture from atomistic, individual units, just as the particle forms the elemental unit in Newtonian mechanics. Accordingly, the attempt has been to explain the whole through its analytical reduction to its presumed microfoundations and component parts.

Many economists pay lip service to methodological individualism and the view that social wholes should be explained solely in terms of the individuals comprising them (Hodgson, 1988, ch. 3). Yet as Lars Udéhn (1987) points out, the complexity of social phenomena means that this methodological practice has never been successfully applied except in trivial cases, and is bound to be unsuccessful in any complex social system.

While mainstream economic theory has long been engaged in an attempt to place economics on secure and individualistic microfoundations, it was quickly realized that the potential diversity among individuals threatened the feasibility of this project. Many types of interaction between the individuals have to be ignored to make the analysis tractable. Indeed, it was not easy to develop a composite picture from a diversity of types of individual agent.

Even with the standard assumptions of rational behaviour, and its drastic psychological and epistemological limitations, severe difficulties are faced. As Arrow (1986, p. S388) has been led to declare: 'In the aggregate, the hypothesis of rational behaviour has in general no implications.' Consequently, it is widely assumed that all individuals have the same utility function. Among other things this denies the possibility of 'gains from trade arising from individual differences (p. S390).

Fabrizio Coricelli and Giovanni Dosi (1988, p. 126) argue that 'the project of building dynamic models with economic content and descriptive power by relying solely on the basic principles of rationality and perfect competition through the market process has generally failed'. Attempts to base macroeconomics on neoclassical microfoundations involve faith in the 'invisible hand' and in the substantive capabilities of individuals to calculate endlessly and make supremely rational choices. Yet the results of this theoretical endeavour show no more than a very crippled hand, incapable of orderly systemic coordination even in relatively simple models:

> Moreover, note that these results are obtained despite an increasing attribution of rational competence and information processing power to individual agents. Certainly ... the attempt to 'explain' macroeconomics solely on the basis of some kind of 'hyper-rationality' of the agents ... and the (pre-analytical) fundamentals of the economy (i.e. given technology and tastes) has failed. (Coricelli and Dosi, 1988, p. 136)

Hence it is no exaggeration to say that in economics the microfoundations enterprise has effectively collapsed, and for reasons well known to and understood by the leading theorists of the genre.[2] The gravity of the present crisis for mainstream economics can be illustrated by considering a few selected topics.[3]

First, theoretical work in game theory and elsewhere has raised questions about the very meaning of 'hard core' notions such as rationality. Yanis

Varoufakis (1990) surveys some of the recent results concerning the problems of rational decision-making in the circumstances where a limited number of other actors are believed to be capable of 'irrational' acts. Such 'irrationality' need not stem from stupidity; it is sufficient to consider the possibilities that rational actors may have incomplete information, limited computational capacities, slight misperceptions of reality, or doubts concerning the attributes of their adversaries. Agents do not have to be substantially irrational for irrationality to matter. Irrational behaviour may emerge simply where some people are uncertain that everybody else is rational.

Second, the intrusion of chaos theory into economics has put paid to the general idea that economics can proceed simply on the criterion of 'correct predictions'. With non-linear models, outcomes are oversensitive to initial conditions and thereby reliable predictions are impossible to make concerning any extended period. In particular, chaos theory has confounded the rational-expectations theorists by showing that even where most agents know the basic structure of the economic model, in general they cannot derive reliable predictions of outcomes and thereby form any meaningful 'rational expectations' of the future (Grandmont, 1986).

Third, recent research into the problems of the uniqueness and stability of general equilibria have shown that they may be indeterminate and unstable unless very strong assumptions are made, such as the supposition that society as a whole behaves as if it were a single individual (Hodgson and Screpanti, 1991, p. 2). Essentially, this demolished the entire microfoundations project. Facing such profound problems, Alan Kirman (1992, p. 118) writes: 'there is no plausible formal justification for the assumption that the aggregate of individuals, even maximizers, acts itself like an individual maximizer'. He concludes: 'If we are to progress further we may well be forced to theorize in terms of groups who have collectively coherent behaviour. ... The idea that we should start at the level of the isolated individual is one which we may well have to abandon' (Kirman, 1989, p. 138). The theoretical implications of these uniqueness and stability results for general equilibrium theory are devastating. The indeterminacy and instability results produced by contemporary theory lead to the conclusion that an economy made up simply of self-contained individual agents has not structure enough to survive.

Typically, the textbook macroeconomics that is spun out of neoclassical theory goes well beyond the rigours of general equilibrium theory, to make bold and general claims concerning the relationship between wages and unemployment, and inflation and the money supply. Only the more honest and careful neoclassical theorists have questioned such macroeconomic derivations from microeconomic assumptions. For instance, Arrow (1986, p. S386) states that he knows 'of no serious derivation of the demand for money from a rational optimization'.

## The Ubiquitous Problem of Analytical Intractability

As in other sciences, a strong reductionist tradition still survives in biology. In the nineteenth century, after the publication of Charles Darwin's *Origin of Species*, there was a prominent tendency on behalf of his followers to assume that explanations of social phenomena were reducible to biological terms. One of the best-known equivalent cases in the twentieth century is the work of Richard Dawkins (1976) where he maintains that the behaviours of organisms, groups and whole species can be largely explained in terms of their genes. Similarly, sociobiologists such as Edward Wilson (1975) attempt to explain the social behaviour of animals and humans in terms of the constituent genes, without sufficient recognition of the explanatory autonomy of social culture. It may be the case that biology is of relevance for the study of social phenomena (Hirst and Woolley, 1982) but the extreme view that they can be understood wholly or largely in biological terms has been rightly challenged.

Yet biological reductionism has unmanageable computational problems. Consider the prediction of evolution with multiple loci or alleles:

> even the simplest multi-locus case of two alleles at each of two loci is analytically intractable. This should not be surprising: the problem of dimensionality nine (there are nine possible genotypes, with independently specifiable fitness parameters) is already more complicated than the three-body problem of classical mechanics. (Wimsatt, 1980, p. 223)

Like the three-body problem, this biological computation has been solved for a variety of special cases (Roughgarden, 1979, pp. 111–33) but has not been solved in general. Similar problems of intractability arise from the Schrödinger equations for subatomic particles.

Consider the apparently simple case of the three-body problem in mechanics. While this problem has been solved for two bodies, the differential equations that result from applying these laws to three bodies are so complicated that a general solution has not been found. Instead, partial solutions have been achieved by resorting to approximations or constraints of various kinds, such as the assumption that one body has negligible mass (Stewart, 1989, pp. 66–72). Hence mathematical solutions cannot be found to configurations of this very first level of complexity, involving just three bodies. This indicates the operational limits of reductionism, even in mechanics. The hope that predictions can be made with such a simple three-body system is in vain. There is here no consolation for the biological or economic reductionist who aims to predict by breaking down all complex phenomena to the interactive behaviour of atomistic or individual parts.

Chaos theorists have shown that in non-linear systems, tiny changes in crucial parameters can lead to dramatic consequences (Gleick, 1988; Stewart, 1989). The result is not simply to make prediction difficult or impossible; there are serious implications for the notion of reductive explanation in science. We cannot with absolute confidence associate a given outcome with a given set of initial conditions, because we can never be sure that the computations traced out from those initial conditions are precise enough, and that the initial conditions themselves have been defined with sufficient precision. Hence in chaos theory the very notion of explanation of a phenomenon by reference to a system and its initial conditions is challenged.

As leading mathematicians of chaos have themselves proclaimed, chaos theory 'brings a new challenge to the reductionist view that a system can be understood by breaking it down and studying each piece' (Crutchfield *et al.*, 1986, p. 48). The impact of chaos theory for science as a whole is likely to be profound. Not only is the common obsession with precise prediction confounded; the whole atomistic tradition in science of attempting to reduce each phenomenon to its component parts is placed into question.

However, this does not mean that such non-linear equations relating to a lower level of analysis are worthless. Although they may be of limited computational or predictive use, they retain some explanatory power. Furthermore, as noted later below, chaotic systems do exhibit some kind of order about which deductions may be drawn.

## The Limitations and Biases of the Counter-Strategies

Strategies have been devised to attempt to deal with the general analytical problems associated with complex systems. For instance, Herbert Simon (1968) has examined 'the hypothesis of near decomposability' through which it is assumed that a complex system can be decomposed into a set of subsystems. For this to be feasible, all strong interactions must be contained within the boundaries of subsystems, and interactions between variables or entities in different subsystems must be appreciably weaker than those relating variables or entities in the same subsystem. If this is the case then a short-run approximation to the behaviour of the system can be made by ignoring the interactions between subsystems, and analysing each one as if it were isolated.

However, the general applicability of this principle is in doubt. Apart from the remaining problem of long-term interactions, biologists have shown that under feasible conditions there can be permanent and substantial linkage disequilibrium between subsystems (Maynard Smith, 1978; ch. 5; Roughgarden, 1979). This suggests that systems can be treated as being nearly decomposable only in a limited number of special cases.

In a seminal work of genetic reductionism in biology, George C. Williams (1966) claims that reductive problems can be solved one locus at a time and then extended to a global solution by 'iterating over all loci'. This is now recognized by critics as invalid. Williams wrongly presumes that gene frequency alone is an adequate basis for a deterministic theory of evolutionary change, and ignores context dependence. This refers to a situation where the fitness or behaviour of an organism may be significantly dependent on its environmental context, often leading to two-way interactions between a unit and its environment. As William Wimsatt (1980, p. 240) argues, 'Illegitimate assumptions of context-independence are a frequent error in reductionist analyses.'

In the course of his argument, Wimsatt (1980, p. 241) highlights 'the practical impossibility of generating an exhaustive, quasi-algorithmic, or exact analysis of the behaviour of the system and its environment'. In response to this complexity,

> the reductionist must start simplifying. In general, simplifying assumptions will have to be made everywhere, but given his interest in studying relations *internal* to the system, he will tend to order his list of economic priorities so as to simplify, first and more extremely, in his description, observation, control, and analysis of the environment than in the system he is studying. After all, simplifications internal to the system face the danger of simplifying out of existence the very phenomena and mechanisms he wishes to study (ibid., p. 241).

However, there are clear pitfalls in ignoring the complexities of the environment and some of its interactions with the system in question. Therefore the reductionist research strategy, Wimsatt rightly concludes, has an inbuilt bias towards the inclusion of certain types of relations and the exclusion of others.

It should be pointed out that the general idea of a reduction to parts is not being overturned here. Some degree of reduction to elemental units is inevitable. Even measurement or classification are acts of reductionism. Science cannot proceed without some dissection and some analysis of parts. However, although some reductionism is inevitable and desirable, complete reductionism is both impossible and a philosophically dogmatic diversion. What is important to stress is that the process of analysis cannot be extended to the most elementary subatomic particles presently known to science, or even to individuals in economics or genes in biology. Complete reductionism would be hopeless and interminable. As Karl Popper has declared, 'I do not think that there are any examples of a successful reduction' to elemental units in science (Popper and Eccles, 1977, p. 18). Reduction is necessary to some extent, but it can never be complete. What is contentious is not reductionism *per se*, but its chosen scope and extent, and the ultimate reliance placed on it in comparison with, or to the exclusion of, other general methodological procedures.

## 2. THE ROLE OF METAPHOR

Faced with this problem of complexity and the failure of complete reductionism, some other methodological approach is required. As Brian Arthur has explained,

> If you have a truly complex system, then the exact patterns are not repeatable. And yet there are themes that are recognizable. In history, for example, you can talk about 'revolutions', even though one revolution might be quite different from another. So we assign metaphors. (Quoted in Waldrop, 1992, p. 334)

Among the preliminary tasks of scientific analysis are taxonomy and classification, involving the assignment of sameness and difference. Classification, by bringing together entities in discrete groups, must refer to common qualities. To peer into the complex reality and make some sense of it we are guided inevitably by frameworks and habits of thought that we inherit from our past. We construct 'ideal types' (Dyke, 1985). We use metaphor. As Arjo Klamer and Thomas Leonard (1994, p. 31) put it: 'Science needs metaphor since it provides the cognitive means to chart the unknown.'

In contrast, scientists often regard metaphors as mere literary ornaments. It is sometimes suggested that they should be removed to reveal the essential theory below. For instance, in economics, Joseph Schumpeter (1954, pp. 17–18, 30, 119, 211, 537, 788–90) persistently alleged that analogies with physics or biology were at best an irrelevant diversion and at worst completely misleading.[4] He wrote at a time when positivistic views of science were at their apogee, and metaphor and analogy were thus regarded as an obstruction on some hypothetico-deductive road to truth.

Typically, in economics and elsewhere, recourse to mathematical modes of expression is motivated in part by a desire to remove all such metaphorical 'literary frills'. However, modern philosophers of science take a very different view. Mary Hesse (1980, p. 111) complains that 'It is still unfortunately necessary to argue that metaphor is more than a decorative literary device, and that it has cognitive implications whose nature is a proper subject of philosophic discussion.' Similarly, Max Black (1962, p. 237) concludes in a prominent study of metaphor and analogy in science, 'Metaphorical thought is a distinctive mode of achieving insight, not to be construed as an ornamental substitute for plain thought.'

Clearly, for a positivist, a formalist or a nominalist the use of metaphor is a superficial matter, even a distraction: a confusing renaming of entities that can have nothing to do with their essence. But this kind of response is challenged by modern philosophers who argue that metaphor is constitutive and perhaps even indispensable for science. Now we are 'beyond positivism' (Caldwell, 1982) in the methodology – if not the perceived practice – of economics and other sciences. We cannot found theory simply on facts; the facts do not 'speak for themselves', and can neither verify nor strictly falsify our theories. Metaphor is not an ornament: it is an unavoidable means of constituting and ordering our thoughts. As Friedrich Nietzsche wrote in the nineteenth century,

> What, then, is truth? A mobile army of metaphors, metonyms, and anthropomorphisms – in short, a sum of human relations, which have been enhanced, transposed, and embellished poetically and rhetorically, and which after long use seem firm, canonical, and obligatory to all people. (In Kaufman, 1982)

Metaphors may lead or mislead. By their nature, they are never complete, precise, or literal mappings. If they were precise representations they would not be metaphors, and the juxtaposition of similar but different conceptual frameworks would be lost. This juxtaposition, involving a degree of similarity and dissimilarity, can have both creative and damaging effects.

Metaphors are more than similes. For example, to describe the economy as 'evolving' is not simply to state that the economy develops like an organism or a species in the natural world. It also may prompt the investigator to consider the many meanings and ambiguities in the term 'evolve' and the many extensions and facets of the implicit analogy between the natural and the social world.

In economics the triumph of formalism has done nothing to limit the extensive use of metaphor, with terms such as 'human capital', 'market forces', 'consumer sovereignty' and 'natural rates of unemployment'. The use of metaphor affects not merely the phrasing, but the structure and substance of the discipline (Samuels, 1990). Yet the metaphorical references may be partially obscured by the progress of formalism in economics. As mathematical symbols replace words, the analogies may seem to disappear. This is an illusion. As Donald McCloskey (1985, p. 74) puts it: 'Noneconomists find it easier to see the metaphors than do economists, habituated as the economists are by daily use to the idea that of course production comes from a "function" and of course business moves in "cycles".'

## The Role of the Mechanistic Metaphor in Economics

The use of metaphor in economics has often been explicit. Even at the foundation of modern economic science, Adam Smith appealed specifically to metaphor and Newtonian mechanics in his essay on *The Principles which*

*Lead and Direct Philosophical Enquiries: Illustrated by the History of Astronomy*. As Brian Loasby points out, Smith used Newtonian astronomy as primarily a set of 'connecting principles' (Loasby, 1989, pp. 1–5; 1991, pp. 6–8). These were held to make sense of his experience and were deemed to be fitting for his own theoretical work. Indeed, Smith was remarkably candid about the role of metaphor and 'imagination' in science. In the tradition of Descartes and Newton, the aim must be to simplify, to reduce to elemental laws, to render 'nature a coherent spectacle' made up of a few 'primary and elementary objects' (Smith, 1869, p. 386).

It has been argued extensively, by Philip Mirowski (1989b) and others that modern economics is still dominated by the metaphor of a mechanistic system. Many commentators typify the kind of mechanistic ideas that permeate economics as essentially Newtonian, although Mirowski sees as crucial the additional influence of the energetics movement in physics in the latter half of the nineteenth century. Whatever the precise details of the account, the consensus is that modern economics is still heavily influenced by the kind of mechanistic thinking that dominated physics around the middle decades of the nineteenth century. In particular, the evidence for the substantial influence of physics on the architects of the 'marginal revolution' is substantial. As Mirowski shows, the founders of modern mainstream economic theory all made explicit reference to the mechanistic metaphor, and indicated that their work was guided by such a vision of constitution and structure.

However, the precise details of the transfer of metaphor need to be examined. Here some questions can be raised about Mirowski's account in his *More Heat Than Light*. He argues that the transfer was overt and generally self-conscious, supposing that the economists involved were continuously aping physics and its every twist and theoretical turn.

There are at least two flaws in this version of the story. First, it underestimates the subtlety of the process of metaphorical transfer. Whilst there are cases of the direct appropriation of concepts and mathematical formalisms – amply documented by Mirowski – the constitutive transfers are at a deeper and less conscious level, affecting the ontology, epistemology and methodology of the subject. With such 'deep level' transfers the contamination of economics by mechanistic thinking is even more profound than Mirowski suggests.

The second flaw is that Mirowski disregards the sociology of the economics profession. We may illustrate this by considering later developments in physics in the twentieth century and their influence on economics. For instance, Mirowski makes a case that quantum theory has had an effect on econometric practice from the 1930s (Mirowski, 1989a). Apart from this, however, the general effect of post-quantum physics on economics since 1930 has not been crucial.

If economics has been driven by physics in the direct and overt manner suggested by Mirowski then he would have to account for the fact that the deeper implications of modern quantum theory have not been incorporated. Indeed, the organicist and indeterminist aspects of modern quantum theory are in profound contradiction to the Cartesianism, reductionism and atomism at the root of both the earlier physics and of modern economics.

Consideration of these points suggests a slightly different story, although it cannot be discussed in detail here. Although Walras, Jevons, Edgeworth and Pareto did ape the physics of their time, the professionalization and institutionalization of economics since then has locked the subject into that particular genre. Once the new norms of scientific activity became established in the emergent economic journals and economics departments of the late nineteenth and early twentieth century then they set down the self-reinforcing standards for subsequent research. Scholars seeking publication or promotion had a better chance of success if they conformed to these norms. The canon of mathematical formalization was endowed with particular prestige. As in other cases of institutional evolution, the phenomenon of locked-in behaviour depending much on initial circumstances is normal rather than exceptional.

Accordingly, the initial role of physics was crucial – in contributing greatly to the initial intellectual environment and in legitimating the allegedly scientific credentials of the subject – but since the early decades of the twentieth century economics has been driven less by physics than by its own momentum. It is institutional practice, including a very outdated view of science and an over-obsession with mathematical formalism, that drives economics along its present groove – not an overt and unabating desire to replicate everything going on in modern physics or other natural sciences.[5] This does not mean that the role of the mechanistic metaphor in economics is diminished. Far from it: it is subtle and ubiquitous.

Although no other social science has used mathematical techniques as extensively as economics, the cache of mathematical tools employed has typically been rather limited. Nineteenth-century physics did not only offer 'scientific' credentials: it provided an armoury of formal techniques, with differential calculus in pride of place. It is only recently that the kind of mathematics bestowed in the last third of the nineteenth century is beginning to be overshadowed by other formal developments, particularly game theory. Notably, it is now recognized that its application threatens core tenets such as the axioms of rationality (Sugden, 1991).

In overt terms, however, modern economics has almost forgotten the source of the crucial metaphor from which it gained so much formal and theoretical inspiration during the eighteenth and nineteenth centuries. The history of economic thought, now generally and almost completely disregarded by economists, is noticeably absent from undergraduate syllabi and professional job descriptions. With the ever sharper focus on mathematical form rather than conceptual substance, attention is has been shifted away from the nature and origin of core assumptions in economics.

This is one reason why the exposure of the role of metaphor is so important. It can reveal deeply embedded structures of thought, and provide a clue to why the subject develops along one path rather than another. The reforming theoretician can then identify, and attempt to remove or alter, the malign features at the theoretical core. If we ignore metaphor, or regard it like Schumpeter as a useless diversion, we are impelled to place all our faith in facts and *a priori* argument. By this neglect we are condemned to remain with current orthodoxy. The facts themselves are structured by the dominant theories, and orthodoxy offers us a highly restricted choice of axioms upon which theory may be built.

Whilst Mirowski claims that mainstream economics has continued consciously to ape physics, his ironic thrust is to suggest that they often got the physics wrong. Yet the intellectual aptitudes of economic theorists in a foreign discipline are really of little relevance. The whole point of metaphor, as the history of science reveals, is that ideas from elsewhere do not have to be perfectly understood or entirely appropriate in order to inspire novelty.[6]

Our revised version of Mirowski's story has a better and deeper irony. In the 1870s neoclassical economics attempted to gain the accolade of a science by adopting a thoroughly reductionist research programme, based on the tenet of methodological individualism. In Newtonian spirit, the idea was to found economics on allegedly 'self-evident' axioms about human behaviour, and to develop the formal theoretical apparatus from there. Such a view of science contrasts with the self-conscious application of metaphors to complex systems, the intuitive insight, or the *gestalt*. The deeper irony was that precisely at the moment of foundation of the neoclassical system its architects were forced to make extensive use of metaphor from another domain of study. On reflection, this is a deep embarrassment to the Cartesian or Newtonian way of doing things. It is no accident that, far from chasing every turn in physics, subsequent neoclassical economists quickly forgot this source of original inspiration.

Contrary to Mirowski, the problem for economics is not the general appropriation of metaphor from the natural sciences but more fundamentally the adoption of a positivist conception of science in which the role of metaphor is specifically denied. In this manner the source of the constitutive assumptions of modern economics has been ignored, despite their continuous transmission through the orthodox mathematical formalisms and their reinforcement through the sociological structure of the economics profession. For this reason, the ingrained mechanistic metaphor in economics is even more difficult to remove and to replace.

The argument that metaphors are indispensable in scientific discourse counters the mistaken and positivist view of a metaphor-free science. In addition, and concerning particular subjects such as economics, it would lead us to the self-conscious evaluation of metaphor, rather than the futile attempt to remove it entirely as found in the work of Schumpeter and many others.[7]

## From the Mechanistic to the Biological Metaphor in Economics

The deficiencies of the metaphor taken from classical mechanics have been discussed by a number of authors (Georgescu-Roegen, 1971; Gowdy, 1985; Hodgson, 1993; Norgaard, 1989; Sebba, 1953; Thoben, 1982; Veblen, 1919). There are a number of perennial problems involved, all relating to the limitations of Cartesian philosophy and Newtonian principles. For instance, movement is reversible in the 'conserved system' of Newtonian mechanics; there is no arrow of time. 'Classical mechanics only knows motion, whereas at the same time the processes of motion are completely reversible and in no way give rise to any qualitative changes' (Thoben, 1982, pp. 292–306, 293). Although in some non-conserved, mechanistic theoretical systems the possibility of irreversibility emerges – such as with the addition of friction – the reasons are quite different from those in more complex systems. Above all, with mechanistic presuppositions, cause and effect can be mirrored by logical syllogism, and logical replaces historical time (Robinson, 1974).

It is easy to trace the derivation of the ideas of rationality and equilibria, the core concepts of neoclassical economics, from the inheritance of mechanistic thought:

> Classical mechanics considers a system of material points upon which directional forces operate at a distance according to calculable laws of motion. The choice of paths is governed by the principle of least action, which may be termed the economic principle if we take the term in its widest sense as denoting a maximum–minimum principle. (Sebba, 1953)

Hence, subject to a combination of forces, economic agents optimize to the point of equilibrium as if they were mere particles obeying mechanical laws.

In addition, there is a general difficulty of incorporating information, learning and knowledge in a mechanistic scheme. In classical mechanics there is no place for thoughts and ideas: all is mere matter, subject to Newtonian laws. As Norbert Weiner (1954, p. 29) remarked, 'In nineteenth-century physics it seemed to cost nothing to get information.'

It is not proposed here that the use of mechanistic thinking in economics has been entirely without value. Nevertheless, the limitations are severe. In sum, the mechanistic metaphor excludes knowledge, qualitative change and irreversibility through time. It entraps economics in an equilibrium schema where there are no systematic errors and no cumulative development. Clearly much is missing here. The strength of the alternative, biological, metaphor is that a place can be found for these important features of economic life.

Another extremely important reason why ideas from biology are of relevance to economics is that both economic and biotic systems are highly complex. They both encompass tangled structures and causalities, involve continuous change and embrace huge variety. Partly for this reason, there is the problem of levels of abstraction and appropriate units of analysis. This has been faced up to and debated by a number of prominent biologists, but far less attention has been given to this vital issue in economics. The adoption of biological metaphors may help to redress the balance.

Taking recourse to biology is not simply a tactic. It is held that real-world economic phenomena have much more in common with biological organisms and processes than with the mechanistic world of billiard balls and planets. After all, the economy involves living human beings, not merely particles, forces and energy. Nevertheless, there are risks involved in this trade; biology has been often abused by social scientists in the past, sometimes with horrendous social and political consequences.

It is still widely assumed that evolutionary thinking leads to the rejection of any kind of state subsidy or intervention, and the support for *laissez-faire* on the basis of the idea of 'survival of the fittest'. However, it is wrong to assume that evolutionary theorizing always points to the optimality of competitive outcomes, or to laws of evolutionary 'progress', or to the sagacity of *laissez-faire*. According to modern theory, evolutionary processes do not necessarily lead to – by any reasonable definition – optimal consequences. Similar arguments apply in the economic as well as the biotic context (Gould and Lewontin, 1979; Hodgson, 1993, ch. 13).

Moreover, it should be emphasized that biology has internal problems of its own; it is not panacea. Indeed, biology is not itself free of mechanistic metaphor and reductionist methods. A large number of biologists are committed to reductionism, even concerned to explained biological phenomena in physical terms. Within its boundaries, however, there are also pronounced attempts to transcend such strains of thought.

Furthermore, the explicit recognition of the underlying metaphor can perhaps help the theorist to develop 'auto-immune systems' against a rejected strain of thought. For instance, attention to the problem of excessive formalism would lead to the consideration and development of appropriately descriptive and historical approaches to counter an emerging infatuation with the tools and techniques of mathematical biology. Whilst the adoption of a biological metaphor rather than a mechanical one does not itself cure the problem of excessive formalism,[8] the recognition of the complexity and irreducibility of socio-economic reality should warn against this addiction.

It is important to emphasize that all metaphors create difficulties as well as solutions. Accordingly a precise transfer of ideas is neither possible nor desirable. As Renate Mayntz (1992, pp. 68–9) puts it,

> What we do ... is not to use the natural science theory to explain social phenomena, but the natural science theory stimulates a new way of viewing the social phenomena that, guided by some rather abstract notions, triggers a process of social science theory building. Strictly speaking, the potentially most productive mode of borrowing is therefore one where transfer in a direct way does not take place at all.

A preeminent problem with both the biological and the mechanical analogy is the conceptualization of the human agent. It has been argued by several critical economists that – despite the rhetoric – orthodox and mechanistic economics provides no room for real individual choice (Loasby, 1976). Biological natural selection invokes genetic replication and random variation or mutation, but seemingly affords no role for intentionality, purposefulness or choice.

The problem of 'vitalism', involving choice, will and purpose, has been persistent within biology. Although 'vitalism' is now out of fashion, it raises real issues of importance, even if the notion is shunned by biologists who confine themselves to causal rather than intentional explanations. Dissenters to strict Darwinism, including Arthur Koestler, have tried to instate concepts of will and purpose in the science, but with limited effect. This whole problem should not be ignored or underestimated: It is addressed at length elsewhere (Koestler, 1967; Hodgson, 1993, ch. 14).

Despite all the problems and dangers, it is suggested here that modern biology provides a rich source of ideas and approaches from which a revitalized economics may draw. In all, the application of an evolutionary approach to economics seems to involve a number of advantages and improvements over the orthodox and mechanistic paradigm. For instance, it enhances a concern with irreversible and ongoing processes in time,[9] with long-run development rather than short-run marginal adjustments, with qualitative as well as quantitative change, with variation and diversity, with non-equilibrium as well as equilibrium situations, and with the possibility of persistent and systematic error-making and thereby non-optimizing behaviour.

In short, an evolutionary paradigm provides an alternative to the neoclassical 'hard core' idea of mechanistic maximization under static constraints. The theory of rational choice at the core of mainstream economics relies on static assumptions, the notion of an eventually constant decision environment, and the idea of global rationality, which are all challenged by evolutionary theory (Cooper, 1989; Goldberg, 1975; Hodgson, 1994).[10]

Finally, connecting economics with biology may also result from a recognition that as human beings we are part of the natural world. Although the levels and modes of analysis in the two disciplines are quite different, reflecting the emergent properties in each sphere, the provision of conceptual and theoretical links pays respect to the common reality (Bhaskar, 1979; Hirst and Woolley, 1982).

## 3. IN CONCLUSION: THEORETICAL PLURALISM

The Latin word *cogito* comes from *coagitare*, to shake together. Much creativity in science comes from the integration of hitherto unrelated ideas or frames of thought. Examples are plentiful (Koestler, 1964). Pythagoras observed a blacksmith at work and noticed that iron bars of different lengths gave out sounds of different pitch under the strokes of the hammer: conceptions of sound and length, of music and measure, were amalgamated. In 1820 Hans Christian Oersted saw that an electric current flowing through a wire deflected a nearby compass. He thus discovered the hitherto unrecognized link between magnetism and electricity, created the concept of electromagnetism and inspired the development of the electric motor. Michael Faraday set himself the problem of finding the connections between light, heat, magnetism and electricity and developed a unified theory of electromagnetic radiation. Energy and matter became later unified in Albert Einstein's theory of relativity.

The founder of pragmatism, Charles Sanders Peirce (1958, pp. 123–5) argued that an important source of creativity in science was the 'abductive' transfer of metaphor from one scientific discourse to another. 'Abduction' was Peirce's addition to the traditional dichotomy of induction and deduction. It concerned the creative process of forming an explanatory hypothesis. According to Peirce (1934, p. 90), induction 'never can originate any idea whatever. No more can deduction. All the ideas of science come to it by the way of abduction.' Hence abduction alone could account for creativity and progress in science. By abduction, Peirce seems to have in mind the spark of intellectual creativity or intuition, kindled in the tinder of assimilated facts. He writes:

> The abductive suggestion comes to us like a flash. It is an act of *insight*, although of extremely fallible insight. It is true that the different elements of the hypothesis were in our minds before; but it is the idea of putting together what we had never before dreamed of putting together which flashes the new suggestion before our contemplation. (Peirce, 1934, p. 113)

For Peirce, the 'abduction' via metaphor of ideas from another context enables us to put together 'what we had never before dreamed of putting together'.[11] As long ago as 1882, Peirce (1958, p. 46) wrote:

> But the higher places in science in the coming years are for those who succeed in adapting the methods of one science to the investigation of another. That is what the greatest progress of the passing generation has consisted in. Darwin adapted biology to the methods of Malthus and the economists; Maxwell adapted to the theory of gases the methods of the doctrines of chances, and to electricity the methods of hydrodynamics. Wundt adapts to psychology the methods of physiology; Galton adapts to the same study the methods of the theory of errors; Morgan adapted to history a method from biology; Cournot adapted to political economy the calculus of variations.

Ultimately, the clashes and tensions between different approaches in a subject provide the sources of creativity and novelty. A possible source of creativity in science is through the juxtaposition of two different frames of reference, so that already existing but previously separate ideas can cross-fertilize. Accordingly, Larry Laudan (1977, p. 103) argues that the amalgamation of different research traditions may produce a sum greater than the constituent parts. Arthur Koestler (1964) has coined the term 'bisociation' to describe the kind of adjoining of different ideas that occurs in the act of scientific creation. Providing such a bridge between different discourses and contexts, metaphor can thus be both creative and constitutive.

There is no guarantee that metaphor can play a creative role. Conceivably in a given context there is a large set of metaphors that would be employed to no positive benefit. However, the inspired choice of metaphor seems to be a major source of theoretical innovation in science.

Compare the degree of theoretical pluralism inside modern economics with that in modern biology. Although both disciplines are still strongly affected by a reductionist imperative in the culture of modern science, in biology there are debates concerning methodology and core propositions. For instance, in biology there is a debate about the nature and boundaries of the subject, embracing a discourse concerning reductionism and the appropriate units of evolutionary selection and also over the viability of further reduction from genetics down to molecular biology, and even below to chemistry and physics (Sober, 1984). In contrast, confident in the Newtonian metaphor of the indivisible, 'individual' particle, mainstream economics traditionally proscribes discussion of the psychological or social foundations of individual purposes and preferences as being beyond the bounds of the discipline.

The internal lack of consensus within biology is itself refreshing. A variety of forces and tensions within that subject point to an organicist ontology, a less rigid methodology, and the transcendence of mechanistic thinking. These indicators are discussed in the work of leading mainstream biologists such as Theodosius Dobzhansky and Ernst Mayr, as well as more heterodox scientists such as Niles Eldredge and Stephen Jay Gould, along with historians of biology such as Edward Manier (Dobzhansky, 1968; Eldredge, 1985; Gould, 1982; Manier, 1978; Mayr, 1985a).

Partly because of the acknowledged complexity of the phenomena that it attempts to analyse, biological science exhibits a theoretical pluralism (Gould and Lewontin, 1979; Mayr, 1985b). Substantially, this involves a break from the Newtonian practice of single explanations that are supposed to displace all superfluity. Characteristically, Darwin himself placed great stress on his argument that natural selection was not the only possible element in evolution. In the last edition of the *Origin of Species* he wrote:

> As my conclusions have lately been much misrepresented, and it has been stated that I attribute the modification of species exclusively to natural selection, I may be permitted to remark that in the first edition of this work, and subsequently, I placed in a most conspicuous position – namely at the close of the Introduction – the following words: 'I am convinced that natural selection has been the main, but not the exclusive means of modification.' (Darwin, 1872, p. 395)

Hence Darwin accommodates the possibility of a plurality of different but complementary theories. Note that this kind of pluralism is that of 'theory complements', rather than of 'theory substitutes' where different and incompatible theories are involved.[12] Furthermore, as David Hull (1973, pp. 3–36) points out, Darwin's methodology is not rigidly axiomatic. There is a rigorous deductive core, but it is deemed to prove little on its own and it is thus placed in the context of a mass of empirical material. Again this contrasts with the Cartesian–Newtonian tradition in science.

Hence in biology there are deductive arguments combined with contingent empirical premises and conclusions. Typically, in biology a number of theories and explanations compete in their claims to identify the main, rather than the exclusive, cause in given real circumstances. Fortunately, biology does not present the near-monopoly of methods and approaches that threatens to stifle economics today.

Faced with these problems there is no instant solution. Neither is there an adequate and well-formed heterodoxy waiting in the wings. Austrian economics, post-Keynesian economics, Marxian economics, institutional economics: they are all afflicted with deep internal theoretical problems of their own. We have to be candid about the limitations of even our most favoured approach in economics, whatever it may be.

An obvious but crucial argument for theoretical pluralism in science can be derived from biology itself. Darwinian evolution depends on variety, and variety is the evolutionary fuel. Without the maintenance and regeneration of a variety of forms evolution would come to a stop. The evolution of scientific ideas requires diversity and pluralism as does evolution in nature. Let a thousand flowers bloom.

Clearly this applies to economics as well as other sciences. In this spirit we can do little better than follow the example of the self-avowed 'neoclassical' economist Frank Hahn (1984, pp. 7–8):

> The most strongly held of my views … is that neither is there a single best way for understanding in economics nor is it possible to hold any conclusions, other than purely logical deductions, with certainty. I have since my earliest days in the subject been astonished that this view is not widely shared. Indeed, we are encompassed by passionately held beliefs. … In fact all these 'certainties' and all the 'schools' which they spawn are a sure sign of our ignorance … we do not possess much certain knowledge about the economic world and … our best chance of gaining more is to try in all sorts of directions and by all sorts of means. This will not be furthered by strident commitments of faith.

Hahn's welcome comment seems to endorse a theoretical pluralism embracing both neoclassical and non-neoclassical approaches. This pluralism contrasts with the prevailing view that economics is defined in terms of a single, and neoclassical, method or approach. Particularly since the famous essay by Lionel Robbins (1932), among economists the prevailing practice has been to regard this subject as being defined by a single type of method or analysis, with an associated set of core assumptions. If the subject is defined in this way then not much theoretical pluralism within economics is possible; we are stuck with a single type of theory or approach.

In economics today there is increasing standardization of thought and the core assumptions are defended with renewed zeal. Perhaps the most optimistic interpretation possible of the widespread phenomenon is suggested by Hahn (1991, p. 49) who writes: 'After all in other spheres, say religion, one often encounters increased orthodoxy amongst some just when religion is on the decline.' Yet even this statement is not that optimistic: a religion under threat can lead to an Inquisition rather than a Renaissance. Yet unless renewed variety is generated within the discipline its degeneration into a narrow, over-abstract, and practically non-operational formalism will continue apace.

Strictly speaking, however, this pluralism concerns the policy of institutions toward the funding and nurturing of science. It is 'pluralism of the academy' and it does not concern the *individual practices* of science itself. There is much to be said for tolerance of many different and even antagonistic scientific research programmes within a department, university or nation. But we should not tolerate the existence of inconsistent ideas within our own heads. The role of diversity is not to sanctify or foster contradiction. Tolerance of the right of a scientist to practise, even when we may disagree with his or her views, does not imply tolerance of any method and proposition. The policy toward science must be pluralistic and tolerant, but science itself cannot be so. Pluralism does not mean that 'anything goes'.[13]

Methodological anarchism means the tyranny of the strong, and the strongest are those currently in power. Hence, despite anarchistic appearances, the precept of 'anything goes' is ultimately conservative. In contrast, the policy of academic pluralism provides a relentless challenge to orthodoxy and heterodoxy alike. We have to recognize the immense and enduring value of pluralism within the discipline without abandoning precision and rigour in our own work.

## ACKNOWLEDGEMENTS

The author is very grateful to Philip Mirowski, Bruna Ingra, Roy Weintraub, Uskali Mäki, Tony Lawson, Ernesto Screpanti and several other participants at the workshop on 'Pluralism in Economics', in Bergamo, Italy in June 1994 for critical and helpful comments on an earlier draft.

## NOTES

1. Whilst central to the argument here, the concept of complexity has proved notoriously difficult to define. Stent (1985, pp. 215–16) makes a useful stab at the problem, arguing that 'the complexity of a phenomenon is not to be measured by the number of component events of which it is constituted, but rather by the diversity of the interactions among its component events'. See Lloyd (1990) for a review of definitions of complexity.
2. See also Lavoie (1992, pp. 36–41), Rizvi (1194), Screpanti and Zamagni (1993, pp. 344–53).
3. There are many other problems in modern economics and the crisis in economic theory afflicts heterodox as well as orthodox traditions. However, for reasons of brevity the other topics and schools of thought are not discussed in detail here.
4. By contrast, Veblen (1919) and later American institutional economists embraced the analogy with biological evolution, making them the true inheritors of the 'evolutionary' epithet in economics.
5. As Peter Allen and M. Lesser (1991, p. 166) have wittily suggested, the evolution of economics as an academic profession is a case of lock-in comparable to the evolution of the peacock's tail. Although the male's beautiful tail makes it more successful in mating and producing offspring, there is no useful function or enhancement of fitness in terms of finding food or escaping predators. Just as the beautiful tail evolves with the peacock, economics has evolved an ever more intricate and beautiful mathematical formalism, similarly with little or no functional advantage for the development of economic policy. The developers of abstract theorems and proofs are awarded with prestige and resources, although there is an increasing suspicion by those on the outside that economics has less and less to do with real economies.
6. Examples of this are legion in both the physical and the social services. The unconvinced should read Koestler (1959) and take – as one of several examples in that brilliant book –

Kepler's obsessive belief in the false idea that everything in the universe is built around some basic geometrical symmetries and the way in which it led to the birth of modern cosmology. Likewise, in economics, Marx adopted from the classical economists the untenable notion of 'value' as a substance, and one generated by labour alone: with it he constructed the wonderful theoretical edifice of *Capital*. Yet essentially this theoretical structure survives without any labour (or substance) theory of value (Hodgson, 1982), and still provides some of the best insights into the workings of modern capitalism.

7. Mayntz (1992, p. 53) notes that in the past sociologists used the metaphor of natural selection, but because 'no attempt at conscious theory transfer was made ... the question of how biological and sociocultual evolution might differ was not explicitly raised'. This is surely an object lesson for all those who want to keep their metaphors at arm's length.
8. Note the disturbing degree of mathematical formalism in the – otherwise often useful and innovative – *Journal of Evolutionary Economics*.
9. It should not be assumed, however, that all evolutionary processes in biology are irreversible: see Mani (1991). An extended discussion of irreversibility in economics is given by Dosi and Metcalfe (1991).
10. Furthermore, as Nicolai Foss (1994) has argued, there is a key ontological difference between neoclassical and the kind of 'evolutionary' economics exemplified by Nelson and Winter (1982) and Witt (1987). Whereas evolutionary economics theorizes on the basis of a universe that is open, with novelties and emergent properties, neoclassical economics suppresses novelty. The importance of such open systems and emergent properties is stressed by philosophical realists such as Bhaskar (1979) and Lawson (1989). See also Dyke (1985) who also discusses the problem of closure in complex phenomena. The existence of open systems and emergent properties is incidentally another major reason why the reductionist project in science is confounded.
11. One of the clearest recent attempts to elucidate the notion of abduction, in a realist philosophical framework which is specifically related to economics, is by Tony Lawson (1989, pp. 68–73). In his chapter 4 of this volume, Warren Samuels suggests that the advocacy of methodological pluralism implies the non-existence of a given reality. A contrasting point is made here. As no theoretical analysis of a reality can completely represent or mirror that reality in all its complexity, therefore we cannot rule out other viable and complementary analyses in principle. Philosophical realism and the assertion of a given reality 'out there' are perfectly compatible with such a proposition.
12. Note the useful taxonomy of types of pluralism offered by Uskali Mäki in the present volume (chapter 2). The kind of pluralism advocated here is further qualified below.
13. This statement concurs with the convincing argument by Sheila Dow in chapter 5 of this volume.

## REFERENCES


Allen, Peter M. and Lesser, M. (1991), 'Evolutionary Human Systems: Learning, Ignorance and Subjectivity', in P.P. Saviotti and J.S. Metcalfe (eds), *Evolutionary Theories of Economic and Technological Change: Present Status and Future Prospects*, Reading, Harwood, pp. 160–71.

Arrow, Kenneth J. (1986), 'Rationality of Self and Others in an Economic System', *Journal of Business*, **59** (4.2), October, pp. S385–S399. Reprinted in R.M. Hogarth and M.W. Reder (eds), *Rational Choice: The Contrast Between Economics and Psychology*, Chicago, University of Chicago Press, 1987.

Bhaskar, Roy (1979), *The Possibility of Naturalism: A Philosophic Critique of the Contemporary Human Sciences*, Brighton: Harvester.

Black, Max (1962), *Models and Metaphors: Studies in Language and Philosophy*, Ithaca: Cornell University Press.

Caldwell, Bruce J. (1982), *Beyond Positivism: Economic Methodology in the Twentieth Century*, London: Allen & Unwin.
Cooper, W.S. (1989), 'How Evolutionary Biology Challenges the Classical Theory of Rational Choice', *Biology and Philosophy*, **4** (4), October, pp. 457–81.
Coricelli, F. and Dosi, G. (1988), 'Coordination and Order in Economic Change and the Interpretative Power of Economic Theory', in Giovanni Dosi, Christopher Freeman, Richard Nelson, Gerald Silverberg and Luc Soete (eds), *Technical Change and Economic Theory*, London: Pinter, pp. 124–47. Reprinted in Geoffrey M. Hodgson (ed.) (1993), *The Economics of Institutions*, Aldershot: Edward Elgar, 1988.
Crutchfield, James P., Farmer, J. Doyne, Packard, Norman H. and Shaw, Robert S. (1986), 'Chaos', *Scientific American*, **255** (6), December, pp. 38–49.
Darwin, Charles (1872), *On the Origin of Species by Means of Natural Selection*, last edn, London: John Murray.
Dawkins, Richard (1976), *The Selfish Gene*, Oxford: Oxford University Press.
Dobzhansky, Theodosius (1968), 'On Some Fundamental Concepts of Darwinian Biology', in Theodosius Dobzhansky, M.K. Hecht, M.K. Steere and W.C. Steere (eds), *Evolutionary Biology*, Amsterdam: North-Holland, pp. 1–34.
Dosi, Giovanni and Metcalfe, J. Stanley (1991), 'On Some Notions of Irreversibility in Economics', in P.P. Saviotti and J.S. Metcalfe (eds), *Evolutionary Theories of Economic and Technological Change: Present Status and Future Prospects*, Reading, Harwood, pp. 133–59.
Dyke, C. (1985), 'Complexity and Closure', in D.J. Depew and B.H. Weber (eds), *Evolution at the Crossroads: The New Biology and the New Philosophy of Science*, Cambridge, MA: MIT Press, pp. 97–131.
Eldredge, Niles (1985), *Unfinished Synthesis: Biological Hierarchies and Modern Evolutionary Thought*, Oxford: Oxford University Press.
Foss, Nicolai Juul (1994), 'Realism and Evolutionary Economics', *Journal of Social and Evolutionary Systems*, **17** (1), pp. 21–40.
Georgescu-Roegen, Nicholas (1971), *The Entropy Law and the Economic Process*, Cambridge, MA: Harvard University Press.
Gleick, James (1988), *Chaos: Making a New Science*, London: Heinemann.
Goldberg, M.A. (1975), 'On the Inefficiency of Being Efficient', *Environment and Planning*, **7** (8), pp. 921–39.
Gould, Stephen Jay (1982), 'The Meaning of Punctuated Equilibrium and its Role in Validating a Hierarchical Approach to Macroevolution', in Roger Milkman (ed.), *Perspectives on Evolution*, Sunderland, MA: Sinauer Associates, pp. 83–104.
Gould, Stephen Jay and Lewontin, R.C. (1979), 'The Spandrels of San Marco and the Panglossian Paradigm: A Critique of the Adaptationist Programme', *Proceedings of the Royal Society of London*, Series B, 205, pp. 581–98. Reprinted in E. Sober (ed.), *Conceptual Issues in Evolutionary Biology: An Anthology*, Cambridge, MA: MIT Press, 1984.
Gowdy, John M. (1985), 'Evolutionary Theory and Economic Theory: Some Methodological Issues', *Review of Social Economy*, **43**, pp. 316–24.
Grandmont, Jean-Michel (1986), 'Stabilizing Competitive Business Cycles', *Journal of Economic Theory*, **40** (1), October, pp. 57–76. Reprinted in Jean-Michel Grandmont (ed.), *Nonlinear Economic Dynamics*, New York: Academic Press, 1987.
Hahn, Frank H. (1984), *Equilibrium and Macroeconomics*, Oxford: Blackwell.
Hahn, Frank H. (1991), 'The Next Hundred Years', *Economic Journal*, **101** (1), January, pp. 47–50.

Hesse, Mary B. (1980), *Revolutions and Reconstructions in the Philosophy of Science*, Brighton: Harvester Press.
Hirst, Paul Q. and Woolley, Penny (1982), *Social Relations and Human Attributes*, London: Tavistock.
Hodgson, Geoffrey M. (1982), 'Marx Without the Labour Theory of Value', *Review of Radical Political Economics*, **14** (2), Summer, pp. 59–67. Reprinted in J.C. Wood (ed.), *Karl Marx's Economics: Critical Assessments*, Croom Helm, Beckenham, 1987, and in Geoffrey M. Hodgson, *After Marx and Sraffa: Essays in Political Economy*, London: Macmillan, 1991.
Hodgson, Geoffrey M. (1988), *Economics and Institutions: A Manifesto for a Modern Institutional Economics*, Cambridge and Philadelphia: Polity Press and University of Pennsylvania Press.
Hodgson, Geoffrey M. (1993), *Economics and Evolution: Bringing Life Back Into Economics*, Cambridge, UK and Ann Arbor, MI: Polity Press and University of Michigan Press.
Hodgson, Geoffrey, M. (1994), 'Optimisation and Evolution: Winter's Critique of Friedman Revisited', *Cambridge Journal of Economics*, **16** (4), August, pp. 413–30.
Hodgson, Geoffrey, M. and Screpanti, Ernesto (1991), 'Introduction' to G.M. Hodgson and E. Screpanti (eds), *Rethinking Economics: Markets, Technology and Economic Evolution*, Aldershot: Edward Elgar, pp. 1–15.
Hull, David L. (1973), *Darwin and His Critics: The Reception of Darwin's Theory of Evolution by the Scientific Community*, Cambridge, MA: Harvard University Press.
Kaufman, W. (ed.) (1982), *The Portable Nietzsche*, Harmondsworth: Penguin.
Kirman, Alan P. (1989), 'The Intrinsic Limits of Modern Economic Theory: The Emperor Has No Clothes', *Economic Journal (Conference Papers)*, **99**, pp. 126–39.
Kirman, Alan P. (1992), 'Whom or What Does the Representative Individual Represent?', *Journal of Economic Perspectives*, **6** (2), Spring, pp. 117–36.
Klamer, Arjo and Leonard, Thomas C. (1994), 'So What's an Economic Metaphor?', in Philip Mirowski (ed.), *Natural Images in Economic Thought: Markets Read in Tooth and Claw*, Cambridge and New York: Cambridge University Press, pp. 20–51.
Koestler, Arthur (1959), *The Sleepwalkers: A History of Man's Changing Vision of the Universe*, London: Hutchinson.
Koestler, Arthur (1964), *The Act of Creation*, London: Hutchinson.
Koestler, Arthur (1967), *The Ghost in the Machine*, London: Hutchinson.
Laudan, Larry (1977), *Progress and its Problems: Towards a Theory of Scientific Growth*, London: Routledge & Kegan Paul.
Lavoie, Marc (1992), *Foundations of Post-Keynesian Economic Analysis*, Aldershot: Edward Elgar.
Lawson, Antony (1989), 'Abstraction, Tendencies and Stylised Facts: A Realist Approach to Economic Analysis', *Cambridge Journal of Economics*, **13** (1), March, pp. 59–78. Reprinted in A. Lawson, J.G. Palma and J. Sender (eds), *Kaldor's Political Economy*, London: Academic Press, 1989.
Lewin, Roger (1993), *Complexity*, Phoenix: Orion Books.
Loasby, Brian J. (1976), *Choice, Complexity and Ignorance: An Enquiry into Economic Theory and the Practice of Decision Making*, Cambridge: Cambridge University Press.
Loasby, Brian J. (1989), *The Mind and Method of the Economist: A Critical Appraisal of Major Economists in the Twentieth Century*, Aldershot: Edward Elgar.

Loasby, Brian J. (1991), *Equilibrium and Evolution: An Exploration of Connecting Principles in Economics*, Manchester: Manchester University Press.
Lloyd, Seth (1990), 'The Calculus of Intricacy', *The Sciences*, pp. 38–44.
McCloskey, Donald N. (1985), *The Rhetoric of Economics*, Madison: University of Wisconsin Press.
Mani, G.S. (1991), 'Is There a General Theory of Biological Evolution?', in P.P. Saviotti and J.S. Metcalfe (eds), *Evolutionary Theories of Economic and Technological Change: Present Status and Future Prospects*, Reading: Harwood, pp. 31–57.
Manier, Edward (1978), *The Young Darwin and his Cultural Circle: A Study of Influences which helped Shape the Language and Logic of the First Drafts of the Theory of Natural Selection*, Dordrecht: Reidel.
Maynard Smith, John (1978), *The Evolution of Sex*, London: Cambridge University Press.
Mayntz, Renate (1992), 'The Influence of Natural Science Theories on Contemporary Social Science', in Meinolf Dierkes and Bernd Bievert (eds), *European Social Science in Transition: Assessment and Outlook*, Frankfurt am Main and Boulder, CO: Campus Verlag and Westview Press, pp. 27–79.
Mayr, Ernst (1985a), 'How Biology Differs from the Physical Sciences', in D.J. Depew and B.H. Weber (eds), *Evolution at the Crossroads: The New Biology and the New Philosophy of Science*, Cambridge, MA: MIT Press, pp. 43–63.
Mayr, Ernst (1985b), 'Darwin's Five Theories of Evolution', in D. Kohn (ed.), *The Darwinian Heritage*, Princeton: Princeton University Press, pp. 755–72.
Mirowski, Philip (1989a), 'The Probabilistic Counter-Revolution, or How Stochastic Concepts Came to Neoclassical Theory', *Oxford Economic Papers*, **41** (2), April, pp. 217–35.
Mirowski, Philip (1989b), *More Heat Than Light: Economics as Social Physics, Physics as Nature's Economics*, Cambridge: Cambridge University Press.
Nelson, Richard R. and Winter, S.G. (1982), *An Evolutionary Theory of Economic Change*, Cambridge, MA: Harvard University Press.
Norgaard, Richard B. (1989), 'The Case for Methodological Pluralism', *Ecological Economics*, **1** (1), February, pp. 37–57.
Peirce, Charles Sanders (1934), *Collected Papers of Charles Sanders Peirce, Volume V, Pragmatism and Pragmaticism*, edited by C. Hartshorne and P. Weiss, Cambridge, MA: Harvard University Press.
Peirce, Charles Sanders (1958), *Collected Papers of Charles Sanders Peirce, Volume VII, Science and Philosophy*, edited by A.W. Burks, Cambridge, MA: Harvard University Press.
Popper, Karl R. and Eccles, John C. (1977), *The Self and Its Brain*, Berlin: Springer International.
Rizvi, S. Abu Turab (1994), 'The Microfoundations Project in General Equilibrium Theory', *Cambridge Journal of Economics*, **18** (4), August, pp. 357–77.
Robbins, Lionel (1932), *An Essay on the Nature and Significance of Economic Science*, first edn, London: Macmillan.
Robinson, Joan (1974), *History Versus Equilibrium*, London: Thames Papers in Political Economy.
Roughgarden, Jonathan (1979), *Theory of Population Genetics and Evolutionary Ecology: An Introduction*, New York: Macmillan.
Samuels, Warren J. (ed.) (1990), *Economics as Discourse: An Analysis of the Language of Economists*, Boston: Kluwer.

Schumpeter, Joseph A. (1954), *History of Economic Analysis*, New York: Oxford University Press.
Screpanti, Ernesto and Zamagni, Stefano (1993), *An Outline of the History of Economic Thought*, Oxford: Clarendon Press.
Sebba, G. (1953), 'The Development of the Concepts of Mechanism and Model in Physical Science and Economic Thought', *American Economic Review (Papers and Proceedings)*, **43** (2), May, pp. 259–68.
Simon, Herbert A. (1968), *The Sciences of the Artificial*, Cambridge, MA: MIT Press.
Smith, Adam (1869), *Essays of Adam Smith*, London: John Murray.
Smith, Adam (1980), 'The Principles Which Lead and Direct Philosophical Enquiries: Illustrated by the History of Astronomy', in *Essays on Philosophical Subjects*, edited by W.P.D. Wightman, Oxford: Clarendon.
Sober, Elliott (ed.) (1984), *Conceptual Issues in Evolutionary Biology: An Anthology*, Cambridge, MA: MIT Press.
Stent, Gunther, S. (1985), 'Hermeneutics and the Analysis of Complex Biological Systems', in D.J. Depew and B.H. Weber (eds), *Evolution at the Crossroads: The New Biology and the New Philosophy of Science*, Cambridge, MA: MIT Press, pp. 209–25.
Stewart, Ian (1989), *Does God Play Dice? The Mathematics of Chaos*, Oxford: Basil Blackwell.
Sugden, Robert (1991), 'Rational Choice: A Survey of Contributions from Economics and Philosophy', *Economic Journal*, **101** (4), July, 751–85.
Thoben, H. (1982), 'Mechanistic and Organistic Analogies in Economics Reconsidered', *Kyklos*, **35**, Fasc. 2, pp. 292–306.
Udéhn, Lars (1987), *Methodological Individualism: A Critical Appraisal*, Uppsala: Uppsala University Reprographics Centre.
Varoufakis, Y. (1990), 'Conflict in Equilibrium', in Y. Varoufakis and D. Young (eds), *Conflict in Economics*, Hemel Hempstead: Harvester Wheatsheaf, pp. 39–67.
Veblen, Thorstein B. (1919), *The Place of Science in Modern Civilisation and Other Essays*, New York: Huebsch. Reprinted 1990 with a new introduction by W.J. Samuels, New Brunswick: Transaction Publishers.
Waldrop, M. Mitchell (1992), *Complexity: The Emerging Science at the Edge of Order and Chaos*, New York: Simon & Schuster.
Weiner, Norbert (1954), *The Human Use of Human Beings*, second edn, New York: Houghton Mifflin.
Williams, George C. (1966), *Adaptation and Natural Selection*, Princeton, NJ: Princeton University Press.
Wilson, Edward O. (1975), *Sociobiology*, Cambridge, MA: Harvard University Press.
Wimsatt, William C. (1980), 'Reductionist Research Strategies and Their Biases in the Units of Selection Controversy', in T. Nickles (ed.), *Scientific Discovery, Volume II, Historical and Scientific Case Studies*, Dordrecht, Holland: Reidel, pp. 213–59. Reprinted in E. Sober (ed.), *Conceptual Issues in Evolutionary Biology: An Anthology*, Cambridge, MA: MIT Press.
Witt, Ulrich (1987), *Individualistiche Grundlagen der evolutorischen Ökonomie*, Tübingen: Mohr.

# COMMENT

**Philip Mirowski**

> Leopards break into the temple and drink to the dregs what is in the sacrificial pitchers; this is repeated over and over again; finally it can be calculated in advance, and it becomes a part of the ceremony.
>
> (Franz Kafka, *Parables and Paradoxes*)

Geoffrey Hodgson is one of the foremost interpreters of the use of biology in the history of economic thought; he is also the prime mover behind the revival of institutionalist economics in Europe. Given that the differences between Geoff and myself on most major issues in economics are of the order of magnitude of epsilon, whereas with most other economists, it is orders of magnitude higher, it is only with great misgivings and trepidation that I venture to say anything at all critical about his chapter. But he has raised some issues with regard to my own work therein, and I have some confidence that he and others may regard this as an early moment in an ongoing dialogue about issues that should concern us all.

Hodgson asserts in his chapter that reductionism in science is more or less moribund and that neoclassical economics has been severely hobbled by this and other *fin de-siècle* crises. The appropriate response, he argues, is simply to acknowledge that metaphorical reasoning is pervasive in science, and therefore the time has come to transfer our allegiences to biological metaphors and enjoy their salubrious consequences, which will include greater pluralism and tolerance in matters methodological and theoretical. I am afraid I harbour a much darker view of the same set of observations, which I have already outlined in my review of his book *Economics and Evolution* (1995). To put the objection in much too brief a format, I believe that the widespread turn to biology for metaphorical inspiration, far from threatening neoclassicism, can be regarded as simply more of the same scientism which was so important for its nineteenth-century genesis and twentieth-century dominance – it is the incorporation of the leopard's transgression into the sacred ceremony. Far from neglecting the sociology of the economics profession and the 'deeper' aspects of metaphorical transfer, as he claims, my objections are predicated upon precisely these grounds.

For Hodgson, the real problem for economics is 'not the general appropriation of metaphor from the natural sciences but more fundamentally the adoption of a positivist conception of science' (p. 141). I could not disagree more. Not just economists, but also physicists and biologists, have had no persistently solid communal idea of the true nature of 'science'; all they know at various junctures are the traditions and practices with which they were indoctrinated, plus some general cultural prejudices characteristic of their times. This is why all of the sciences supposedly were 'positivist' in the 1930s to 1960s; and why they all now are supposedly more wholist, indeterminist and constructivist these days. What matter much more are some images of progressive and successful sciences, which then colour everyone's metaphorical appropriations: in the seventeenth century it was astronomy; in the nineteenth and early twentieth centuries it was physics; and now, in our lifetime, it is biology. It is not simply the economists who are promiscuous – it is most disciplinary formations. As Ian Hacking has said, we are living in an era in which the Triumph of Capitalism and the Human Genome Project are becoming fused into one great Theory of Everything.

The implications of this cultural phenomenon are not necessarily propitious for a pluralistic economics. As Hodgson knows, much of biology is still pigheadedly reductionist and individualistic; and as I tried to explain in *More Heat than Light* (1989, pp. 117–19), evolutionary biology, energy physics and neoclassical economics all share a core doctrine of constrained optimization, which makes it all the more effortless to shift back and forth between them in metaphorical appropriation. Indeed, Depew and Weber (1995) have shown that the very meaning of 'evolutionary Darwinism' has changed content dramatically over the past century, largely under the prior influence of changes in the treatment of dynamical systems in physics. This is why everyone from Armen Alchian to Jack Hirshleifer to Robert Aumann can claim evolutionary biology for their own legitimation. At this point, one might respond to Hodgson with a *tu quoque*: What difference would it make for the economists to get the biology 'wrong' in any sense of the word? Since they all plead not guilty when one asks them to get specific about distinctions between genotype and phenotype, between organism and environment, or between arguments from selection and those from random drift, it does not seem very likely that even someone of Hodgson's demonstrated sophistication in the field could hold them to much of any programmatic guidelines at all. In that case, what is the real significance of the rush to biological metaphor which one can observe in the *American Economic Review* just as well as in the *Journal of Evolutionary Economics*?

I would argue that the answer resides more directly in sociological than conceptual consideration. All I ask at this stage is that Hodgson look that fact much more squarely in the face. I am as sympathetic as he to various conceptual moves that one can find in the biological literature: population thinking, a less teleological approach to explanation, a celebration of diversity and variance, a sense of the intricate complexity of phenomena in their fundamentally temporal unfolding. But there is nothing in all this that suggests that neoclassicism will not be able in its inimitable polymorphously perverse fashion to absorb some of the metaphorical cachet of this quintessentially cultural seachange, yet with the mythic optimization of utility ultimately emerging unscathed. Indeed, the recent events at the Santa Fe Institute suggest that neoclassicals could reach an accommodation with novel cultural currents by renewing their tryst with the physicists, by-passing the biologists altogether (Mirowski, 1993). All sorts of alliances are possible. It would seem that the real issue is: What are the actual dynamics of appropriation of scientific legitimacy in the history of economics, rather than the specifics of the transfer of concepts across disciplines? I would maintain that this is the real subject of *More Heat*, though one which Hodgson has not yet sufficiently taken to heart.

## References

Depew, David and Weber, Bruce (1995), *Darwinism Evolving*, Cambridge: MIT Press.

Kafka, Franz (1961), *Parables and Paradoxes*, New York: Schocken.

Mirowski, Philip (1989), *More Heat than Light*, New York: Cambridge University Press.

Mirowski, Philip (1993), 'The Goalkeeper's Anxiety at the Penalty Kick', in Neil De Marchi (ed.), *Non-Natural Social Science*, Durham: Duke University Press.

Mirowski, Philip (1995), 'Review of Geoffrey Hodgson's *Economics and Evolution*', *Economics and Philosophy*, **11**, pp. 366–70.

# 8. Analytical descriptions and theoretical pluralism in economics

**Roberto Scazzieri**

## 1. INTRODUCTORY REMARKS

It is well known that Joseph Alois Schumpeter, in his *History of Economic Analysis*, emphasized the role of semantics (and related features of conceptualization) in any given cognitive field by introducing the concept of pre-analytic 'vision':

> in order to be able to posit to ourselves any problems at all, we should first have to visualize a distinct set of coherent phenomena as a worth-while object of our analytic efforts. In other words, analytic effort is of necessity preceded by a preanalytic cognitive act that supplies the raw material for the analytic effort. In this book, this preanalytic cognitive act will be called Vision. It is interesting to note that vision of this kind not only must precede historically the emergence of analytic effort in any field but also may re-enter the history of every established science each time somebody teaches us to *see* things in a light of which the source is not to be found in the facts, methods, and results of the pre-existing state of science. (Schumpeter, 1954, p. 41)

The logical, rather than merely pre-scientific and 'cultural', role played by the human faculty that may be called 'reasonable imagination' has more recently been described by Nicholas Georgescu-Roegen, according to whom,

> it is we who endow nature with rationality so that our rational minds may grasp it. There is no wonder then that the more we learn about the behaviour of nature, the more we discover how irrational nature is. The miracle – as Louis de Broglie observed – is that even a compartmental and limited concordance between natural phenomena and our mental representation of them is nevertheless possible. (Georgescu-Roegen, 1971, p. 35)

Georgescu-Roegen has considered this issue once again when examining the logical steps required in order to set up a suitable *analytical representation* of productive activity:

> [e]verywhere there is some action, some change, some vibration, far too many happenings for a manageable description. To remedy the situation we must take an absolutely necessary jump in the dark, as it were, from dialectics into analysis. In analysis a process must be defined by a substantial and temporary boundary .... *If there is no such boundary, there is no analytic process.* Where the boundary is drawn depends on the interest of the analyst. In nature we find no seams to guide our carving, it all depends on our knowledge and purpose. (Georgescu-Roegen, 1990, p. 207)

The effectiveness of scientific investigation (as well as the firmness of its empirical foundation) is greatly enhanced by selection and utilization of the 'best' (that is, most suitable) analytical representations:

> [t]hanks to [the analytical habit], experimenting ceases to be a routine procedure by which the factual truth-value of logically derived propositions is established. By stimulating the imagination of the experimenting scholar, the analytical habit is alone responsible for the fact that theoretical experimenting is far luckier than mere experimenting. In the experimental undertaking, as Pasteur once observed, chance favours only the prepared minds. (Georgescu-Roegen, 1966, p. 14)

Analytical representations are descriptive devices such that the relevant features of reality are selected on the basis of a conjecture concerning the important factors that one needs to consider in order to solve the problem at hand. It follows that analytical representations cannot be purely syntactic devices, that is logical devices concerning the admissible combinations of propositions independently of meaning (see Carnap, 1934, para. 1). Any given analytical representation is related to the assignment of meaning. In other words, it is related to the process by which a given object is rationally represented in order to become intelligible within a particular community of speakers (or readers). (See Sextus Empiricus's essay *Adversus Mathematicos* (viii, 12) for an early presentation of this view; see also Frege (1892) and Peirce (1958, written in 1903) for the association between meaning assignment and interpretation.)

The above point of view entails the conception of analytical representation as a cognitive device by which phenomena are made intelligible within a given community. It follows that analytical representations are necessary to the formation and accumulation of knowledge, but that they should not be considered as purely subjective or idiosyncratic constructions. For any given description to be a proper analytical representation within its own domain, it has to provide the foundation (or the starting point) of a conceptual system, that is, of a system of propositions derived from one another by means of formal (though not necessarily symbolic) rules of inference. In practice, no analytical representation may be accepted as such (rather than being considered as a mere description) unless its 'object' is rooted in the linguistic and conceptual structure of a particular community of scholars.

The concept of 'economic structure' has a critical role to perform within the above framework, since it provides the benchmark of any given analytical representation. In other words, economic structure may be considered as a *cognitive device* by which economic processes are given a form that makes them suitable to theoretical investigation. It may be argued that the above conception of structure is compatible with a non-conventionalist approach and is, at the same time, conducive to theoretical pluralism in the field of economic inquiry.

## 2. STRUCTURES OF INQUIRY AND ECONOMIC THEORY

The above argument entails that the way in which we 'give form' to any particular object of investigation, even by means of a simple description, is a most critical step that is likely to influence in a significant way the subsequent construction of theories, quite independently of the amount of 'naive' empirical work that we may undertake. In particular, the consideration of any particular analytical representation of economic processes (that is, the consideration of a particular economic structure) entails that we identify the space of *virtual processes* that may be investigated on the basis of a given description (or set of 'stylized facts'). And identification of a space of virtual processes is an essential prerequisite in order to achieve (to approximate) theoretical understanding of any given object of inquiry.

The above standpoint has recently been formulated as follows by René Thom:

> if science is *more* than just naive description, this is due to the fact that it has constructed a set of 'virtual' (i.e. imaginary) processes among which it is capable of selecting the real, observable ones. Hence the criterion for true scientificity lies not in the veracity of observation or in its accuracy, nor in the use of instruments to help increase the set of observable facts, but in the building of a virtuality of phenomena from which the real ones can be selected by a well defined logical or mathematical procedure. (Thom, 1989, p. 40)

Long before Thom, the critical role of virtual phenomena and processes in the formation of theories had been emphasized by the mathematician and philosopher Federigo Enriques, who maintained that 'the scientific fact takes on the form of a *simplified fact, a type of a series of possible facts* '(Enriques, 1914, p. 81). The above perspective entails that real processes, in so far as they are intelligible, have to be understood in terms of virtual processes. The selection of one particular real process from within a space of virtual processes is a characteristic feature of explanation in science.

The concept of 'economic structure' may be discussed at two different levels:

1. The level of the general conceptual frameworks, or *structures of inquiry*, that is, at the level at which any given space of virtual processes may be identified.
2. The level of actual events and real processes.

The latter may be explained in terms of a particular space of virtual processes or, quite often, in terms of the intersection between different such spaces. In other words, any particular event or real process is made intelligible by reducing it to a special case within a general class of conceivable events or processes. As a result, the analytical representation of any given process is related to real processes at least as a condition for their intelligibility.

Economic structure in the conceptual sense (that is, economic structure as the analytical representation of economic reality) is thus related to economic structure in the real sense (the relatively persistent network of actual processes) by means of an epistemic connection: knowledge of the real structure may only be approximated by means of a conceptual structure in which actual processes appear to be special cases within a wider range of possible outcomes.

The above argument entails that the availability of *multiple* possible representations of given processes, or networks of processes, may be considered as an essential conceptual device in the interpretation and explanation of such processes. The plurality of ways in which given events (or processes) may be described encroaches upon our ability to understand them in terms of *virtual* events and processes. For real processes may often be conceived (that is, analytically represented) in terms of the intersection between different spaces of virtual phenomena. As a result, theoretical pluralism may extend our ability to cope with the complexity of nature and history.

## 3. INTERSECTION OF CONCEPTUAL SPACES AND THE INTERPRETATION OF ECONOMIC PROCESSES

I have argued that the understanding of real processes and structures involves the identification of a suitable set of virtual events, and sometimes of a suitable intersection between different sets of virtual events.

The multiplicity of conceptual structures (that is, of the analytical representations that may be considered) is an inherent feature of economic knowledge (and perhaps of scientific knowledge in general).

Such a multiplicity relates primarily to the mental apprehension of known events and processes, but may also be of great importance in discovering and explaining new events and processes. For our ability to describe the same event (or process) as an element of two or more virtual spaces enhances our capability of conceiving a suitable intersection of conceptual spaces in which a specific event (or process) may be explained from a genetic point of view, and *new* events (or processes) may be discovered by the principle of analogy.

It may be worth emphasizing that the above perspective suggests a particular interpretation of the process of induction, in which empirical regularities recede to the background and the identification of relevant singularities comes to the fore. As William Whewell maintained in his *Philosophy of Discovery*, a scientific discovery is generally such that

> a new conception [is] applied in order to bind together observed facts. And though the conjunction of the observed facts [is] in each case an example of logical *Induction*, it [is] not the induction process merely, but the novelty of the result in each case which [gives] its peculiar character to [the history of inductive sciences]. (Whewell, 1860, p. v)

The above framework may be useful in order to assess the relationship between distinct and apparently contradictory logical frameworks in economic analysis. In this connection, we may refer to the distinction, which was originally proposed by Luigi Pasinetti (1965) and John Hicks (1975, 1976), between the logical set-ups of a simplified 'pure production economy', and of a simplified 'pure exchange economy'. As Luigi Pasinetti has maintained:

> The concept of trade is, so to speak, a static concept. It is associated with a situation in which a plurality of economic systems (or of individuals) are endowed with particular resources or products and try to gain advantages by exchange. The interest that such a situation arouses in an economist concerns the problem of how to reach the best allocation of given resources, namely of how to make the best use of what one has already. … The problem involved is a problem of rationality, which may be expressed by a mathematical function to be maximised under certain constraints. The concept of, and the problems entailed by, industry are quite different. Industry is, so to speak, a dynamic concept. It means production, i.e. the engagement and the application of man's ingenuity to make and shape the products he wants. But since by doing and experiencing man learns, it is implied in the very nature of carrying on a production activity that new and better methods of production will be discovered. Of course, to find new methods takes time, and takes time in a persistent way. The economist is faced here no longer with a problem of rationality, but with a process of learning. (Pasinetti, 1965, pp. 574–5)

A similar distinction was introduced by John Hicks when discussing the features of the 'marginalist' revolution, and the main differences between the 'marginalist' and the 'classical' economists. In Hicks's view, the fundamental theme of classical political economy is the identification of national wealth with the flow of production, and the assumption that this latter 'is so far homogeneous that it can be greater or less' (Hicks, 1976, p. 210). This point of view made it necessary 'to distinguish between market values (which might not be significant as a means of valuation) and "natural" or normal values which should be' (Hicks, 1976, p. 211). In addition, as Hicks points out, the classical economists found it necessary 'to find a "standard of value" so as to be able to correct for changes in the value of money' (Hicks, 1976, p. 211). In particular, 'already in Smith, *political economy* is based upon a theory of value' whose primary purpose 'is not to explain prices, that is to say, to explain the working of markets', but rather 'to identify the values which are needed for the *weighing* of the social product, the reduction of the heterogeneous commodities which compose it to a common measure' (ibid., p. 211). The above approach is distinguished from the perspective adopted by the marginalist economists. In their case,

> The essential novelty ... was that instead of basing their economics on production and distribution, they based it on exchange ... There is, of course, no doubt that exchange is a basic feature of economic life, at least in a 'free', or what Marx would have called a 'capitalist' economy. By none of the classical economists would that have been denied. By while the classics looked at the economic system primarily from the production angle, the catallactists [Hicks's preferred name for the marginalists] looked at it primarily from the side of exchange. It was possible, they found, to construct a 'vision' of economic life out of the theory of exchange, as the classics had done out of the social product. It was quite a different vision. (ibid., p. 212)

Hicks concludes that catallactics and political economy are based upon quite different 'concentrations of attention' and that 'they do not fit together' (Hicks, 1975, p. 325). However, a possible conciliation is found, from a pragmatic point of view, in the belief that

> since it is a changing world that we are studying, a theory which illumines the right things at one time may illumine the wrong things at another. This may happen because of changes in the world (the things neglected may have gained in importance relatively to the things considered) or because of changes in ourselves (the things in which we are interested may have changed). There is, there can be, no economic theory which will do for us everything we want all the time. (ibid., p. 320)

A somehow similar way of finding a conciliation between the 'pure production' and the 'pure exchange' models has been proposed by Luigi Pasinetti in his discussion of the related distinction (which he now thinks to be more appropriate) between the 'pure preference' and the 'pure labour' models (see Pasinetti, 1986). Here Pasinetti maintains that the simplification of economic reality that is implied by the consideration of a particular analytical representation (a necessary step in theory building) poses 'a problem at the stage of applicability and utilization' (Pasinetti, 1986, p. 428). In this connection, Pasinetti maintains that

> [g]iven the crude simplifications that economists are compelled to make, some considerable dose of humility about the merits and applicability of one's theories, and at the same time the avoidance of quite unwarranted attitudes of intolerance against other theorists' theories, would seem a code of behaviour much more appropriate to the state and nature of knowledge in economics

and that 'the coexistence of competing paradigms, even for long periods of time, far from being regarded as a sign of anomaly, might well come to be recognized as the normal way of proceeding in the development of economic theory' (Pasinetti, 1986, pp. 429–30).

In a sense, both Hicks and Pasinetti seem to regard the 'stage of application' of economic theories as the critical benchmark in the assessment of the scope and relative merits of different conceptual frameworks. This perspective highlights the role both of economic history and of economic policy in determining the field of interaction between different conceptual spaces when economic theories are being evaluated. In particular, distinct economic theories (that are based upon different analytical representations of economic reality) may provide the intellectual materials out of which complex processes may be reconstructed and effective actions may be carried out. Theoretical pluralism would thus be an essential condition for the identification of intersections of conceptual spaces that may be useful in the interpretation of actual processes and in the realization of policy objectives.[1] A most important function of theories is the discovery of facts. The intersection of conceptual spaces is essentially a regulative idea, that is, something we should strive for in order to expand the domain of theoretical investigation. In this way, the same argument may be used to support both the constructive and deductive use of theories and theoretical pluralism.

## 4. CAUSAL CLUSTERS AND CAUSAL POWERS

The above argument entails that emphasis upon the heuristic role of analytical representation (and upon the role of 'verisimilitude' in the field of induction; see Popper, 1963, ch. X) may be associated with emphasis upon theoretical pluralism as a particularly effective device in dealing with the interpretation of economic history and the formulation of economic policy (that is, with real events and processes).

The 'pure exchange' and 'pure production' models previously considered provide characteristic examples of conceptual spaces based upon the identification of subjective and objective structures respectively. Subjective structures may essentially be considered as communication networks among economic agents. Material and institutional factors here play the role of providing restrictions upon the behaviour of individuals, so that certain actions are admissible, others are not.

Objective structures, on the other hand, emphasize the importance of the interdependence among objective conditions in moulding the 'system of events' to which human actions belong. In particular, objective structures relate to the way in which social interaction brings into being a space of interaction such that certain events are possible, others are not, and certain events are more likely than others simply because social interaction leaves a mark in terms of the 'historical heritage' that is transferred from one generation to another. (For example, the existing structure of human and mechanical skills, of the capital equipment and of materials-in-process often influences in an important way the subsequent evolution of the economic system, quite independently of the agents' purposive behaviour.)

To sum up, subjective structures relate to agents *having a purpose;* objective structures, on the other hand, relate to circumstances *serving a purpose*, that is, making certain events more likely than others in certain phases of their evolution.[2] In this connection, a 'causal cluster' (of subjective and objective causes) may be defined as a set of causal powers that may in principle be ascribed to different conceptual spaces but could also operate in conjunction in order to bring about a specific historical constellation of events.

The 'causal cluster principle' could be an important analytical criterion in explaining a number of characteristic features of economic processes, such as: (1) the lack of perfect reversibility of sequences of economic events, due to the multiplicity of causal factors and the chance character of joint occurrences[3]; (2) the role of 'middle principles' (that is, of historical or institutional contingent factors) in identifying specific 'causal clusters', such as particular joint occurrences within the subjective and objective spheres, and their influence upon the *working mode* of the economic system under consideration.[4]

In general, more than one cluster of subjective and objective features is compatible with the persistence of any given economic system characterized by a particular institutional set-up (that is, by a particular set of 'middle principles'). However, there may be classes of subjective features that must be excluded if certain objective features are assumed and, similarly, there may be classes of objective features that one must exclude if certain subjective features (such as moral values, cultural habits, and so on) are taken for granted. It follows that the working mode of any given economic system may generally be reconstructed as the outcome of contingent interaction between subjective and objective structures. This makes generalization and theorizing based upon the alleged existence of uniformities very difficult indeed. But there will, of course, be ample scope for economic theorizing, considered as the construction of conceptual frameworks, and for historical work as an investigation of joint occurrences *and* the discovery of specific causal clusters from within the set of logical possibilities that economic theorists may identify.

## 5. 'MIDDLE PRINCIPLES' AND THEORETICAL PLURALISM: SOME CONCLUDING REMARKS

The role of causal clusters, which has been briefly outlined above, is closely related to the multiplicity of processes at work behind historical reality, and to the utilization of theories (sometimes rooted in distinct conceptual frameworks) in order to identify such clusters.

Some recent theoretical work has been directly addressing the economic analysis of institutional and historical issues by examining in which way 'middle principles' may specify the role of economic theory in providing interpretations of the actual working mode of any given economic system.[5]

The 'critical analysis' of economic structures has been advocated by Luigi Pasinetti in his *Structural Economic Dynamics* (Pasinetti, 1993), as well as in his previous *Structural Change and Economic Dynamics* (Pasinetti, 1981) In this case, theoretical work consists in selecting a particular layer of economic structure as the 'natural' one, and in assessing different institutional set-ups in terms of their 'distance' from the natural structure thus identified.

The 'instrumental analysis' of economic structures, which is especially related to the work by Adolph Lowe *(On Economic Knowledge*, 1965; *The Path of Economic Growth*, 1976) consists in selecting a certain cluster of features as the desired *terminal state* for the economic system under consideration, and in devising an appropriate path of structural transformations that may lead from the initial to the terminal state. In particular, the consideration of objective structure allows for the identification of a set of feasible transformation paths, and the subsequent consideration of a specific cluster of objective and subjective (institutional) features makes the selection of a particular transformation path possible.

Finally, the 'descriptive-analytical' investigation of economic structure consists in identifying and describing particular clusters of subjective and objective features, in attempting an identification of the process by which such clusters came about, and in assessing certain features of future development, even if only by means of *exclusion.*[6] This approach has found a notable application in the late work on economic dynamics by John Hicks (see, in particular, *Capital and Time*, 1973).

The above contributions are inclined to see historical clusters of institutional or behavioural features as the starting point of a theoretical investigation, rather than the *product* of it. However, the intersection of theories may suggest ways in which new, relevant 'causal clusters' may be identified and economic processes reconstructed.

## ACKNOWLEDGEMENT

This chapter was originally presented as a paper at the International Workshop, 'Pluralism in Economics: Theory, History and Methodology' (University of Bergamo, 26–8 May 1994). Stimulating criticism by a number of workshop participants, and in particular by Wade Hands, is gratefully acknowledged.

## NOTES

1. The relationship between economic policy and the need to consider singularities was emphasized long ago by Luigi Valeriani, when he noted that effective economic policy requires the application of general economic theory to 'transversal data of place, time, circumstances' (Valeriani, 1804, p. xliii). In this connection, Valeriani also pointed out that economic policy 'can be reduced to an increasingly accurate theory, that is to the knowledge of more specific data, none of which can be overlooked if we want the practical result to coincide with the theoretical one, even if all other conditions are as required' (ibid., p. xxv).
2. I am indebted to Professor Timothy McDermott of Clare Hall, Cambridge for enlightening conversation on this particular issue.
3. It may be interesting to note, in this connection, that irreversibility is closely associated with the joint operation of a multiplicity of causal factors, *and* to their chance conjunction. The 'chance conjunction' requirement is essential in order to make multiple causation compatible with the indeterminacy and irreversibility of historical paths, punctuated as they are by irrepeatable singularities.
4. The role of 'middle principles' was carefully examined by Adolph Lowe, particularly in his lectures at the London School of Economics on 'Economics and Sociology' (see Lowe, 1935).
5. It may be interesting to recall that the role of middle principles is related to the field of intermediate generalization, that is, to a class of statements akin to the 'derivative laws' considered by John Elliott Cairnes (Cairnes, 1874, p. 135) in his discussion of value: 'I propose to call attention ... to some examples of value which I think may not improperly be called "derivative laws" of that phenomenon I refer to those changes in the values of different kinds of commodities which occur when the general laws of value, such as we have found them to be, come into operation under the actual circumstances of progressive societies' (Cairnes, 1874, p. 135).
6. Characteristically, this type of structural analysis is one in which the logic of *abduction* is used (see Peirce, 1931–58). This approach, which is akin to William Whewell's conception

of induction (see above), makes new conceptions essential in order to 'bind together observed facts' in a novel way (see Whewell, 1860, p. v).

## REFERENCES


Cairnes, J.E. (1874), *Some Leading Principles of Political Economy. Newly Expounded*, London: Macmillan.

Carnap, R. (1934), *Logische Syntax der Sprache*, Vienna: Springer Verlag.

Enriques, F. (1914), *Problems of Science* (1st edn 1906), Chicago: Open Court.

Frege, G. (1892), 'Uber Sinn und Bedeutung', *Zeitschrift für Philosophie und Philosophische Kritik*, pp. 25–50.

Georgescu-Roegen, N. (1966), *Analytical Economics. Issues and Problems*, Cambridge, MA: Harvard University Press.

Georgescu-Roegen, N. (1971), *The Entropy Law and the Economic Process*, Cambridge, MA: Harvard University Press.

Georgescu-Roegen, N. (1990), 'Production Process and Economic Dynamics', in M. Baranzini and R. Scazzieri (eds), *The Economic Theory of Structure and Change*, Cambridge: Cambridge University Press, pp. 198–226.

Hicks, J. (1973), *Capital and Time. A Neo-Austrian Theory*, Oxford: Clarendon Press.

Hicks, J. (1975), 'The Scope and Status of Welfare Economics', *Oxford Economic Papers*, **27**, pp. 307–26.

Hicks, J. (1976) '"Revolutions" in Economics', in S.J. Latsis (ed.), *Method and Appraisal in Economics*, Cambridge: Cambridge University Press, pp. 207–18.

Lowe, A. (1935), *Economics and Sociology A Plea for Co-operation in the Social Sciences*, London: Allen & Unwin.

Lowe, A. (1965), *On Economic Knowledge. Toward a Science of Political Economics*, New York/Evanston: Harper & Row.

Lowe, A. (1976), *The Path of Economic Growth*, Cambridge: Cambridge University Press.

Pasinetti, L.L. (1965), 'A New Theoretical Approach to the Problems of Economic Growth', in *Econometric Approach to Development Planning*, Amsterdam: North-Holland Publishing Company, pp. 571–696.

Pasinetti, L.L. (1981), *Structural Change and Economic Growth. A Theoretical Essay on the Dynamics of the Wealth of Nations*, Cambridge: Cambridge University Press.

Pasinetti, L.L. (1986), 'Theory of Value – a Source of Alternative Paradigms in Economic Analysis', in M. Baranzini and R. Scazzieri (eds), *Foundations of Economics. Structures of Inquiry and Economic Theory*, Oxford and New York: Basil Blackwell, pp. 409–31.

Pasinetti, L.L. (1993), *Structural Economic Dynamics. A Theory of the Economic Consequences of Human Learning*, Cambridge: Cambridge University Press.

Peirce, C. (1931–58), *Collected Papers*, vols. I–VI, edited by C. Hartshorne and P. Weiss, 1931–5; vols. VII–VIII, edited by A.W. Burks, 1958, Cambridge, MA: Harvard University Press.

Popper, K. (1963), *Conjectures and Refutations. The Growth of Scientific Knowledge*, London and Henley: Routledge & Kegan Paul.

Schumpeter, J.A. (1954), *History of Economic Analysis*, edited from manuscript by Elizabeth Boody Schumpeter, New York: Oxford University Press.

Sextus Empiricus (AD 100–200), *Adversus Mathematicos*, edited by J. Mau, Leipzig: Teubner, 1954.

Thom, R. (1989), 'Causality and Finality in Theoretical Biology: A Possible Picture', in J. Casti and A. Karlqvist (eds), *Newton to Aristotle: Toward a Theory of Models for Living Systems*, Boston: Birkhauser, pp. 39–45.

Valeriani, L. (1804), *Lezione inaugurale di pubblica economia*, Bologna: a S. Tommaso d'Aquino.

Whewell, W. (1860), *On the Philosophy of Discovery. Chapters Historical and Critical,* London: Parker & Son.

# COMMENT

**D. Wade Hands**

Professor Scazzieri's chapter deals with a difficult and important problem in economic methodology (and philosophy of science more generally). The problem is that while we must admit that our conceptual frameworks (or paradigms, or analytical visions) determine what we 'see' and what is intelligible to us, we want these conceptual frameworks to be grounded in the objective properties of the world, and not be, as he puts it, 'purely subjective and idiosyncratic constructions'. The goal of the chapter seems to be to find a solution to (or dissolution of) this problem in a way that also supports theoretical pluralism.

While the chapter is innovative and thoughtful, I do not believe that it accomplishes its intended goal. This is not to say that the author's position cannot be defended in future work. This chapter appears to be the first step in a much larger research project, and my criticisms are only intended to point out the weak points in this early argumentation and not indict the entire project. Before I discuss these criticisms let me briefly summarize (what I believe to be) the author's main argument.

The initial claim is that our conceptual frameworks provide interpretative filters through which we see the world and render it intelligible; analytic representations are devices that select certain aspects of reality and prepare it for our understanding. These analytic representations involve the 'assignment of meaning' and are inexorably intertwined with the interests and interpretative strategies of those sharing the vision or conceptual framework. Real processes only come to be understood within the context of such interpretative frameworks. Economic structures, as perceived from the viewpoint of various economic research programmes, are an example of such analytic representations.

The next step in the author's argument is to emphasize that *intersections* of analytical representations are particularly important; additional insight can be gained when a real process is described from the perspective of two (or more) alternative conceptual frameworks. Since the number of potential intersections increases with the number of different conceptual frameworks that are available, the argument for theoretical pluralism – a multiplicity of such frameworks – follows quite easily. The example discussed is the policy insight that can be gained by viewing various aspects of economic life from the perspective of, or as the intersection of, the neoclassical 'pure exchange' (agency/subjective/price) and the classical 'pure production' (structure/objective/value) theoretical paradigms. He argues that particular economic events are often caused (or can best be seen as caused) by a 'cluster' of such influences, each with its own causal powers. The argument is that we need a plurality of different theories because economic events are best reconstructed as the 'contingent interaction' of the various causal powers identified by different theoretical frameworks.

One might associate this particular defence of theoretical pluralism with the defence given by Paul Feyerabend in his early work (Feyerabend, 1968 for example); but the argument is really much different. Feyerabend argues that since empirical facts are determined by scientific theories (fact are 'theory-laden'), if one wants to be a good empiricist – if one wants to have a wide range of facts with which to falsify theories – then one needs to have many theories. Scazzieri's argument is much less empiricist and much more essentialist in orientation; he speaks of pluralism in terms of increasing our understanding of the underlying (and interacting) causal powers, rather than in terms of increasing the number of potentially falsifying instances.

Assuming that I have not drastically misinterpreted the author's position, there seem to be a number of problems with his argument. Let me discuss just two of these: those that I find to be the most problematic.

First, I think there is a real question about whether paradigms or conceptual framework *even have intersections* in their empirical domains. If one follows the arguments about the theory-ladenness (or social-ladenness) of empirical observations from the recent literature in the philosophy of science then it is not at all clear that different paradigms will share any elements of their empirical basis at all – this is what 'incommensurability' is all about. If there are no 'intersections' then there seems little to support the author's claims regarding the benefits of a multiplicity of different approaches. Of course one could reject the arguments about theory-ladenness and incommensurability, and argue that there is a single objective observational domain, but then all of Scazzieri's arguments in the first few pages seem to be much less convincing. When he first introduces the problem it certainly sounds like he accepts the position that various conceptual frameworks determine the facts in their domain; if this is not something he accepts then one is hard pressed to understand why the multiplicity of theories are needed in the first place. The problem is that if one accepts the incommensurability thesis then there is not necessarily any reason for 'intersections' to exist, on the other hand, if one does not think that incommensurability is a problem, then one could simply test the available theories against the objective empirical evidence in order to find the single best theory, thus removing any argument for having more than one theory. It may be that Scazzieri is not actually concerned with the issue of theory-ladenness (despite the way the first few pages read), but rather is concerned with the impact of identifying interacting causal powers; if that is the case his position needs to be made clear from the beginning.

Second, supposing that we accept his arguments about 'intersections' and the possibility of viewing the same real economic process or structure in two alternative ways, there is still a question about why this should help us with policy or with economic understanding more generally. Whether one thinks in empiricist terms and considers the intersections as cases of empirical event regularities consistent with two different theoretical approaches, or whether one thinks more in essentialist/realist terms and considers the intersections to be events produced by the interaction of two different causal powers, the issue is the same; there is no reason for the two theories to give the same policy prescriptions or the same understanding. In a pure exchange economy changes in taste change prices while in a classical economy they do not; it is not clear how thinking in terms of causal clusters would help us conduct policy in an economy characterized by the intersection of these two theories. A more obvious choice would be to take the Marshallian path and propose a new theory that subsumes both the neoclassical pure exchange model and the classical pure production model as special cases. I am not claiming that Marshall's, or later, efforts at subsumption were entirely successful, only pointing out that being able to view the same economic event from two different theoretical perspectives may not help us in any of the activities that we normally say we want economic theories for. Scazzieri repeatedly asserts that such causal clusters will help us understand complex economic phenomena and to be more successful in policy analysis, but his argument seems to be just proof by repeated assertion. He does not provide a convincing argument about why these overlapping and intersecting, but fundamentally different, theories must necessarily serve us better than just getting the one right (perhaps new) theory in the first place. Again, as with my first criticism, there may be a way to make the case within the framework the author sets out but, at the very least, additional argumentation will be needed.

As I said in the beginning, this is an innovative and thoughtful chapter on a difficult and important topic, but I do not find the argument persuasive in its current form. Perhaps the best way to address my first criticism would be to make the author's philosophical presuppositions (empiricist or essentialist/realist) more clear from the outset. The best response to the second criticism would be more, and more convincing, examples.

## References

Feyerabend, P.K. (1968), 'How to be a Good Empiricist – A Plea for Tolerance in Matters Epistemological', in P.H. Nidditch (ed.), *The Philosophy of Science*, Oxford: Oxford University Press, pp. 12–39.

# PART II

# Case Studies in History and Methodology

# 9. The taste-less theory of consumer choice meets novelty

**Marina Bianchi and Neil De Marchi**

## INTRODUCTION

Increasingly, the firm has been rescued from consideration along a single, purely technological, dimension. Economists have begun to analyse the implications of acknowledging that the organizational structure that is the firm must be capable of anticipating and responding to change, able to generate innovative strategies, and active as an investor in creating its own markets – the institutions (networks, rules) and organizations necessary for sustaining ongoing transactions (Milgrom and Roberts, 1992; Loasby, 1993; Langlois, 1994). Strangely, however, the consumer continues to be seen as just a passive maximizer, optimizing over options that are constructed elsewhere and by others, and simply put before him or her. No explanation is given as to why preferences might be as they are; no learning occurs; and the consumer does nothing that alters the available alternatives or creates new options – novelty is not part of the choice set, nor of consumer wellbeing (for the *opposite* view, see Scitovsky, 1976). Even in the alternative approaches of the not-so-distant past (exemplars: Veblen and Galbraith) the de-emphasis on the rationality of individual choice only served to strengthen the sense of passivity and openness to manipulation of the consumer.

There are exceptions. An active consumer, decomposing goods into characteristics, which may then be recomposed in preferred ways, has been introduced by Lancaster (1991). Independently, Stigler and Becker (1977) turned the consumer into an active *producer*, of 'objects of choice' called 'commodities' (a category larger than 'market goods'). In neither of these new approaches, however, is novelty as such treated as an argument in the utility function; there is a continued absence of concern with the way tastes might be formed, as distinct from strengthened (or weakened) once acquired, and, as a direct result, an inability to deal with things that have always been found troublesome by price theorists such as art (especially old masters) and fashion.

In this essay we exploit the notion that consumers can and do actively combine and recombine properties or characteristics of goods, as part of their ongoing search for and experimentation with the novel. This enables us to break away from the traditional reductionist approach to consumer choice which treats choices as strictly determined by prices and income, with tastes as given. Once it is allowed that consumers may alter their options in the very process of choosing, a plurality of added aspects comes within the analyst's purview: the study of learning capabilities; the formation and content of tastes; innovation and change. Not surprisingly, this altered view of the consumer is in line with new approaches to the firm, which have introduced history, cybernetics, learning theory and biological metaphors into the analysis (see, for example, Earl 1986, and especially Loasby, 1993 and Langlois, 1991, 1993, 1994).

In the first section, we take Stigler and Becker (1977) as a point of reference but also as a point of departure. They show how idiosyncratic choices, under which might be included those involving fashion goods, fads and addictions, can be reconciled with traditional price theory. The strengths and limitations of their approach are brought out. In the section following, a contrast is more openly drawn with an approach which makes the search for novelty central to the formation *and* exercise of choice, in line with though also going beyond Lancaster. In the final substantive section two illustrations of the alternative approach we espouse are offered, both dealing with what have become known generally as manias: the taste for Swatch watches in the past decade, and tulips in the seventeenth century.

## THE ACTIVE CONSUMER AS PRODUCER

Stigler and Becker's agenda is to account for those forms of consumer behaviour that seem, at first glance, to betray a change in tastes. Traditional economic analysis assumes that tastes are capricious (unstable) and therefore inscrutable, and stops inquiry just at the point where it becomes important to sort out whether tastes have or have not changed (Stigler and Becker, 1977, p. 76). The Stigler–Becker improvement on this is to transform the consumer into an active maximizer who, no differently from the firm, is also engaged in production and investment decisions. They insist strongly that preferences are the same for all people and are stable. Maximization takes place against that background. Their innovative analytical move is to separate clearly preferences from resources and to suggest that utility comes from acquiring objects of choice, called commodities, which households produce using market goods, their own time, skills, knowledge, and other inputs.

With this modified utility function in place, Stigler and Becker are able to show that shifts in behaviour, or choices, which show traces of habit or addiction, or seem explicable only as fads, fashion and the persuasive power of advertising, are not the result of volatile or irrational preferences; instead, they are responses to changes in shadow prices or the opportunity costs of *producing* the objects of choice themselves. As the authors say, they have translated what are called unstable tastes into variables in the household production function for commodities, thus allowing changes in behaviour to be accounted for solely by changes in prices and incomes, 'precisely the variables that organize and give power to economic analysis' (ibid., p. 89).

The logic of this argument is stringent and very palatable to most economists. Still, problems remain, of which we notice two. One is connected to the fact that, while they avoid the 'endless degrees of freedom' exploited by believers in the instability of preferences (ibid.), Stigler and Becker invoke something not all that dissimilar, namely an infinite multiplicity of production functions capable of generating household utility, with shadow prices and choices specific to each household. That is to say, they *allow* for such a multiplicity without, however, explaining where the different production functions might come from.

The individual household as active chooser is in fact only nominally the focus of the new analysis. As Becker in his own work makes especially clear, what is gained by treating the household as 'an organizational entity... like the firm' (Becker, 1976, p. 141) is a new field of application for all the standard tools and concepts of production theory (ibid., p. 147); and in traditional production-theoretic analysis of the firm what counts are technical features of the production function, such as homogeneity, and the elasticity of factor supply and substitutability, in a hypothesized setting of competition or monopoly. Market equilibrium, hence 'industry'-wide behaviour, is frequently invoked, but there is no presumption made about what motivates individual firms. Similarly, in the new theory of consumer behaviour, despite Stigler and Becker having set up a framework within which differences between households can be expressed, these differences in fact play little part in the examples they analyse dealing with addiction or fashion; and in these same areas, their predictions and the sort of data relevant to testing them tend to be rather aggregative. That is to say, they offer an account of why addiction need not be thought of in terms of a change in tastes; and of fashion as investment in social distinction; but these are treated as rationalizations of observed behaviour on the part of aggregates of households. They do not try to account for why certain goods (or characteristics) appeal to certain households and not others, why some become 'addicted' to classical music and others to hip hop, why some smoke marijuana while others snort cocaine.

The second problem is related to this. Stigler and Becker enlarge the commodity space to include commodities such as appreciation for music and desire for distinction or 'style'. These replace 'taste for', and are meant to make that vague expression amenable to strictly economic analysis. The new expressions, however, hide precisely the same sorts of complexities as the original one. For these commodities are very different from single-purpose market goods. Just like tastes, they seem to be composites, and even to function as meta-commodities which organize and orientate choices, and whose effects spread over many goods – a taste for art deco design affects the table settings one prefers, the vases one buys, the sort of antique shops one frequents. One does not escape these strong complementarities by reformulating 'taste for' as the production of 'addiction to' this or some other type of antique.

Not only is it true that externalities – here meaning complementarities, spillover effects and interdependencies among goods – are important in consumer choice, but one starts to see also the possibility of developing different links between goods, and these in turn make it less useful to identify a good with a single, or even a primary, purpose. Stigler and Becker are not free to abandon such narrow typing, however, because, having reduced consumer choice to a matter of combining productive inputs, costs have to be attachable to a readily identifiable entity, and inputs and outputs have to be definable in strong ways, lest the whole notion of a production function fail. Within their framework, therefore, commodities are taken as unproblematic, described sufficiently by the principal use for which they were designed, but not allowing for the possibility that the consumer might seek and discover uses for single goods, and for goods in combination, that were never dreamed of by their designers and producers.[1] Thus are excluded exactly the things we wish to emphasize about choice.

To anticipate a portion of the discussion to come, a watch may be said to have the principal function of telling us the time; if its cost of production is reduced, as has steadily happened, that particular sort of information also costs less. But what is one to make of a watch whose face and hands are black, making the hands all but invisible, a distinct inconvenience; or of watches which have only a minute hand, or only an hour hand; or whose dials have no numbers, making accurate time-telling impossible though the mechanism itself incorporates quantum improvements in accuracy over the watches of just a few years ago? It seems clear that multiple possible 'uses' are involved here, though the commodity, along a principal dimension, is recognizably constant. Or, to pick up again the theme of externalities, what of a watch whose decoration (in the case we have in mind, a sort of *puntinismo)* inspires furniture incorporating the same pattern and where both clearly are meant to recall impressionism and one of the impressionists' techniques for handling light? What exactly is the object of choice here? To what precise commodity are costs to be attached?

The cost/production focus of Stigler and Becker, in short, with its narrow identifications of commodities by single function, ignores one of the more important freedoms of the active (producing) consumer, to explore the possibilities of combining and recombining component commodities, possibilities that sometimes appear almost endless – think of music composition deploying various electronic aids; of the components of dress; or imagine wire-less communication which could intermingle voice, data and images. It also ignores any analysis of externalities, though it is plain that the production of drug euphoria, to take just one of their subjects of analysis, involves the communication of disease, street crime, child neglect, and so on.

## CAPABILITIES AND EXPERIMENTATION IN CONSUMPTION

If the decision process of the consumer is one that involves also the search for and production of novelty, there can be no meaningful representative consumer. This is not the usual objection, which runs in terms of the lack of an agreed basis for defining groups which can be represented; from our perspective, the main difficulty is that any definition will break in one's hands, because consumers create new options in the process of choosing. Lancaster has not addressed this problem, but he has gone some way towards addressing the need to explain why commodities are desired in the first place, by promoting the idea of choice over characteristics rather than products (see Lancaster, 1991).

Choice over characteristics transforms goods prices or resources (shadow) prices into hedonic prices, and hedonic price indexes in principle render the choice over characteristics operational. Lancaster himself is mainly interested in the welfare implications of situations where consumers are *not* able to combine characteristics in their most preferred way (ibid., ch. 11), whereas the potential and freedom to combine and recombine is exactly what we would prefer to stress. Moreover, in all other respects his method is standard: preferences are given and known, characteristics are amenable to objective measurement, and both production and consumption technologies are well-behaved (smooth and, respectively, concave and convex). By contrast, if one emphasizes novelty and an explorative element in consumer behaviour, smoothness disappears and local optima eclipse the significance usually given to global equilibrium positions.

How should one give expression to the dissident notions that commodities may have multiple appeals, that interdependencies are important, and, above all, that consumers actively seek new uses of and combinations between goods? A classification of goods that identifies possible links and uses and thus helps pinpoint where innovation is likely to arise seems a good place to start. A useful first step is to distinguish between goods which may be called first-order goods and those which may be called second-order goods. That may sound a bit like Menger's 'roundaboutness', but it is not similar in anything but terminology. Our focus is strictly on consumption; moreover, we are seeking a way to locate where 'problems' exist for the consumer and where consequently novel solutions are called for. This is closest in lineage to Popper's approach to learning.

First-order goods are things like food, housing, clothing, health, while second-order goods include things which help organize, enable, or even produce those things, such as knowledge, information, tastes, skills, capabilities and the like.

A further distinction useful for our purposes is between both sorts of goods just mentioned, which as represented are general, composite, or global goods, and their specific elements, or component member goods, such as jam and cabbage (food), newspapers and labels (information), furs and T-shirts (clothing), or aerobics and secondary smoke (health). See Figure 9.1.

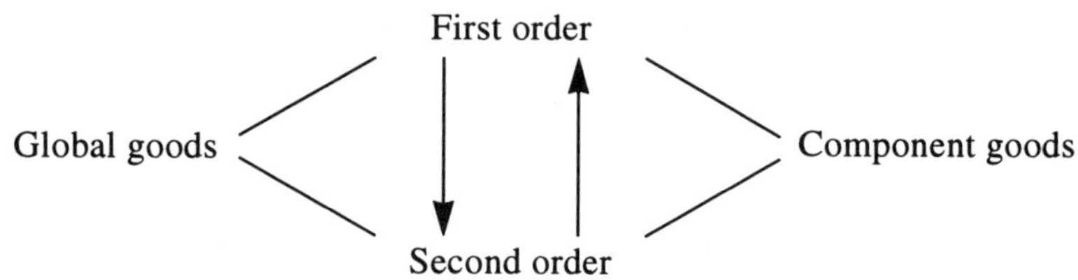


*Figure 9.1 Generalities and specifics: first- and second-order goods*

We use these distinctions to say something about novelty and spillover effects in consumption. First, then, the distinctions clarify where change and innovation occur. An obvious form of change is when new first-order member goods replace old ones: for example, pasta replaces potatoes in the Californian version of *nouvelle cuisine. Less* obvious is the change that occurs as a result of a simple recombining of member goods within global ones: different recipes or altered combinations of items of clothing. Here the global good – food, clothing – has remained the same, but a different configuration of its components has made it new.

Cast in this way, newness and novelty explain a familiar feature of consumer experience. At the level of single, isolated component goods, repeated exposure produces decreasing returns, but at the level of global goods, both first and second order, increasing returns are everywhere. For example, the desire for food in terms of the third dish of pasta is surely less than that for food in terms of a sequence in which prosciutto precedes pasta, which precedes vegetables, which are followed by cake. Desire for novelty suffices to explain this. My greater willingness to pay for the initial quantities of a good is due to the fact that those first amounts, relative to the other goods in my possession, make a difference, cause a change, produce a sense of newness. One may even argue that the urgent response to new items known to be in short supply is a way of protecting oneself from the risk of being deprived of the novel.

Novelty has not been seriously considered by economists as an element in the utility function. Certain behavioural psychologists, however, have treated novelty and its components – surprise, change, uncertainty – as a central motivating force of behaviour. D.E Berlyne, in particular, has shown that novelty, within bounds, can increase pleasure. As to the bounds, sameness and routinization, on the one hand, and excessive complexity and uncertainty, on the other, are both experienced as unpleasant and therefore call for action to either increase novelty or reduce it (Berlyne, 1971). The potential implications for equilibrium analysis are startling, though to date only Scitovsky among economists has shown much appreciation for how novelty might change the way we think about consumption (see his 1976; and, for an elaboration of some of the analytical implications, the Introduction to Bianchi, forthcoming).

Modern neglect notwithstanding, in stressing novelty we are recalling what writers since the time of Pufendorf and Barbon have recognized as self-evident: that there are a few goods related to physical needs and an infinite category of goods of the mind. Satiation has long been thought not to belong to goods of the mind, *as a category*. We are merely emphasizing that local increasing returns may apply to goods in general, physical as well as mental, first order or second order, because of the consumer's capability of recombining their components so as to create novelty.

A second useful feature of the classification we have introduced is that it stresses the strong interrelations that exist among goods and which cause there to be externalities, both positive and negative. A member good, for example, is not only related to other member goods by links of complementarity and substitutability, but can simultaneously be a member of different global goods. Thus beer is a substitute for water; but it may also, and simultaneously, satisfy a certain need for nourishment, serve as a social lubricant and contribute a degree of risk to driving safety. Both linkages and conflicts among them are easy to spot when one turns to concrete examples (Figure 9.2).

The existence of these strong links between goods is important also for another reason. We have suggested that each good can be decomposed into multiple dimensions, attributes or characteristics which may also place it at different levels of goods classification: a watch, we have asserted, measures time – that is its primary functional use – but it can also belong to the goods art, status, rarity, fancy, even play. Thus a good's function can be renewed,

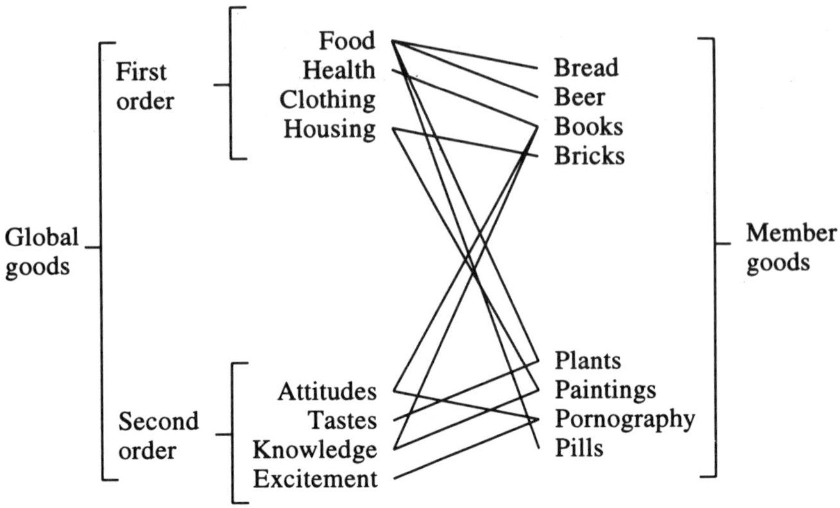


*Figure 9.2 Interrelations between goods*

altered, or extended simply by discovering and changing its combinatory position with others. Take something as apparently straightforward as dishes. They may be containers for holding food, but their colour and shape can also enhance, or decrease, the pleasure derived from the food itself, while combining them in various ways can add purely aesthetic pleasure, a sense of newness in the midst of daily routine needs. Scitovsky (1976), once again makes great play of just these possibilities, and our approach at this point owes a good deal to his insights (see too Veblen, 1930, p. 71).

At the level of global goods the recombinatory impact of a change is even more plain. These goods, because they represent a sort of organizing principle for their components, can add and subtract functions with respect to other goods, by isolating and re-aggregating them, and by building on the strong cross links that exist among goods. To enlarge upon what was said earlier about a taste for art deco design, appreciation for design in general may influence and reinforce a preference for the dimensions, colour and shape of goods such as lamps, chairs, tables, TV sets, telephones and so on. In addition, it may cause one to design a chair and have it realized in crystal (a tripling of function, for those who find crystal objects beautiful in themselves and who also can admire the ingenuity of the design and its realization in an unexpected medium), or to buy an old radio for display although it no longer works (functions!).

In sum, the power of the combinatory relations between goods explains where both conflicts and the potential for innovation arise, and tells us that even with zero change in the range of products available, novelty can still be created by the consumer, who experiments with various links between existing goods.

In the next section we adapt these simple notions to produce a modified reading of 'fashion and fad', drawing on some particulars of the fad for tulips in the seventeenth century and the rise of Swatch watches over the past decade. 'Fashion and fad' has a nice alliterative quality, but the two have always been placed together for a deeper reason, namely, that adherence to fashion has seemed to separate economic analysis from any firm foundation, a prejudice that not even the sage Galiani avoided, and which Stigler and Becker have commendably sought to undermine. Unlike them, however, we do not need to introduce something like an unexplained desire for social distinction to account for fashion, though that is almost certainly relevant, as are elements such as manipulation, passive imitation and so on; we simply accept what is readily confirmed by observation, that a desire for newness, change – in a word, for fashion – is a permanent element in consumers' ways of forming and exercising their freedom of choice. The active consumer, though of course in varying degrees, is an explorer and experimenter.

## PLASTIC WATCHES AND DISEASED TULIP BULBS

When phenomena are considered such as the desire for tulips in Holland in the early seventeenth century, or the more recent passion for Swatch watches, particularly among Italian consumers, there is a tendency to tame the presumed underlying element of irrationality by making them, as far as possible, into 'rational' bubbles (Garber, 1990), or informational 'cascades' (Bikhchandani *et al.*, 1992). Such accounts, reflecting the standard approach to consumer choice, fail to address why the goods involved are perceived as, and become, desired in the first place. Part of the promise of an approach that focuses on novelty is that it can go some way towards filling this gap.

In the case of Swatches, the parent company, the Swiss Corporation for Microelectronics and Watchmaking (SMH), deliberately set out to cause consumers to *think* differently about the familiar first-order member good 'watch'. They did this by focusing consumers' attention in the first instance not on the primary function of a watch, time-telling, but on a global, second-order good, individual and social identity. They linked characteristics such as Swiss-made (an allusion to traditions of miniaturization, high quality, precision), plus elements of cultural history (many models incorporate references to art, music, design, sport), with the function of time-telling. Moreover, they offered a watch that was cheap and throwaway (Swatches cannot be repaired), and could readily be purchased in large numbers (the average Swatch owner has a mini-inventory of six), so that one bought also the fun and challenge of combining a different watch with various combinations of clothes.

This was a radical change: from the one-dimensional view of a watch as a commodity whose function is to tell the time, consumers were invited to consider the possibility of viewing a watch as a focal point, around which to organize, deploy, and re-deploy in novel combinations, the components of dress and personal style, while identifying with particular elements of cultural history. In the process of offering an aid to articulating identity, SMH managed to alter existing preferences for 'timepieces'. In the words of the president of SMH, Nicolas Hayek, what Swatch has sought to offer is not a 'fashion' good, but an emotional, cultural attractor.

> We are not just offering people a style. We are offering a message … . Fashion is about image … . Emotional products [among which Swatch] are about message … . There are many elements that make up the Swatch message. High quality. Low cost. [Swatches too are] Provocative … [offering something] funny, fanciful, a joke – joy of life. (Interview, *Harvard Business Review*, March–April, 1993, p. 103)

Hayek explains further that he does not view the Swatch primarily as a market good, nor does he consider SMH to be engaged in market goods competition. Japanese-made watches, and watches assembled in Hong Kong, may be 10 and 20 per cent cheaper, but price does not determine sales; what sells is a way of identifying with a particular culture and cultural history (ibid., pp. 99–100, 103).

Swatch management, having initially decomposed the commodity 'watch' into its cultural and symbolic elements, devised design and production strategies for recomposing these elements in multiple ways which provide a constant source of variations and differentiation. The operational face of the strategy is that a design laboratory in Milan feeds designs for two new collections per year to the management committee in Switzerland. Roughly 70 watches per collection are selected for production, using automated assembly and mechanisms and parts designed and engineered in Switzerland.

Specific elements of production, pricing and distribution strategy contribute to maintaining the appeal of the watches. For example, production runs are limited, and once a model is sold out no more are produced, adding a potential element of scarcity value to every style chosen for production. Price was downplayed – prices for the basic Swatch remained unchanged in Swiss franc terms for a decade after its introduction in 1983 – but craftsmanship and micro-engineering were emphasized, so that value for money became a given. There is a collectors' club, and certain styles are designated collectors' pieces. This adds to the general sense of cultural identity attaching to Swatch an element of special group identity, with just a hint too of uniqueness.

But perhaps most important is the way in which the Design Lab itself consciously facilitates the cultural identity aspect of Swatch, while contributing directly to the potential for multiple uses of the product through providing a constant flow of novel styles. The members of the Lab rotate quickly; this guarantees a changing set of ideas from outside, but while at the Lab the designers also expose themselves to a huge range of artistic and cultural manifestations, through books, magazines, performances, exhibitions and personal contact with artists and communication media of all sorts. As a result, Swatch can play the role of interpreter and decodifier of social languages, both historical and new. The analogy is to a museum, which organizes and catalogues, and constantly recatalogues, so as to give a changing range of contexts to art, history, literature, ethnic traditions, architecture, craft and language. Or perhaps one might think of a newspaper, which selects, combines and structures different messages while maintaining a distinctive editorial imprint.

The history of the tulip in seventeenth-century Holland confirms this account in certain particulars. Variability, scarcity and aesthetic appeal are three such. Admiration was expressed by contemporaries for the rich and variegated colours – a challenge to the palette of the most talented artist; but there were also certain bulbs considered collectible. The flowers of these were unusual in another way: petals of white, red or yellow were bordered, streaked or flamed with crimson, or yellow, or red, respectively. These effects were caused by an aphid virus which affected some bulbs; the prized patterned flowers could not be reproduced from seed, only by introducing the virus into the bulbs of a single-colour tulip (in this and other details we have followed Krelage, 1942). But the effects of the virus, called 'breaking' – the breaking of plain colours – were not predictable in detail in newly diseased bulbs, and the variations in colour patternings were therefore considerable even within a given sort of tulip.

Novelty, beauty and uniqueness combined to drive prices astonishingly high for the bulbs responsible for intriguing new broken colourings, until reproduction (and eventual success in seed cultivation) made them more common. That pattern both preceded and continued long after the short-lived 'mania' which has commanded the exclusive attention of modern economists. The horticulturists catering to the collectors' tastes contributed to the price phenomenon by planting not large numbers of a few plain colours but a few bulbs each of a vast variety of types displaying the broken-colour effects.

Collections of curiosities of all sorts were common among various elites in seventeenth-century Holland, as elsewhere. The aim, so far as we can gather, was not to place exotic objects within a system or classification derived from laws or empirical patterns; it was enough that an object was new, rare, strange or beautiful. 'Broken' tulips fit the bill, and had the added advantage over tropical parrots, stuffed alligators and shells, that they could be multiplied with relative ease, and with constantly varying effects.

The tulip eventually lost its place as the flower of preference to the double hyacinth. The hyacinth too was prized for its relative scarcity; but admirers were quite as pleased with its absolute predictability and regularity of form – the exact opposite of what had proved attractive in 'broken' tulips – and the longevity of its bulbs, compared with those of tulips; though they also enjoyed the large range of very subtle shades that could be produced. This subtlety offset, so it would seem, the predictability of form and colour.

The combination of familiarity and novelty is one that Swatch has exploited well, with its constant supply of new models but predictable price, reliability and quality of mechanism.

In the effort to discover whether the tulip mania was 'rational' or not, no attention has been paid to why the flower was found desirable in the first place. Just as there are Swatch competitors – Timex, Casio, Benetton and others have got into the cheap, decorative watch market – so too the tulip vied with the carnation, and later with the hyacinth, ranunculus (buttercup, crowfoot), and anemone, as can be seen from still-life paintings of flower arrangements. Why was it preferred? Rivalrous social distinction is no doubt part of what caused tulips to be desirable. To the basic aesthetic appeal of the tulip was added, however, the unusual effects produced by diseased bulbs. That created variants of startling visual attractiveness. Moreover, the broken tulips were scarce, while they were capable of constantly surprising with novel effects. This made the bulbs a gardener's delight and a collector's item *par excellence*, in an age when, to use Daston's phrase, 'ravening curiosity' was an acceptable form of *consumer*, as well as of intellectual, display.

## CONCLUSION

When one acknowledges that the consumer, in the very process of choosing, is confronted with and even selects for novelty and change, new questions arise, questions that cannot be forced into the narrow framework in which consumer theory has been modelled but which require instead help from several quarters: the analysis of learning, taste formation and the production of capabilities for dealing with change, among others. This essay is an example of how one might broaden the analysis; if one prefers, it is an illustration of how pluralities of parallel, discrete analyses, using somewhat different methods and pursuing different questions, can enrich economics.

## ACKNOWLEDGEMENT

We have benefited from the comments of audiences in Bergamo, Italy, and Witten/Herdecke, Germany.

## NOTE

1. Becker is aware that commodities such as envy and prestige are more encompassing than a lot of the market goods economists traditionally have dealt with (1976, p. 147), but this awareness does not relieve the tension introduced by applying production function analysis to such 'global' commodities.

## REFERENCES

Becker, Gary S. (1976), *The Economic Approach to Human Behavior*, Chicago: University of Chicago Press.

Berlyne, D.E. (1971), *Aesthetics and Psychobiology*, New York: Appleton-Century-Crofts.

Bianchi, Marina (ed.), *The Active Consumer. Novelty and Surprise in Consumer Choice*, forthcoming.

Bikhchandani, S., Hirschleifer, H. and Welch, I. (1992), 'A Theory of Fads, Fashion, Custom, and Cultural Change as Informational Cascades', *Journal of Political Economy*, **100**, pp. 992–1026.

Daston, Lorraine (1993), 'Ravening Curiosity, Gawking Wonder, and the Study of Nature', University of Chicago, mimeo.

Earl, Peter (1986), *Lifestyle Economics. Consumer Behavior in a Turbulent World*, New York: St Martin's Press.

Garber, Peter M. (1990). 'Famous First Bubbles', *Journal of Economic Perspectives* **4**, pp. 35–54.

Krelage, E.H. (1942), *Bloemenspeculatie in Nederland. De Tulpomanie van* 1636–'37 *en de Hyacintenhandel* 1720–'36, Amsterdam: P.N. Van Kampen & Son.

Lancaster, Kelvin (1991), *Modern Consumer Theory*, Aldershot: Edward Elgar.

Langlois, Richard N. (1991), 'The Capabilities of Industrial Capitalism', *Critical Review*, **4**, pp. 513–30.

Langlois, Richard N. (1993), 'Capabilities and Coherence in Firms and Markets', University of Connecticut, mimeo.

Langlois, Richard N. (1994), 'Cognition and Capabilities: Opportunities Seized and Missed in the History of the Computer Industry', University of Connecticut, mimeo.

Loasby, Brian J. (1993), 'Understanding Markets', University of Stirling, mimeo.

Milgrom, P. and Roberts, J. (1992), *Economics Organization, and Management*, Englewood Cliffs, N.J.: Prentice Hall.

Scitovsky, Tibor (1976), *The Joyless Economy*, New York: Oxford University Press.
Stigler, George J. and Becker, Gary S. (1977), 'De Gustibus Non Est Disputandum', *American Economic Review,* **67**, pp. 76–90.
Taylor, William (1993), 'Message and Muscle: An Interview with Swatch Titan Nicolas Hayek', *Harvard Business Review* (March–April), pp. 99–110.
Veblen, Thorstein (1930), *The Place of Science in Modern Civilisation, and Other Essays*, New York: Viking.

# COMMENT

**Maria Cristina Marcuzzo**

Bianchi and de Marchi challenge the view presented by Stigler and Becker (1977) that there is no need to change the postulate that tastes are given in order to explain phenomena such as addiction, habitual behaviour, advertising and fashions, because once the appropriate variables are introduced into the utility function and budget constraint, standard maximization provides most of the answer.

According to Stigler and Becker, utility comes from acquiring objects of choice, called commodities, which households produce using market goods, their own time, skills and knowledge. Thus, choices showing traces of habit or addiction, or that seem explicable only as fashion need not be interpreted as changes in taste, but as responses to changes in shadow prices or in the opportunity costs of producing the choices themselves. In particular, far from being in contradiction with stable preferences and given tastes, fashions and fads are adequately explained by changes in prices and incomes, once it is understood that 'the commodity produced by fashion goods is social distinction' (Stigler and Becker, 1977, p. 87).

Once the individual's demand for fashions is made dependent on the individual's social environment and his/her own efforts, then standard microeconomic analysis applies: each individual maximizes the 'social distinction' function, subject to a budget constraint that depends on his income and on a given social environment. An increase in the individual's income, at constant prices, increases his/her demand for social distinction. If the social environment remains unchanged, the increase in distinction is brought about by his/her own contribution. If there is an exogenous decline in the individual's social environment – because other persons increase their contribution to their own distinction – there may be an induced response by the individual to spend more on his/her distinction, since social distinction is 'an incentive to individuality and a source of conformity' (Stigler and Becker, 1977, p. 88).

Bianchi and de Marchi criticize the Stigler–Becker approach mainly on the ground that fashions are treated as rationalizations of observed behaviour on the part of aggregates of households and there is no account for why certain goods appeal to certain households and not others. They argue against reducing the explanation of why something becomes a fashionable commodity or a habit to nothing more than prices and income, with tastes taken as given and they claim to be able to explain particular instances of fashion, such as the present-day Swatch mania and the fad for diseased tulips in seventeenth-century Holland, by breaking away from the traditional assumption of 'given tastes'.

The basis of their claim rests on (1) introducing the 'desire for novelty' as an argument in the utility function and (2) on considering tastes and preferences as a meta-commodity which organizes and orientates choice. These, they argue, should be the main elements of the framework to address *in general* the question of why some goods become desired rather than others.

To eliminate the assumption of stability in tastes, their explanation invokes, on the one hand, the existence of a multidimensional space where objects of choice are located and new capabilities are produced and, on the other hand, assumes 'novelty' as an object of choice in itself. My objection is that in their approach 'novelty' is again assumed as a constant in behaviour, which cannot – any more than constant tastes – account for differences in individual behaviour. Furthermore, 'desire for novelty' does not seem to differ much from 'desire for social distinction'; a shadow price for it and income and price effects could easily be accommodated within the Becker–Stigler approach. Thus, it seems to me that their *general* question – which variables explain why certain items become objects of choice and gain widespread acceptance – remains unanswered.

I believe that constraining any explanation of observed social behaviour to the requirement of generality – postulating utility – optimizing individuals seeking social distinction or active consumers building new capabilities in pursuing novelty – does not produce really powerful results. The reason is that there is a trade-off between historical accuracy and generalizations, i.e. between interpreting a phenomenon by drawing from a broad spectrum of knowledge, insights and factual information and by applying a theory which is necessarily confined within its limited scope. The broader the domain encompassed, the greater will be the explanatory power of an interpretation of an historical occurrence, while the narrower the domain (the number of variables) where the explanation is sought the lesser it will prove.

The test for a convincing, as opposed to an unconvincing interpretation of an historical occurrence of generalized behaviour cannot be the number of variables invoked: the fewer the better. Nor can it be an appeal to an entity such as desire for 'social distinction' or for 'novelty', which are not explanations but just another way of phrasing 'fashions and fads'.

If we want to explain why generalized behaviour favours a particular object of choice in a particular historical instance, we want to look not only to the active consumers, but also (or especially) to the active producers. As Bianchi and de Marchi rightly point out, the demand for novelty must be met by the supply. Swatch managers and designers, no less than seventeenth-century Dutch gardeners must be ready to supply the commodity 'novelty' and to monitor the scarcity value which must accompany it. It is not a matter of how much the consumer is active or passive, but rather whether the demand for novelty can be profitably catered for in the market. Heroin addiction is best understood as an instance of *production* of wants by the suppliers of the drug rather than by the consumers of it.

The mania for fancy watches by modern consumers and for diseased tulip bulbs by seventeenth-century consumers is best accounted for by exploring the context in which each particular behaviour pattern is set. The grasp of the circumstances Bianchi and de Marchi display is more fruitful and rewarding to the reader than their reductionist exercise in finding an explanatory variable of wide generality.

## Reference

Stigler, G.J. and Becker, G.S. (1977), 'De Gustibus Non Est Disputandum', *American Economic Review*, **67** (2), March, pp. 76–90.

# 10. Frank Knight's pluralism

**D. Wade Hands**

Behind every fact is a theory and behind that an interest.

(Frank Knight, 1922)

Monism is moonshine!

(Frank Knight, 1925)

## 1. INTRODUCTION: THE CHANGING FACE OF PLURALISM IN ECONOMICS

The plea for pluralism in economics has been a frequent refrain throughout the history of modern economic thought. This refrain has usually been voiced by those who were outside, and critical of, the mainstream in modern economics. It is not surprising that economists who consider themselves to be excluded or marginalized – those of the Marxist, institutionalist, Austrian, or other heterodox persuasion for example – would protest the uniformity and lack of diversity that exists in both the theory and the method of mainstream economics. In a few cases these critics have focused their attention on the *epistemology* or *methodology* of mainstream economics (or at least the views that the mainstream purports to hold on such issues) – examples include the synthetic *a priori* of the Misesian Austrians and the historical materialism of traditional Marxism – but the most common plea is simply for an alternative *theory*, and not for an alternative approach to theorizing. In other words, the recurrent exhortation for pluralism in economics has traditionally been a plea for theoretical pluralism rather than a plea for the (potentially more radical) pluralism of a methodological, an epistemological, or even an ontological sort. The critics have generally agreed with the mainstream about ontology (there is only one economy), about there being only one path to the discovery of truth about the economy (economic science), and about methodology (follow the 'scientific method') – the disagreement has been about the profession's lack of theoretical diversity.

Recent trends in the philosophy of science, and intellectual life more generally, have started to change the situation in economics. Whether one focuses on the 'paradigms' of Thomas Kuhn, the 'interests' of the Strong Programme in the sociology of scientific knowledge, the 'language games' of Wittgenstein, or Richard Rorty's deconstruction of the 'mirror nature', it is clear that recent philosophical trends have moved in the direction of *contextualism.* Increasingly the universal and the necessary are being replaced by the perspectival and the contingent; that which was once viewed as foundational – a place to stand outside of the human context – is increasingly seen as situated, socially constituted, and deprivileged.[1] This contemporary contextualism has started to change the face of 'pluralism in economics'.

One example of this change is the methodological pluralism that Bruce Caldwell defended in the final chapter of *Beyond Positivism* (1982). Caldwell's pluralism is clearly motivated by the impact of contextualism in the philosophy of science; it surrenders the traditional methodological problem of finding rules for theory choice and it endorses theoretical pluralism, although it does still retain a type of epistemic monism based on Popperian critical rationalism.[2] The 'rhetoric of economics' approach of Donald McCloskey and others is a different response to contextualism in economics.[3] The rhetoric of economics literature uses arguments similar to those of Richard Rorty (1979) to motivate the complete rejection of traditional epistemology in favour of rhetoric and discourse analysis. While the rhetorical perspective is certainly not inconsistent with theoretical pluralism, McCloskey's economic practice suggests that it need not imply it.[4] Still other recent responses to contemporary contextualism include the Marxist overdetermination view of Stephen Resnick and Richard Wolff (1987)[5], the social constructivist reading of the history of general equilibrium theory by Roy Weintraub (1991), and the various feminist strategies for economic theorizing presented in Ferber and Nelson (1993).

All of these recent approaches are informed by contextualism, and all of them advocate a pluralism that is philosophically more radical than the simple theoretical pluralism that has traditionally been the concern of those advocating pluralism in economics. We are confronted with a plurality of new approaches that advocate pluralism in economics, but the relationship between these various views is unclear and, more importantly, it is not clear what the implications of these more radical views are for the more traditional question of theoretical pluralism. Do these contextualist-inspired perspectives support the view, held by most of those who have advocated pluralism in the history of economic thought, that the economics profession should encourage a wider range of theoretical strategies?

While I am certainly not going to provide an answer to such a general question in the context of this brief chapter, I will attempt to get some insight into the question by turning backward to a figure in the history of economic thought who was also concerned with many of these same issues.

The figure is Frank Knight. Knight stated repeatedly that he was a 'pluralist'. It is also clear that he was concerned with a number of issues that would now be considered 'contextualist'; he was anti-positivist, relatively hermeneutic and anti-scientistic about social science, and sensitive to the idea of social constructivism. He was not though, a theoretical pluralist about economic theory. This mix, an explicit pluralist with elements of contextualism who advocated a theoretical monism in economics, makes Knight a figure who is potentially relevant to the current debate regarding pluralism in economics.

## 2. KNIGHT AND CONTEMPORARY CONTEXTUALISM

Before I attempt to unpact Knight's use of the term 'pluralism', I would like to consider a few of the many contextualist aspects of his general position. In particular I will focus on three – interrelated but still separable – aspects of Knight's perspective that are consistent with the spirit of contemporary contextualism: his anti-scientism, his emphasis on the theory-ladenness of empirical observations, and his recognition of the social aspect of human knowledge.

Contemporary contextualism is not simply 'a theory' or 'a point of view'; it is a loose amalgam of partially conflicting insights and conceptualizations that share a few common themes. One of these common themes is the rejection of the scientific world view as advocated by the Vienna Circle in the late 1920s.[6] According to the Vienna Circle there is one and only one path to knowledge about the world, it is the path of natural science based on empiricism and logicism. Metaphysics, or any form of reasoning that resembles metaphysical speculation, is simply nonsense. This view lends support to those who promote a unified science, the claim that all human and social sciences should strictly follow the method of, and where possible be reduced to, the physical sciences.

The Vienna Circle's scientistic view of social science was vehemently rejected by Frank Knight. As Knight frequently argued, this type of scientism leads to a rigid behaviourism where human agents are devoid of motives, intentionality, free will and, ultimately, all mental life. For Knight the behaviour of human agents is goal directed and intentional; it is driven by motives that are not empirically observable and can not be reduced to mere physical or biological processes; any successful social science must fully recognize this human fact.[7] Positivist human science is simply impossible – 'it just cannot be done' (Knight, 1946, p. 109) – and this is a good thing because if it were possible it would mean that humans were not really humans at all, but simply mechanisms.

> To begin with, it is well to recognize explicitly that behaviorism is in fact the application of scientific method in the strict sense, as developed in the natural sciences, to the study of human phenomena, … . In opposition to this view I propose … that we *cannot* treat human beings as unconscious organisms or mechanisms, and that we do not want to do so even if it were possible. (Knight, 1925, pp. 247–8; emphasis in original)

> It seems to us that science is a special technique developed for and applicable to the control of physical nature, but that the ideal so constantly preached and reiterated, of carrying its procedure over into the field of the social phenomena rests on a serious misapprehension. (Knight, 1935a, p. 133)

Knight's alternative to the positivist view of human science was a 'common-sense' view of intentional, motivated behaviour that is much closer to the continental *Verstehen* and hermeneutic schools than to scientistic or behaviourist social science. While Knight's characterization of social science as motivation-based might not seem very radical by contemporary contextualist standards, his rejection of the positivist view of unified science and his support for a more interpretive approach to human behaviour is a position that many contextualists would also endorse.

A second common theme in contemporary contextualism is that empirical observations are theory-laden. The theory-ladenness thesis asserts that scientific theories – or the conceptual frameworks employed by any other group of systematic inquirers – determines what the investigators will and will not 'see'. The implication is that there does not exist a separate and theory-neutral domain of empirical observations that can be used for the objective evaluation of scientific theories; there may exist something that can be called 'the empirical' but it is relative to, and at least partially constituted by, the particular community of scientific inquirers.

Knight clearly recognized the problem of the theory-ladenness of observations. The example that he referred to a number of different papers was the problem of 'force' in physics. Force is the product of mass times acceleration (f = ma), but 'mass is not measured and not experienced directly, but only as force' (Knight, 1944, p. 306).[8] The implication that Knight saw for economics was that since theory-ladenness exists in all sciences, the common complaint that 'utility' is not independently observable is not nearly as incriminating to the discipline of economics as is frequently suggested. For Knight, the entire issue of what is observed and what the observer contributes is less than clear cut. In his words, 'no one has ever proposed a distinction acceptable to critical common sense between what we perceive and what we infer' (Knight, 1944, p. 306).[9]

Knight's recognition of the problem of theory-ladenness is simply the adjunct of another, more radical, aspect of his overall view: the notion that knowledge is socially constructed. This is a third aspect of Knight's position that has much in common with contemporary contextualism. For Knight all knowledge is social knowledge and the empirical testing of scientific observations 'is chiefly, and always ultimately, a social activity' (Knight, 1956, p. 156); this means that 'all knowledge of the world of sense observation, whether that of the plain man or that of the scientist (not to mention knowledge of social data)' is actually a 'social activity and a social phenomenon' (ibid.).[10] Knight's main argument for the social construction of knowledge is the interaction and intercommunication that is always involved in the human learning process. Learning is a process that takes place through interaction with other individuals who share a common language and social context.

> There can be no question that we build up our knowledge of an external world through the interchange of experience with our fellow beings. The individual learns from others to perceive and observe, to interpret the 'buzzing booming confusion' which experience in the raw must be ... into a world of objects, movements, relations, and forces. ... [O]bservation itself, understood in anything approaching its scientific meaning, is a power socially developed and trained in the individual, and produced in the course of history by accumulation of communicated and compared experiences. Only in this way do we learn even to see with anything like accuracy. And always we see largely what we expect to see, what fits into our organized knowledge of the world. And the structure of our thinking is notoriously that of our language, our medium of communication. ... Observation in the scientific sense is therefore restricted to the limits of possible communication; and nothing very far from the common experience and symbolized by speech forms, could be observed even if it existed. (Knight, 1935b, p. 96)[11]

Knight's social constructivism extends to his notion of truth. For Knight, truth is neither an absolute nor completely relative; it is a consensus. The consensus theory of truth endorsed by Knight is the pragmatic notion derived from Charles Sanders Peirce; it is that '*the truth is simply "the limit of inquiry", that is, what the scientific enterprise will discover in the idealized long run*' (Rescher, 1993, p. 23; emphasis in original). In Knight's own words:

> The point is that illusion is what we agree is illusion, and reality what we agree is reality, because in each case it is shown to be so by tests which we agree are valid. It is ultimately a matter of agreement, of common-sense. Truth is established by consensus as much as beauty. In both cases, to be sure, it is a consensus of the 'competent.' But the competent are selected by agreement, another consensus; and ultimately we must come to principles agreed upon by the great mass of mankind. (Knight, 1925, p. 253)

Again, this particular (Peircean) consensus theory of truth may be relatively tame when compared to some contemporary contextualist positions, but nonetheless it places Knight squarely within the general contextualist genre.

## 3. KNIGHT'S PLURALISM

Knight stated repeatedly that he was a pluralist. Since he was typically writing about economics and the other human sciences, his pluralism was almost always presented in the context of his views on the philosophy of social science. This is not to deny (or assert) that Knight's pluralism went deeper than merely his views on social science; it is only to assert that this is the context in which his opinions about pluralism were most often stated. Given this frequency, and given that my particular focus is economics, I will restrict my attention to Knight's characterization of pluralism as a philosophy of social science.

Knight's fundamental claim is that 'Economics deals with human beings, and their study demands a *pluralistic* approach' (Knight, 1961, p. 188; emphasis in original). This pluralism is based on the argument that human beings are not simple systems; they have a number of fundamentally different, and mutually irreducible, aspects. Human beings are at once, physical, biological, intentional and social entities. Any knowledge we have of human behaviour or society must, according to Knight, acknowledge these different aspects of human existence.[12]

In his discussions of social science and social policy Knight frequently divided the various aspects of human phenomena into (at least) the following six categories.[13]

I. Positivistic
   1. Physical
   2. Historical or institutionalist
   3. Biological

II. Motivated or problem-solving
   1. Economic behaviour
   2. Abstract or socially motivated action
   3. Value deliberation

The first three categories – physical, historical, and biological – are listed under the general rubric 'positivistic' because they are aspects of human behaviour that are capable of being treated in a scientific way, that is, as a science in the positivist sense; they are phenomena that exhibit discoverable universal empirical regularities. The first of these categories, physical laws, seems to be straightforward. The second category is perhaps less familiar; it would include the type of empirical social regularities that could be uncovered by historical, sociological or anthropological studies. In the case of economics this second category would include some studies by institutionalist economists (I suspect Knight would consider Mitchell's work and NBER-type studies to be in this category) as well as the work of the German Historical School. Knight did not say too much about biology, but he seemed to place it in the positivist category with some reluctance.

Knight put *economic science* in the second category of 'motivated' or 'problem-solving' approaches. His definition of economic science was quite narrow; it was 'using given means to achieve given ends' (Knight, 1935a, p. 105). Economics, for Knight, was about 'economizing', using the most effective means to achieve *given ends*. In contemporary terminology, Knight characterized economics as the science of instrumental rationality: finding the most efficient way of achieving (often maximizing or minimizing) a given objective (or objective function). Knight's use of the term 'economic science' for this type of economic theorizing should be interpreted carefully; it is a type of science but it is not a positivistic science like those in the first category. Because economics involves motivated behaviour and given ends (goals, desires, etc.), it is an intentional or common-sense science, not a positivistic one; such a 'science' is capable of explanation and, at least to a limited sense, prediction, but it is not a science like those in the first category.[14] As Knight says,

> a treatment of economics as defined by this basic notion cannot be an 'empirical' science in the literal sense of that word. Effectiveness, a synonym for economy, is inherently relative to some purpose, motive or intention, and these are not known, by one person for himself or for others, through sense observation; nor yet through experiment, in a direct or scientific meaning. (Knight, 1961, p. 187)

For Knight, economics is a science that is narrowly concerned with efficiently achieving given ends – such as the maximization of utility or profit. It is a science, but it is an intentional, not a positivistic, science.

The distinction between the second and third categories under the heading of 'motivated or problem-solving' behaviour is more subtle. The second category, abstract or socially motivated action, is human behaviour that is not explicitly goal directed (economic), but is also not concerned with value formation (not 'value deliberative'). Examples include behaviour that is done 'simply out of curiosity' or is 'purely exploratory' (Knight, 1935c, p. 5) – things like 'sport' and 'play'. Such activities do not involve achieving any specific goal; they are just done for entertainment or for exploration. The third category, value deliberative, is a very important category for Knight; it is behaviour that is 'value-seeking' or 'value-defining'. Humans, unlike other animals, choose their values; they decide what is right, what is good, and what they want to want. In Knight's words,

> But man is also a problem-solving entity at the higher level of critical deliberation about ends, or free choice of ends on the basis of thinking .... That is, he is a being

> who seeks, and in a real sense creates, values. The essential significance of this is the fact that man is interested in changing himself, even to changing the ultimate core of his being. … In contrast with natural objects – even with higher animals – man is unique in that he is dissatisfied with himself; he is the discontented animal, the romantic, argumentative, aspiring animal. (Knight, 1982, pp. 281–2)

The main point of Knight's pluralism is that when *considering human beings, and particularly when considering social policy, it is necessary to consider all six of these categories*. Human behaviour can not be reduced to the categories of positivistic science since humans are motivated and intentional agents – economic, goal-directed behaviour matters. By the same token, there is much more to a science of social policy than merely economics; in addition to being rational goal-seeking agents (and physical, and biological, systems) human beings also 'play' and choose their own values. Humans are physical, biological, historically contingent, rational-purposeful, arbitrary, social, and value determining; any knowledge we have of human society must recognize this pluralism.

While Knight was primarily concerned with the mistake of carrying over the 'categories of natural science into the field of social relations' and the 'supreme catastrophe' or 'suicide' of 'intelligence itself' (Knight, 1935c, p. 20) such scientism would entail, he was also critical of any attempt to discuss social policy from the narrow perspective of only one of these points of view: including economic theory. The rational economic man of neoclassical economic theory is, for Knight, a useful abstraction that is fundamental to economics as a (motivational) science, but it is just one tool for understanding human society. Knight freely admits the restricted vision of pure economics.

> Economic laws in any very strict and distinctive meaning are reached through isolating by abstraction a particular aspect of conduct and ignoring much that is quite as real and important: The economic view is important, intellectually and practically, but we must not make applications that disregard other and equally significant considerations. Account must be taken of all views or approaches, in their proper relations and perspective. (Knight, 1946, p. 111)[15]

Although a detailed discussion of Knight's view of social policy is beyond the scope of this chapter – it would require an inquiry into the nature of his particular brand of 'liberalism' and his views on democracy and democratic consensus[16] – it is clear that his view is inexorably intertwined with his pluralism about humans and human society. He is a pluralist about the categories of human inquiry, and a pluralist about the variety of approaches that must be involved in social policy, but he is not a pluralist about economic theory. Economic science is the narrow investigation of goal-directed rationality: the actions of rational economic man. For Knight it is this type of rational goal-directed activity that defines 'the economic'. But Knight also recognized that there is much more to human life than that which is purely economic.

## 4. CONCLUSION

In conclusion I would like to point out just two of the many possible lessons that can be learned from Knight's pluralism and its relationship to contemporary contextualist ideas.

First, *much of contemporary contextualism is not new*. Although philosophers writing in this genre are usually quite clear about this – witness Rorty's (1979) frequent references to Nietzsche, Heidegger and Dewey – economists eager to apply the most recent philosophical developments often seem to lose sight of this fact. This is particularly troublesome when the author is advocating a more historically sensitive approach to the discipline of economics – history should begin at home. In the above discussion I have shown that many aspects of Frank Knight's philosophical position are quite consistent with recent contextualist trends.[17] Although I focused exclusively on Knight, I suspect that a similar story could be told for many other twentieth-century economists who were influential prior to the post-war hegemony of mathematical economics and econometrics. There is much to learn from this earlier generation of economists, and that includes some things about contemporary contextualism.

Second, I think it is important to note that Knight's pluralism did not imply a theoretical pluralism about pure economic theory. Knight retained a relatively pristine view of economics while recognizing the extraordinary complexity of the social world. Perhaps there is a tension here that is problematic for Knight,[18] but perhaps not. The point is not really about Knight, it is about the 'inevitability' of theoretical pluralism. The question is whether theoretical pluralism – or at least the support for a theoretical view that is fundamentally different from rational choice theory – is necessarily an implication of being sympathetic to contemporary contextualism. Knight's work clearly indicates that this quite common presumption needs to be carefully re-examined.

## NOTES

1. As Jürgen Habermas characterizes the situation, '[C]ontextualism has become a manifestation of the spirit of the times. Transcendental thinking once concerned itself with a stable stock of forms for which there were no recognizable alternatives. Today, in contrast, the experience of contingency is a whirlpool into which everything is pulled: everything could also be otherwise, the categories of understanding, the principles of socialization and of morals, the constitution of subjectivity, the foundation of rationality itself' (Habermas, 1992, p. 139).

2. See Caldwell (1988 and 1991) and Hands (1993a).
3. McCloskey (1985 and 1994) and Klamer *et al.* (1988).
4. The variety of theoretical views consistent with the rhetoric of economics is clear in Klamer and McCloskey (1989).
5. See Amariglio, Resnick and Wolff (1993) for a discussion of how these authors view the relationship between their position and other epistemological and theoretical strategies in economics.
6. The single best statement of this view remains the original statement by Hahn *et al.* (1973).
7. The argument that economics is based on unobservable intentional concepts is a main theme in Alexander Rosenberg's recent book (1992). For Rosenberg though, unlike Knight, this presents a problem for economics. For Knight, economics is intentional and thus different from natural science, but that is not something problematic for economics; the human sciences are, should be, and must be, different from the natural sciences. I speculated about how Knight would respond to Rosenberg's critique in Hands (1993b).
8. Also see Knight (1931, pp. 62–3; 1935b, p. 81; 1946, p. 109; and 1961, p. 161).
9. Knight's recognition of the problem of theory-ladenness is discussed by Daniel Hammond in his article on Knight's anti-positivism. 'Knight claimed that the primary observational data of the external world require testing themselves and that this testing is inherently a theoretical exercise. Therefore observational data cannot be prior to theory, and influence must run both from data to theory and from theory to data' (Hammond, 1991, p. 371).
10. McKinney (1977) argues that Knight's social constructivism is at odds with his individualistic economic theory; he calls 'Knight's combination of radical individualism and sociological determinism the basic *pluralistic paradox*' (p. 1445; emphasis mine). In relating Knight's work to contemporary debates it is interesting to note that McKinney's criticism of Knight is essentially the same as Mirowski's (1987, 1992) criticism of McCloskey.
11. Hammond discusses Knight's social constructivism in the context of Knight's criticism of MacIver's *Social Causation* (1942): 'Knight's major criticism of MacIver was that he had not adequately confronted the social character of knowledge. Knight emphasized that *all* knowledge not just knowledge of society, is social. In all of our inquiries we are confronted by the fact that we simultaneously stand outside and inside our object' (Hammond, 1991, p. 376; emphasis in original).
12. Pluralism is a sufficiently dominant theme that it is often discussed in the secondary literature on Knight's work. For example:

    > From James, Knight takes the concept of *pluralism*, which becomes the dominant theme of his moral and social philosophy. ... Each of these 'universes' has its own kind of truth which may contradict the truth of other universes. (McKinney, 1977, p. 1439; emphasis in original)

    > He had the uncommon gift (and the curse!) of the compound eye; human society appeared to his perception through many angles of view which compelled a projection that was a mosaic of great riches, complexity, and ultimately, mystery. (Gordon, 1974, p. 571)

    > He applied his philosophical ideas to develop a pluralistic theory of human nature and conduct, a notion that influenced his views regarding the social aspects of economic activity and the proper method of ethical analysis. (Kasper, 1993, pp. 414–15)

13. This particular form of the six-way classification is from Knight (1956, p. 173), but variations of the scheme appear in a number of different papers: 1935c, p. 2; 1935d, p. 327; and 1982, pp. 286–7 for example.
14. Knight makes it very difficult for his readers because he uses the term 'science' in at least three different ways. First, and most narrowly, is 'positivist science'; this is science that could be done, and perhaps is done, in the way that science is characterized by the Vienna Circle. Knight wants to argue that sciences like physics are positivistic sciences, and yet

he also argues that even physics is not as 'positivistic', in particular not as 'empiricist', as the positivist philosophers seem to think. The second, much broader, category is what I would call 'theoretical science'; this includes almost any theoretical inquiry that attempts to predict and explain empirical phenomena. This second use corresponds most closely to the way that the term 'science' is used in the English language. Knight's third use of the term is even more broad; it corresponds roughly to the continental usage where 'science' means any systematic or rigorous inquiry. This latter use of the term science would also include many fields considered to be 'humanities' in Anglo-American academic culture.

15. As Knight said in a letter to Clarence Ayres dated 25 August 1941,

> I have said 'hundreds of times' that the theory of competition takes the individual as given, as to their 'wants, resources, and technology'; but that it is absurd for either general social theory, or social policy, to take this point of view. It is really from this point onward that I have tried to contribute something, all this seems to me so obvious. (Samuels, 1977, p. 510)

16. I suggest Gordon (1974) and Kasper (1993) on these matters.
17. And given Knight's pragmatist background, his views seem to have the same philosophical origins as the views of a neo-pragmatist such as Rorty.
18. As argued by McKinney (1977); see note 10.

## REFERENCES

Amariglio, J., Resnick, S. and Wolff, R.D. (1993), 'Division and Difference in the "Discipline" of Economics', in E. Messer-Davidow, D.R. Shumway and D.J. Sylvan (eds), *Knowledges: Historical and Critical Studies in Disciplinarity*, Charlottesville, VA: University of Virginia Press, pp. 150–84.

Caldwell, B.J. (1982), *Beyond Positivism: Economic Methodology in the Twentieth Century*, London: Allen & Unwin.

Caldwell, B.J. (1988), 'The Case for Pluralism', in N. De Marchi (ed.), *The Popperian Legacy in Economics*, Cambridge: Cambridge University Press, pp. 231–44.

Caldwell, B.J. (1991), 'Clarifying Popper', *Journal of Economic Literature*, **29**, pp. 1–33.

Ferber, M.A. and Nelson, J.A. (eds) (1993), *Beyond Economic Man: Feminist Theory and Economics*, Chicago: University of Chicago Press.

Gordon, H.S. (1974), 'Frank Knight and the Tradition of Liberalism', *Journal of Political Economy*, **82**, pp. 571–7.

Habermas, J. (1992), *Postmetaphysical Thinking*, Cambridge, MA: MIT Press.

Hahn, H., Neurath, O. and Carnap, R. (1973), *The Scientific Conception of the World: The Vienna Circle*, Dordrecht, Holland: D. Reidel Publishing. (Originally published as 'Wissenschaftliche Weltauffassung: Der Wiener Kres' in 1929.)

Hammond, J.D. (1991), 'Frank Knight's Antipositivism', *History of Political Economy*, **23**, pp. 359–81.

Hands, D.W. (1993a), *Testing, Rationality, and Progress: Essays on the Popperian Tradition in Economic Methodology*, Laham, MD: Rowman & Littlefield.

Hands, D.W. (1993b), 'Frank Knight's Review of Alexander Rosenberg's *Economics: Mathematical Politics or Science of Diminishing Returns?*', University of Puget Sound Department of Economics Working Paper 93–4.

Kasper, S.D. (1993), 'Frank Knight's Case for Laissez Faire: The Patrimony of the

Social Philosophy of the Chicago School', *History of Political Economy*, **25**, pp. 413–33.
Klamer, A., McCloskey, D. and Solow, R.M. (eds) (1988), *The Consequences of Economic Rhetoric*, Cambridge: Cambridge University Press.
Klamer, A. and McCloskey, D. (1989), 'The Rhetoric of Disagreement', *Rethinking Marxism*, **2**, pp. 140–61.
Knight, F. (1922), 'Ethics and the Economic Interpretation', *Quarterly Journal of Economics*, **36**, pp. 454–81.
Knight, F. (1925), 'Fact and Metaphysics in Economic Psychology', *American Economic Review*, **15**, pp. 247–66.
Knight, F. (1931), 'Relation of Utility Theory to Economic Method in the Work of William Stanley Jevons and Others', in Stuart A. Rice (ed.), *Methods in Social Science*, Chicago: University of Chicago Press, pp. 59–69.
Knight, F. (1935a), 'The Limitations of Scientific Method in Economics', in *The Ethics of Competition and Other Essays*, New York: Harper & Brothers, pp. 105–47.
Knight, F. (1935b), 'Economic Psychology and the Value Problem', in *The Ethics of Competition and Other Essays*, New York: Harper & Brothers, pp. 76–104. (Originally published in *The Quarterly Journal of Economics*, **39**, 1925.)
Knight, F. (1935c), 'Social Science and Social Action', *The International Journal of Ethics*, **46**, pp. 1–33.
Knight, F. (1935d), 'Economic Theory and Nationalism', in *The Ethics of Competition and Other Essays*, New York: Harper & Brothers, pp. 277–335.
Knight, F. (1944), 'Realism and Relevance in the Theory of Demand', *Journal of Political Economy*, **52**, pp. 289–318.
Knight, F. (1946), 'Immutable Law in Economics: Its Reality and Limitations', *American Economic Review*, **36**, pp. 93–111.
Knight, F. (1956), '"What Is Truth" in Economics?', in *On The History and Method of Economics*, Chicago: University of Chicago Press, pp. 151–78. (Originally published in *Journal of Political Economy*, **48**, 1940.)
Knight, F. (1961), 'Methodology in Economics – Part I', *Southern Economic Journal*, **27**, pp. 185–95.
Knight, F. (1982), 'Fact and Value in Social Science', in *Freedom and Reform: Essays in Economics and Social Philosophy*, Indianapolis, IN: Liberty Press, pp. 268–92. (Originally published in 1942.)
McCloskey, D. (1985), *The Rhetoric of Economics*, Madison: University of Wisconsin Press.
McCloskey, D. (1994), *Knowledge and Persuasion in Economics*, Cambridge: Cambridge University Press.
MacIver, R.M. (1942), *Social Causation*, Boston: Ginn & Co.
McKinney, J. (1977), 'Frank H. Knight on Uncertainty and Rational Action', *Southern Economic Journal*, **43**, pp. 1438–52.
Mirowski, P. (1987), 'Shall I Compare Thee to a Minkowski–Ricardo–Leontief–Metzler Matrix of the Mosak–Hicks Type?', *Economics and Philosophy*, **3**, pp. 67–96.
Mirowski, P. (1992), 'Three Vignettes on the State of Economic Rhetoric', in N. De Marchi (ed.), *Post-Popperian Methodology of Economics: Recovering Practice*, Boston: Kluwer Academic, pp. 235–59.
Rescher, N. (1993), *Pluralism: Against the Demand for Consensus*, Oxford: Clarendon Press.

Resnick, S. and Wolff, R.D. (1987), *Knowledge and Class: A Marxian Critique of Political Economy*, Chicago: University of Chicago Press.
Rorty, R. (1979), *Philosophy and the Mirror of Nature*, Princeton, NJ: Princeton University Press.
Rosenberg, A. (1992), *Economics – Mathematical Politics or Science of Diminishing Returns?*, Chicago: University of Chicago Press.
Samuels, W.J. (1977), 'The Knight–Ayres Correspondence: The Grounds of Knowledge and Social Action', *Journal of Economic Issues*, **11**, pp. 485–525.
Weintraub, E.R. (1991), *Stabilizing Dynamics: Constructing Economic Knowledge*, Cambridge: Cambridge University Press.

# COMMENT

**John B. Davis**

Wade Hands has given us a valuable and intriguing account of Frank Knight's methodological thinking, arguing that Knight reasoned much as do contemporary 'contextualists', opposing positivism and scientism about social science, and often adopting hermeneutical strategies in a social constructivist manner that served to emphasize the social character of human knowledge. At the same time, Hands notes that Knight's methodological pluralism was accompanied by a theoretical monism. Whereas Knight was a pluralist about the various categories of human inquiry, he also held the traditional neoclassical view that economics is the investigation of goal-directed rationality, where 'economic laws in any very strict and distinctive meaning are reached through isolating by abstraction a particular aspect of conduct and ignoring much that is quite as real and important' (Knight, 1946, p. 111). Other approaches to economic analysis Knight resisted. In particular, Knight was often critical of institutionalist thinking which had a much wider following at the time when he wrote than it does now. Hands suggests that there may be a tension here, and indeed some have argued that this is indeed the case (McKinney, 1977). I would like to argue that Knight's example – the combination of a methodological pluralism and theoretical monism – raises interesting questions regarding the nature of pluralism itself. Many, it seems fair to say, might suppose that the openness methodological pluralism implies should also apply to economic theory. That is, methodological pluralism should go hand in hand with theoretical pluralism. Is this the case?

An important idea behind methodological pluralism is that no single approach seems fully satisfactory as an explication of economic method, whether it is the sort of normative, rule-based approach of the Popperians or rather purely descriptive efforts to understand economists' practice of more recent vintage (e.g., de Marchi, 1992). Given this, economic methodologists should be open to different methodological approaches. A posture of methodological openness would then in turn seem to imply the need for an accompanying theoretical pluralism, since different methodological strategies are likely to give credibility to different kinds of economic theory. One then might be termed a theoretical pluralist were one – contra Knight – to believe that among the different kinds of economic theory none is superior to all others. Different kinds of theory, it might thus be said, suit different explanatory purposes, and since we have many such purposes, we must also have many kinds of economic theory.

A view not unlike this has been expressed by Bruce Caldwell in a discussion of contemporary trends in methodological thinking (1989). Caldwell distinguishes between a traditional methodological thinking meant to tease out the implications of the philosophy of science for economics and more recent efforts on the part of economic methodologists to explain the actual practice of economists. Methodological pluralism emerges in this new environment, because methodologists seem to be less inclined to impose abstract philosophical views on economics, and because they recognize that economists' practices are not easily reducible to pre-given theoretical categories. Indeed, economists' practices often cut across different theoretical approaches. Thus methodological work in economics needs to be pluralist, because the practical strategies and modes of argument of economists are themselves diverse and irreducible to one another.

I think there is considerable plausibility to this view, but wonder whether economists and particularly economic theorists are likely to be as sympathetic to the idea of being pluralistic and openminded in the way that many economic methodologists have now argued is desirable. Knight is a case in point. If we give him the benefit of the doubt, and suppose that he was reasonably well aware of the particular combination of postures he embraced – methodological pluralism and theoretical monism – then we must conclude that he likely rejected arguments like the ones advanced above, and thought rather that a methodological pluralism should go hand in hand with theoretical monism. How might he have argued such a thing?

One might conclude that methodological pluralism goes hand in hand with theoretical monism were one to argue as follows. We again say that different methodological strategies are likely to give credibility to different types of economic theory. Now suppose additionally that different types of economic theory are essentially distinct in that they share no substantive concepts or principles, while economic theorists deny that no theory is fully adequate. Indeed, different economic theorists believe that their own theories are correct, and that those of others are mistaken. Then, if it is still believed that no methodological approaches are fully adequate, economic theorists may be both theoretical monists and methodological pluralists. They accept that there is no method for demonstrating the superiority of their own theoretical views, but nonetheless continue to believe in that superiority. As Warren Samuels, in his contribution to this volume and conference, puts the situation, methodological pluralism involves not a *theoretical tolerance*, but rather a *practical tolerance*. Because we do not agree about different types of economic theory, we agree to adopt a 'live and let live' strategy at a methodological level, and accordingly methodological pluralism only arises in the context of competing theoretical monisms. Indeed, were we all truly theoretical pluralists and believed different theories all simultaneously correct, then it seems it would be redundant to call for a methodology of openness in the first place.

This argument, no doubt, may seem counter-intuitive to many. Somehow, if one is open methodologically, one should also be open theoretically. But as Hands notes, many of those who are the strongest proponents of methodological pluralism – heterodox economists – are entirely critical of neoclassical economics. Their motivation, I would conjecture, is not that their own theoretical approaches are *also* correct – a theoretical pluralist view – but rather that neoclassical economics is mistaken and misguided in its most basic assumptions, and that their own approaches remedy the deficiencies of neoclassicism – a theoretical monist view. In practice, then, theoretical monism often seems to accompany methodological pluralism. Heterodox economists and neoclassical economists dispute the worth of each other's approaches, and sometimes also the worth of their associated methodological strategies, but tend to maintain an openness on the latter score, because methodological disputes appear irresolvable while economic theories are thought distinct and non-overlapping.

Where does Caldwell's view stand in relation to all of this? Recall that his view is focused on practices rather than on the sort of paradigmatic approaches to theory implicitly referred to above. Practices, it is probably fair to say, can be shared across paradigms, which themselves arguably do not share substantive concepts and principles. For example, both neo-Ricardian and neoclassical theory rely on the practice of reasoning in general equilibrium terms, but are at the same time radically different in that the former uses a production-based approach to value, where the latter uses an exchange-based approach to value. We could of course speak of a theoretical pluralism at the level of practices, and in that sense methodological pluralism and theoretical pluralism would presumably go hand in hand. But thinking about economic theory usually involves paradigm-specific level concepts and principles, and in this sense it seems that the isolation of theories as paradigms from one another implies methodological pluralism is better understood as a *practical tolerance for theoretical intolerance.*

Put in these terms, however, we can perhaps begin to see how the argument that methodological pluralism combined with theoretical monism manages to reach its conclusion. When economists dismiss other economists' paradigmatic approaches, they often tend to exaggerate those approaches and their own as monolithic, tightly structured, self-contained, non-communicating systems of theorization. They thus lend credibility to the second premise of our argument for the methodological pluralism–theoretical monism combination, namely, that different paradigms do not share substantive concepts or principles. But of course though theories can be represented by assumptions regarded as paradigm-specific, assumptions also tend to be subject to different interpretations. Indeed assumptions subject to different interpretations often distinguish different camps *within* broader approaches or paradigms, such as when different types of Keynesians are distinguished by competing interpretations of assumptions about labour markets. This suggests that theories or paradigms may not really have the self-contained, non-communicating character that is needed to drive the Knightian, pluralism–monism argument above to its conclusion. If different approaches within paradigms share assumptions differently interpreted, then it is also reasonable to think that entirely different paradigms share assumptions differently interpreted. On this view, paradigms are rarely as distinct as they are often made out to be, so that it turns out that the business of describing what theoretical monism amounts to is not all that clear.

I want to suggest that these conclusions point toward an interesting comment on methodological pluralism and pluralism in general. Theoretical monist projects of compartmentalizing kinds of theory, it seems, can be said to depend upon our having what may be termed *identity criteria* for individuating different paradigms or discourses as distinct and non-communicating. That is, just as one distinguishes and differentiates individuals by establishing criteria for how we identify and distinguish one person from another, so speaking of individual paradigms or discourses in economic theory or other disciplines requires that we explain the terms on which we identify and distinguish one paradigm or discourse from another. Can it be said that there do indeed exist identity conditions for individuating discourses from one to the next as the Knight position requires? The irony is that in supposing we might achieve agreement on identity conditions for individuating discourses as seemingly non-communicating we thereby presuppose some shared meta-discourse, the existence of which would itself bring into question the project of distinguishing discourses as distinct and non-communicating. And surely any shared meta-discourse regarding what distinguishes different paradigms in economics would require a background field of substantive concepts and notions common to different paradigms as the principal resource for making the distinctions registered between paradigms. Paradigms on this reading would then be only relatively distinct, and their non-communication would then chiefly be a matter of the *practical* intolerance of different theorists towards each other's different approaches.

It seems, then, that Knight was mistaken in adopting a strong theoretical monist view of economic theory, and that he would have done well to think further about the relationship between methodology and theory. But on the argument here this would not imply that one should simply fall back upon the methodological pluralism–theoretical pluralism position first advanced above. Indeed, given what has just been argued, there is still some truth to Knight's view of the relation between methodology and theory. First, when theorists stress the autonomy and adequacy of their respective approaches, they automatically invite methodologists' commentary on identity conditions for paradigms and encourage the argument that theories are only relatively autonomous. Their theoretical monism is thus leavened with an element of pluralism. Second, when methodologists emphasize their openness to different methodological strategies in regard to the credibility these strategies offer to different kinds of theory, they implicitly place themselves in agreement with one another on the need to elaborate identity conditions to distinguish different kinds of theory. Their methodological pluralism is thus leavened with an element of monism. Both theorists and methodologists, that is, really have more hybrid sorts of views than initially appears the case, and this takes us beyond both of the views advanced above.

Is there a straightforward way to characterize this third combination of methodology and theory? Methodologists need to be aware that there are limits to openness. Theorists need to be aware that there are limits to closemindedness. In effect methodological pluralists need to develop rational forms of intolerance, and theorists would be better off being a bit more tolerant towards one another. For the former this is a theoretical matter, the business of elaborating a shared discourse regarding identity criteria for paradigms. For the latter this is a matter of civility and good conduct toward others, essentially a practical concern. Our final position thus combines something of a theoretically intolerant methodological pluralism with a more practically tolerant theoretical monism. The first half of this pair sets an agenda for future development of methodological pluralism.

## References

Caldwell, Bruce (1989), 'The Trend of Methodological Thinking', *Ricerche Economiche,* **XLIII** (1–2), pp. 8–20.

De Marchi, Neil (ed.) (1992), *Post-Popperian Methodology of Economics: Recovering Practice,* Dordrecht: Kluwer.

Knight, Frank (1946), 'Immutable Laws in Economics: Its Reality and Limitations', *American Economic Review*, **36**, pp. 93–111.

McKinney, J. (1977), 'Frank H. Knight on Uncertainty and Rational Action', *Southern Economic Journal*, **43**, pp. 1438–52.

# 11. Is 'is a precursor of' a transitive relation?

**E. Roy Weintraub**

## 1. INTRODUCTION

In a number of recent papers,[1] and in my recent book,[2] I have explored the implications of the idea that the history of economics is neither found nor discovered. I have argued that history is a creation,[3] a construction by the community of economists. The facts of the history are fluid and mutable since relevant ideas change as the identity and interests of readers and hearers change and as the community of economists itself is concerned with first one, then another, local and contingent problem.

One of the ways in which this construction of the past occurs is through the scholarly disputations of historians of economics. Other changes transpire through the efforts of expositors who seek to explain specialized economic arguments to broader classes of economist-readers. But less well understood is the way in which the past is transformed in the economist-community's understanding through the actions of economists: that is, in constructing a bit of economic analysis, and placing it in the hands of other members of the community who appreciate the craft and can be changed in their thinking by the piece of work, individual economists frequently appeal to the past and to shared understandings of that past.

In usual practice, a scholarly paper partakes of a shared vision of what is understood, but that shared vision must be asserted and, by the assertion, it implicitly problematizes alternative understandings. To make this point, I intend to show how the creation of a model simultaneously creates and is created by history. Of course this history is a creation of and by language, but it has some of its own dimensions, and the historiographic questions are not entirely addressed in their linguistic dimension. This historiographic element of discussions about methodology is hardly ever remarked upon.

## 2. THE ARROW–HURWICZ PAPER

Sometimes 'Science' is best examined through the trail of scientific papers. That is, if we wish to study a bit of science, we may read and study the scientific paper as the primary instantiation of scientific practice. If we seek to understand economic model building, we are well advised to begin by reading economic articles which purport to construct models. That is where I too will start.

To make matters specific, I shall consider a paper written several decades ago, but one which had a significant impact on its particular subdiscipline, or research programme; the paper thus lived on as it were in other works which were written later. Because I have written recently on the history of stability ideas, I shall consider the paper 'On the Stability of the Competitive Equilibrium, I' by Kenneth J. Arrow and Leonid Hurwicz which appeared in *Econometrica* in 1958. This paper, together with its companions 'On the Stability of the Competitive Equilibrium, II' (with the additional author, the mathematician H.D. Block) are generally taken to define the conclusion of a sequence of attempts to establish the stability of the competitive equilibrium, a problem outstanding in the economic theory literature.

The paper, of nearly 30 pages, has a six-section Introduction: section 1 sets out the context; 2, dynamic concepts, sets out the mathematical definitions of equilibrium and stability; 3, the adjustment process, suggests two explicit models of market dynamics and frames them in the mathematics of dynamical systems; 4 and 5, on excess demands, connect the dynamic process so defined to the underlying market behaviours; and 6 presents a summary of results. It is the two-paragraph untitled introductory remarks to the Introduction which I want to consider. For convenience, I reproduce it here:

> A great deal of work has been done recently on what one may call the static aspects of competitive equilibrium, its existence, uniqueness, and optimality. [footnote 2] This work is characterized, in the main, by being based on models whose assumptions are formulated in terms of certain properties of the individual economic units, although in the last analysis it is the nature of the aggregate excess demand functions that determines the properties of equilibria.
>
> With regard to dynamics, especially the stability of equilibrium, much remains to be done. The concept of stability, used already by the nineteenth century economists [footnote 3] in its modern sense, did not receive systematic treatment in the context of economic dynamics until Samuelson's paper of 1941. Samuelson, however, did not fully explore the implications of the assumptions underlying the perfectly competitive model. He (as well as Lange, Metzler, and Morishima) focused attention on the relationship between 'true dynamic stability' and the concept of 'stability' as defined by Hicks in *Value and Capital,* rather than on whether under a given set of assumptions stability (in either sense) would prevail or not. [footnote 4] Even though the Hicksian concept does not, in general,

> coincide with that of 'true dynamic stability', it is of considerable interest to us for two reasons: first, as shown by the writers just cited, there are situations where the two concepts are equivalent; second, because the equilibrium whose 'stability' Hicks studied is indeed competitive equilibrium. [footnote 5] But again, little is known about conditions under which Hicksian stability prevails. There is thus a gap in this field and our aim is to help fill it. The task consists in constructing a formal dynamic model whose characteristics reflect the nature of the competitive process and in examining its stability properties, given assumptions as to the properties of the individual units or of the aggregate excess demand functions. The results here presented cover certain special classes of cases and many important questions remain open.

The Introduction's first sentence notes the previous work on what the authors call static equilibrium theory, and refers (footnote 2) to results by Wald, Hotelling, Lange, Debreu, Arrow, Arrow and Debreu, McKenzie, Nikaido, Gale and Uzawa. This sentence defines the immediate context of this paper as a successor to the work done on existence, uniqueness and optimality of the competitive equilibrium by the named authors. The second sentence characterizes that work as having been concerned with the characteristics of the particular equilibrium that emerges in models based on individual economic units, or agents, and implicitly on the market behaviours that are linked to the individual behaviours. The one interesting point to note here, in this history, is that although the papers written by Abraham Wald in the early 1930s are cited, the paper by John von Neumann of 1936 on equilibrium is not cited, reflecting perhaps the author's belief that that paper was not part of the sequence of investigations which led to the Arrow–Debreu–McKenzie model and proofs of existence of a competitive equilibrium. Certainly the papers by Nikaido, Gale and Uzawa were extensions, and refinements, of the papers on existence done by Arrow and Debreu and McKenzie.

The second paragraph leaves issues of static equilibrium. The first sentence sets up the reader's expectations for the current paper with its claim that with regard to dynamics, especially stability, 'much remains to be done'. Note first that stability is here presented as a subcategory, a subproblem, in the larger context of dynamics. Second, it is left unargued that statics is now settled, while stability is unsettled, leaving the reader to expect that that problem is now, in the paper being read, to be taken up and at least partially settled. Recall the title has a comma followed by a 'I', which suggests at least 'II' if not 'III' to follow in due course.

Although Wald had written 25 years earlier than 1958, the historicization of the Arrow–Hurwicz argument appears in the next sentence most clearly where it is asserted that stability was 'used already by the nineteenth century economists in its modern sense'. Here we are given page references to Cournot, Walras and Marshall.

Going back to these references, we see indeed that in Cournot there is a reference to 'no other system of values but the one resulting from these equations being compatible with a state of stable equilibrium'.[4] And in Walras we read that

> Such an equilibrium is exactly similar to that of a suspended body of which the centre of gravity lies directly beneath the point of suspension, so if this centre of gravity were displaced from the vertical line beneath the point of suspension, it would automatically return to its original position through the force of gravitation. This equilibrium is, therefore, stable.[5]

The last word here has a translator's note of some significance. That note 5 to Walras's Lesson 7 has been a major source of controversy in the Walras industry, for in it Jaffee cites Walras's contentious claim to priority in discussing stability, and Marshall's counterclaim, and Samuelson's assertion that Walras did not really understand the issues very clearly at all. In Marshall, we read in Appendix H about supply and demand curves intersecting in several points, and are led to characterize the various equilibria (intersections) as stable and unstable in the famous passage:

> When demand and supply are in unstable equilibrium then if the scale of production be disturbed ever so little from its equilibrium position, it will move rapidly away to one of its positions of stable equilibrium; as an egg if balanced on one of its ends would at the smallest shake fall down and lie lengthways …[6]

The second half of the Arrow–Hurwicz sentence suggests that these nineteenth-century contributions must be considered as unsystematic, for stability did not appear in the context of economic dynamics until Samuelson's paper of 1941. But that paper too had a defect since it did not explore the connections between, presumably, the dynamic processes and the 'underlying perfectly competitive model'. Samuelson, as well as Lange, Metzler and Morishima had rather, according to Arrow and Hurwicz, examine the 'relationship between "true dynamic stability" and the concept of "stability" as defined by Hicks in *Value and Capital*.' The reader is led thus to ask why this was the particular problem attacked by the cited economists. Why was there not the more natural examination of the problem 'whether under a given set of assumptions stability (in either sense) would prevail or not)'? The Arrow–Hurwicz footnote here allows that Samuelson had, in one specific case, done what was being called for, but they imply that the problem remained unsolved at that date in its full generality.

The next sentence begins to create the paper's central problematic, for it argues that the Hicks conception, imperfect though it appears, 'is of considerable interest to us for two reasons'. The use of 'us', the first time the authors use the first person pronoun, brings the reader to a direct view of the authors' perspective: we are invited to share in their vision, to see Hicks's contribution, as they themselves do, as an approach to the true solution to the real problem of establishing stability in an economic model. For although sometimes the Hicksian and true stability ideas coincide, it is also true that Hicks established stability, of his type, for an 'indeed competitive equilibrium'. Just so. The footnote here, number 5, historicizes the assertion, claiming that in the case of two goods this Hicksian problem was 'studied by Walras [in the section discussed above] although without a formal dynamic framework'. This leaves Arrow and Hurwicz's reader to ponder the incompleteness of the Walrasian analysis, a tension created by the use of the Whiggish 'although'. 'But again, little is known about conditions under which Hicksian stability prevails' leads immediately to the reader's expectation that shortly thereafter the authors will provide such conditions. The next sentence satisfies the expectation and leaves matters clearer: 'There is thus a gap in this field and our aim is to help fill it.' Again, the first person enlists the reader's trust, trust that not only is the claim that there is a problematic 'gap' accurate, but that the authors will, not fill it but rather a bit more modestly, 'help fill it'.

The penultimate sentence of this section then defines 'The task' ahead in the paper, the set of expectations that measures the article's success or failure by completion of the named task to construct 'a formal dynamic model' with certain assumptions, characteristics and properties. The final sentence reins in those expectations, qualifies them as it were, by restricting the paper's attention to 'certain special cases' and thus leaves the reader to appreciate that overall the task is difficult for 'many important questions remain open', and will not be answered in the paper the reader is about to study.

## 3. MEMORIES

One way to begin to reconstruct the history of any scientific paper is to encourage the authors themselves to recall just what they were doing when they wrote the paper. In the case of the 1958 stability paper, we are in the fortunate position that both Arrow and Hurwicz have recently been asked quite directly, in interviews, to reconstruct the circumstances and motivations that were responsible for the stability paper's being written.[7] In response to a question from the interviewer, George Feiwel, about the 'genesis and essence of your work on stability' Arrow replied as follows:

> That, of course, is more derivative than some of my other work. Stability theory is actually a very old theme, really first discussed by Mill … . Samuelson provided a formalization that in fact captured in a general equilibrium sense the intuitive

ideas of stability that had been expressed for the most part in a partial equilibrium context. Of course, Walras had made an attempt at a general equilibrium formalization of stability. So, in that sense, the problem had been set forth by Samuelson in his papers in 1941.

In a way, what Leo Hurwicz and I and others were trying to do was essentially to carry out the Samuelson programme and to extend it. Samuelson had a few cases of stability; we tried to extend this in various ways (Metzler had made a very important contribution there). One of the things Leo and I were trying to do was to extend it to global analysis rather than local analysis. Actually, one of the immediate impulses was a somewhat different kind of stability, namely, in programming problems. That again was due to Samuelson. Samuelson had discussed stability, using economic ideas, in the context of linear programming methods. Of course, you are aware that there was an important strand of thought about stability in a socialist system which was in a way between stability of a competitive equilibrium and stability of a programming problem which is a method of optimization. Paul had argued that if you apply straightforward methods in a linear programming system you get cycles.

Leo and I started out by re-examining that question and, in particular, to extend it also to non-linear programming. We got some important results in this simpler context of general equilibrium. Having done that we got interested in the stability concept in the broader context of general equilibrium theory. We used the standard method in stability theory that had not been used in economics – the so-called Lyapunov method for analyzing global stability.

The other author of the stability paper, Leonid Hurwicz, remembered the nature and development of the stability paper collaboration in the following way:

The three areas [of programming, stability, and design of resource allocation mechanisms] were closely related, at least in their technical aspects: While the first topic dealt with the static aspects of non-linear programming, we then proceeded to the dynamic aspects of linear and non-linear programming … . When we shifted to a study of stability of competitive equilibrium, we started out with the thought of applying the techniques we had developed … namely the so-called gradient method. (It was Samuelson who had pioneered the use of the gradient method in programming models.) We thought that that method, originally designed for the programming problems would also work in the context of competitive equilibrium and would enable us to determine whether, and under what conditions, competitive equilibrium is or is not stable. So we sort of got into competitive equilibrium theory through programming theory, and we got into dynamics through our initial work on statics … . [It] was natural to interpret the dynamics of programming as a certain kind of mechanism for resource allocation. It then became very clear that this kind of interpretation brought us very close to the earlier work of two groups of economists.

One group was composed of people who talked a lot about stability, the main ones being Hicks and Samuelson; the other group consisted of people like Lange and Lerner who were designing a certain kind of economic system. As we started looking at the work of the first group we were struck by the following: On the one hand, you have the work of Hicks which did utilize the concept of competitive

> equilibrium ... but whose concepts of stability were not in accordance with the modern notion of what stability means in a dynamic sense. On the other hand, the work of Samuelson was modern in spirit as far as the dynamics was concerned, but it did not exploit fully the specific properties of stability of competitive equilibrium as opposed to any other kind of equilibrium. We noticed there was a gap in the economists' understanding of this problem ...

There are a number of interesting features of these interviews. Most importantly for our understanding of context is the recollection that the context of the stability paper was not what the paper construed as context in its introductory section. The programming context is missing. Also missing is the context of the design of resource allocation mechanisms. Both authors of this paper recollect a bit differently of course, with Arrow placing a bit less emphasis than does Hurwicz on the 'design' history which subject has so engaged Hurwicz's later intellectual career. Both though recall that their interest grew out of a concern with the difficulties of the gradient process as solution technique for solving programming problems. The question which one must ask is 'Why is the programming context of the 1958 stability paper not present in the paper, and why is the design of the resource allocation mechanism context not present in the paper?' Put another way, why was the problematic of the 1958 paper restricted to the 'gap' between the Hicks and Samuelson treatments of stability of equilibrium?

It is important to be clear here, for it is not the case that I am accusing Arrow and Hurwicz of inaccuracy or faulty memory, nor am I accusing them of falsifying the historical record in such a way that only an alert historian of economics can set the historical record straight for posterity. What we have is a conflict between, on the one hand, the paper's self-construction of the context for its creation and publication and, on the other hand, a later recollection of a threefold set of ideas which Arrow and Hurwicz contend had organized, and generated, the concerns of that 1958 paper on stability of a competitive equilibrium. One way to go about discussing this 'problem' is to take an epistemological stand on Truthfulness and The Facts Of The Matter. But I have no interest in thinking about the problem of which context is the true context. Nor do I believe that this is a problem that requires a solution, if by a solution one means the construction of a metanarrative in which the development of stability theory becomes an exemplar of some larger philosophical point (e.g. that what was really going on was the early stage of a Lakatosian research programme, or that there was a Kuhnian paradigm shift, or a Laudan problem-sequence, etc.). Instead, as a historian, I would suggest that it is possible to handle the disparate accounts of the motivation of the Arrow–Hurwicz paper by constructing a larger context in which the paper's 'history' and the recollected 'history' can be viewed together and related to a more complex version of the history itself. That is, what I wish to suggest is that each of the two versions is appropriate for its own purposes. Different histories are constructed for different purposes, and may be equally reasonable for those different purposes. Along the way to this point I shall construct several other histories which share this feature of problematizing the first two histories presented in the paper, and in the recollection, which make them 'false' as well. The historiographic point will become 'one, two, many histories': pluralistic history if you prefer. With that as the focus, let me return to the paper itself.

## 4. SAMUELSON

Recall the 1958 paper's comment that 'The concept of stability ... did not receive systematic treatment in the context of economic dynamics until Samuelson's paper of 1941'.[8] The authors went on to suggest, though, that 'Samuelson did not fully explore the implications of the assumptions underlying the perfectly competitive model'. This leaves the reader with the quite distinct view that Samuelson had at least partially explored those implications, or at the very least that Samuelson was concerned with the perfectly competitive model. This, however, was not the case at all. The structure of Samuelson's paper, which appeared later as Chapter IX of his 1947 *Foundations of Economic Analysis*, is clear on the point. After an introductory section, there follows a section on comparative statics in which that term is defined in the sense of a formal equilibrium model defined by a set of equations

$$f^i(x_1,\ldots,x_n,a)=0, \quad i=1,\ldots n.$$

The next section takes up the Frisch definitions of statics and dynamics and, for a general set of functional equations which include differential equations systems as a special case, defines what Samuelson calls perfect stability of the first kind, stability of the first kind in the small, and stability of the second kind. The reference for this material is G.D. Birkhoff's *Dynamical Systems*. I have discussed this connection between Samuelson's development of dynamical theory in economics, and his reliance on the works of Birkhoff, Emile Picard, J. Willard Gibbs, A. J. Lotka, Edwin Biddell Wilson, and others at length in another place,[9] so I will not repeat that set of arguments here. Instead, let me point out that the problems that concerned Samuelson were not the problems that concerned Arrow and Hurwicz. To see this, recall that Samuelson argued that 'in order for the comparative-statics analysis to yield fruitful results, we must first develop a theory of dynamics.' To the point, Samuelson's interest in dynamics was specifically associated with his concern to generate comparative statics propositions, for these propositions, he believed, were the operational theorems of economic theory. We could, as economists, operationalize our theories only if we framed them in terms like 'a change in such and such a direction of such and such a parameter would be associated with a rise (or fall) in the equilibrium price (or quantity)'. He argued, and later dubbed this argument the 'Correspondence Principle', that determinate comparative statics results could be derived from the assumption that the dynamic system was stable in some particular sense. The remainder of the section on stability and dynamics was devoted to a set of examples to illustrate this connection between 'dynamic stability' and comparative statics. For example, his case ends as, 'If our stability conditions are realized, the problem originally posed is answered. Price must rise when demand increases' (ibid., p. 103). His other exemplars of this idea are the Marshallian stability conditions, the cobweb, Marshall's trade dynamics, a combined stock-flow dynamic adjustment in a one-commodity market. Only in one section, 'The Stability of Multiple Markets', does Samuelson take up the Hicksian problem. There he simply frames the Hicks discussion in terms of his own stability definitions, and shows that, for example, in the symmetric case, '*Imperfect stability in the Hicks sense necessarily implies perfect stability and conversely*' (ibid., p. 111). The next, and final, section simply goes on to look at the Keynesian system in these same terms of dynamics and comparative statics.

Put most starkly, Samuelson was not concerned with the same set of problems that later concerned Arrow and Hurwicz, and thus to suggest that he left a 'gap' is to reframe Samuelson's contribution to make it part of a different line of inquiry. Samuelson was not a Walrasian, nor was he in any sense a general equilibrium theorist. Unlike Hicks, Samuelson's reading of Pareto was more influenced by the Harvard 'Pareto Circle' of the physiologist Lawrence J. Henderson than it was by the general equilibrium basis of Wicksell and Keynes, which was Hicks's concern. Moreover, Samuelson's view of statics and dynamics was linked more to Gibbs's physical chemistry as interpreted in social systems by E.B. Wilson than it was to Walrasian, or even Keynesian, issues. Thus Samuelson did not write on general equilibrium analysis in the flowering of that theory in the late 1940s and early 1950s, concerning himself instead in his mathematical economics with the mathematizing of capital theory, public goods theory, etc.

## 5. METZLER

Another individual discussed in the tradition called up by Arrow and Hurwicz was Lloyd Metzler (1913–80). In the area of concern to us, Arrow and

Hurwicz recall Metzler for his 1945 paper which examined the conditions under which Hicksian and 'true' stability would be consistent.[10] 'Metzler showed that if multiple markets are stable for any (relative) speeds of adjustment, then they must satisfy Hicks's concept of perfect stability.'[11] What I am interested in suggesting, however, is that this result is less connected to the ideas of the stability of a competitive equilibrium, and more connected to a set of issues about the nature and meaning of equilibrium and stability, issues which look back to the 1930s, not ahead to the 1950s. One of the ways to see this is to try to frame some of the ideas in Metzler's paper in terms of earlier work.

Metzler was a graduate student at Harvard, arriving there in 1937. Paul Samuelson had arrived at Harvard two years earlier, and was, by the late 1930s, finishing his Ph.D. work and enjoying some scholarly freedom as a member of Harvard's Society of Fellows. His influence on the graduate student population was profound, as can be seen from Metzler's classroom notes from Fall, 1938.[12] Metzler, attending Schumpeter's Economics 103 class on theory, received a thorough grounding in the classics of general equilibrium, Walras, Pareto, Barone, *et al.* But the class notes reflect a continuous exchange between Schumpeter and Samuelson who was probably attending the lectures. In November Metzler is reporting '[Schumpeter has an] Argument with Samuelson over Harrod's envelope curve' following an earlier discussion in class that 'Samuelson's original assumption will lead directly to all conditions on indifference curves' in the context of a lecture which concerned the fact that 'Schumpeter says Walras admits multiple equil. tho Marshall doesn't'. This probably refers to the revealed preference assumptions which Samuelson was writing up in 1938.

Most interesting is the hand-written note, dated 17 November, 1938, that 'Walras didn't prove solution was unique or even that it existed at all. Wald has shown that a simplified Walrasian system has a unique solution, Mathematical Colloquy [sic] of the University of Vienna.' This of course suggests that Metzler was informed about the most modern, and sophisticated, work on the existence of equilibrium in the Walrasian tradition. It also suggests that it was Samuelson, and his concerns, which tended to dominate discussions about economic theory at Harvard of what was important and significant in recent theoretical work in economics. Schumpeter, with his European connections, had more catholic intellectual tastes than had E.B. Wilson, Samuelson's unofficial mathematical mentor. And Samuelson was taken up with the problems which concerned Hicks. The Metzler paper of 1945 thus owes much more to Samuelson's influence than it does to the emergent neo-Walrasian programme fortified by Wald and von Neumann's contributions, and linked later to the stability literature noted by Arrow and Hurwicz.

The stability literature of the 1940s attempted to navigate among, and stabilize the meanings to be attached to, the differing systemic views about equilibrium and stability associated with Keynesian concerns about unemployment equilibrium, and market clearing failures which would or would not persist over time. The stability literature of the 1940s was concerned with the 1930s problems of dynamics and statics, and transitions to new equilibria versus returns to pre-existing equilibria. Ultimately of course it was based upon the metaquestion 'Is the capitalist system stable?' It was not an exploration of the stability of the established equilibrium in a formal model of the competitive system. It was not, therefore, a working out of the dynamics of a system of equations whose equilibrium solution had already been established in a formal manner. The reconstruction of that 1940s literature as leading to the Arrow and Hurwicz papers of the late 1950s is a Whiggish re-telling of the story which makes the interests of the 1940s economists more connected to future success than could have been known at the time, and which finds more intellectual kinship among authors of papers than can be reasonably posited except after the fact.

To make this point more vivid, consider a letter dated 25 November 1968 from Paul Samuelson to Lloyd Metzler. Remember that Metzler, after the operation for removal of a brain tumour in 1952, was less able to find the same kind of intellectual energy he had in the 1940s. Samuelson, responding to a Metzler letter about stability, wrote at length about Metzler's own contribution to Metzler himself, placing the 1945 paper in his own Samuelsonian context as follows:

> Hicks's (1939) definitions [of stability] are completely in terms of comparative statics. Moreover, in his discussion of comparative statics, both here and in connection with complementarity definitions, his text and Appendix sometimes give slightly different definitions, in which sometimes quantities are the independent variables and sometimes prices.

After a discussion of the ways to formalize the Hicksian argument, Samuelson writes

> Now when we come to dynamics, there is the same asymmetry introduced by choosing one of the goods, say the zeroth, as given in the background. That is, we have a different dynamic sequence in time when we use a different numeraire. Ideally, we would want our dynamic stability to be such that the system is stable for the actual pattern that takes place in the market place. But who knows exactly what that is? We always work with ideal and slightly artificial models ... Hence I write
>
> $$(4'')\dot{p}_i = k_i x_i\,(p_1,\ldots,p_n), \quad i=1,\ldots n \quad k_i > 0$$

> Now here is where you did Hicks a great service, relating his comparative statics conditions to true dynamic conditions. Suppose in (4″), one of the k's gets to be very large, approaching infinity, then by dividing its equation through by that k, say $k_n$, we find that its statical equation is (practically) always satisfied so as to clear the market. Hence, that equation, and all other equations which have very large k's relative to the rest, can be thought of as (practically) having floating prices that have floated instantaneously to clear their markets.
>
> Now consider the opposite extreme. Suppose some k, say $k_2$, is 'terribly small'. Then it is as if that price were frozen; and the same will be true of all such k's that are very small ...

After some additional discussion of a matrix condition, Samuelson concludes his letter to Metzler, written 23 years after the result had appeared, that 'Essentially, there has been no advance on your early theorem.' Of course, one of the reasons why this was the case was that the early theorem was entirely submerged in a tradition in which stability theory was linked to the mathematical theory of stability of dissipative dynamical systems. This was one of the causes, and effects, of the Arrow–Hurwicz paper. But the point here to note is that any claim for Metzler to be in a precursor relationship to the Arrow–Hurwicz concerns does a bit of violence to the auto-construction of the Metzler paper by Metzler, and to the recall of its own context by Samuelson who had certainly helped to shape its Hicksian problematic.

## 6. CONCLUSIONS

Let me review the argument to this point:

1. The particular paper under examination, the Arrow–Hurwicz 1958 paper on stability of a competitive equilibrium, historicized its assertions by placing its own arguments in a context in which other earlier papers were noted as precursors, or earlier presentations of, the material to be developed in the subsequent sections of the paper.
2. Although I have only suggested the point, it is reasonably clear that this historicizing of the paper's assertions is not unique to the particular Arrow–Hurwicz paper.
3. The particular historicization asserted in the Arrow–Hurwicz paper is opposed by (a) the retrospective memory of Kenneth Arrow; (b) the retrospective memory of Leonid Hurwicz; (c) accounts of Samuelson's concerns with stability ideas, and his own interests in the stability problem as reported by himself and others; and (d) accounts of Lloyd Metzler, one of the stability theorists claimed by Arrow and Hurwicz as a precursor.

In order to understand the context of a particular scientific paper, or even a mathematical paper, it is necessary to recapture it from the constructed sequences in which it is said, by its authors, to have taken its place. The idea of 'precursorness' is not itself inherent; a paper is not written with a footnote stating that 'in five years' time the results of the paper will be recognized as an imperfect attempt to solve problem X which is the really important idea even though the author does not have a clue about what is really going on'. To be a precursor of an idea or solution or tradition is to be recognized, after the fact, as having been associated with a line of enquiry which, looking back from one particular perspective, was 'on the right track'.

What though is the meaning to be attached to 'on the right track'? If at time $t$ an author A identifies a contribution created by B at $t$ -1 as having been 'on the right track' we see that A is trying to link B with A. Why would this be done? The primary reason to concern oneself with precursors would be to assert claims of 'Progress'. That is, precursorness is often linked to Whiggish histories in which step by step the past leads inexorably to the present, where reason marches ahead and progress is reason's measure. The idea that science is an accumulation of reasoned argument, and that science is the exemplar of the growth of knowledge, leads naturally to the stages of growth, the passage from less knowledge to more. This concern directs attention to what is common to the growing body, and that leads one to attend to ideational similarities which can be tracked through the progressive sequence of ideas. A precursor then is a temporally earlier right idea, where right is equivalent to 'correct from the present viewpoint'. Science as the exemplar of the march of reason, and economics as science, leads the Whiggish historian of economics, and the normal economic scientist, to think in terms of successes and failures, precursors and blind alleys, heroes sung and unsung, and all manner of retrospective gold medals and booby prizes.

Another reason for invoking the idea of a precursor is more rhetorical, more associated with the construction of arguments which might be persuasive in the economists' community. That is, A's claim that B is a precursor of A may be an assertion that B has a fame which A can utilize to legitimize A's contribution. If I say that my ideas are already present in Keynes, then to the degree I can make the claim I can buttress my claim to legitimacy by Keynes's legitimacy. This is an appeal to authority pure and simple, and most claims to have a famous precursor are claims upon an authority. 'It is all set out there in Marshall, or Adam Smith, or Keynes, although in an unformed way' claims the authority of the eminent for one's own ideas. Thus the notion that B is my precursor is a rhetorical device which attempts to legitimize certain claims the author otherwise seeks to establish by arguments based on accepted rules of argument within the particular language community.

For economists, construction of mathematical models, with formalized assumptions and established lines of arguments to conclusions, is but one of several ways of convincing an economist-reader that the assertions are meritorious. Arguments from authority are no less important, even in mathematical-economics work, than arguments from the data, or from the model, or from the theorem. It is too seldom appreciated that the assertion of a precursor relation is often an argument from authority.

Thus to answer the question posed by the title of this chapter, 'Is a precursor of' is not a transitive relation on the set of ideas contained in papers written by economists. It is not such a relation because the 'set' is not fixed. The ideas of economists are not immutable, even as they are set out in words on a physical page written or printed in the past, for the ideas themselves are continuously recreated. That is, the ideas themselves change in the cascades of representations and re-representations of past work by members of the community of economist-readers. Those economist-scientists choose, for local and contingent reasons, to emphasize or de-emphasize certain features of the past in their own work, and thus recreate that past by confronting its ideas, and constructions, in their own current works. This process never ends. It is one of the ways in which the stock of propositions to which truth-value is assigned changes over time, and one of the ways in which we confer with the larger community of economist-scientists both long dead and yet unborn.

## ACKNOWLEDGEMENTS

This chapter has benefited from comments by Neil De Marchi, Bruna Ingrao, and Wade Hands. It is a revision of the paper presented at the Bergamo conference and, in its current form, it appeared in the literary journal, *The South Atlantic Quarterly*, **94** (2), Spring 1995. That special issue, edited by Barbara Herrnstein Smith and Arkady Plotnitsky, is titled 'Mathematics, Science, and Postclassical Theory'. It is jointly published here with the journal's permission.

## NOTES

1. 'Surveying Dynamics', *The Journal of Post Keynesian Economics*, **13** (4), Summer 1991, pp. 525–44; 'Allais, Stability, and Liapunov Theory', *History of Political Economy*, **23** (3), Fall 1991, pp. 383–96; 'Commentary: Historical Case Studies Are Made, Not Given', N. de Marchi (ed.), *Post-Popperian Methodology of Economics* (Boston, 1992), pp. 355–74; 'Introduction', E. Roy Weintraub (ed.), *Toward a History of Game Theory* (Durham: Duke University Press, 1992), pp. 3-12; 'From Dynamics to Stability', Mark Blaug and Neil de Marchi (eds), *Appraising Economic Theories: Studies in the Methodology of Scientific Research Programmes* (Aldershot: Edward Elgar, 1991), pp. 273–91; 'Comment

on Heilbroner', W. Samuels (ed.), *Economics as Discourse* (Boston: Kluwer, 1990), pp. 117–28; 'Roger Backhouse's Straw Herring', *Methodus*, **4** (2), December 1992, pp. 53–7; 'Comment: Thicker Is Better', *Journal of the History of Economic Thought*, **14** (2), Fall 1992, pp. 271–6.

2. *Stabilizing Dynamics: Constructing Economic Knowledge* (New York: Cambridge University Press, 1991).
3. The best general survey of this set of arguments framed by professional historians can be found in Peter Novick, *That Noble Dream* (Cambridge: Cambridge University Press, 1988). His Chapter 15, 'The Center Does Not Hold', in the lengthy part called 'Objectivity in Crisis', ranges over the various assaults on 'objective' history.
4. Augustin Cournot, *Researches into The Mathematical Principles of the Theory of Wealth*, trans. N. Bacon (Homewood: Irwin Co., 1963 [1897]), p. 85.
5. Leon Walras, *Elements of Pure Economics*, trans. William Jaffe (London: George Allen & Unwin, 1954 [1926]), pp. 109–12.
6. Alfred Marshall, *Principles of Economics*, 8th edition (New York: Macmillan, 1949), p. 806.
7. These interviews are the substance of Chapters 2 (on Arrow) and 4 (on Hurwicz) of George Feiwel (ed.), *Arrow and the Ascent of Modern Economic Theory*, (New York: New York University Press, 1987).
8. Paul A. Samuelson, 'The Stability of Equilibrium: Comparative Statics and Dynamics', *Econometrica*, **9**, January 1941, pp. 97–120.
9. See Chapter 3 in E. Roy Weintraub, *Stabilizing Dynamics: Constructing Economic Knowledge* (New York: Cambridge University Press, 1991).
10. 'The Stability of Multiple Markets: The Hicks Conditions', *Econometrica*, **13** (4), October 1945, pp. 277–92.
11. See p. 460 of the entry by George Horwich and John Pomery, 'Lloyd Appleton Metzler' in John Eatwell, Murray Milgate and Peter Newman (eds), *The New Palgrave: A Dictionary of Economics, Volume 3* (London, 1987), pp. 458–61.
12. These materials are located in The Lloyd Appleton Metzler Papers, Special Collections Department, Duke University Library, Durham, North Carolina. The materials were not filed or otherwise processed as of March 1994. The classroom materials are in (unprocessed) file box No. 8, the letter from Samuelson noted below is in (unprocessed) file box No. 13.

# COMMENT

**Bruna Ingrao**

The focus of Roy Weintraub's chapter is methodological more than historical, although it deals with episodes in the history of mathematical economics in this century. Weintraub argues that the history of economics is a construction by the community of economists. The sequence of 'facts' in the history of the discipline is fluid and mutable, according to the contingent problems with which each community of scholars is concerned. Within each scientific community pieces of history are created under the different perspectives of local and contingent reasons, which prompt the scientists to emphasize or de-emphasize some aspects of their past. Thus history of economics is indeed a fluid 'cascade' of representations of past work.

Within this general conception, Weintraub aims at underlining the specific role of scientific communities in the 'creation' of historical narration. The chapter deals with the way scientists make up (or indeed concoct) the past of their discipline while producing new scientific work. This aim is controversial and the controversy is with the historians, who believe that past knowledge is a step by step, progressive march towards the scientific truth of today.

I have already argued elsewhere my radical disagreement with this methodological approach. Although it rightly aims at criticising the naive, scientist view that conceives thought as linearly progressing towards the more advanced discoveries, it plunges into extreme relativism, thus denying a constructive role for sound interpretation and theoretical appraisal in history writing.

The thesis that human groups create history according to their interests, their prejudices or their biased perspective is not new. It was emphasized both by Marx and by Pareto, among others, as is well known. Both Marx and Pareto argued that historical narration is biased (by 'ideologies' or by 'derivations'). Sharing a positivist faith, they thought the task of the 'true' scientist to be unmasking such manipulation, also when unconscious, thus assuming that it is possible better to ascertain the sequence of 'facts' from another (biased or unbiased) perspective. We know how much both proponents of these views were champions of extreme ideologies.

Hundreds of essays and papers have been written afterwards in the same vein, to immunize both scholars and the general public from the risk to acquiesce blindly to biased histories. It certainly was an essential task in societies poisoned by ideologies, as some European societies have been in the twentieth century. Today, it seems that we run the risk of losing all criteria of truth in historical discourse or the very idea of historical discourse performing a specific function in selecting criteria of truth.

Weintraub, following the radical relativism of deconstruction, insists on the plurality of histories that may be written. No criterion is offered to prefer one to the other; therefore, none seems really relevant for extending our knowledge. The radical relativism is another side of the same scientist view which is under attack. It suggests that when we leave the safe ground of science, we are in the mist. Out of science, there are neither safe criteria of truth, nor sound knowledge.

As a consequence of his strong critique of the 'Whiggish' view of history, Weintraub ends up denying the relevance of core ideas, main research programmes or leading paradigms in the development of economics. In my opinion, Weintraub mixes up the domain of new discovery, new technique, new ideas with the core ideas or the persisting line of thought which these may revitalize. In the effort to emphasize the local and contingent reasons behind each different paper, each research, each result, he seems to suggest that no line of inquiry exists larger than a single paper, or the contribution of a single author in a specific period. The risk is to demean the work of the professional historian by collecting spare episodes, losing sight of cross fertilization of ideas and change in continuity. Since the emphasis is on communities of scientists, and not on ideas, the danger is to downgrade history to the personal recollections of scientists, more or less valuable and consistent depending on the culture or insight the single scientist may have.

Weintraub uses, however, the term 'line of inquiry' (see p. 220) and makes reference indeed to lines of inquiry inspired by large themes of research. Why, then, should it be inappropriate to conceive of lines of inquiry over decades or centuries, as the result of the combined effort of different authors in many works? Contrary to Weintraub's view, I wish to emphasize the great need we have for sound interpretation and theoretical appraisal as they are provided by historical narration organized around core ideas. Both lines of inquiry and cross-fertilization of theories are exceedingly important in the history of economics, since new concepts or fresh techniques are often instruments for rethinking on old themes. One of the main tasks for the historian is to recognize lines of research, as they run through different works and cross or part at crucial theoretical cross-roads.

The theoretical core is, after all, very important and so the historian's ability to focus and appraise it. It is my contention that scientific discourse is one among many sources of human knowledge. Knowledge is reached and enriched by other types of discourse, among which historical narration plays a major role.

To illustrate the methodological point, Weintraub examines the short historical overview on stability in economic literature which is included in the paper 'On the Stability of Competitive Equilibrium' by Arrow and Hurwicz. Quoting recollections by the authors, Weintraub maintains that the scientific context in which their stability results were obtained was not the historical one mentioned in the brief introductory survey. He argues that the 'true' background of Arrow and Hurwicz was the work on linear and non-linear programming, which is missing from their historical account, thus disqualifying their appeal to precursors in the paper itself.

The suggestion is interesting and sound; but Weintraub's explanation seems far-fetched, since in their paper Arrow and Hurwicz did not pretend to write a historical survey aiming at summarizing a whole period of research on dynamics. Rather they pointed to the old domain of problems where it was possible to apply the new mathematical insight, trying to place their work in context by relating it to previous work: a task without which no scholarly contribution is possible. They offered a new focus on a crucial open problem, to rephrase and answer old questions more effectively. So I doubt that there are really two versions of the story, one in the recollections, one in the paper.

However that might be, if history is neither found nor discovered, but is just a fluid cascade of reconstructions by the community of economists, why should Arrow's reconstruction be less valid and relevant than any another one, including what Weintraub is suggesting?

In fact, Weintraub is proposing an *alternative* explanation of the development of ideas in mathematical economics, which he thinks to be more pertinent than the short stability survey. Although he seems to suggest from the opening that many histories may be built on the same set of papers, quite unexpectedly he jumps to the conclusion that there was one strong and dominating line of inquiry. According to Weintraub, this line of inquiry was dominated by the political metaquestion: 'Is the capitalist system stable?'

Thus, the chapter ends up: (a) denying that there was a research programme or a line of inquiry in Walrasian stability at all; (b) stating (but not demonstrating) that instead there was a pervasive, and much more relevant research programme about the microfoundations, aiming at reconciling Keynesian theory and general equilibrium. This research programme was inspired by a political metaquestion. In summary, the chapter suggests that the microfoundation question was 'politically correct' and crucial, while the stability question never was.

I cannot understand why offering a reconstruction based on the hard core of Walrasian theory, including the stability of the price adjustment mechanism should be seen as more Whiggish, than proposing a reconstruction based on the microfoundation approach. Why is the historian who spots the first one biased, while the historian who predicates the second is not? The line of inquiry that Weintraub underlines looks like a research programme, or a paradigm, with its successes and failures and dead-ends. Besides, the two lines of inquiry fail or succeed together, since both are based on the same theoretical core. No Walrasian microfoundations may be sound if the stability and uniqueness questions have not been approached. Weintraub's conclusion is, in the end, quite apologetic of general equilibrium theory, since he strongly disregards the role of global stability to prove the soundness of Walrasian theory.

The richer history that Weintraub is telling is, of course, valuable and interesting. Never should historical narration be reduced to pre-set schemes which admit of no crossing of different strands of thought and research. The illustration, however, is built on a misunderstanding. The interviews that Weintraub quotes point both to the sources of a fresh, technical insight (a new modelling approach, a new mathematical technique) and to a wider context of problems for Walrasian theory (the design of resource allocation). Weintraub does not answer a crucial question: why did the authors choose to apply techniques developed in programming outside their first domain of application? My answer is: because they wished to solve a core of unsolved questions in general equilibrium theory. A new technique or a new approach may be applied to reshape an old thematic question: to offer a new solution which is also reshaping the problem itself.

The wider context for Walrasian theory is also a new variation on old themes: *tâtonnement* was conceived in the twofold meaning of an ideal simulation of the market process or an algorithmic procedure for resource allocation from Walras's first essay on equilibrium theory. This twofold nature was so entrenched in the very idea of *tâtonnement* because of the theoretical structure of the theory: determinism, mathematical modelling, ideally complete *a priori* definition of all conditions for equilibrium; that is, the theoretical hard core that emerged in the debate on socialist calculation and that Hayek so effectively criticized. Where Weintraub sees disjointed paths, I see continuity according to a strong theoretical legacy, although in new language.

This is not to deny that different strands of thought cross in the literature on stability in general equilibrium theory. It is certainly true that Samuelson's interest in dynamics had different sources than Marshall's one, or Cournot's, or Arrow's. It is certainly true that Samuelson did not devote himself to general equilibrium; however, he included general equilibrium in the family of mathematical models as the model of maximum generality. Thus, his contribution was important in the debate on the stability of *tâtonnement.* Here again I cannot see why recognizing and underlining diversity in culture and approach by different scholars should imply denying the existence of any common core of research to which they contributed. On the other hand, when dealing with the debate on statics and dynamics in the 1930s, Weintraub pays quite exclusive attention to Keynesian theory, while many participants in that debate, such as Lindahl and Hayek, were quite critical of it and moving on other paths.

As historians we should not be afraid to draw sequences and patterns in the history of economics around crucial questions, or core ideas, provided that we always respect and emphasize the rich background against which they emerge.

## Bibliography

Ingrao B. (1994a), 'History of economics: Meaning and Method', *History of Economic Ideas*, **II** (2), pp. 147–64.

Ingrao, B. (1994b), 'Does the history of ideas have a future?', review of R. Weintraub's *Stabilizing Dynamics. Constructing Economic Knowledge*, Cambridge: Cambridge University Press, 1991, in *Journal of Economic Methodology,* **1**, June.

# 12. On critics and protective belts

**Heinz D. Kurz and Neri Salvadori**

## 1. INTRODUCTION

In *Vom Kriege* (Of War), published posthumously in 1832, Carl von Clausewitz maintained that '*the defensive form of leading a war is in itself stronger than the attacking one* ' (Clausewitz, 1963, [1832], p. 139; emphasis in the original). He expounded: 'He who is on the attack has only the advantage of the sudden attack, whereas he who is on the defence is able to permanently surprise the enemy in the course of the battle in terms of the strength and forms of his counter-attacks' (ibid., p. 141). It hardly needs to be stressed that academic disputes are not military battles and that the critics of a particular theory and its advocates are not warriors attempting to defeat each other by all means, including the extinction of the adversary. Nevertheless, the view appears to be widespread that there are some similarities between intellectual debates and military battles. Otherwise it would be difficult to understand why the former are frequently described in terms of a vocabulary that derives from the realm of the latter. Two examples suffice to illustrate this. Eugen von Böhm-Bawerk in a heated controversy about alternative theories of value and distribution between advocates of the classical cost of production theory on the one hand and advocates of marginal utility theory on the other spoke of the 'showdown between the old and the new doctrine' (Böhm-Bawerk, 1892, p. 321). And John Maynard Keynes coined the formula that 'Ricardo conquered England as completely as the Holy Inquisition conquered Spain' (Keynes, 1936, p. 32).

In this chapter an attempt will be made to reflect upon Clausewitz's claim that defence is easier than attack with regard to a recent debate in economics: the controversy in the theory of capital and interest, also known as the 'Cambridge controversy' (Harcourt, 1969). This controversy has been chosen for the following reasons. First, many people can be counted upon to have some knowledge about it. Hence the barriers to entry to a fruitful discussion should not be too large to most contemporary economists. Second, the controversy under consideration involved a major challenge to the long-period version of what is frequently called 'mainstream' or 'neoclassical' economics. It saw a clash of schools, which, in the terminology suggested by Mäki in this book, advocated 'strong substitutes' containing 'rival core claims to nothing but the truth about the ontic core' (see Mäki's chapter in this volume). As is well known, long-period neoclassical theory explains all prices and quantities, including the distributive variables: the wage rate(s) and the rate of interest (profit), in terms of 'supply and demand'. Emphasis is on constellations characterized by 'free' or 'perfect' competition. Third, the development the controversy took exemplifies in an almost ideal way the different possibilities of reacting to criticism: the strategies of negligence, misrepresentation, elimination, claiming complementarity, vector addition and unification (cf. also Mäki). It displays a whole set of 'protective belts' utilized by the advocates of the theory under attack. Hence the title of our chapter.

The structure of the argument is as follows. Section 2 gives a simple argument in favour of pluralism in economics. In Section 3 a typology of possible reactions to criticism is provided and some considerations as to the factors affecting the probability of the criticism being successful are put forward. Section 4 summarizes the criticism levelled at traditional long-period neoclassical theory. In Section 5 neoclassical responses will be dealt with. Section 6 contains some concluding remarks.

## 2. IN DEFENCE OF PLURALISM

Max Planck, the famous physicist, is said to have decided not to study economics because he felt it was too difficult for him. The view that economics is an intrinsically difficult subject is also conveyed in the writings of major economists. Notwithstanding this, studying the economic literature one frequently gets the impression that although the questions posed are extremely intricate, it is simple to find the appropriate answers provided one adopts the right perspective, analytical method, intellectual paradigm. While this attitude is understandable as a device to promote a particular point of view, it lacks conviction. The reason for this is obvious. If many of the questions posed in economics are indeed as difficult as people tend to believe, then there is no reason to presume that there are simple answers. There is even less reason to presume that any of the rivalling theories available at a given moment of time could provide a full answer to the question under consideration.

Think about an ordinary and at first sight simple-looking economic problem such as what determines the price of a particular commodity at a given moment of time or the average of the actual prices of that commodity over a certain interval of time. Confronted with a question of this kind the layman would probably come up with a large number of considerations that are pertinent to the question. The economist would presumably add to this some further considerations, systematize the different factors contemplated, reason about their relative importance and possible interactions, etc. He might point out that the price of a commodity may depend on the prices of other commodities and the prices of primary factors of production, he might take into consideration, for example, the impact of state regulations on price formation etc. In short, after a few rounds of reflection upon the problem the answer to an allegedly simple question tends to get out of control: a mass of considerations would be accumulated which nobody could oversee any longer, and worse – there would be no end in sight at which the question would actually be settled.

Economic theory is a device to provide an answer to questions of this kind within a fairly short period of time. In order to be able to do so, economic theory has to focus attention on what are considered to be the main factors affecting the phenomenon that is to be explained. This does not mean that there are no other factors or that those factors as a whole have no impact, because they compensate one another. It only means that they will be set aside in the explanation on the grounds that the impact of these factors is assumed to be negligible. There is no deeper justification for setting aside these factors than the success of the explanation given. Since no theory can take into consideration all factors there is scope for pluralism in economic theory. Theories may be discriminated according to which factors they take into consideration in explaining a certain phenomenon. However, even if two theories were to take into account the same set of factors there would still be scope for pluralism: the importance attributed to each of these factors and their interaction may be conceptualized differently. There is scope for this because the explanation given by each of these theories is of necessity non-exhaustive due to the neglect of some factors. In both cases discussed it could be argued that the alternative theories are not really alternative but complementary, that is, each of them contributes to a better understanding of the phenomenon under discussion. To seek dominance for one theory over all the others with the possible result that all the rival theories are extinguished amounts to advocating scientific regress. To paraphrase Voltaire: In a subject as difficult as economics a state of doubt may not be very comfortable, but a state of certainty would be ridiculous.

What has just been said does not mean that anything goes (or should go). There are criteria which any kind of theory ought to fulfil. These criteria can only be formal, since any kind of substantive imposition would imply that we do know the answer, which we don't. There appears to be wide, although not unanimous, agreement that an important requirement is that the theory be logically coherent. To refer to the example which will concern us in the following, a theory which puts the 'principle of substitution' in the centre of its explanation of economic phenomena should apply that principle in a logically consistent way. In neoclassical long-period analysis that principle, applied to the sphere of production, is said to imply that an increase in the price of factor of production $i$, $p_i$, involves a decrease or at best the constancy of the quantity of that factor used per unit of output, $q_i$, that is,

$$\frac{(\Delta q_i)}{(\Delta p_i)} \leq 0.$$

All propositions of the theory can be traced back to this basic idea. If this is not true in general, then that theory appears to be in trouble. The question then is, how the advocates of that theory respond to the demonstration that this idea cannot be sustained in general. The following section prepares the ground for a treatment of that question.

## 3. HOW TO DEFEND A THEORY: A TYPOLOGY

### 3.1. Different Ways to Cope with Criticism

The history of our subject shows that there are (at least) the following ways to deal with critics and their criticisms against doctrines or theories that are in high esteem in the scientific community in a given period of time. The critics and their criticism may be (i) ignored, (ii) misrepresented, (iii) played down as non-pertinent, (iv) refuted, (v) absorbed by putting the doctrine or theory on a more general basis or (vi) accepted. In this chapter attention will focus on cases (i)–(v).

**Reaction (i): strategy of negligence**

For obvious reasons we can only deal with cases in which the criticism put forward is not permanently ignored, but has been ignored for a certain period of time only. To ignore temporarily new findings that run counter to established doctrines is very common indeed and not difficult to explain. It can be traced back either to a lack of understanding of the new findings and their implications for the received doctrines or to ideological commitments on the part of the majority of scholars or academic bodies supervising their research and teaching. While the politico-ideological aspects do seem to play a considerable role in the process of the production and preservation of theories we shall in the discussion in this section set them aside. Hence in the case under consideration it is the speed with which people are able to learn. This speed depends on a variety of factors, including the technical ability of scholars to come to grips with the new results if these are arrived at by using new techniques, for example new mathematical tools, and the demanding character of these which accounts for the fact that several major findings have been ignored for a long time by large parts of the scientific community. What has been ignored at one time can of course be refuted, absorbed or accepted at another time. Here it suffices to emphasize that the mere fact that learning processes are time consuming activities favours, at least for some time, the survival of existing doctrines that have become obsolete with the discovery of new results.

**Reaction (ii): strategy of misrepresentation**

When a new theory is put forward and particularly when it is perceived as a strong substitute to the going dominant theory, then there is the danger that the new theory will be misrepresented by certain advocates of the incumbent theory. The history of our subject offers many illustrations of this. The misrepresentation may or may not be due to a lack of understanding of the alternative. In the case in which it is, the misrepresentation would vanish as the theory is gradually grasped better. The strategy of false representation is often combined with the following one.

**Reaction (iii): strategy to play down the new results**

Attempts to play down new results and even entire theories that might constitute an alternative to the dominant one(s) are a recurrent phenomenon in the history of our subject. There are essentially two variants of this, one related to the theoretical novelty of the alternative, the other related to its empirical importance. The phenomena which the dominant theory is unable to explain are often played down as cases which, though conceivable, can be ignored because they are said to represent but 'anomalies' or 'perverse cases'. Scepticism is expressed as to the relevance of the alternative. Very often the scepticism is based on a preconception of 'the real world out there'. The novel phenomenon is taken to be empirically unimportant. Hence theories are rejected on grounds of 'relevance', empirical and other. It goes without saying that this is a highly dubious response since its claimant pretends to be possessed of some prior knowledge of the explanandum which is not available to the scientific community at large.

**Reaction (iv): strategy of elimination**

The demonstration that a criticism put forward against a theory is ill-founded may contribute to strengthening the 'belief' in the correctness of the theory and can thus be compared in its effects to a successful vaccination of a person. To be able to show that certain propositions are correct and the objections levelled at them are wrong or not pertinent is the best way to give support to a theory. However, economic theories are not only rejected because of slips in the argument. There are also cases in which certain theoretical possibilities which cannot be denied for the simple reason that they can be shown to exist are rejected on the grounds that they can be ruled out empirically. According to this view the theory under attack is a simplified picture of reality that cannot be challenged by 'exceptions' pointed out by the critics. This way of choosing between different theories or rather of attempting to immunize a theory against its critics appears to be very common indeed. The accusation of being empirically irrelevant has become a major strategy to silence critics. The success of this strategy presupposes that the theory under attack has proved to be long-lived, i.e. characterized by a high fitness to survive. This fitness to survive seems to be closely related to its capacity to absorb certain criticisms either by providing a more general conceptualization of the theory which allows one to take care of the phenomena referred to in the critique, leaving the basic approach of the theory intact, or by changing that approach without, however, dispensing with major features of the theory. To reject a criticism on empirical grounds implies the adoption of the falsificationist's criterion.

**Reaction (v): strategy of vector addition and of unification**
The absorption of a criticism in terms of a combination of a new bit of analysis with the received doctrine or of a more general formulation of the theory appears to be the common route taken in the development of a theory. However, one ought to distinguish between effective and spurious absorptions of arguments within a given analytical framework. There are cases in the history of our subject where a new theory has wrongly been conceived as more general than, and thus including as a special case, an earlier or a different theory.

## 3.2. On the (In)Effectiveness of Criticism(s)

In order to understand why some criticism proved to be effective, whereas some other criticism did not, a few additional considerations should be taken into account. Keynes in his attempt to explain the success of Ricardian economics in England pointed towards a couple of factors that may have played some role.[1] Since the type of factors mentioned are frequently invoked in similar contexts, it is useful to quote Keynes's reasoning in full:

> The completeness of the Ricardian victory is something of a curiosity and a mystery. It must have been due to a complex of suitabilities in the doctrine to the environment into which it was projected. That it reached conclusions quite different from what the ordinary uninstructed person would expect, added, I suppose, to

> its intellectual prestige. That its teaching, translated into practice, was austere and often unpalatable, lent it virtue. That it was adapted to carry a vast and consistent logical superstructure, gave it beauty. That it could explain much social injustice and apparent cruelty as an inevitable incident in the scheme of progress, and the attempt to change such things as likely on the whole to do more harm than good, commended to its authority. That it afforded a measure of justification to the free activities of the individual capitalist, attracted to it the support of the dominant social force behind authority. (Keynes, 1936, pp. 32–3)

So much for the success of the doctrine. What about the causes that gradually undermined its authority? Keynes continues:

> But although the doctrine itself has remained unquestioned by orthodox economists up to a late date, its signal failure for purposes of scientific prediction has greatly impaired, in the course of time, the prestige of its practitioners. For professional economists, after Malthus, were apparently unmoved by the lack of correspondence between the results of their theory and the facts of observation; – a discrepancy which the ordinary man had not failed to observe, with the result of his growing unwillingness to accord to economists that measure of respect which he gives to other groups of scientists whose theoretical results are confirmed by observation when they are applied to the facts. (Ibid., p. 33)

Hence, in Keynes's view the ultimate judgment passed on economic theories is whether or not they possess predictive power.

While there is certainly some truth in the view that economic theories which consistently misread 'reality' are in danger of being jettisoned, there is no reason to presume that this will of necessity be the case. The main reason for this is that it is difficult, even impossible, to falsify a theory. This accounts for the fact that theories, once established, are long-lived. It also helps to explain why new theories normally meet with large difficulties in getting accepted.

As to the problem mentioned last, one aspect deserves to be stressed. There is reason to think that for a criticism to be effective it matters whether it is put forward by someone from within the camp of those who advocate the theory that is being challenged, or whether it is put forward by someone from outside that camp. This may be exemplified in terms of Sraffa's 1926 criticism of partial equilibrium theory on the one hand and Sraffa's 1960 book on the other (Sraffa, 1926 and 1960). While his article triggered the development of the theory of imperfect (monopolistic) competition, which is still an integral part of standard microeconomics textbooks, that is, was absorbed by mainstream economics, the propositions of his book, though generating an enormous literature, did not filter into mainstream texts. A possible explanation of this asymmetric reception is that the latter criticism concerned allegedly a 'family quarrel conducted mainly by Cambridge-trained economists' (Newman, 1960, p. 594). The criticism of Marshallian analysis, on the other hand, was seen to show a way out of the impasse which partial analysis had got into. The author of *The Economics of Imperfect Competition*, Joan Robinson, wrote in the Introduction of her *Collected Economic Papers*: 'Marshall's *Principles* was the Bible, and we knew little beyond it. ... Marshall was economics' (Robinson, 1951, p. vii). It is also true that Sraffa's earlier criticism was not fully understood. It was enough for the participants in the debate to believe to have realized Sraffa's message.[2] A completely different story has to be told in Section 4 with respect to the impact of *Production of Commodities* on mainstream economics. Sraffa's contribution was considered to come from an outsider with the effect that it was largely ignored by the mainstream.

This suggests that successful criticisms are often those put forward by people who have themselves, at one point, strongly advocated the theory they are now attacking. Only in very rare cases are criticisms coming from the outside accepted. While this appears to be a fair statement, it deserves emphasizing that the willingness, or otherwise, of accepting a new result or the criticism of an established theory depends also on whether the scope, method or content of that theory is challenged.

### 3.3. Scope, Method and Content of Theories

Differences in scope generally involve differences in the conceptual framework elaborated in order to answer the questions that define the very scope of an analysis. Differences in scope must however not be mistaken for differences in theory; it may simply reflect a strategy of division of labour. Frequently, analyses characterized by different scopes may be integrated into a single, coherent whole that is, or is not, more general than its parts; we may then speak of strategies of vector addition or integration. The basic principles in terms of which the different phenomena are explained may be the same, that is, derived from a single theory. In Mäki's terminology we face strong or weak complements. Similarly with regard to method. Differences in method lead to different perspectives on and analytical treatments of the same phenomenon. These methods may however be mutually compatible. In other words, differences in method must not be mistaken for differences in theory. For example, the problem of price may be dealt with from a short-period and a long-period analysis in terms of a single theory, as is for example the case with Marshallian theory. It is only content which of necessity involves different theories.

From these considerations it follows that protective belts prove often effective in the case of scope; they are also effective in the case of method, provided there is mutual compatibility. They cannot, as a matter of logic, be effective in the case of content. Yet there is ample evidence that theories survive despite the demonstration that they are flawed. How is this possible? This brings us to our case study: the capital controversy of the 1960s and 1970s.

## 4. THE CRITIQUE OF TRADITIONAL NEOCLASSICAL THEORY

### 4.1. The Aggregate Production Function

The macroeconomic version of neoclassical theory was the target of a criticism put forward by Joan Robinson in her 1953 paper 'The Production Function and the Theory of Capital' (Robinson, 1953), which was the proper beginning of what has become known as the 'Cambridge controversies in the theory of capital' (see Harcourt, 1969, 1972). In the course of investigating the meaning of a production function for total output, Joan Robinson set up what Robert Solow (1963) later dubbed a 'pseudo-production function', consisting of the possible positions of equilibrium, corresponding to alternative levels of the rate of profits, given the set of alternative techniques of production. She showed 'that there is no meaning to be given to a "quantity of capital" apart from the rate of profit, so that the contention that the "marginal product of capital" determines the rate of profit is meaningless' (Robinson, 1970, p. 309). In constructing a 'pseudo-production function' she found that over certain ranges of it the technique that becomes eligible at a lower real wage rate (to which corresponds a higher rate of profits) may be less labour-intensive than that chosen at a higher wage rate (to which corresponds a lower rate of profits). This finding contradicted the 'well-behaved production function', the popular work horse of neoclassical macroeconomic theory, which assumes that a lower real wage rate is always associated with a more labour-intensive technique.

Joan Robinson called this finding a 'perverse relationship' (Robinson, 1956, pp. 109–10), a 'curiosum'. Paul Samuelson (1962), in an attempt to counter Joan Robinson's attack on the aggregate production function, claimed that even in cases with heterogeneous capital goods some rationalization can be provided for the validity of simple neoclassical 'parables' which assume that there is a single homogeneous factor called 'capital', the marginal product of which equals the rate of return. Samuelson based his defence of traditional theory in terms of the construction of a 'surrogate production function' in a model which takes into account heterogeneous capital in a very special way: corn is produced with labour and a machine, which is itself produced by labour and the same machine, but for each process to produce corn there is a different machine. In constructing the 'surrogate production function', Samuelson, alas, assumed equal proportions of labour to the machine in both sectors of the economy for each technique (cf. ibid., pp. 196–7). This implied however that the two goods could not sensibly be discriminated in the sense that the price of the machine in terms of corn is not affected by changes in income distribution. By this token the 'real' economy with heterogeneous goods was turned into the 'imaginary' economy with a homogeneous output, i.e. the 'surrogate production function' was nothing more than the infamous aggregate production function. This was shown, among others, by Garegnani (1970). Samuelson (1966) openly admitted that he was wrong and that what he called the 'Ramsey–Clark parable', i.e. the aggregate production function, cannot generally be sustained. In the introduction to her 1953 paper Joan Robinson stressed that 'the production function has been a powerful instrument of miseducation' (Robinson, 1953, p. 81). The economic literature published since shows that, strangely enough, it still is. Just look into the macroeconomic literature in general and the so-called 'new' theories of economic growth in particular.

## 4.2. 'Capital' as a Factor of Production

The use of the value of capital as a factor of production alongside the factors labour and land which are measured in terms of their own technical units in the production function of single commodities was already rejected by Knut Wicksell. This implied 'arguing in a circle' (Wicksell, 1934 [1901], p. 149), since capital and the rate of interest enter as a cost in the production of capital goods themselves. Hence the value of the capital goods inserted in the production function depends on the rate of interest and will generally change with it. Following Joan Robinson (1953, p. 95), the dependence of prices on distribution was discussed under the heading of 'price Wicksell effects'.[3]

However, even though the phenomenon under consideration had been well known since the classical economists and was referred to also by several neoclassical authors, especially Wicksell (e.g., 1934 [1901], pp. 147–51), the earlier authors were not fully aware of the complications involved. In particular, they were of the opinion that with a rise in the rate of profits, $r$, given the system of production, the ratio of prices of any two commodities would stay constant *or* rise *or* fall, throughout the range of variation of $r$. This opinion was closely related to the hypothesis that the capital–labour or capital–output ratios of the different industries could be brought into a ranking that is independent of distribution. Yet, as Sraffa has shown, this is generally not possible, i.e. 'the prices of a product ... may rise or it may fall, or it may even alternate in rising and falling, relative to its means of production' (Sraffa, 1960, p. 15). Therefore, to characterize an industry as 'capital intensive' or 'labour intensive' in general makes no sense unless the level of the rate of profits is specified at which this characterization is supposed to apply.

According to Marshall the applications of the principle of substitution 'extend over almost every field of economic inquiry' (1920, p. 284). This principle forms the very basis of the marginalist theory of value and distribution. Hence any criticism of that theory has to deal with the problem of choice from a set of alternatives contemplated by the principle of substitution. In the Cambridge controversy in the theory of capital emphasis was naturally on the problem of the choice of technique rather than that of consumer choice.

*Reswitching* is a situation in which a technique is cost-minimizing at two disconnected ranges of the rate of profits and not so in between these ranges. Samuelson has recognized that 'this phenomenon can be called "perverse" only in the sense that the conventional parables did not prepare us for it' (1966, p. 578). The implication of the possibility of the reswitching of techniques is that the direction of change of the 'input proportions' cannot be related unambiguously to changes of the so-called 'factor prices'. The central element of the neoclassical explanation of distribution in terms of supply and demand is thus revealed as defective. The demonstration that a fall in the wage rate (i.e. a rise in the rate of profits) may lead to the adoption of the less 'labour-intensive', i.e. more 'capital-intensive', of the two techniques destroyed, in the minds of the critics of traditional neoclassical theory, the whole basis for the neoclassical view of substitution in production. Moreover, since a fall in the wage rate may cheapen some of the commodities, the production of which at a higher level of the wage rate was characterized by a relatively low 'labour intensity', the substitution among consumption goods contemplated by the traditional theory of consumer demand may result in a higher, as well as a lower, 'labour intensity'. It follows that the principle of substitution in consumption cannot offset the breakdown of the principle of substitution in production. It should be noted, however, that in order for the input use per unit of output to be positively related to the price of the input, reswitching is not needed. Hence, the inequality stated in Section 2 cannot generally be taken for granted.

We talk of *reverse capital deepening* when the relationship between the value of capital (per capita) and the rate of profits is increasing. The negative implication of reswitching and reverse capital deepening for traditional theory can be illustrated by means of the example of Figure 12.1, in which the value of capital ($K$) corresponding to the full employment level of labour is plotted against the rate of profits ($r$). Obviously, if with traditional analysis we conceived the curve $KK'$ as the 'demand curve' for capital, which, together with the corresponding 'supply curve' $K^*K^{*\prime}$, is taken to determine the equilibrium value of the rate of profits, we would have to conclude that this

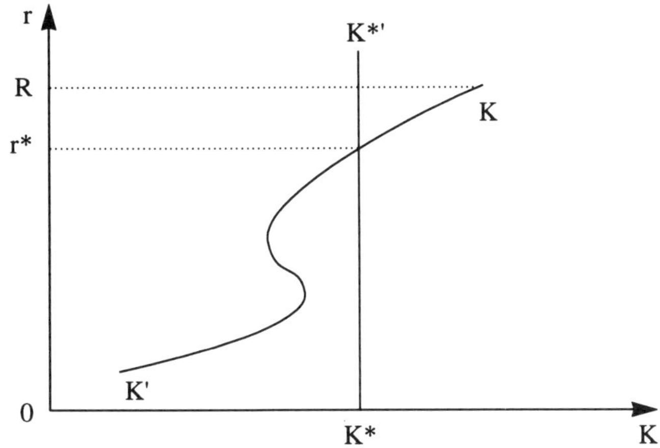


*Figure 12.1*

equilibrium, although unique, is unstable. With free competition, conceived, as it is in neoclassical theory, as including the perfect flexibility of the distributive variables, a deviation of $r$ from $r^*$ would lead to the absurd conclusion that one of the two income categories, wages and profits, would disappear. According to the critics of traditional neoclassical theory, this result demonstrates all the more impressively the failure of the supply and demand approach to the theory of normal distribution, prices and quantities.

## 5. NEOCLASSICAL RESPONSES

It is hardly surprising that the protagonists of the supply and demand approach should have shown so much concern when confronted with the critique. In what follows, we shall briefly summarize their consecutive responses to the critique. We may distinguish broadly between two types of responses: (i) attempts to defend traditional neoclassical theory and (ii) counter-attacks on the alternative theory from which the criticism had been developed. Historically, the answers belonging to the first type generally preceded those belonging to the second.

### 5.1. In Defence of Traditional Neoclassical Theory

The very first reaction followed Christian Morgenstern's famous dictum that 'it cannot be what must not be'; that is, it amounted to the strategy of elimination. In 1965 David Levhari, a student of Paul Samuelson's, claimed to have demonstrated that reswitching was impossible, i.e. that systems of production can be ordered according to 'degrees of mechanization' (cf. Levhari, 1965). This claim was shown to be false by Luigi Pasinetti, who was encouraged to do so by Piero Sraffa (cf. Baranzini and Harcourt, 1993, p. 9), in a paper presented at the First World Congress of the Econometric Society in Rome in 1965. A revised version of Pasinetti's paper was then published in the November 1966 issue of the *Quarterly Journal of Economics* (Pasinetti, 1966) together with papers by Levhari and Samuelson (1966), Morishima (1966), Bruno *et al.* (1966), Garegnani (1966) and Samuelson (1966).[4] Samuelson and Levhari in their joint paper and Samuelson in his 'summing up' paper frankly admitted that the no-reswitching theorem was wrong. Samuelson also gave some numerical examples which illustrated in simple terms why reswitching and capital reversing are possible. See also Burmeister and Turnovsky (1972).[5]

Since the possibility of reswitching and reverse capital deepening could no longer be denied, doubts were raised as to its empirical importance (see, for example, Ferguson, 1969). The adopted strategy of negligence consisted of playing down the importance of the new results, thereby insinuating that neoclassical theory was a simplified picture of reality, the basic correctness of which could not be endangered by 'exceptions' of the kind analysed in the capital debate.[6] This sort of reasoning was implicitly dealt with by Sraffa in an oral intervention at the 1958 Corfu conference on the theory of capital. Counterposing the statistician's measure with measurement in theory, which should be able to take into account all possible cases, i.e. universally applicable, Sraffa emphasized:

> The theoretical measures required absolute precision. ... The work of J.B. Clark, Böhm-Bawerk and others was intended to produce pure definitions of capital, as required by their theories, not as a guide to actual measurement. If we found contradictions, then these pointed to defects in the theory, and an inability to define measures of capital accurately. (Cf. Lutz and Hague, 1961, pp. 305–6)

Furthermore, it should be clear that attempts to disprove reswitching in terms of wage–profit curves constructed from input–output data for different years (cf. Krelle, 1977, and Ochoa, 1989; see also Petrovič, 1991) are fundamentally mistaken. Leaving aside data problems and the conceptual difficulties concerning the required 'translation' of empirical 'facts' into the categories of the analytical framework, the finding that the $w$–$r$ curves associated with the techniques of 1988 and 1993, for example, do not possess several switch-points cannot be considered an empirical counterexample to reswitching, since the latter refers to the technical knowledge *at a given moment of time.*[7]

Some authors attempted to preserve the traditional neoclassical theory by simply ruling out reswitching and other 'perverse', i.e. non-conventional, phenomena in terms of sufficiently bold assumptions about available techniques. This route was followed, for example, by Sato (1974). It should come as no surprise that given these assumptions the central neoclassical postulate of the inverse relation between the capital–labour ratio and the rate of profits should re-emerge as 'one of the most powerful theorems in economic theory' (Sato, 1974, p. 355). However, in order to be clear about this move it deserves to be stressed that it was motivated, as one author expressly admits, by the fact that 'regular economies' have 'desirable properties' (Burmeister, 1980, p. 124).[8]

Other advocates of the neoclassical approach were conscious of how defective the attempts were to avoid reswitching and capital reversing or to play down their importance using the 'empirical' route. Since the phenomenon was irrefutable it had to be absorbed and shown to be compatible with the more sophisticated versions of the theory, i.e. those at the 'frontier of knowledge' (cf. Hahn, 1975, p. 363). In responses of the second type the criticism of traditional neoclassical theory is therefore generally accepted. Instead of defending what cannot be defended, the alternative classical theory is examined. It is claimed that the latter does not constitute an alternative to the *modern* versions of neoclassical theory, i.e. those based on the notions of temporary or intertemporal equilibrium (strategy of complementarity or of unification). This was argued by Christopher Bliss (1975), Edwin Burmeister (1980), and especially by Frank Hahn (1975, 1982). Their responses can be said to reflect Clausewitz's dictum: 'he who is on the defence is able to permanently surprise the enemy in the course of the battle in terms of the strength and forms of his counter-attacks'.

## 5.2. 'General' vs. 'Special' Theories

Hahn frankly admitted that the Sraffa-based critique is correct with respect to 'many writers whom we regard as neoclassical who have either made mistakes of reasoning or based themselves on special assumptions which have themselves nothing to do with neoclassical theory' (Hahn, 1982, p. 354). He also expressed the opinion that 'Sraffa's book contains no formal propositions which I consider to be wrong although here and there it contains remarks which I consider to be false' (ibid., p. 353). However, the main point of Hahn's argument is a different one: 'I assert the following: there is not a single formal proposition in Sraffa's book which is not also true in a General Equilibrium model constructed on his assumptions' (Hahn, 1975, p. 362; similarly 1982, p. 353). This has the following implications stressed by Hahn. First, the criticism of traditional neoclassical theory has no bearing upon general equilibrium theory of the Arrow–Debreu variety.[9] Secondly, it is contended that Sraffa's analysis represents but a 'special case' of the latter.

Both propositions are ultimately traced back to the fact that in modern general equilibrium theory the distribution of income is determined in terms of arbitrarily given *physical* endowments of agents. Since the endowment of the economy with capital goods is not given a scalar representation, as in traditional theory, the capital critique is said not to be applicable. Moreover, since in general equilibrium there will generally be as many 'own' rates of return as there are different assets in the endowment set, Sraffa's analysis which revolves around the uniformity of profit rates is said to be concerned with 'a very special state of the economy' (ibid., p. 363).

To qualify the analyses of other schools of thought as special cases of one's own analysis is a time-honoured device in intellectual controversy amongst economists. Keynes, for example, presented his own theory, which allows for persistent unemployment, as the *General Theory*, implying that the conventional full employment theory is a 'special case' (Keynes, 1936, p. 3). Representatives of the 'neoclassical synthesis' in macroeconomics on the other hand maintained that Keynes's analysis lacks generality, because it is based on special assumptions concerning the flexibility of wages, etc. But does this method carry us very far? While there can be no doubt that in some cases it is appropriate, in others it is not. For example, it is well known that a model of a non-Euclidean geometry can be built up within the axioms of Euclidean geometry. Does this entitle us to consider the non-Euclidean geometry a 'special case' of the Euclidean one? Similarly, take a model inspired by Sraffa's analysis in which there are different qualities of land but there is neither capital nor labour. This model is very similar to a neoclassical model in which income distribution is determined by the relative scarcities of the 'factors of production'. Do we have to conclude from this that the neoclassical analysis is a 'special case' of 'classical' analysis?

There is an obvious way to decide whether a particular analysis is, or is not, a special case of the Arrow–Debreu model. If it were, it would start from the *same* set of data but impose special restrictions on this set. The set of data, or exogenous variables, on which modern general equilibrium theory is based is summarized by Hahn in the following definition of what he means by a 'neoclassical theory':

> I shall call a theory neoclassical if (a) an economy is fully described by the preferences and endowments of agents and by the production sets of firms; (b) all agents treat prices parametrically (perfect competition); and (c) all agents are rational and given prices will take that action (or set of actions) from amongst those available to them which is best for them given their preferences. (Firms prefer more profit to less.) (Hahn, 1982, p. 354)

Attention has to focus on element (a), since the other two elements (regarding competition and rationality) are also to be found in classical analysis, with the concept of 'free competition' replacing that of 'perfect competition'. In element (a) we encounter (i) preferences, (ii) initial endowments (labour powers, lands, capital goods, etc.) and the distribution of property rights among agents, and (iii) technical alternatives. The main difference between neoclassical and classical theory of value and distribution concerns item (ii), that is, the assumption entertained in neoclassical theory of given endowments of capital goods.

Hahn is thus confronted with the task of showing that Sraffa, very much like modern general equilibrium theory, starts from given initial endowments, and in addition, very much like a special case of that theory, presupposes a particular composition of those endowments (see also Garegnani, 1990b, pp. 113–15). Yet this cannot be demonstrated for the simple reason that Sraffa, following the classical approach to the theory of value and distribution, develops his analysis in terms of a *different* set of data, thus putting forward a *different* theory. The difficulty of the task Hahn has put to himself can be seen in the way he attempts to tackle it. As to the first aspect of this task, i.e. that of discovering *some* assumption about endowments in Sraffa, Hahn simply *claims* that 'it cannot be part of the doctrine that you are uninterested whether there [are enough commodities in a given year that can be used as means of production] to meet demand' (Hahn, 1982, p. 365). In the immediately following sentence Hahn admits, however, that his claim is contradicted by Sraffa's analysis: 'Yet Mr Sraffa does not consider this matter' (ibid.). Interestingly, this finding does not prompt Hahn to question his 'special case' interpretation. It rather makes him seek to establish its correctness by adopting a different route: instead of providing direct evidence in support of the claim that Sraffa started from given endowments, he looks out for indirect evidence. He believes to have found it in Sraffa's concern with a uniform rate of profits. Clearly, to impose a uniform rate of profits on a general equilibrium system would render it overdetermined. Hence, data (i), (ii) or (iii) mentioned above cannot be taken as independent variables. Now it is Hahn's contention that at the basis of Sraffa's price equations there must be a special proportion between the initial endowments, i.e. (ii) is tacitly assumed to be specified accordingly. 'So the neoclassical economist who is always happy to consider interesting special cases sets to work to find a proper equilibrium for Mr Sraffa' (ibid.). Combining the familiar assumptions of general equilibrium theory of given preferences and technical alternatives with the unfamiliar one of a given and uniform rate of profits implies that the composition of the capital stock cannot be taken as independently determined, but must be seen as depending on the givens mentioned: as Hahn emphasizes with regard to the two-commodity illustrations of his argument, 'we must make one of [the two endowments] into an unknown' (ibid.). This concludes Hahn's attempt to demonstrate that the 'special case' interpretation of Sraffa's analysis is correct.

Hahn's interpretation does not stand up to close examination. First, it deserves to be stressed that Sraffa does *not* start from given endowments of capital goods, i.e. produced means of production, in order to determine distribution and normal prices. He rather takes as given *gross outputs* and one of the distributive variables. The quantities of the capital goods available in the system are considered as dependent rather than independent variables. Following the classical economists, he assumes that the capital stocks installed in the different industries are adjusted to these outputs and the given level of the distributive variable, by an appropriate choice of technique, such that these outputs can be produced at minimum costs. The tendency towards normal capital utilization and a uniform rate of profits is taken to be the outcome of the working of competition. Sraffa's is a different theory of value and distribution which manages to meet its objective, i.e. to determine relative prices and the remaining distributive variable(s) in term of *these* data. Secondly, what Hahn thinks to be an adequate interpretation of Sraffa's analysis is in fact a reiteration of a finding in older neoclassical authors: as has been seen in Section 4, several representatives of traditional neoclassical theory were aware that in order to be consistent with the notion of a competitive equilibrium the capital endowment could only be given in value terms, with the physical composition to be determined endogenously. Hence, ironically, Hahn attributes to Sraffa what Sraffa had identified as the major difficulty of traditional neoclassical theory, i.e. that the 'quantity of capital' and the distribution of income cannot be ascertained independently of one another.

In what follows two further observations on the 'special case' interpretation will be provided. To claim that the Arrow–Debreu model is general, whereas Sraffa's analysis is special, misses the fact that the former is short-period and the latter is long-period. Thus, in dealing with a 'private ownership economy', Debreu (1959, pp. 39 and 78) assumes a *given* number of producers and *given* shares of the profit of the various producers received by consumers. While these assumptions are necessary within the schema of Debreu's short-period theory, there is no room for them in the different schema of Sraffa's analysis.

Duménil and Lévy (1985) (see also Dana *et al.,* 1989) take intertemporal general equilibrium theory as it is and ask whether it is possible to locate in its formalism the concept of 'natural' prices, or prices of production, and a uniform rate of profits. They show that under certain conditions, over an infinite horizon, prices in the intertemporal model tend toward 'natural' prices as the relative prices progressively stabilize. They conclude:

> What can be conserved in the intertemporal equilibrium is only its asymptotic behaviour position, i.e. *that which coincides with the classical conception of equilibrium*! Therefore, prices of production are not an uninteresting particular case of the neoclassical model. On the contrary, every price described in the

> neoclassical story which does not correspond to prices of production is totally deprived of any economic significance. (Ibid. p. 343, original emphasis.)

In their view the tracks of 'natural' prices are clearly discernible in the neoclassical equilibrium model. This undermines, they conclude, the claim that the latter is the general case and the classical long-period theory the special one.[10]

Finally, it should be noted that there is an asymmetry in the way in which Sraffa's analysis is perceived by advocates of general equilibrium theory and the way in which that theory is perceived by advocates of the Sraffian, i.e. 'classical', analysis. From the point of view of the former Sraffa's analysis, though correct, is but a 'special case' of general equilibrium theory. Yet from the point of view of the latter, general equilibrium theory is not only different from Sraffa's analysis but also difficult to sustain. More particularly, it is argued that temporary and intertemporal theory, not differently from traditional neoclassical theory, cannot avoid the problem of capital. We shall come back to this claim towards the end of the following subsection.

### 5.3. Temporary and Intertemporal Equilibrium and the Problem of Capital

We may conclude this section by way of summarizing what we consider to be the main features of intertemporal and temporary equilibrium models, as far as the problem of capital and interest is concerned. We begin with a discussion of temporary equilibrium.

Temporary equilibrium models are characterized by a seemingly complete evaporation of the concept of capital. Markets exist only for the exchange of commodities at the present date. Supply and demand determine present prices at which individual plans are mutually consistent, given the initial data which include individual agents' expectations about future prices.[11] Nothing guarantees that these expectations will be realized, so that individual plans will be revised as actual prices are found to differ from what was anticipated. In each single period capital goods cannot be seen differently than natural resources inherited from the preceding period which earn their proprietor a rent if and only if they are scarce. However, while it is true that in these models the concept of capital as a *stock* magnitude has been dispensed with, the concept of capital as a *flow* magnitude is still there. To see this, we have to leave the capital market and turn to the investment savings market.

Similarly in intertemporal models, in which the problem of capital is also seemingly removed from the scene: the capital goods available at the beginning of the first period have the character of 'primary' factors of production and can thus be treated on a par with scarce natural resources, such as land.

The income a capital good yields its owner is again similar to the rent of land. These capital goods, together with the other primary factors, are used to produce consumption goods and new means of production in correspondence with intertemporal preferences of consumers, coping with the ever present problem of scarcity as well as possible, given the initial endowments and the available technical alternatives. As the offsprings of rent-yielding assets the newly produced means of production bear the stamp of their origin and are also rent-yielding factors. Some uneasiness about the treatment of produced means of production and the asymmetric treatment of the past and the presence in intertemporal equilibrium models is expressed by Geanakoplos:

> the assumption of a finite number of commodities (and hence of dates) forces upon the model the interpretation of the economic process as a one-way activity of converting given primary resources into consumption goods. If there is universal agreement about when the world will end, there can be no question about the reproduction of the capital stock. In equilibrium it will be run down to zero. … One certainly cannot speak about the production of all commodities by commodities (Sraffa, 1960), since at date zero there must be commodities which have not been produced by commodities. (Geanakoplos, 1987, p. 122)

What can at most be said is that along the avenue leading from original factor services to consumption goods, intermediate goods will emerge which gradually transmute themselves into final goods. To all appearances, the problem of capital is again successfully circumnavigated.

Yet as with temporary equilibrium, these appearances are deceptive. As Malinvaud pointed out in his entry, 'Intertemporal Equilibrium and Efficiency', in *The New Palgrave* (cf. Malinvaud, 1987), 'it is now realized that the rate of interest is related in a very complex way to the many exogenous determinants of equilibrium and that changes of relative prices, which are associated with changes of interest, may be responsible for paradoxical effects' (ibid., p. 960). This admitted, the challenge to intertemporal equilibrium theory posed by these findings is right away played down using the (infamous) 'empirical' route (cf. subsection 5.1 above): 'The significance of these various negative theoretical results should of course [!] not be overstated. While reflecting the basic complexity of the relationship between the full system of discounted prices and its determinants, the results do not prove that "pathological cases" are often empirically relevant' (ibid., p. 960).

To see more clearly why the modern versions of neoclassical theory are not immune to the criticism of the traditional neoclassical notion of 'capital' (as summarized in section 4), a few additional considerations may prove useful. In this context it is worth mentioning that it was particularly Garegnani (most recently 1990a, 1993) who argued that, notwithstanding the fact that capital is resolved into a set of physical factors, the modern versions cannot evade the problem of capital. First, recall that the demand and supply functions for capital, a stock, in the older theories were assumed to operate over time through a sequence of demand functions for gross investment confronted with supply functions for gross savings, i.e. flows. The interest elasticity of these demand functions for investment was seen to reflect the interest elasticity of the demand for capital as a stock. Once this is understood, 'it also becomes clear that the difficulties associated with the demand for "capital" in the traditional long-period versions have to be present also in the contemporary short-period versions of the theory' (Garegnani, 1990a, p. 60). For these short-period versions cannot do without (gross) investment and (gross) saving functions, i.e. functions which refer to 'capital' in its 'free' form. In equilibrium investment equals savings, i.e. the aggregate demand for the outputs of means of production equals the aggregate supply. However, there is no guarantee that the equilibrium is stable. With reswitching and capital reversing there is no reason to presume that with a fall (rise) in the effective rate of interest investment demand will increase (decrease). In short, the presence of these phenomena would be reflected in a multiplicity of equilibria, one or several of which would be unstable. However, as was argued in section 4 with regard to 'perversely' shaped, i.e. upward sloping, factor-demand functions, this possibility would question the validity of the entire economic analysis in terms of demand and supply.[12]

The above considerations should have made clear the following. First, there is no presumption that the neoclassical theories of intertemporal or temporary equilibrium are 'general', whereas the classical theory is 'special'. The truth is that these theories are *different*: while the former are short-period, the latter is long-period. Secondly, although in the modern neoclassical theories there is no single 'quantity of capital' representing the endowment of the economy with produced means of production, the problem of capital is not avoided: it reappears in the investment–savings market and is reflected in the instability of equilibrium. Finally, the modern version of the demand and supply approach are beset with several methodological and conceptual difficulties which raise serious doubts about their usefulness.

## 6. CONCLUDING REMARKS

This chapter has illustrated Clausewitz's dictum that 'defence is easier than attack' in terms of the capital controversy in the 1960s and 1970s. It has been shown that if a dominant theory is challenged by a strong substitute, then its advocates will try to defend that theory by producing protective belts or engaging in counter-attacks. While in that controversy it was conclusively shown that the view long-period neoclassical theory takes of the relationship between input use (per unit of output) and the price of the input cannot generally be sustained, surprisingly that view has not been jettisoned. This chapter attempts to contribute to an explanation of this in terms of a detailed account of the different aspects of that debate. The disquieting fact remains that in economics propositions that have been proved wrong are still used by many (the majority?) of its practitioners.

## NOTES

1. It goes without saying that Keynes's account of the situation in the time after Ricardo's death up to the 1930s is grossly exaggerated. Even 'Say's Law' was not as widely accepted and correspondingly some sort of 'principle of effective demand' rejected, as Keynes insinuated.
2. Interestingly, Joan Robinson dedicated a copy of her *Economics of Imperfect Competition* to Sraffa with the words 'To the Piero of 1933 from a disciple of the Sraffa of 1926'.
3. See, for example, Bhaduri (1966), Samuelson (1966), Harcourt (1972, pp. 39–45) and Bliss (1975, pp. 114–17). From the point of view of the history of economic thought this terminology is unfortunate, since the first author ever to analyse in some depth the influence of distribution on relative prices was Ricardo (see, in particular, Ricardo, 1951 [1817], pp. 30–43).
4. The numerical counterexample provided by Pasinetti in 1965 did not meet all the assumptions underlying Levhari's argument, whereas the one published in 1966 did.
5. Some authors claimed that there is an analogy between reswitching and the long-known possibility of the existence of multiple internal rates of return. They remarked, quoting the Bible: 'there is no new thing under the sun' (Bruno *et al.*, 1966, p. 553). However, whereas the phenomenon of multiple internal rates of return is a discovery within the *partial* framework of microeconomic theory of investment, reswitching presupposes a *general* framework. On multiple internal rates of return, see especially Irving Fisher (1930). Interestingly, there are passages in Fisher which indicate that he was aware that prices may vary, possibly in a complex way, with variations in the rate of interest. He contended, however, that this complication is 'more intricate than important' (ibid., pp. 170–71).
6. Occasionally, reswitching was compared to the 'Giffen good' case in consumer theory (cf. Hicks, 1965, p. 154, and Stiglitz, 1974). On the fallacy of this analogy, see Garegnani (1990a, p. 72).
7. More recently there have been attempts to define and then assess the 'probability' of reswitching (or capital reversing) in a given analytical framework; see on this D'Ippolito (1987, 1989) and Mainwaring and Steedman (1993). These attempts are not to be confounded with the applied works referred to above.
8. A 'regular economy' is defined as one for which the 'real Wicksell effect' is always negative (cf. Burmeister, 1980, p. 101), where a 'real Wicksell effect' gives the change in the value of capital due to the fact that steady state capital stocks vary with the rate of profits. That is, the value of capital is taken to be inversely related to the rate of profits. The notion of a 'regular economy' is also called 'a necessary and sufficient condition to preclude paradoxical behavior' (ibid., p. 119). 'Such economies exhibit behavior that in some important qualitative respects is similar to that of the standard one-sector model', which in turn is said to be tentatively acceptable 'on the basis of empirical evidence' (ibid., p. 101).
9. In another place Hahn admitted that he himself 'every so often slipped into the aggregate version of the neo-classical model' (Hahn, 1972, p. 8).
10. Comparing the classical notion of gravitation of market prices to 'natural' prices and the

asymptotic behaviour of prices in intertemporal equilibrium theory, Duménil and Lévy contended that the latter could at most be considered 'an uninteresting particular case of the classical convergence process' (1989, p. 343 fn.).

11. A weakness of the theories of temporary equilibrium concerns the necessarily arbitrary choice of hypotheses about individual price expectations. Indeed, as Burmeister stressed, 'all too often "nearly anything can happen" is the only possible unqualified conclusion' (Burmeister, 1980, p. 215). Moreover, the stability properties of this kind of equilibrium are unclear, since small perturbations caused by accidental factors may entail changes in expectations, which define that very equilibrium.
12. The above considerations also show the futility of Solow's attempt, inspired by Fisher (1930), to avoid the problem of capital in terms of the concept of the 'social rate of return' which gives the ratio of the present value of the additional stream of future income generated by investment and that investment; see Solow (1963, 1967). For a criticism of that concept, see Pasinetti (1969).

## REFERENCES


Baranzini, M. and Harcourt, G.C. (1993), 'Introduction', in M. Baranzini and G.C. Harcourt (eds), *The Dynamics of the Wealth of Nations. Growth, Distribution and Structural Change. Essays in Honour of Luigi Pasinetti*, New York: St Martin's Press, pp. 1–42.

Bhaduri, A. (1966), 'The Concept of the Marginal Productivity of Capital and the Wicksell Effect', *Oxford Economic Papers*, **18**, pp. 284–8.

Bharadwaj, K. and Schefold, B. (eds) (1990), *Essays on Piero Sraffa: Critical Perspectives on the Revival of Classical Theory*, London: Unwin Hyman.

Bliss, C.J. (1975), *Capital Theory and the Distribution of Income*, Amsterdam: North-Holland.

Böhm-Bawerk, E. v. (1892), 'Wert, Kosten und Grenznutzen', *Jahrbücher für Nationalökonomie und Statistik* (3rd series), **3**, pp. 321–67.

Bruno, M., Burmeister, E. and Sheshinski, E. (1966), 'The Nature and Implications of the Reswitching of Techniques', *Quarterly Journal of Economics*, **80**, pp. 526–53.

Burmeister, E. (1980), *Capital Theory and Dynamics*, Cambridge: Cambridge University Press.

Burmeister, E. and Turnovsky, S.J. (1972), 'Capital Deepening Response in an Economy with Heterogeneous Capital Goods', *American Economic Review*, **65**, pp. 842–53.

Clausewitz, C. von (1963), *Vom Kriege*, first published in 1832, in *Rowohlts Klassiker der Literatur und Wissenschaft*, vol. 12, Munich: Rowohlt.

Dana, R.A., Florenzano, M., Le Van, C. and Lévy, D. (1989), 'Asymptotic Properties of a Leontief Economy', *Journal of Economic Dynamics and Control*, **13**, pp. 553–68.

Debreu, G. (1959), *Theory of Value: An Axiomatic Analysis of Economic Equilibrium*, New York: John Wiley & Sons.

D'Ippolito, G. (1987), 'Probabilità di perverso comportamento del capitale al variare del saggio dei profitti: il modello embrionale a due settori', *Note Economiche*, **2**, pp. 5–37.

D'Ippolito, G. (1989), 'Delimitazione dell'area dei casi di comportamento perverso del capitale in un punto di mutamento della tecnica', in L.L. Pasinetti (ed.), *Aspetti controversi della teoria del valore*, Bologna: Il Mulino, pp. 191–7.

Duménil, G. and Lévy, D. (1985), 'The Classicals and the Neo-Classicals: A Rejoinder to Frank Hahn', *Cambridge Journal of Economics*, **9**, pp. 327–45.
Ferguson, C.E. (1969), *The Neo-Classical Theory of Production and Distribution*, Cambridge: Cambridge University Press.
Fisher, I. (1930), *The Theory of Interest*, New York: Macmillan.
Garegnani, P. (1966), 'Switching of Techniques', *Quarterly Journal of Economics*, **80**, pp. 554–67.
Garegnani, P. (1970), 'Heterogeneous Capital, the Production Function and the Theory of Distribution', *Review of Economic Studies*, **37**, 407–36.
Garegnani, P. (1990a), 'Quantity of Capital', in J. Eatwell, M. Milgate and P. Newman (eds), *Capital Theory*, London: Macmillan, pp. 1–78.
Garegnani, P. (1990b), 'Sraffa: Classical versus Marginalist Analysis', in K. Bharadwaj and B. Schefold (eds), *Essays on Piero Sraffa: Critical Perspectives on the Revival of Classical Theory*, London: Unwin Hyman, pp. 112–41.
Garegnani, P. (1993), Sraffa Lecture, mimeo.
Geanakoplos, J. (1987), 'Arrow–Debreu Model of General Equilibrium', in J. Eatwell, M. Milgate and P. Newman (eds), *The New Palgrave. A Dictionary of Economics*, London: Macmillan, vol. 1, pp. 116–24.
Hahn, F.H. (1972), *The Share of Wages in the National Income: An Enquiry into the Theory of Distribution*, London: Weidenfeld and Nicolson.
Hahn, F.H. (1975), 'Revival of Political Economy: The Wrong Issues and the Wrong Argument', *Economic Record*, **51**, pp. 360–64.
Hahn, F.H. (1982), 'The Neo-Ricardians', *Cambridge Journal of Economics*, **6**, pp. 353–74.
Harcourt, G.C. (1969), 'Some Cambridge Controversies in the Theory of Capital', *Journal of Economic Literature*, **7**, pp. 369–405.
Harcourt, G.C. (1972), *Some Cambridge Controversies in the Theory of Capital*, Cambridge: Cambridge University Press.
Harrod, R.F. (1961), 'Production of Commodities', *Economic Journal*, **71**, pp. 783–7.
Hicks, J.R. (1965), *Capital and Growth*, Oxford: Clarendon Press.
Jevons, W.S. (1871), *The Theory of Political Economy*, London: Macmillan.
Keynes, J.M. (1936), *The General Theory of Employment, Interest and Money*, London: Macmillan.
Krelle, W. (1977), 'Basic Facts in Capital Theory. Some Lessons from the Controversy in Capital Theory', *Révue d'Economie Politique*, **87**, pp. 282–329.
Levhari, D. (1965), 'A Non Substitution Theorem and Switching of Techniques', *Quarterly Journal of Economics*, **79**, pp. 98–105.
Levhari, D. and Samuelson, P.A. (1966), 'The Nonswitching Theorem is False', *Quarterly Journal of Economics*, **80**, pp. 518–19.
Lutz, F.A. and Hague, D.C. (eds) (1961), *The Theory of Capital*, London: Macmillan.
Mainwaring, L. and Steedman, I. (1993), 'On the Probability of Reswitching and Capital Reversing in a Two-Sector Sraffian Model', Manchester, mimeo.
Malinvaud, E. (1987), 'Intertemporal Equilibrium and Efficiency', in J. Eatwell, M. Milgate and P. Newman (eds), *The New Palgrave. A Dictionary of Economics*, London: Macmillan, vol. 2, pp. 958–62.
Marshall, A. (1920), *Principles of Economics*, 1st edn 1890, 8th edn 1920. Reprint, reset, London: Macmillan, 1977.
Morishima, M. (1966), 'Refutation of the Nonswitching Theorem', *Quarterly Journal of Economics*, **80**, pp. 520–25.

Newman, P. (1960), 'The Erosion of Marshall's Theory of Value', *Quarterly Journal of Economics*, **74**, pp. 587–600.
Ochoa, E.M. (1989), 'Values, Prices and Wage Profit Curves in the US Economy', *Cambridge Journal of Economics*, **13**, pp. 413–29.
Pasinetti, L.L. (1966), 'Changes in the Rate of Profit and Switches of Techniques', *Quarterly Journal of Economics*, **80**, pp. 503–17.
Pasinetti, L.L. (1969), 'Switches of Techniques and the "Rate of Return" in Capital Theory', *Economic Journal*, **79**, pp. 508–31.
Petrovič, P. (1991), 'Shape of a Wage–Profit Curve: Some Methodology and Empirical Evidence', *Metroeconomica*, **42**, pp. 93–112.
Ricardo, D. (1951), *On the Principles of Political Economy and Taxation* (1st edn 1817), edited by P. Sraffa with the collaboration of M.H. Dobb, Cambridge: Cambridge University Press.
Robinson, J.V. (1951), *Collected Economic Papers*, Oxford: Basil Blackwell.
Robinson, J.V. (1953), 'The Production Function and the Theory of Capital', *Review of Economic Studies*, **21**, pp. 81–106
Robinson, J.V. (1956), *The Accumulation of Capital*, London: Macmillan.
Robinson, J.V. (1970), 'Capital Theory Up to Date', *Canadian Journal of Economics*, **3**, pp. 309–17.
Samuelson, P.A. (1962), 'Parable and Realism in Capital Theory: The Surrogate Production Function', *Review of Economic Studies*, **29**, pp. 193–206.
Samuelson, P.A. (1966), 'A Summing Up', *Quarterly Journal of Economics*, **80**, pp. 568–83.
Sato, K. (1974), 'The Neo-Classical Postulate and the Technology Frontier in Capital Theory', *Quarterly Journal of Economics*, **88**, pp. 353–84.
Solow, R.M. (1963), *Capital Theory and the Rate of Return*, Amsterdam: North-Holland.
Solow, R.M. (1967), 'The Interest Rate and the Transition Between Techniques', in C.H. Feinstein (ed.), *Socialism, Capitalism and Economic Growth. Essays Presented to Maurice Dobb*, Cambridge: Cambridge University Press, pp. 30–9.
Sraffa, P. (1926), 'The Laws of Returns Under Competitive Conditions', *Economic Journal*, **36**, pp. 535–50.
Sraffa, P. (1960), *Production of Commodities by Means of Commodities. Prelude to a Critique of Economic Theory*, Cambridge: Cambridge University Press.
Sraffa, P. (1962), 'Production of Commodities: A Comment', *Economic Journal*, **72**, pp. 477–9.
Stiglitz, J.E. (1974), 'The Cambridge–Controversy in the Theory of Capital: A View From New Haven. A Review Article', *Journal of Political Economy*, **82**, pp. 893–903.
Wicksell, K. (1901), *Föreläsingar i Nationalekonomi*, vol. I, Lund: Berlingska Boktrycheriet. English translation in Wicksell (1934).
Wicksell, K. (1934), *Lectures on Political Economy*, vol. I, London: George Routledge & Sons. Translation of Wicksell (1901) by E. Classen and edited, with an introduction, by Lionel Robbins.

## COMMENT

**Andrea Salanti**

Kurz and Salvadori take the 'Cambridge controversy' on capital theory as an example of economic debates arising from the plurality of theories existing within economics. I must say from the outset that I have nothing to add to their sensible reconstruction of such a debate (about which a huge amount of secondary literature is also already available), and, furthermore, that I completely agree with their conclusion on p. 251: 'there is no presumption that the neoclassical theories of intertemporal or temporary equilibrium are "general", whereas the classical theory is "special". The truth is that these theories are *different*'(italics in the original). I take this judgement to imply that it is impossible to reduce one theory to another (in the sense of reductionism) merely by means of formal manipulations, and that those, like Hahn (1982), who try to perform such an exercise are inevitably led to introduce in at least one of the two different theories some assumptions which are actually alien to it.

What I find somewhat unconvincing, however, is the last sentence of the chapter (with some of its implications). In their concluding remarks, Kurz and Salvadori alert us to 'the disquieting fact ... that in economics propositions that have been *proved* wrong are still used by many (the majority?) of its practitioners' (p. 252, italics added). In this respect, my question is simply the following: how is it possible to *prove* (conclusively) a piece of economic theory to be wrong, if, as Kurz and Salvadori themselves justly recognize throughout their chapter that (1) there exists a plurality of continuously competing theories and (2) appeal to 'facts' is seldom conclusive (or even possible) in our discipline?

Note that what the authors do in their attempt to offer 'a simple argument in favour of pluralism in economics' (see section 2) amounts to nothing but a restatement of the Millian thesis of the intrinsic 'inexactness' of economic theory, based upon the apparent impossibility of taking into simultaneous consideration *all* factors potentially concurring to the explanation of a certain phenomenon. Consistently, they also reject the possibility of applying falsificationism in economics (cf. p. 238).[1] The only limit they impose to the variety of possible theories (in order to avoid, among other things, the disturbing conclusion that 'anything goes') is the criterion of logical coherence. In their words (p. 234):

> There are criteria which any kind of theory ought to fulfil. These criteria can only be formal, since any kind of substantive imposition would imply that we know the answer, which we don't. There appears to be wide, although not unanimous, agreement that an important requirement is that the theory be logically coherent.

From all this, therefore, I have to conclude that according to Kurz and Salvadori the 'proof' of the weakness of the neoclassical theory of capital consists in the demonstration of its logical inconsistency. In this respect two kinds of observations are in order. First, it cannot be forgotten that logical consistency, desirable as it may be, is neither sufficient nor even necessary in order to establish the factual truth of the conclusions of any theory. Apart from the well-known examples in the textbooks of formal logic,[2] this point becomes even more important if we embrace the Millian thesis of the 'inexactness' of economic theory. Indeed, precisely because of the unavoidable incompleteness of the considered factors, we might well have factually true premises (or, if you prefer, assumptions), a logically correct process of deduction, but nevertheless factually false conclusions (and/or predictions).

In addition to this kind of consideration, which applies to all economic theory (and perhaps to all fields of scientific research),[3] there is a second kind of observation particularly relevant for the particular case we are discussing here. As I tried to argue elsewhere (Salanti, 1989), economists' confidence in the power of 'internal' criticism, uniquely directed at the logical structure of a theoretical framework, is open to question. When debating controversial questions we are supposed to make a clear distinction between 'internal' critiques, uniquely concerned with the logical consistency of a theory, and 'external' critiques, dealing with the factual truth of assumptions, conclusions and/or predictions. This would require, however, an equally clear-cut distinction between what is simply a matter of logic and what is a matter of empirical judgement, but such a distinction is much more intricate and of much more difficult application to actual theories (and therefore the ensuing critiques are much less conclusive) than they are usually taken to be.

Indeed, if we look more closely at such kinds of critiques, we soon discover that they are directed not solely at the bare mathematical structure of a theory, but also at the corresponding (economic) 'interpretation'. The critique of neoclassical capital theory based on reswitching of techniques and related issues is a typical case in point. We should admit that a mathematician innocent of economics would not fully understand what is at stake: how is it possible, indeed, to show the (logical) inconsistency of the *one-sector* neoclassical model of growth and distribution by claiming that conclusions drawn from it no longer hold in a *multisectoral* (linear) model of production. The familiar argument makes sense only if we agree on the following two points: (1) one of the obvious features of capital goods is their heterogeneity (and, at least to a certain degree, their complementarity rather than their substitutability), which implies that we regard multisectoral models as particularly suited to deal with the implications of such a characteristic; and (2) because in economic theory the choice of the 'right' model is always somewhat arbitrary, we are more confident in the obtained results when we can replicate them within different classes of models.

The latter is a methodological rule of conventionalist type, while the former may be considered a sort of 'correspondence rule', that is a proposition whose function is to establish a link between the formalized theoretical core and empirical propositions derived from it. Consequently, the effectiveness of the 'reswitching' critique does not rest only on its being concerned with a purely logical argument in the strict sense of the term, but is also due to its being grounded on a correspondence rule which is virtually impossible to reject.

On the one hand, therefore, I agree with Kurz and Salvadori in finding quite 'disquieting' the continuous use, in spite of the well-known demonstrations of its inconsistency, of the aggregate production function in macroeconomic models. The only possible justification, I presume, might be of a purely instrumentalist kind. On the other hand, if my emphasis on the importance of correspondence rules for criticism of this kind is correct, then we ought not to be surprised by the weaker impact of criticisms (like those echoed in section 5.3 of their chapter) directed at temporary and intertemporal (general) equilibrium models. In that case the involved 'correspondence rules' have to deal with the concept of equilibrium, and we have not incontrovertible characterizations of equilibrium easily available.

We don't know if the 'world out there' is ever in equilibrium, yet we suspect that it never is so. In any case, questions like the desirability of stable and unique (rather than unstable and multiple) equilibria, or the nature of expectations, are subject to methodological decisions, and different methodological views on these matters convey different judgements on the relative merits of various competing theories. I would suggest, consequently, that it is the wide spectrum of possible methodological attitudes which in some sense justifies the existence of a plurality of theories.[4]

## Notes

1. For a lengthy discussion of the reasons why the Millian thesis of economics as an 'inexact' and 'separate' science is incompatible with a falsificationist methodology, see Hausman (1992).
2. It is quite easy, for instance, to construct examples in which, from factually false premises, and through either a logically valid or invalid inference, we may obtain conclusions either true or false.
3. It is precisely because of Millian 'inexactness' that economists were induced to set forth the famous distinction between the (positive/normative) 'science' of economics and the 'art' of economic policy. But such a situation, contrary to what economists often seem to believe, is

not peculiar of economics. After all, the job of engineers can be understood only if we admit the existence of a similar gulf between the theoretical core of natural sciences and their corresponding 'applications' in the various fields of applied technology.

4. It is common sense that in social sciences there is more disagreement among different 'schools' (or, if you prefer, more 'pluralism') than is usually the case within natural sciences. An implication of what is maintained here is that such a wider variety of theoretical approaches could be due, among other things, to a wider array of possible methodological perspectives.

## References

Hahn, F.H. (1982), 'The Neo-Ricardians', *Cambridge Journal of Economics*, **6**, pp. 353–74.

Hausman, D. (1992), *The Inexact and Separate Science of Economics*, Cambridge: University Press.

Salanti, A. (1989), 'Internal criticisms in economic theory: are they really conclusive?', *Economic Notes*, **19**, pp. 1–15. Also in B. Caldwell (ed.), *The Philosophy and Methodology of Economics*. Aldershot: Edward Elgar, 1993, Vol. III, pp. 445–59.

# 13. The attribution of quantitative error and the erasure of plural interpretations in various sciences

**Philip Mirowski**

> To be exact, to make calculations balance is something modern. In all previous ages numerical statements are always only approximate. Anyone who is at all acquainted with calculations in the Middle Ages knows that if you check the columns the general thing is to find the totals quite incorrect. Mistakes in arithmetic were common occurrences … . All these errors are clearly seen in the so-called bookeeping of the Middle Ages. If you look through the books of a Töllner, a Viko von Geldersen, a Wittenborg, or an Ott Ruhland, you will find it exceedingly difficult to believe that the writers were all great merchants of their generation.
>
> (Sombart, 1915, p. 18)

Recent breakthroughs in the history and sociology of science have begun to make us appreciate the vast complexity and intricate character of empirical endeavours in the sciences. The days when one could gesture towards 'observation statements' or 'falsification' as though they were some readily understood set of procedures are gone, happily.[1] This does not just mean waving about the Duhem–Quine thesis as a shibboleth: we are now much more sensitive to (for instance) the immense difficulties of establishing viable claims to replication, or the absence of selectivity bias, or convincing others of adequacy of experimental controls. Yet, even so, I would still venture to assert that modern science studies, with only a few exceptions, have ignored the problem of the constitution of error in the context of precision quantitative measurement. More distressingly, in economics and economic methodology, we have not even got so far as the researchers in science studies. Once we have briefly sketched out the requisite backgrounds in the history and philosophy of error which have ben elaborated in greater detail elsewhere,[2] we shall draw out a few unpleasant implications for the present status of empiricism in economics, and some even more unpleasant prognostications for the future of pluralism in economics.

## 1. A BUDGET OF ERRORS

Many economists seem to think that quantitative error is adequately taken care of by statistics or advanced econometrics. This has been most readily apparent in the rational expectations movement in macroeconomics, which swept the field by positing a symmetry between the economic actor and the econometrician in their processing of inference and prediction.[3] In the Neyman–Pearson version, so despised by philosophers but still taught in econometrics texts, one assigns distributions to both a null and auxiliary hypothesis, calculates the power of a test *a priori*, and resorts to assignments of costs of Type I versus Type II error in order to designate regions of acceptance or rejection of the null. Neyman himself was rather free with the use of economic metaphors when motivating his theory of inference and statistical test. In the Bayesian camp, on the other hand, the theory of subjective probability is itself based upon the economic notion of the Dutch Book, or the pecuniary ability to punish individuals sporting inconsistent probability assignments, so that Bayes's Rule can have a stable interpersonal referent. So it would seem that economics and conceptions of the treatment of error have enjoyed rather intimate relations.

Perhaps the prevalence of economic intuitions can be traced to the fact that these two predominant schools of statistical inference were both launched by writers quite familiar with economics (Neyman and Ramsey), and some version of their handiwork is now ensconced in everyone's desktop PC software, so that the idea of the unproblematic taming of error comes as readily as the idea of an unproblematic marketplace of ideas to an orthodox economist. The acceptance of the null or the convergence of updated priors are as much second nature as Pareto optimality, and all cooperate in fostering a certain placid equanimity in the face of chaos and error. But let us entertain, just for the moment, the hypothesis that all this bland self-confidence is built upon sand. Indeed, a case can be made that econometrics is experiencing a bout of severe loss of nerve at present – a phenomenon we shall simply take for granted for the purposes of argument.[4] In such a climate, where we are importuned on all sides to 'take the con out of econometrics' and to put some confidence back in the confidence interval, where can the average practitioner turn in order to get some guidance on the meaning and implications of the attribution of error in their quotidian empirical exercises?

Not, I fear, to the self-styled 'methodologist'. If these souls say anything about econometrics, it consists primarily of endless disputations about whether falsificationism is or is not possible, is or is not practised, is or is not wise (Backhouse, 1994). There is very little here of any practical import for the average economist. Neither can the practitioner in the trenches glean much in the way of understanding of their predicament from the high priests of theoretical econometrics, the Hendrys or the Leamers of this world. When they are not suggesting that the problem lies with the inability of the empirical workers to keep up with their latest and glitziest technical innovations, they spend much of their time trading quips about the relative superiority of their respective computer packages, without really getting to the heart of the seemingly interminable controversy between subjectivists and frequentists. I will make an attempt to break this deadlock by suggesting a third approach to the constitution of error, one which should have immediate payoffs in terms of reorientation of real practices by real economists.

The point of departure for my proposed alternative is to suggest that a novel approach to error also can be prompted by an economic metaphor, but one very different from those which inspire Bayesians and 'classical' statisticians. The fundamental problem with both is that they begin by imagining that all quantitative error is adequately rectified solely within the skull of the lone researcher: the empirical inquirer cranks through the formulas, assigns the error probabilities, and reports the outcome, all as a hermetically self-contained procedure. Other researchers then encounter this initial report in the marketplace of ideas, and assign their own error attributions within their own skulls. The similarity of this story to the neoclassical image of market coordination, where everyone pre-reconciles their desires through a solipsistic constrained maximization, and where competition is a passive state rather than an active occupation, is probably no accident. My proposed reconceptualization of quantitative inference requires a different sort of economic metaphor, one not so concertedly individualistic, and one more explicit about the nature and character of the process of coordination. That metaphor is one of *arbitrage*.

The theory of arbitrage which informs my account is not that of orthodox finance theory (rendering my rhetorical task all the more difficult); rather, it is a theory of the constitution of numerical value invariance by means of chains of virtual or actual exchanges which preserve relative prices when they return to their origin. There exists a mathematical elaboration of this theory,[5] but it is unnecessary for our present purposes. In the economic theory of arbitrage, some actors serve to maintain the integrity of the quantitative structure of prices by seeking out inconsistencies in that structure, trading upon them, and reaping arbitrage profits. Since the quantitative units that they seek to maintain are precisely the same units in which their reward is denominated, there is a sense in which self-interest can render the system homeostatic, within certain broad bounds. Maintenance of a quantitative value system which channels incentives and warns of scarcities can possess some claim to efficacy if it can underwrite all the necessary intermediate calculations of self-interest.

It is important to acknowledge at the outset that, while I will posit an analogous situation in the sphere of quantitative measurement, there will be one very palpable disanalogy between the laboratory and the marketplace which will be central to the subsequent narrative. Whilst economic actors seek to accumulate arbitrage profits in the marketplace because they are realized in the form of money, there is no parallel entity in the laboratory which actors seek to accrue. That is because no researcher wants to collect a sequence of error bars attendant upon a sequence of virtual or actual measurements of physical constants; there is no 'credit' or gain from such an activity. No one gets a Nobel prize for piling up measurement errors.

If the 'moral economy of measurement' breaks down at such a critical juncture, then what can be the purpose of proposing a comparison of market arbitrage and error arbitrage? Consider Figure 13.1. It portrays a set of physical constants, and arrays them on the nodes of a graph, with the arcs representing actual theoretical connections between them. The first point to notice is that any well-developed mathematical discipline, and here physics serves as my exemplar, will define its quantitative constants in terms of its other quantitative constants. (Here one begins to prosecute the analogy with

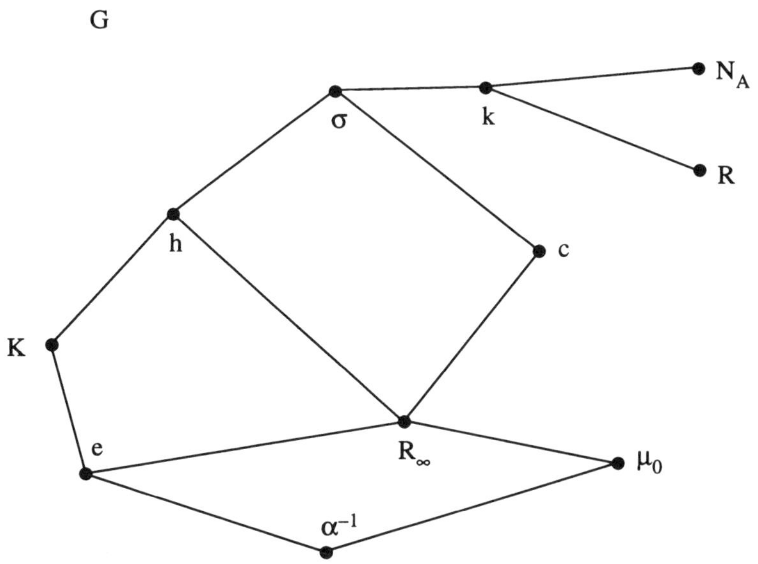


*Notes*:
G – gravitational constant; σ – Stefan Boltzmann constant; K Boltzmann constant; $N_A$ – Avogadro constant; R – gas constant; H – Planck constant; c – speed of light; K – Josephson constant; e – electron charge; $R_\infty$ – Rydberg constant; $\mu_0$ – permeability of vacuum; $\alpha^{-1}$ – fine structure constant.

*Figure 13.1 A simplified graph of some physical constants*

relative prices). This means that any experimental endeavour to gauge the magnitude of a specific quantitative constant must take the value of the other constants as given. But indeed, there is the rub. If error infects all empirical attempts at quantitative measurement, then we can imagine a situation where one lab takes one particular error assessment as given, while a second lab, starting from a different constant, ends up with a different error assessment, producing a divergent quantitative reading of the same constant. The net result will be a system of numerically inconsistent values distributed across various researchers. (The analogy to multiple prices for the same good should be apparent.)

Is this really such a problem? The physicist Raymond Birge thought so, as late as the 1930s:

> A distinguished scientist would obtain a value of some such constant, which he believed more accurate than any previously found. He would make such a claim in a published paper, and thereafter, for some longer or shorter period, his value would be generally accepted and used throughout the scientific world … . In that case there was only one exhaustive investigation. Another situation tended to develop when research workers residing in two or more countries were involved. If, for instance, a distinguished German scientist obtained one value, and a distinguished French scientist another value of the same constant, one usually found the German value used subsequently in German papers and texts, and the French value in French papers and texts … . Another unfortunate aspect of the situation, as I found it, was that the generally adopted value of each constant was chosen quite independently of the value of other, often related constants, so that no *consistent* set of values of the general constants existed … . There have been instances of two *different* values of an auxiliary constant (the velocity of light) used in the *same* equation … . (Birge, 1957, pp. 40–41)

So this situation has actually happened before in physics.

The second point to glean from Figure 13.1 is that, if it adequately represents the situation of the science at a specific juncture, then once that science has managed to evolve beyond its most inchoate beginnings it is practically impossible for any single laboratory to control the attribution of error across the entire constellation of constants; in other words, no lab can encompass and validate the measurement of all the needed constants under its own roof. This simply reiterates the point made above: it is the unobtrusive assumption of methodological individualism which has been the main obstacle to understanding the actual allocation of error in quantitative measurement. Scientists, especially when they cast their questions is the form of number and quantity, are caught in a vast web of interpersonal relations from which they cannot extricate themselves, short of absenting themselves from science altogether.

But we have yet to specify the process by which this multi-lateral reconciliation of measurement comes about. Here is where the metaphor of arbitrage comes home to roost; it is the third idea to be gleaned from Figure 13.1. The key concept is the interconnectedness of the graph of the constants (itself a function of the theories which mathematically connect the constants). In any well-developed science, there will be many 'loops' or circular pathways through which one can 'travel', starting at any arbitrary constant and eventually arriving back at that same constant.[6] The actual counterpart to this 'trip' is a sequence of measurements made along the path of the graph, remembering that each successive constant is defined in terms of those preceeding it in the path. The easiest way to gauge the extent of consistency of the constellation of constants is to (virtually) travel around a selection of loops and measure whether the implied value of the constant at the end of the circuit is 'close' to the initial value. Since measurement error is inevitable, the divergence will never be zero; hence the objective of this exercise is to 'distribute' the measurement error around the loop in such a manner so as to minimize the divergence. This is what happens when an arbitrageur intervenes to profit from divergences in prices.

But we cannot depend upon market incentives in the analogous case of quantitative measurement, because no one is motivated to accumulate the 'error bars' for their own sake. This creates special coordination problems for scientific organizations, and deep conundrums for simple advocacy of tolerance for pluralism in science. To put the case crudely, while market arbitrage was commonplace in Europe from the Italian Rennaissance onwards, numerical measurement arbitrage was essentially absent until the twentieth century in every science. The history, described in detail elsewhere,[7] is a fascinating tale of the evolution of the very conception of error from something that was eminently a personal and moral phenomenon, to something physically inherent in our bodies, to something which could be partitioned in the lab between 'systematic' and 'random' components (with the latter component neutralized by 'statistics'), to its transformation in the twentieth century into a truly corporate phenomenon.

These changes were made manifest in the divergent methods of reporting quantitative measurements through time. In the seventeenth and eighteenth centuries, experimenters would report one lone number, without any qualifications of significant digits or error bars: the reason was that the extirpation of error was a personal and moral phenomenon, something that happened in a private encounter with Nature. Good physicists produced good numbers. Only in the nineteenth century was it noticed that even the most virtuous of virtuosi could not come to exact quantitative agreement in their astronomical observations; and the moral economy of measurement slowly gave way to a physiological conception, with each corporeal observer saddled with a 'personal equation' describing his own ideosyncratic tendencies to error. In the face of such a pathetic collection of flawed and imperfect creatures (many of whom could no longer depend upon face to face contact in order to gauge the dependability of their counterparts), science had to become less individualistic and more regimented or industrialized in character. This accounts for the beginning of precision lab pedagogy in the 1870s, which first took root in Germany and America, and then spread to the rest of the world. Central to this pedagogy was the belief that observation itself could be mechanically regimented in such a way that one could partition systematic error due to theoretical considerations ('accuracy') from random error due to unfathomable limitations ('precision'). With the spread of this pedagogy, we get the parallel development of the rhetoric of the scientific paper, which reports multiple readings, significant digits and probable errors.

Yet even at the turn of the century, these innovations were not sufficient to stabilize the definition of quantitative error, as observed in the quote from Raymond Birge above. The problem, as he stated it, was that no one was checking for consistency across the various domains of measurement, or as we would put it, no one was performing the role of arbitrageur. The answer, first developed by Birge in physics in the 1930s, and then diffused to other sciences after World War Two, was the creation of the persona of the *meta-analyst* or metrologist. The job of the meta-analyst is to collect quantitative estimates of some empirical constant (both published and unpublished), subject each of them to scrutiny and criticism, seek out inconsistencies, and finally, attribute error bars to all the 'best practice' values. Since political, social and logistical considerations militate against any active research lab allocating the error budget by itself and imposing its values upon other labs, it became apparent quite early on that there would have to be a special institution whose primary purpose was to carry out the relevant meta-analyses. Birge laid the foundations at Berkeley for one such unit, the Particle Data Group (PDG), which since 1958 has pronounced upon the best practice values of many physical constants most relevant to the subatomic sphere (Rosenfeld, 1975; Petley, 1985). The level of stabilization is best represented by a wallet-sized card issued by the PDG containing the best-practice values of the best-loved physical constants.

The history of the spread of metrology and meta-analysis has yet to be written,[8] but one can describe its spare outlines in at least one social science, namely, psychology. In the 1950s there arose a self-consciously 'statistical' literature concerning the combination of tests of significance across studies, most usually in a vaguely Neyman–Pearson framework, largely in a psychological or medical empirical context. As objections mounted to the validity of the outpouring of psychological experimentation in the late 1960s, Eugene Glass and his associates began to insist upon the necessity of assessment and combination of quantitative 'effect sizes' of various studies. In 1981 they issued the first textbook of *Meta-analysis in Social Research* (Glass *et al.*, 1981); and the field is now well established in psychology, with its own journal and specialists. All dissention has not been banished, and meta-analysis draws its share of detractors; but the desirability of arbitrage and oversight has been accepted in principle.

## 2. WHAT ABOUT ECONOMICS?

Yes, indeed, what about economics? I will wager that very few economists, and no methodologists, will admit to knowing any of the narrative provided above. The reason is simple. Until recently, if someone enrolled in a graduate programme in economics, they soon learned that the sum total of empirical practice was contained in knowledge about something known as 'econometrics', a set of statistical practices surrounded by vague notions of the 'power of a test' or the Bayesian updating of some unexplained priors. While a very few might become fascinated with the philosophical niceties of the battle between the Bayesians and the 'classical statisticians',[9] most just wanted to get on with their empirical work. This work consisted of lone researchers running scads of regression on data provided by someone else, individually choosing the specifications most coherent with their own expectations, and publishing the isolated result as having passed some species of 'test'. There was no experimental design, no randomization, little comparison of alternative estimators, little reporting of alternative auxiliary hypotheses, desultory reportage of the empirical practices of others and much ceremonial rejoicing at the 'significance' of a coefficient beyond the 0.05 or 0.10 level. With the help of her computer and a little bit of patience, the individual had settled upon her best estimate of the number in question however she deemed fit; and the rest was up to the reader.

The moral of our little fable should now become clear. The project of econometrics, in so far as it represents the epitome of empirical endeavour for the average economist, has remained mired in images of the treatment of quantitative error characteristic of physics in the seventeenth century. The only activity incumbent upon the empirical economist is to provide a good number in his or her own private estimation; it is up to the audience, the free marketplace of ideas, the moral economy of measurement, to somehow single out the uniquely correct value. Evidences of personal virtue might include facility with mathematics or glitzy novel econometric techniques, a 24-carat degree, an affiliation with a top-20 university or research institute like the NBER, or even open fealty to the orthodoxy; but none of these attributes changes the basic structure of the process. The narrative is classic: a lone empirical economist undergoes an unmediated asocial encounter with some quantitative incarnation of the Economy, and comes back, braver and wiser, to recount the tale to her hale and hearty fellows.

This caricature may seem a little overdrawn; but unlike many purveyors of methodology, I assert that this portrayal can itself set in motion an empirical research programme. In this chapter, I merely want to suggest that differing approaches to the treatment of quantitative error lead directly to measurable differences in the degree of agreement of measured constants in the various sciences. This observation is hardly novel; rather, it is derived from the techniques and practices already developed in disciplines with a long tradition of meta-analysis. While there exist many difficult and interesting statistical questions raised by the very practice of meta-analysis, we shall avoid them here, and resort to the simplest of measures, in order to demonstrate the fruitfulness of this approach. For our comparison, we shall harken back to the grandfather of meta-analysis, Raymond Birge.

Birge, as already noted, was concerned to evaluate the best-practice values and appropriate error attributions of the physical constants. Such a procedure required a diagnostic tool to assess how badly individual labs diverged in their estimations of the relevant measurement errors, as a prelude to the process or error arbitrage. Birge proposed a very simple ratio to gauge the relative consistency of internal (within-lab) to external (between-lab) measurement errors (Petley, 1985, p. 304). Suppose an experimenter reports an estimated value $X_i$ of some theoretical constant in conjunction with their own estimate of the standard error $\sigma_i$. Suppose further meta-analyst compiles $N$ such instances of published experiments in a specific science, all claiming to measure the same constant, and uses them to construct the mean estimate $\bar{X}$. To construct a,Birge ratio, define external error consistency as

$$E^* = \left( \sum_{i=1}^{N} (X_i - \bar{X})^2 / \sigma_i^2 \right) \left( (N-1) \sum_{i=1}^{N} 8 \frac{1}{\sigma_i^2} \right)^{-1}$$

If one then defines $b^*$ as the mean of the reciprocals of the individually estimated squared standard errors, the Birge ratio will then be defined as $B = E^*/b^*$. To get some intuitive sense of its meaning, consider the case when B = 1. There is a situation where the individual assessments of within-experiment error bars could readily account for the spread of estimates of the constant between experimenters or labs; or, in other words, error is being successfully arbitraged in this instance. If $B << 1$, then what seems to be happening is that individual researchers are overly cautious, attributing error bars much larger than those warranted by the distribution of values produced by many experimenters. However, if $B >> 1$, then the entire measurement process is deeply flawed, with individual researchers severely underestimating the uncertainty surrounding the value of $X$, or else some other systematic distortion is present, such as violation of the usual assumption of joint independence of the individual experimental determinations of $X$. Especially in this last case, the meta-analyst views the Birge ratio as a warning signal, and will be alerted to search out the sources of between-experimenter inconsistencies. In our terminology, profits are to be made by eliminating some experiments from the average, re-estimation of the magnitudes and errors of some of the network of constants, or, in the worst-case scenario, reconfiguration of the entire theoretical network. It is important to note that the Birge ratio does *not* indicate which of these adjustments is to be preferred.

I offer here some selected Birge ratios for the different sciences of physics, psychology and economics, not to set myself up as instant meta-analyst – the whole thrust of my argument is indeed that such an activity is very difficult and intrinsically communal – but rather to raise methodological questions about the present and future status of empiricism in economics. For the cases of physics and psychology, I take the Birge ratios from existing meta-analysis papers; while for economics, I had to collect and calculate them for myself. The details behind such calculations and sources can be found in my other papers on this subject, as well as in an appendix available from the author.

In Table 13.1 we have two samples of Birge ratios, one for the fundamental physical constants over longer periods of time, and one for some recent subatomic constants, measured over shorter timeframes. The first aspect of

*Table 13.1 Birge ratios, physics*

| *Constant* | *Dates* | *B* | *N*[a] |
|---|---|---|---|
| Speed of light | 1875–1958 | 1.42 | 27 |
| Gravitational | 1798–1983 | 1.38 | 14 |
| Magnetic moment proton | 1949–67 | 1.44 | 7 |
| Fine structure[b] | n.d. | 2.95 | 24 |
| Fine structure[c] | n.d. | 1.26 | 14 |
| | | | |
| Muon lifetime | 1957–80 | 3.28 | 10 |
| Charged pion mass | 1957–80 | 2.23 | 10 |
| Lambda mass | 1957–80 | 4.34 | 10 |
| Lambda lifetime | 1957–80 | 2.72 | 27 |
| Sigma lifetime | 1957–80 | 1.62 | 16 |
| Omega mass | 1957–80 | 0.86 | 11 |

*Notes*:
[a] Number of studies estimating value of constant.
[b] 'High accuracy' measurements of inverse fine structure constant. No dates given.
[c] 'Low accuracy' measurements of inverse fine structure constant. No dates given.

*Sources*: First panel, Henrion and Fischoff (1986, p. 794); second panel, Hedges (1987, p. 447).

the table which jumps out at the novice is the fact that most Birge ratios in physics exceed unity. This might seem a counter-intuitive result, were it not for the brief historical considerations broached in the previous section. To repeat, there always exist inconsistencies in any densely connected network of quantitative constants, and no individual experimenter can effectively allocate error over the entire net. In economic terms, arbitrage opportunities are always present in precision measurement; it is only a question of their greater or lesser magnitude. Furthermore, for many reasons discussed in my other papers, between-experimenter error in physics tends to exceed individual estimates of error bars; people persist in their optimism concerning the taming of error even when the historical record persistently belies their faith.

Our second sample of Birge ratios (Table 13.2), compiled by an educational psychologist specializing in meta-analysis, reports comparable results for 'constants' identified by the experimental psychology community. While a few ratios exceed four, one might claim that the magnitude of quantitative agreement, or the extent of 'arbitrage', was roughly comparable to that found in physics; this was indeed the interpretation of the compiler of these statistics (Hedges, 1987). Again we observe that a preponderance of Birge ratios exceed unity in this community, probably for many of the same reasons as for the physics community. Because the number of studies involved is much larger, we would, if anything, feel even more confident of these magnitudes of Birge ratios. Acknowledging that economists, with their persistent superiority complex relative to the other social sciences, would tend to greater scepticism concerning Table 13.2, we would simply remind them that many different types of phenomena could account for low Birge ratios, and one should not confuse low Birge ratios with unqualified evidence of the validity of the cited theoretical entities.

*Table 13.2 Birge ratios, experimental psychology*

| *Subject* | *B* | *N* |
|---|---|---|
| Sex/spatial perception | 1.64 | 62 |
| Sex/spatial visualization | 1.27 | 81 |
| Sex/verbal ability | 4.09 | 11 |
| Sex/field articulation | 1.75 | 14 |
| Open ed./reading | 1.75 | 14 |
| Open ed./math achievement | 2.73 | 17 |
| Open ed./school aptitude | 2.16 | 11 |
| Open ed./self-concept | 1.39 | 18 |

*Source*: Hedges (1987, p. 449).

*Table 13.3 Birge ratios, economics*

| *Model* | *N* | *Years* | *Birge* |
|---|---|---|---|
| US money demand elasticity | 9 | 1971–88 | 49.66 |
| UK money demand elasticity | 7 | 1971–91 | 73.34 |
| Purchasing power parity, 1920s FF/$ | 6 | 1973–88 | 3.14 |
| US import income elasticity | 14 | 1974–90 | 29.87 |
| US import price elasticity | 10 | 1974–90 | 5.49 |
| US export income elasticity | 13 | 1963–90 | 24.90 |
| US export price elasticity | 9 | 1963–90 | 4.89 |
| Employment–output elasticity, US manufacturing | 6 | 1967–74 | 22.70 |
| Male labour supply | 5 | 1971–6 | 1.26 |
| Welfare spell length and race | 5 | 1986–92 | 2.23 |

*Source*: Philip Mirowski, 'What Could Replication Mean in Econometrics?', unpublished paper.

Table 13.3 reports Birge ratios from some of my own work on the empirical practices of post-1945 neoclassical economists. We would acknowledge at the outset that these 'constants' differ from those in the previous tables in that they are not the product of controlled experiments, but rather the output of econometric packages. The relationship of econometrics to more conventional experimentation has been a contentious issue for the last century; but for many economists, it is often taken for granted that statistical devices can substitute for controlled experimentation.[10] Again for the sake of brevity, let us simply take these convictions for granted, so that we can carry out the comparison with respect to others' practices of error arbitrage. In that case, we discover that Birge ratios in econometrics are orders of magnitude larger than those found in physics and psychology. It seems there exist a myriad of opportunities for error arbitrage in the neoclassical community – $50 bills, contrary to folklore, lie about on the sidewalk in the near neighbourhood of Max U's residence.

Whenever I have presented this evidence to economists, the invidious comparison to the physicists and the psychologists is deemed so galling that I am immediately awash in a plethora of off-the-cuff explanations for the seeming divergence. These responses are themselves extremely revealing of the state of empirical practice in the discipline. There are those, usually theorists of one sort or another, who say: 'So what? We already knew that high theory (perhaps Arrow–Debreu, perhaps Nash non-cooperative game theory, perhaps something else, depending upon location) does not underwrite the constancy of any of the entities you call constants!' Those folks essentially wash their hands of any empirical correlate to their endeavours. Then there are the more empirical practitioners, who find the comparison more directly threatening, and therefore try and come up with reasons why the various studies should not have been subjected to meta-analysis: perhaps the regression coefficients were not strictly comparable, or the use of time series versus cross-sections bespeaks a certain indifference to changing circumstances, or perhaps the real objective of econometricians is not actual estimation of a number, but rather the claim that some coefficient is significantly negative, positive, or different from zero. All of these assertions, if true, create severe cognitive dissonance about what econometricians claim to be doing; but the last is particularly damning, since it involves what is called the 'vote-counting approach' in meta-analysis, something that is known to possess no dependable statistical properties in aggregate research (Glass *et al.*, 1981, pp. 94 *et seq.*). Some others in the audience, perhaps acquainted with my previous work, immediately deploy the *ad hominem* response, claiming that I must have purposely and perversely selected a sample of studies which would place neoclassical economists in the least flattering light.

None of these objections get at the major reason why Birge ratios in economics are so wildly out of line with those found in other quantitative disciplines. As outlined in the previous section, the key to understanding quantitative measurement is to realize that error is structural, not personal, and what counts as error is a function of the social and institutional structures characteristic of the particular science at a particular juncture in its history. As we have demonstrated, physics had evolved the structures of meta-analysis and metrology by the 1940s, whereas psychology achieved something comparable by the 1970s/1980s. Orthodox economics, in contrast, has yet to evolve anything commensurate to those institutions. Indeed, I should go further and assert that economics American-style (which has come to dominate graduate eduction in many countries) is blithely mired in a conception of quantitative error more characteristic of the seventeenth than the late twentieth century. For most economists, a good number is what a virtuous economist says it is. Can Martin Feldstein be harmed by provision of a bad number, ridiculed for his careless empirical practices? No, he cannot; instead he is named chair of the Council of Economic Advisors. Can David Hendry be brought to see that his work can never adequately 'encompass' that of the monetarists whom he opposes? No he cannot. Can a *t*-statistic of 2 or 20 or 200 cause someone to relinquish their adherence to an economic theory? No, it cannot. And contrary to Don (Dierdre) McCloskey, this is not simply a matter of flawed rhetoric.

Is this too pat, too outrageous? I no longer think so. When I first began this project three years ago, like so many others I thought it would be relatively easy to collect numerous estimates of various 'constants' and subject them to meta-analysis. All that would be needed would be to consult some competent review article, say, those found in the *Journal of Economic Literature*. Upon embarking on such an inquiry, I discovered to my dismay *only one* article in the JEL in ten years even bothered to report rival econometric estimates of the particular number in question. But the situation is even worse than that. I have had three graduate research assistants at work on this project, scouring journals for candidates for Birge ratios for three years, and the pathetic number of instances in Table 13.3 is the sum total of what I can report. The reason, contrary to all our untutored folk wisdom, has also been noted by a few others: 'Perhaps the most striking serendipitous finding to us was the relative scarcity of formal hypothesis testing in major [economic] journals. In the absence of RESTAT and the papers and proceedings issue of the AER, papers organized around formal tests of central null hypotheses would be scarce' (de Long and Lang, 1992, p. 1265). The truth of the matter is that full regression equations with clearly identified relevant standard errors, much less adequate documentation of the various sources of data and choices of estimation techniques, are conspicuous in their absence, once you start looking for them. I challenge any reader to collect more than ten instances of individual regression estimates of any number they believe to be concensus values of any economic coefficient. If you do succeed, and I wish you well, please send them to me.

## 3. PLURALISM AND THE FREE MARKET OF IDEAS

What is it about the economics profession that has allowed it to maintain the facade of a 'hard' science in the face of empirical practices which would seem to situate it amongst the most backwards of all quantitative sciences? This question cannot be answered in my simplistic unicausal manner and, moreover, the final word can only be had in an historical narrative. Some of the story will ultimately hinge upon the way economic theory mimicked the outward trappings of physics without taking its core insights to heart (Mirowski, 1989). But, to a first approximation, there is something special about neoclassical economics which could account for its chequered empirical career outlined above. It has to do with the way theories of the economic actor are often turned around to explain the behaviour of the scientist as well.

As everyone knows, neoclassical economics is fundamentally a vision of one version of the invisible hand, where the market mechanism manages to reconcile various self-interested behaviours and produce coherent results as an unintended consequence. This is the old saw, taken from Smith, of our lack of indebtedness to the benevolence of the butcher and the baker. It is a vision of social life which is concertedly methodologically individualist, devoted to a thin notion of formal rationality, and not a little mystical when it comes to specifying the process whereby the coordination is brought about. This is also the way many orthodox economists think about science, and their own careers. It is often expressed by using market metaphors: the marginal product of a colleague, retailing an idea, the free marketplace of ideas. The image is one of numerous individuals concocting bits of intellectual property, sending them out into the marketplace, and having them all find their true value, culminating in all and sundry at a Pareto optimum of knowledge.

It is this root metaphor, resonating with the economic metaphors inherent in the Neyman–Pearson and Bayesian inferential traditions, that leads the average economist to believe that the econometric journal literature is full of concensus estimates of important economic constants, even though the 'facts' in their own narrow area of speciality may be subject to a myriad of technical objections. What is known is not perfect, but free discourse amongst equals guarantees that what is known is the best available information. And it is this, more than anything else, that explains the revulsion of academic economists towards the institution of meta-analysis, once they may learn of its existence. More than once, when I have described the lack of a meta-analytic tradition in economics, I have garnered the response: 'Do you really want Big Brother?' 'How dare anyone censor my regressions!' 'Don't mess with the free marketplace of ideas!'

I believe this is all an artifact of images of science specific to economics, rather than indicative of any solid understanding of the nature of quantitative error. In fact, the supposed pluralism of the free market of ideas serves to mask a rigid hierarchical control of access to journals and grants in the American context, in conjunction with the most eggregiously lax attitudes towards the quality of reporting of empirical endeavour found in any science. The problem is that pluralism reigns in econometrics precisely in the limited sphere where it is most destructive and harmful, namely, the arbitrage of quantitative error. There is no escaping the fact that the sciences are stacked with social structures inimicable to plural interpretations of their doctrines; yet economics has managed to maintain its monolithic reputation by means of the most curious of conjunctures: ruthless policing of mathematical theoretical conformity in conjunction with anarchy in the empirical regime, all framed within an ideology of absolute freedom of inquiry. It is a formidable achievement, not found anywhere else in the gamut of academic inquiry, with the possible exception of cosmology or post-structuralist literary theory. Perhaps it is the apotheosis of Modernism.

## ACKNOWLEDGEMENTS

I should like to thank Wade Hands, Roy Weintraub, Neil de Marchi, Dan Hausman and Geoff Hodgson for helpful discussions. All the sticky bits which remain are due to my own recalcitrance. A somewhat altered version of this chapter will appear in the philosophy journal *Dialogue*.

## NOTES

1. For the recent work in history and sociology, see, for instance, (Collins, 1985; Franklin, 1990; Gooding *et al.*, 1989; Latour, 1987; MacKenzie, 1991). Unfortunately, some methodologists persist in acting like the last two decades haven't happened: see Blaug in Blackhouse (1994).
2. See (Mirowski, 1994b, 1995; and (O'Connell, 1993; Hon, 1989).
3. An excellent description of this process in the case of one of the protagonists, Thomas Sargent, can be found in Sent (1994).
4. One bellweather of this phenomenon is the chastened history of Cowles found in Christ (1994). Another is the movement of graduate students at top-rated institutions out of the field.
5. See Ellerman (1994); Mirowski (1994a).
6. This notion of 'connectedness' as of all the subsequent concepts in the text, have formal expressions in graph theory. To access a sketch of those translations, see Mirowski (1994b).
7. See Tiling (1973); Olesko (1988, 1991); Gooday (1990); Mirowski (1994b); Sheynin (1993).
8. But see O'Connell (1993); Olkin in Wachter and Straf (1990); Danzinger (1990).
9. A misnomer if there ever was one. The fact that textbooks never adequately represented either the Neyman–Pearson or Bayesian positions is ably argued in Gigerenzer and Murray (1987).
10. For some claims along these lines, see Morgan (1990) and Cartwright (1989).

## REFERENCES

Backhouse, Roger (ed.) (1994), *New Directions in Economic Methodology*, London: Routledge

Birge, Raymond (1957), 'A Survey of the Systematic Evaluation of the Universal Physical Constants', *Nuovo Cimento*, Supp. 6, pp. 39–67.

Cartwright, Nancy (1989), *Nature's Capacities and their Measurement*, Oxford: Oxford University Press.

Christ, Carl (1994), 'The Cowles Commission's Contributions to Econometrics at Chicago, 1939–55, *Journal of Economic Literature*, **32**, pp. 30–59.

Collins, Harry (1985), *Changing Order*, London: Sage.

Danziger, Kurt (1990), *Constructing the Subject*, New York: Cambridge University Press.

de Long, B. and Lang, Kevin (1992), 'Are all Economic Hypotheses False?', *Journal of Political Economy,* **100**, pp. 1257–72.

Dewald, W., Thursby, J. and Anderson, R. (1986), 'Replication in Empirical Economics', *American Economic Review*, **76**, pp. 587–603.

Ellerman, David (1994), *Essays in Intellectual Trespassing*, Totawa: Rowman & Littlefield.

Franklin, Allen (1990), *Experiment Right or Wrong*, New York: Cambridge University Press.

Gigerenzer, G. and Murray, D. (1987), *Cognition as Intuitive Statistics*, Hillsdale: Lawrence Erlbaum.

Gigerenzer, G., Daston, L., Porter, T. and Beatty, L. (1989), *The Empire of Chance*, New York: Cambridge University Press.

Glass, G., McGaw, B. and Smith, M. (1981), *Meta-Analysis in Social Research*, Beverly Hills: Sage.

Gooday, Grahame (1990), 'Precision Measurement and the Genesis of Physics Teaching Laboratories', *British Journal for the History of Science*, **23**, pp. 25–51.

Gooding, D., Pinch, T. and Schaffer, S. (1989), *The Uses of Experiment*, Cambridge: Cambridge University Press.

Hedges, Larry (1987), 'How Hard is Hard Science, How Soft is Soft Science?', *American Psychologist*, **42**, pp. 443–55.

Hedges, Larry and Olkin, Ingram (1985), *Statistical Methods for Meta-analysis*, New York: Academic Press.

Henrion, Max and Fischoff, Baruch (1986), 'Assessing Uncertainty in the Physical Constants', *American Journal of Physics*, **54**, pp. 791–7.

Helmholtz, Carl (1990), 'Raymond Thayer Birge', in *Biographical Memoirs of the National Academy of Sciences*, vol. 59, pp. 73–84.

Hon, Giora (1989), 'Toward a Typology of Experimental Errors', *Studies in the History and Philosophy of Sciences*, **20**, pp. 469–504.

Latour, Bruno (1987), *Science in Action*, Cambridge: Harvard University Press.

MacKenzie, Donald (1991), *Inventing Accuracy*, Cambridge, MA: MIT Press.

Mirowski, Philip (1989), *More Heat than Light*, New York: Cambridge University Press.

Mirowski, Philip (1994a), 'Arbitrage, Symmetries and the Social Theory of Value', in Amitava Dutt (ed.), *New Directions in Analytical Political Economy*, Aldershot: Edward Elgar.

Mirowski, Philip (1994b), 'A Visible Hand in the Marketplace of Ideas', *Science in Context*, **7** (3), pp. 563–89.

Mirowski, Philip (1995), 'Three Ways to Think about Testing in Econometrics', *Journal of Econometrics*, **76**, pp. 25–46.

Morgan, Mary (1990), *A History of Econometrics*, Cambridge: Cambridge University Press.

O'Connell, Joseph (1993), 'Metrology', *Social Studies of Science*, **23**, pp. 129–74.

Olesko, Kathryn (1988), 'Michelson and the Reform of Physics Instruction', in S. Goldgerg and R. Steuewer (eds), *The Michelson Era in American Physics*, New York: American Institute of Physics.

Olesko, Kathyrn (1991), *Physics as a Calling*, Ithaca: Cornell University Press.

Petley, Brian (1985), *The Fundamental Physical Constants and the Frontiers of Measurement*, Bristol: Adam Hilger.

Rosenfeld, Arthur (1975), 'The Particle Data Group', *Annual Review of Nuclear Science*, **25**, pp. 555–98.

Sent, Esther-Mirjam (1994), 'Resisting Sargent ', unpublished Ph.D. thesis, Stanford University.

Sheynin, Oscar (1993), 'The Treatment of Observations in Early Astronomy', *Archive for the History of the Exact Sciences*, **46**, pp. 153–89.

Sombart, Werner (1915), *The Quintessence of Capitalism*, London: Allen & Unwin.
Stanley, T. and Jarrel, S. (1989), 'Meta-regression analysis: A Quantitative Method of Literature Surveys', *Journal of Economic Surveys*, **3**, pp. 161–70.
Stigler, Stephen (1986), *A History of Statistics*, Cambridge: Harvard University Press.
Tiling, Laura (1973), 'The Interpretation of Observational Errors in the 18th and Early 19th Centuries', unpublished Ph.D. thesis, University of London.
Wachter, Kenneth and Straf, Myron (eds) (1990), *The Future of Meta-analysis*, New York: Russell Sage.

## COMMENT

**Carlo A. Favero**

This chapter proposes to apply meta-analysis to econometrics by producing Birge's ratio to evaluate best-practice values and appropriate error attributions for estimated parameters of interest in economics. According to the author, the results of his investigation are disappointing for applied economists in two respects: not only are the Birge's ratios in this field very high, denoting high variability across experiments and casting a shade of doubt on the concept of 'constant parameters' in economics, but the Birge's ratios are also very difficult to compute, because of lack of data. On the second source of disappointment I do not have very much to say; it is very worrying that someone who has three research assistants at work on a project, scouring journals for candidates for Birge ratios for three years, come out with 'the pathetic number of instances in Table 13.3'. There is a challenge here to establish if this fact is worrying for the profession or for the research assistants, but I shall not make this point the issue of my discussion.[1] I shall concentrate instead on the first source of disappointment, to illustrate why Birge ratios in econometrics should be taken with more care than in other sciences, and why Birge ratios may be expected to be high in time series econometrics (all the Birge ratios reported in Table 13.3 refer to studies based on time series).

In time series econometrics the estimated values of parameters are dependent on the specification of the estimated model. The applied econometrician does not know the Data Generating Process (DGP) and all he can do is to approximate it with some (linear) parsimonious model; the choice of the specification of the model affects the outcome of the estimation procedure. Suppose that we have two models: one is correctly specified (it does not omit relevant variables) the other is not. As a consequence of mis-specification, the estimated parameter in the second model is very far removed from the estimated parameter in the first one and we are likely to obtain a very high Birge ratio. However, the Birge ratio, in this case, does not suggest anything on the level of the uncertainty with which 'constants' are estimated in economics, it just confirms the importance of validating a model before basing any inference on it.

To illustrate this point further I shall consider two applications, relevant to interpreting the outcome of a conspicuous body of research in applied econometrics.

## Application 1

Let us consider the following DGP, where are all the variables are expressed in logarithms:

$$\begin{aligned} y_t &= a_0 + a_1 y_{t-1} + b_0 x_t + b_1 x_{t-1} + u_t \\ x_t &= c_0 + c_1 x_{t-1} + \varepsilon_t \quad 0 \leq c_1 \leq 1 \end{aligned} \tag{1}$$

Where the residuals are white noise processes, not contemporaneously correlated, therefore $x$ is strongly exogenous (Hendry, 1994) for the estimation of the parameter capturing the contemporaneous relation between $y$ and $x$. The investigator estimates a single equation model to explain the behaviour of $y$, but omits the first order dynamics from his model:

$$y_t = \beta x_t + u_t \tag{2}$$

It is very easy to show that the mis-specification will prevent the OLS estimator of the parameter $\beta$ from being consistent. In fact, we have:

$$plim\, \hat{\beta} = \frac{b_0 + b_1 c_1}{1 - a_1 c_1} \tag{3}$$

Where *plim* denotes the probability limit of the estimator. Equation (3) makes clear that the effect of mis-specification is the identification of an estimated elasticity of $y$ to $x$ which lies in between the short-run elasticity ($b_0$) and the long-run elasticity $[(b_0 + b_1)/(1 - a_1)]$. It is worth noting that, for short memory of the process generating $x$, the estimated elasticity is close to the short-run elasticity, whilst, when the process generating $x$ gets closer to a process with a unit root, the estimated elasticity converges to the long-run elasticity. Given that the long-run elasticity and the short-run elasticity might very well be far removed, it follows that mis-specification is a potential explanation for very high Birge ratios.

## Application 2

Let us consider the following DGP:

$$\begin{aligned} C_t &= \sum_{i=0}^{\infty} Y_{t+i}^{e} \\ Y_t &= a_1 Y_{t-1} + u_t \end{aligned} \tag{4}$$

Where $C$ is consumption, $Y$ is income and $u$ is a white noise error term. Then the DGP for consumption represents a very stylized life-cycle model with an autoregressive model for income.

The investigator estimates the following static model for consumption:

$$C_t = \alpha + \beta Y_t + \varepsilon_t \tag{5}$$

In the case we have:

$$plim\,\hat{\beta} = \frac{1}{1 - a_1} \tag{6}$$

therefore the static model produces an estimate of the marginal propensity to consume which depends on the parameters driving the process generating income. Every break in the process generating income should be reflected in the estimated marginal propensity to consume. In other words income is not super-exogenous for the estimation of the parameter of interest and the static consumption function is subject to the Lucas (1976) critique. Estimating backward-looking models when the DGP is forward-looking is another recipe for high Birge ratios.

The two applications we have just considered illustrate that care should be taken before computing mechanically Birge ratios for econometric estimates. However, I am convinced that the chapter by Mirowski has an important message to convey on the application of meta-analysis to econometrics. For instance one could apply meta-analysis to assess the results of alternative approaches to time series econometrics. Reconsidering the second application I have discussed I see some room to apply meta-analysis to evaluate the comparative reliability of feedback and feedforward econometric specifications (Hendry, 1988; Favero and Hendry, 1992). As we have seen, whenever the Lucas critique is relevant, feedback models should feature high Birge ratios. On the other hand, estimates of the parameter in Euler Equations derived by the Generalized Method of Moments (Hansen, 1982); (Hansen and Singleton, 1984); (Oliner *et al.*, 1992), being able to separate the deep parameter from the expectational parameter, should produce a lower Birge ratio. The comparison of the estimates obtained from feedback and feedforward models through Birges ratios, once the issue of specification has been controlled for, could be an interesting and alternative way to provide indirect evidence on the merit of alternative econometric approaches.

## Note

1. Prof. Mirowski himself remarks that at the beginning of his project he thought it would have been relatively easy to collect numerous estimates of various 'constants' in economics and subject them to meta-analysis.

## References

Favero, C.A. and Hendry, D.F. (1992), 'Testing the Lucas Critique. A Survey', *Econometric Reviews*, **2**, pp. 265–318.

Hansen, L. (1982), 'Large Sample Properties of The Generalized Method of Moments Estimators', *Econometrica,* **4** (50), pp. 1029–53.

Hansen, L. and Singleton, K. (1982), 'Generalized Instrumental Variables Estimation of Nonlinear Rational Expectations Models', *Econometrica*, **50** (5), pp. 1269–91.

Hendry, D.F. (1988), 'The Encompassing Implications of Feedback versus Feedforward Mechanisms in Econometrics', *Oxford Economic Papers*, **4** (1), pp. 133–47.

Hendry, D.F. (1995), *Dynamic Econometrics*, Oxford: Oxford University Press.

Lucas, R.E. (1976), 'Econometric Policy Evaluation. A Critique', in Brunner and Meltzer (eds), *The Phillips Curve and the Labour Market* ', Carnegie-Rochester Conference Series on Public Policy, vol. 1, Amsterdam, North-Holland.

Oliner S., Rudebusch, G. and Sichel, D. (1992), *The Lucas Critique Revisited: Assessing the Stability of Empirical Euler Equations*, Board of Governors of the Federal Reserve System, D.P. 130.

# 14. The economic consequences of pluralism

**Shaun P. Hargreaves Heap**

## 1. INTRODUCTION

Let us suppose we live in a society where people (or groups) value things differently and where we also value this diversity. There is, so to speak, not just a plurality, there is also what I shall refer to as a political commitment to pluralism. The question addressed by this chapter is: what institutional arrangements will best respect the diversity of view? In other words, what institutional arrangements will encode our shared political commitment to pluralism? In particular, I focus on this question for the difficult case of societies which are marked by maximum disagreement: that is, where the only thing held in common by the different groups is the political commitment to pluralism.

The market seems an obvious choice. After all, the apparent virtue of a market exchange is that neither party has to give up or modify its views regarding what is useful or worthwhile as an exchange only occurs when each party believes that they gain according to their own way of looking at things. There is no need, for instance, for the agents to agree on anything like why the object of the exchange should be valued. Indeed the greater the disagreement in this sense the better, as this is likely to expand the trading opportunities. All that must be agreed is that each should be allowed to hold and pursue their own views so long as it does not undermine those of others and then the market will seem perfectly suited for the task.

To pursue this thought, it is not just the market which seems the obvious choice: it is the 'free' market. Interventions in markets would not necessarily be ruled out, but it seems they could only be sanctioned when all agreed on the point of intervention; and in a thoroughgoing plurality this seems likely only around issues of efficiency where all views stand to gain. There could be no interventions on distributional matters, for instance, because the intervention would amount to a privileging of one person or group's view over another and this goes against the grain of our political commitment to pluralism. In effect, we value the right of everyone to hold whatever beliefs they like so long as they do not seek to impose them on others because this is the condition under which a plurality of views is sustained. Hence we are bound to be uncomfortable whenever any public agency decides between views in order to favour one over another.

Thus on this account one might expect the advance of the political idea of pluralism to go hand in hand with the extension of the 'free' market. In this chapter, I shall argue that this account is deeply misleading.

In the next section, I sketch what seems to be wrong with this portrayal of the market as an institution which allows agents, so to speak, to 'agree to disagree'. The question then becomes, if not 'free markets', what? The third and fourth sections take up this issue by considering how a political commitment to pluralism might lead to certain constraints being placed on the operation of markets. Rawls is an obvious starting point in section 3 because he has recently recast his theory of justice as a political theory which applies to pluralist societies and it carries clear implications for the institutional arrangements of such a society. However, he also appears to assume that agents agree about rather more than the 'agreement to disagree'. Of course, the contingent fact of further agreement, although not necessarily the Rawlsian form, is far from implausible and is probably characteristic of most pluralist societies. But I am concerned with the most difficult case where groups literally agree about nothing except the commitment to pluralism and section 4 sketches an alternative principle of justice which could complement markets in support of the political valuation of pluralism in these circumstances.

## 2. MARKETS IN VACUO

The competitive model of markets is probably the source of what is misleading about the view I have just sketched. In such models, agents receive the price at which trades occur, courtesy of something like the Walrasian auctioneer, and so the terms of the exchange are liable to seem in some degree perfectly 'normal'. In most markets, however, the absence of anything approximating the information generating device of the Walrasian auctioneer means that prices are set by human hands; and typically information and transaction costs give the parties to the exchange something to bargain over. As a result bargaining models become indispensible for our understanding of market processes and this is where the trouble begins.

There are two approaches to the bargaining problem in the economics literature: the axiomatic and the non-cooperative game theoretic approaches. Both used to provide support for a unique solution to the bargaining problem: the so-called Nash solution that maximizes the product of the utility gains of each party which come from agreement. The problem as far as the earlier argument is concerned is that neither seems as secure in this result as was once the case. There seems, for instance, to be no obvious reason to associate the 'independence of irrelevant alternatives' and 'symmetry' axioms with the assumptions of instrumental rationality and common knowledge of this rationality which are the mainstays of modern game theory. Likewise, the non-cooperative support seems to depend too much on the precise protocols of the bargaining procedure and a controversial reliance on the principle of backward induction for any general comfort (see Sugden, 1991 and Varoufakis, 1991).

The grounds for this new scepticism regarding the Nash solution are not hard to find. When you strip most bargaining problems down to their bare basics, you have something which involves two parties making a claim to a share of a pie. If their shares sum to 100 per cent, then they each get what they claimed; whereas if they do not there is still more bargaining to be done before the cake can be divided (either because the sum exceeds 100 per cent or because they sum to less than 100 per cent and so leave a part of the pie still to be divided). As a result when one player claims x per cent this is a Nash equilibrium (cf. the Nash bargaining solution) in the non-cooperative game so long as the other player claims 100-x per cent. Hence there are any number of Nash equilibria in this game: one for each value of 'x'.

Since most game theorists believe that a Nash equilibrium is (at best) what is entailed by the usual game theoretic assumptions of instrumental rationality and common knowledge of this rationality, this means the outcome of the bargaining problem looks uncomfortably indeterminate. In other words, the bargaining game yields multiple Nash equilibria and without a theory of equilibrium selection we shall not be able to say what will happen in many markets.

There seem to be two ways out of this problem. One is to reflect deeper on what follows from the assumptions of instrumental rationality and common knowledge of this rationality. This defines what is usually known as the Nash refinement project in game theory; and it seems to have failed to produce anything which commands common assent (see Kreps, 1990). The other involves introducing something into the analysis which has previously been taken to be 'extraneous' to the conventional game theoretic description. It will have to be 'extraneous' if it is to identify one equilibrium from among the many because the conventional description provides no way of distinguishing between them – that is why there is the problem of equilibrium selection. Furthermore, whatever extraneous feature is used in this way, it will have to be used by the bargainers in the same way. Otherwise it will not select the same equilibrium for each player. In shorthand, it is sometimes said that the bargainers will have to draw on shared resources of 'extraneous information'.

The reasons for my scepticism regarding the institutional suitability of 'free' markets to a world where agents 'agree to disagree' will now be apparent. If markets are to work when they involve bargaining, then there must be a way of selecting one equilibrium from the many potential ones. Otherwise the market participants will not be able, in effect, to agree on a price. And to select one equilibrium in this way, it appears the agents must draw on some shared sources of 'extraneous information'. So they must agree on something beyond the fact that they are 'agreeing to disagree'.

In other words, 'agreeing only to disagree' in markets is a recipe for disagreement and markets do not work without agreements over such central variables as price. This seems to be the message from the theory of bargaining problems and to check very coarsely that this is not just a theoretical curiosity, it is perhaps worth taking a quick glance at the cross-country data on relative strike frequency in Table 14.1.

Of course, there are well-known difficulties with such comparisons and I am not inclined to make much of them. But it is surprising if it is just coincidence that those societies like the US, Canada, the UK and Australia which are most closely associated with the tradition of political pluralism are also those which seem to be most strike-prone (i.e. the ones which seem to find it most difficult to secure agreements in one important area of bargaining).

*Table 14.1* *Volume of strike activity by country (annual days lost per 1,000 workers)*

| *Country* | *1955–62* | *1963–73* | *1974–9* | *1980–88* |
|---|---|---|---|---|
| Italy | 412 | 870 | 1 067 | 465 |
| Canada | 284 | 590 | 878 | 444 |
| Eire | 139 | 464 | 620 | 316 |
| US | 435 | 464 | 312 | 106 |
| Australia | 228 | 297 | 601 | 302 |
| UK | 185 | 296 | 491 | 333 |
| Belgium | 282 | 146 | 193 | 60 |
| France | 116 | 162 | 160 | 57 |
| Denmark | 282 | 171 | 71 | 169 |
| Sweden | 1 | 37 | 25 | 176 |
| Japan | 121 | 76 | 78 | 8 |
| Norway | 150 | 24 | 55 | 97 |
| Germany | 25 | 27 | 42 | 26 |
| Netherlands | 30 | 26 | 21 | 14 |

*Source*: Cornwall (1993).

Plainly none of these societies is pluralist in the sense that they only 'agree to disagree'. They often agree on a lot more than this. The point of the illustration is that the frequency of disagreement does seem to be associated with the degree of pluralism. In this sense then, there seem to be both theoretical and (casual) empirical reasons for doubting the advance of pluralism will reinforce the claims of the 'free' market. Indeed, a move towards pluralism, rather than highlighting the virtues of 'free' markets, is more likely to contribute to their malperformance through strikes and the like.

Is this the only conclusion to be drawn? The issue is perhaps not as clear cut as I have tried to make it. It all depends on whether the commitment to pluralism is accompanied by any further shared beliefs. In practice, of course, many pluralist societies are marked by a range of shared beliefs that are encoded in institutions which complement the operation of markets. However, I am concerned with whether such shared beliefs are entailed by the commitment to pluralism or are merely contingently found in pluralist societies. In other words, suppose nothing is shared except the commitment to pluralism, would this commitment entail any further shared beliefs which might help secure agreements in bargaining games by acting as 'shared sources of extraneous information'?

What sort of beliefs might we be looking for here? In the context of the bargaining games, the most obvious candidate for a shared source of extraneous information seems to be a shared sense of justice since the selection of one equilibrium rather than another will determine how the benefits from trade are distributed between the players. (There is also some support for this from the experimental literature on bargaining games; see Roth, 1988). Consequently, in the remainder of this chapter I shall focus on whether a political commitment to pluralism has any clear entailments regarding a theory of justice.

A word of explanation is perhaps in order before making this change in direction. I began by talking in terms of the institutions that are appropriate to societies which value pluralism and I am now considering the sources of shared extraneous information which might obtain in a community that values pluralism. The change from institutions to beliefs is more apparent than real. Shared sources of extraneous information are typically encoded in the rules of behaviour (either informal or formal) which make up an institution. Thus when considering the possible shared sources of extraneous information, I am in effect discussing the character rather than the detail of the institutions (formal and informal) to associate with plural societies.

## 3. PLURALISM AND JUSTICE AS FAIRNESS

Rawls (1992) has recently recast his famous Theory of Justice as a political rather than a moral theory. It is a theory which he now concedes applies only to those societies which embody what he refers to as a 'reasonable' pluralism. It is not always clear what Rawls has in mind when he uses this term 'reasonable' pluralism, but I shall take it to be a society containing diverse viewpoints which all nevertheless value pluralism. So this is not just a society where there are many viewpoints, rather it is a society where each viewpoint values belonging to a plural grouping. In other words, I shall take it to mean what I referred to at the beginning as a political commitment to pluralism. This is, of course, somewhat self-serving, given the task that I have in mind, but it does not seem to do Rawls a major injustice.

Thus if we accept Rawls's argument (or my version of it), then it seems we have a ready made theory of justice to accompany the political commitment to pluralism. It contains two principles. The first provides for the full range of liberal freedoms which can be consistently enjoyed by all. The second is the difference (or maximin) principle which allows us to choose between different social arrangements which embody the first principle.

For the purposes of the argument in this chapter, where I am concerned (only) with the economic institutions of pluralism, it is probably uncontentious if the first principle is held to be satisfied by the institutions of markets when they allow for voluntary exchange between individuals who are guaranteed the same rights before the law. In this way, the second principle is left to do the work of selecting the equilibrium in our bargaining games; and so Rawls provides the perfect answer to our problem. He supplies a theory which first supports the original intuition that markets are well suited to plural societies and then it also gives us the shared something else (encoded either formally or informally in institutions) which will enable markets to function by guiding agents towards a particular equilibrium.

This simple mapping of the two principles on to our problem of 'markets plus what?' might require more careful argument if it was to be taken further. However, there are reasons for doubting the argument before we even reach this point. The problem for Rawls's theory really arises at an earlier stage in the derivation of the second principle. His recent work offers no alternative account of why we should select the arrangement that provides the best outcome for those who are least well-off and so we are left with his original explanation of the maximin rule. This had two parts.

The first is the argument that agents with 'moral personalities' will seek arrangements that are impartial in their operation and which he uses to justify considering things from behind a 'veil of ignorance'. I have no objection to this part of the argument. In particular, the condition of impartiality seems to follow naturally from the commitment to pluralism (at least as well as it does from the presumption of 'moral personalities', and I shall have more to say on this below). My only query with the device of the veil of ignorance is whether it is capable of delivering unambiguous guidance. This leads on to the second part of his argument, where he suggests that people, from behind the veil of ignorance, will use the maximin principle when deciding between arrangements. This is the difficult bit. First, it presumes that each person when they go behind the veil of ignorance will actually evaluate the outcome for each actual person under each possible arrangement in the same way. You can see why this must be the case, otherwise it would be perfectly possible for different people behind the veil of ignorance to rank social arrangements differently even though they are using the same decision rule (for the simple reason that they see each arrangement differently). Secondly, it assumes that maximin is the decision rule that rational agents will employ when making decisions under this kind of uncertainty.

Both presumptions seem difficult to justify in plural societies unless they are built-in by assumption as further sources of agreement. But why should this be the case in genuinely plural societies? Consider, for example, the last assumption over the decision rule. Rawls and many moral philosophers may think this is what rational agents will do, but most economists, for instance, are unhappy with the maximin principle and would prefer some expected 'value' calculation to guide action. So even within the academy there is not likely to be an agreement over this decision rule!

Of course, there is also a procedural solution for generating agreement in pluralist societies which is perhaps worth mentioning in this context because it is often linked with pluralist beliefs: the ballot box. In other words, it is sometimes argued that in the absence of agreement over the substantive character of the institutions (shared beliefs), there is still the possibility of an agreement over the procedures that will determine these institutions. Thus people will agree to abide by the results of the ballot box. This, however, is unlikely for several reasons. For instance, there are problems associated with the Arrow Impossibility Theorem and the problems of minorities (see Riker, 1982); both of which make it unlikely that people will generally agree to this procedural solution when there are significant differences of view.

## 4. PLURALISM AND EQUAL RELATIVE CONCESSION

Although I am suspicious for these reasons of the particular claim made by Rawls and the traditional link between pluralism and democracy, I am not disheartened by the prospect of a growing political commitment to pluralism because there are other ways of cashing-in this commitment. For example,

O'Neill (1989a, b), drawing more directly from Kant than Rawls, suggests that a commitment to pluralism within a society generates principles of justice which must be universalizable. Thus she asks, 'What does justice require of such a plurality?' and replies:

> At least we can claim that their most basic principles must be ones that *could* be adopted by all. If they were not, at least some agents would have to be excluded from the plurality for whom the principle can hold, whose boundaries would have to be drawn more narrowly. (1989b, p. 18)

In other words, unless a principle for action is universalizable, its use would undermine the plurality to which we are committed. The link with Kant's moral philosophy and the categorical imperative will be obvious, but it also runs deeper in a way which illumines why we might be committed to the value of pluralism. For Kant the crucial insight of reason is that it knows its own limits – this is why the books were titled 'critiques of reason'. For instance, he rejects the Cartesian enterprise of introspection because it exempts one's own life from radical doubt. Like all attempts to build knowledge on secure foundations, it begs questions about the justification of the foundation. And to answer the question by an appeal to some more 'fundamental' foundation (in the spirit of foundationalism) is to initiate a process of infinite regress as the same question is asked of these more 'fundamental' foundations, and so on. Instead, Kant is looking for how knowledge can be shared and constituted among a plurality of different agents, each with a different voice and each with a different view. His answer is weak in the sense that it does not tell us directly what knowledge consists of, but he does supply a negative constraint which any principle of knowledge must satisfy if it is to be shared by a community of people: any principle of thought must be capable of being followed by all if it is to be constitutive of knowledge in a group of rational agents.

Thus we may, in effect, come to value pluralism because we recognize that all knowledge is uncertain (as a result, for instance, of the problems of foundationalism) and so we do not want to make claims of certainty for one position over all others. Nevertheless this does not mean that any view should be respected. Only views which satisfy the condition of universalizability could possibly be the objects of knowledge since any piece of knowledge must be capable of being shared by rational agents. Again O'Neill (1989a, p. 27) puts the point in the following way:

> [Kant] denies not only that we have access to transcendent metaphysical truths, such as the claims of rational theology, but also that reason has intrinsic or transcendent vindication, or is given in consciousness. He does not deify reason. The only route by which we can vindicate certain ways of thinking and acting,

> and claim that those ways have authority, is by considering how we must discipline our thinking if we are to think or act at all. This disciplining leads us not to algorithms of reason, but to certain constraints on all thinking, communication and interaction among any plurality. In particular we are led to the principle of rejecting thought, act or communication that is guided by principles that others cannot adopt, and so to the Categorical Imperative.

This seems reasonable enough but does a condition of universalizability carry any bite in the sense, to return to the ground with a bump, that it might provide a source of shared 'extraneous beliefs' in bargaining problems? For O'Neill, it has the great virtue of preventing a commitment to pluralism collapsing into relativism because it rules out the practices of Nazis (since they denied moral status to the Jews and other groups and so their principles were never designed to be universalizable), but does it do anything more? Will it for instance enable two agents holding very different but 'reasonable' views of what is just, in the sense that each view satisfies the condition of being potentially universalizable, to come to an agreement?

At first sight the answer does not look very promising as one of the traditional criticisms of Kantian ethics is precisely that too many principles satisfy the condition of universalizability for it to be at all helpful. However, it does carry surprising bite under certain conditions. When the two agents literally agree about nothing, including the description of the problem itself, then there is only one principle that is universalizable. This is the principle of equal relative concession.

To illustrate this principle and the conditions in more detail, let us suppose that there is a conflict between two groups over, say, the development of a resource which arises because they have very different conceptions of the 'good' or justice. Further, we assume that each view of the world is coherent in the sense that it can evaluate the relative merits of the various ways that the resource might be developed by attaching a utility number to each outcome (where these numbers are arbitrary up to any positive linear transformation). In other words, each group has a cardinal 'utility' ordering over the possible uses of the resource. Such numbers are, of course, strictly incommensurable between groups (as indeed they must be if we are to keep with the commitment to pluralism). The utility numbers for the groups in the event of non-development are $d_1$, $d_2$. Now suppose the best possible development for group 1 which leaves group 2 feeling no better-off than non-development yields that group $I_1$. Likewise the maximum return possible for group 2 is $I_2$. Various compromise paths of development between these two extremes are possible and they yield a continuous set of possible utility combinations for the two groups, given by the frontier in Figure 14.1.

This is a standard representation of a bargaining problem and we would like to be able to choose one of the paths represented by a point on the utility

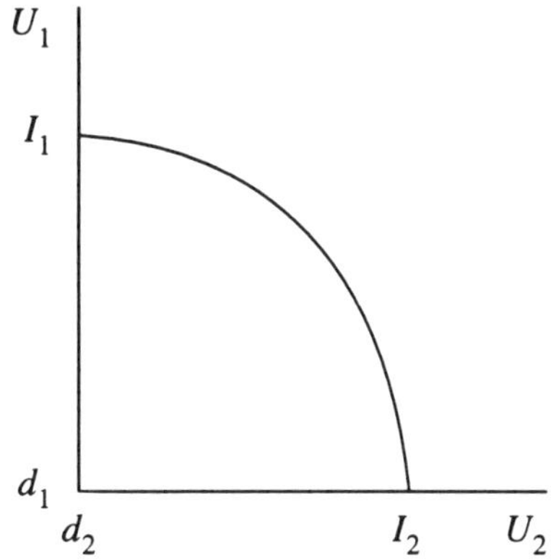


*Figure 14.1 Conflict between two groups*

frontier as this represents an improvement for both groups over non-development. The problem is that the groups do not share the same views with respect to justice or the good and so they cannot use such a view to adjudicate in this dispute over how to develop this resource – indeed the dispute here arises precisely because they do not share such a view. However, I shall assume that both groups value pluralism and so seek a rule for dispute resolution which can be universalized. If I further require that the rule operates for a group only on the preferences that the group itself holds (because I want to consider conditions of maximum disagreement and so I do not want to build in implicit agreements over the description of the problem itself by allowing rules for an agent which operate on both its and the other agent's utility information), then there is only one rule that universalizes. It is the Kalai–Smorodinsky (1975) principle of equal relative concession. This principle selects that option for development which yields the utility pair $(u_1, u_2)$ on the frontier such that

$$(u_1 - d_1) / (I_1 - d_1) = (u_2 - d_2) / (I_2 - d_2)$$

It will be obvious that this satisfies the condition of universalizability since it requires every group to be treated in the same relative way. Thus any group's relative concession is matched by all other group's concessions and so the application of the principle to one group does not preclude its application to another group. What is perhaps less obvious is why this is the only principle which is universalizable. The quick explanation is as follows (see Hargreaves Heap, 1994, for a full discussion). The assumption of cardinality means that we can represent the maximum and minimum utilities by '1' and '0' respectively without any loss of generality. The condition that the rule operates for each agent on that agent's utility information means that the rule must select a fraction for each agent when it operates on that agent's (0,1) utility interval. In other words, admissable rules select fractions individually and the condition of universalizability means that any fraction selected must be capable of being selected for all agents. Thus we are looking for equal fractions; and this is exactly what the equal relative concession principle requires.[1]

In other words, the political commitment to pluralism under conditions of what otherwise amounts to complete disagreement entails a commitment to a shared principle of justice (equal relative concession); and when this principle is encoded either formally or informally in institutions that guide market behaviour, it will secure determinate market outcomes. Of course, in many actual pluralist societies, the disagreements may be less far-reaching; with the result that the agreement occurs around a different principle of justice and the characters of the institutions which complement markets are correspondingly different.

## 5. CONCLUSION

I want to claim two things in this chapter. The first is that it is misleading to imagine that a commitment to pluralism and 'free' markets walk hand-in-hand. Markets will only work when the participants share some background beliefs, particularly, I suspect, with respect to justice. In this sense, a form of pluralism where people literally 'agree only to disagree' would be a poor accompaniment to the institution of the market. There must be additional accompanying institutions (either formal or informal) which encode some further shared beliefs and which will help guide behaviour in markets.

Secondly, and perhaps somewhat surprisingly in view of the first point, I am not pessimistic about the conjunction of markets and the advance of pluralism. This is because there is scope for further types of agreement in pluralist societies and these in turn can form the basis for the shared background beliefs (or institutions) which enable markets to work.

In part these arguments arise because there seem, in practice, to be considerable overlaps in beliefs even in relatively thoroughgoing pluralist societies. In other words, societies rarely literally 'agree only to disagree'. This is a rather obvious point and so I have not dwelt upon it here. Instead, I have focused on the case where groups do indeed 'agree only to disagree' and I have argued that even this weak agreement entails a further commitment to a principle of justice which will be helpful to the operation of markets. This is not Rawl's Theory of Justice, even though it is sometimes cast in this role. Instead, it is the principle of equal relative concession. This principle should appeal to agents who are politically committed to pluralism but share no other substantive view because it is the only principle which satisfies the condition of universalizability under these conditions. Consequently institutions which embody this principle will seem ideally suited to societies that value pluralism but which are in all other respects deeply divided.

## ACKNOWLEDGEMENTS

This chapter was originally prepared as a paper for the Conference on Pluralism in Economics, at which many useful comments were made. I am particularly appreciative of the comments from the discussant of the paper, Maurice Lagueux, and I hope to have responded to some of his points in this version of the paper.

## NOTE

1. This is not the place for a detailed discussion of the principle of equal relative concession, but two comments are worth making to anticipate some possible objections. First, the application of the principle requires that each party's preferences should be publicly known and this might seem to be a weakness. Of course, this is not unusual in discussions of the bargaining problem and it might be defended by appealing to the various schemes economists have proposed for encouraging truthful revelation of preferences. Alternatively it might be defended as the first step from which we can develop more practical versions. In other words it is a first-best exercise which can be modified later, if necessary, for a second-best world where this information is not readily available. Secondly, the principle of equal relative concession does not always satisfy the condition of Pareto optimality in three or more person bargaining games; and this too is sometimes regarded as a weakness. However, the bargaining games where this problem arises are quite peculiar and while transgressions of the Pareto principle may worry economists, the principle has never appealed to political theorists in the same way because it fails to respect individual rights.

## REFERENCES

Cornwall, J. (1993), *The Theory of Economic Breakdown*, New York: M.E. Sharpe.

Hargreaves Heap, S. (1994), 'Conflict resolution in plural (and post-modern) societies', University of East Anglia Discussion Paper.

Kreps, D. (1990), *Game Theory and Economic Modeling*, New York: Oxford University Press.

O'Neill, O. (1989a), *Constructions of Reason: Explorations of Kant's Practical Philosophy*, Cambridge: Cambridge University Press.

O'Neill, O. (1989b), *Justice, Gender and International Boundaries*, WIDER Working Paper, 68.

Rawls, J. (1992), *Political Liberalism*, New York: Colombia University Press.

Riker, W. (1982), *Liberalism against Populism*, New York: W.H. Freeman.

Roth, Alvin (1988), 'Laboratory experimentation in economics: a methodological overview', *Economic Journal*, **98**, pp. 974–1031.
Sugden, R. (1991), 'Rational bargaining', in S. Hurley and M. Bacharach (eds), *Foundations of Decision Theory*, Oxford: Basil Blackwell.
Varoufakis, Y. (1991), *Rational Conflict*, Oxford: Basil Blackwell.

# COMMENT

**Maurice Lagueux**

By contrast with most chapters in this volume, Shaun Hargreaves Heap's chapter is concerned not with pluralism in the context of methodology, but rather with pluralism in the context of socio-political relations. The chapter addresses the question of which institutional arrangements would be most consonant with a society where people agreed on nothing but the right to disagree, taking this as the limiting case of a pluralistic society.

But what is this pluralism about? Depending on the context, the chapter refers either to a plurality of tastes or to a plurality of interests, but more often to pluralities of views, ideas and principles. And, what is considered an 'institutional arrangement'? A free market is clearly a straightforward example of such a thing, but it is important to note that the author has in mind quite varied types of institutional factors including what he describes as 'extraneous information' encoded in behaviour.

After devoting a sizable part of his chapter to discarding both an unrestricted free market and institutions derived from Rawls's principles as appropriate institutional arrangements for fully satisfying the requirements of such a pluralistic society, Hargreaves Heap concludes that the institutional acceptance of the principle of equal relative concession would constitute the only universalizable solution to this problem – and consequently the only acceptable one. I shall not discuss the author's views concerning the free market or concerning Rawls's principles, and shall instead concentrate on his solution. Before providing a useful formalization of the principle of equal relative concession in terms of cardinal utility, Hargreaves Heap correctly underscores the fact that utility numbers are 'strictly incommensurable between groups', especially in a pluralistic society. Consequently, interpersonal comparisons of utility must absolutely be avoided. To deal with cardinal utility in such a context, the gambit embodied in the principle is to equate not quanta of utility but ratios of utility which are pure numbers. It is not quite clear, however, that the interpersonal trap can be avoided in this way. The formula suggests that the part of A's possible gains in utility which has to be equalized with some part of B's possible gains in utility is, for both, the third part, for example. However, it is not clear that the reasons for avoiding interpersonal comparisons of utility do not also command us to avoid the interpersonal comparisons of such ratios which, after all, have to be privately derived by each member of society.

Let us try to use an example to see whether the principle of equal relative concession could work in a strictly pluralistic society. Suppose that A is a radical ecologist who claims that no nuclear reactor should ever be built and, accordingly, devotes his whole life to attaining this goal. And suppose that B is an industrial developer convinced that the future welfare of humanity depends on the multiplication of nuclear reactors. If we suppose further than both readily agree only to disagree, these two opposite views would be quite acceptable in Hargreaves Heap's pluralistic society. Now, if the principle of equal relative concession were to be encoded in the behaviour of both agents, A would tend to say, 'My firm conviction is that I must fight with my last breath against the construction of even a single nuclear reactor, but if you are right to claim that you both can and will build ten of them, I would accept that, let us say, five of them be constructed in so far as you agree to abandon the other five. Indeed, the utility I would obtain by this restriction to your nuclear reactor programme is merely a fraction of the utility I would obtain by a total ban on your ten reactors, but I estimate this fraction to be roughly the same as the fraction of the utility you will get by constructing five reactors in relation to the utility that ten would have provided. I hope that you will make more or less the same estimate.' If such a reaction really illustrates the type of behaviour that results from the general acceptance of the principle of equal relative concession in a pluralistic society, this means that there would no longer be any room in that society for extremist views. Both extremist and moderate ecologists would be similar in their equally reasonable popensity to compromise; consequently, this society would no longer be a pluralistic society.

Since there is no reason to fix the trade-off bar at five reactors rather than any other point between zero and ten, a sensible trade-off would suppose a private assessment by each party of various levels of *possible* utility. But how would B determine the level of utility he would gain by constructing the essentially indeterminate number of nuclear reactors he can reasonably expect to build over his whole lifetime? In this bargaining situation, extremists would naturally tend to hide their preferences. It is true, as Hargreaves Heap mentions in a footnote, that economists have proposed various schemes 'for encouraging truthful revelation of preferences', but I doubt that these schemes could cope with the above situation. Indeed, the problem is not so much a matter of sincerity but of the private assessment of preferences regarding an ideal which allows for no compromise. Since the principle supposes the comparison of a fraction of A's private assessment of utility attached by A to the realization of such an ideal with a fraction of B's private assessment of the utility attached by B to an opposite but equally radical ideal, I do not see how the problem of interpersonal comparisons can be avoided.

A large part of the trouble arises because the problem of pluralism is treated as a case of pie-sharing between two individuals with unequal taste for pie. In such a situation, a 'gentlemen's agreement' based on the principle of equal relative concession would be quite acceptable. But in a pluralistic society where many of its members are opposed on matters of principle, there is no point in looking for a 'gentlemen's agreement'. Naturally, the principle can serve as a useful guideline for a referee in a position to make *mandatory* decisions, but in such a case, we would no longer find ourselves in a strictly pluralistic society.

But what about the idea of looking for a universalizable rule? This idea is well-grounded in so far as it refers to a very general rule that everybody is in a position to apply. Those referred to by Kant, Hayek and Rawls are of this type. By contrast, a rule such as 'act in such a way that a general equilibrium will prevail' does not qualify; this is not because it cannot be adopted in principle by everybody but because there is no point in requiring everybody to apply it. According to me, it is for similar reasons that the principle of equal relative concession is largely unapplicable, especially in a pluralistic society made up of a large number of people defending a variety of views including extremist views on matters of principle.

Without a doubt, Shaun Hargreaves Heap has argued convincingly against the too-easy association often made between political pluralism and a free market, but this does not mean that he has convincingly made a case for the principle of equal relative concession.

# Afterword: can methodological pluralism be a methodological canon?

**Ernesto Screpanti**

## 1. INTRODUCTION

The answer is no. And this is the case, whether one follows a realist or a postmodern approach. Scientific realism and postmodernism are two philosophical attitudes toward methodological matters which are polarizing the attention of scholars in these times of post-methodology.

Realist approaches are based on some strong foundations concerning both ontology and epistemology.[1] Objective reality is believed to be endowed with a structure which can be known independently of the subjective viewpoints of the scientists. It is furthermore maintained that, although scientists adopt different theoretical systems and although their knowledge might by theory-laden and uncertain, checking with observational data gathered from objective reality is nevertheless a deciding criterion of truth. The goal of science is to assert true propositions about reality, and propositions are considered true if reality is in fact as they state. In this perspective there can be but one truth. It is towards truth that science, albeit asymptotically and dubiously, tends. The existence of a plurality of methods and theories may be recognized, but cannot be considered as intrinsically desirable. Indeed it is admitted only as a consequence of the complexity of reality and the limitations of human reason. Science must, however, aim to overcome it. From a realist point of view, pluralism cannot be encouraged, and endeavours are recommended to get over it. This is argued in section 2.

In postmodern approaches ontology ceases to be a problem.[2] While it is recognized that each particular theoretical system refers to its own specific set of ontological assumptions, it is denied that the Methodologist, Epistemologist, Philosopher or any other kind of meta-theorist is able to postulate an ontology that is not theory-laden and which is therefore above the specific theoretical systems elaborated by scientists. Even the legitimacy of the profession of the Methodologist, as a theorist *super partes,* is denied. It is maintained that it is impossible to get away from the partiality of discourses, let alone to provide methodological canons from outside scientific research. No meta-scientific prescriptions are admitted. So, while acknowledging the existence of a plurality of methods, it must also be recognized that, from a postmodernist standpoint, not even pluralism can be prescribed as a methodological canon. This is argued in section 3.

In the conclusions the author takes a stand in the dispute between realists and postmodernists, showing that the postmodern deconstruction of Methodology is the only way out of the difficulties occasioned by the realist obsession with ontology.

## 2. METHODOLOGICAL PLURALISM AGAINST REALISM

The insistence on ontology by contemporary realist epistemologists originates from an urgency to react to an alleged postmodern scepticism. These philosophers believe that it is necessary to refer to an objective reality if scepticism and relativism, not to mention idealism, are to be avoided. From this comes the 'great axiom of ontology': a reality exists which is independent of the subjectivity of the scientists investigating it. What this axiom says is that an objective reality exists and is unique. And this is plain, if not trivial; nobody would deny it. Even those who insist on the multifariousness of the real world (Dow, Chapter 5 in this volume) do not mean that many real worlds exist, but only that the one world is multifaceted. Thus what really matters, here, is not the content of the axiom but the necessity to posit it. The realists need to postulate the great ontological axiom in order to found a realist epistemology.

In fact there is yet another fundamental proposition which, in realist stances, is always associated with the axiom of ontology. It is a proposition with fundamental methodological implications and which could thus be called the 'great axiom of methodology'. It goes like this: the validity of a theory can be justified on the ground of a matching with observational data inferred from objective reality. In the light of this axiom it is easier to understand the importance of that relating to ontology and, above all, the necessity for it from the viewpoint of a realist foundation of methodology. It is evident that without an absolute ontology there can be no realist methodology. From a realist point of view any methodological recommendation must be founded ontologically.

Is it possible to reconcile this position with methodological pluralism? The realist philosopher who professes methodological pluralism may claim that encouraging the development of a plurality of methods is a methodological canon which contributes to getting closer to the truth. A canon of this kind is often justified on the ground of two assumptions. On the one hand it is held that reality, although unique, is multifaceted and variable. On the other hand, the uncertain nature and theory-ladenness of knowledge is recognized, and is at times accounted for in terms of weakness of induction (no proposition on reality can be inductively demonstrated with certainty), and at times in terms of bounded rationality (the human mind is too limited when confronted with the complexity of the real world).

It should, however, be noted that while these two assumptions can easily account for methodological *plurality*, i.e. the *de facto* existence of a plurality of methods, they are unable to justify a stance in favour of methodological pluralism in a realist view. In fact, if there is one reality which can be known independently of the subjective viewpoints of scientists, there must be but one truth. If truth can be ascertained through checking with data, the theory that asserts it can be but one. And if reality is multifaceted, then many partial truths may exist, visions of the same world from different perspectives. But they will, however, be complementary truths, parts of one potentially general truth. The plurality of methods and theories with which the various parts of reality are approached does not imply substitutability. It remains true that if two truths are complementary they can be integrated in, or subsumed under, a more general theory, whereas if they are alternative they cannot both be true. If difficulties are encountered in an attempt to integrate two partial theories, it may be due to the subject's limited cognitive capacities. But this limitation and the ensuing plurality of theories and methods cannot be considered as a positive fact. On the contrary: the only canon admissible from a realist point of view, faced with the existence of a plurality of theories and methods, is to make efforts ultimately to overcome it. Methodological plurality may be recognized as a lamentable necessity but methodological pluralism can only be condemned. Even if it is accepted that methodological plurality is a situation which continually returns, so that it is impossible to definitely overcome it, the methodological prescription can only be directed towards getting over it. Only methodological monism can be founded on the great axiom of ontology and the great axiom of methodology. Methodological monism may be as virtual and imperfect as you like, but it is still necessary as a precept for overcoming the plurality of methods and theories.

It might seem that a way out of this impasse would be to admit that the complexity of the world is so great and epistemological uncertainty so radical that it is impossible to confirm a truth or a theory by appealing to data that reflect in some way objective reality. In this case it is acknowledged that any form of scientific verification, or even falsification, is inexorably afflicted by radical uncertainty. An apparently plausible foundation would emerge: the multiplication of methods and theories devised to attack the complexity of reality could at least serve to increase the probability of striking the right conjecture.[3] Maybe rather a bold foundation but the only one that seems compatible with realism. This attitude is typical of 'fallibilism', an approach in which methodological pluralism is accepted as a *critical* tool. But in so far as fallibilism is coupled with realism it inevitably leads to methodological monism. Fallibilists like Caldwell, for example, endeavour to seek plurality and then try to reduce it through criticism. At any rate, this is a weakened form of realism: a realist philosophy which, while remaining faithful to the great axiom of ontology, is prepared to give up that of methodology. But what use is the ontological axiom when one gives up the methodological one, if it is true that the necessity for positing the former derives from the will to safeguard the latter? It is precisely from the reply to this question that the postmodern attitude towards ontology originates.

## 3. POSTMODERNISM AGAINST METHODOLOGICAL PLURALISM

To mitigate the realists' preoccupations it must be made clear from the outset that no serious postmodern philosopher has ever denied the existence of objective reality. What is denied is that knowledge is independent of scientists' particular points of view. It is not objective reality but objective *truth* that is denied by postmodernists. And this is perhaps one of the few strong propositions that unite all the diverse postmodern approaches to the methodological problem.

On the other hand, neither do postmodern philosophers deny the fact that in their research activity scientists almost invariably, perhaps even inevitably, resort to hypotheses of an ontological kind – hypotheses which in the majority of cases are often assumed *a priori*, real forms of metaphysics. What is denied is that these forms of metaphysics are univocal. On the contrary it is recognized that different, even discordant, but undoubtedly numerous, forms of metaphysics exist within each discipline.

These forms of metaphysics are accepted as valid within the context of the specific theoretical systems that generate them. For this reason we could call them 'local metaphysics'. They perform two primary functions, a heuristic and a methodological one: they help in defining the field of research and justifying the truths reached. It is natural therefore that the existence of a plurality of local metaphysics must be matched with the existence of a similar plurality of local methods, i.e. methods accepted as valid only within specific theoretical systems.

It should be stressed that this plurality of methods and metaphysics not only spans across the disciplines, but also within each discipline. It may therefore be a matter of plurality of substitutes rather than complements. On the other hand, it is substitutability, not complementarity, that makes the phenomenon of methodological plurality interesting and worth studying.

It goes without saying that each single form of local metaphysics must espouse the great axiom of ontology. Thus this axiom is of use to someone. In point of fact it is of some use to scientists. And this is recognized by postmodern philosophers. What is denied, however, is that it could be of use to methodologists or, better, that it could be used as a foundation for Methodology. For a better understanding of this argument it is necessary to enter into the postmodern explanation of methodological plurality.

To account for the existence of a plurality of methods and theories, it is not to a property of objective reality that recourse is made but to some properties of scientific subjects. Arguments about complexity and radical uncertainty are not refused, but they are justified in a peculiar way.

In fact, complexity is explained as a product of the subjects' activity. It is not the world in itself that is complex but rather the way in which subjects perceive it (Delorme, Chapter 6 in this volume). And here the hypothesis of bounded rationality comes to the fore. Because of their poor ability to collect and elaborate information, scientists perceive the world as complex.

More important for the problem at issue, however, is how radical uncertainty is accounted for. There are four characteristics of scientific activity which in different ways and with varying degrees of awareness are brought to light by various postmodern approaches.

The first is *sociality*. Scientific research is not a product of the individual scientist's mind. It is instead the result of a collective activity and is necessarily influenced by the various social contexts in which it takes place. These social contexts are structured in concentric circles which go from the restricted scientific community of those colleagues with whom the scientist directly interacts to the wider community defined by cultural communication apparatuses (journals, books, conferences, etc.); but they go further afield, even as far as to include the community that upholds the cultural tradition to which the scientist refers, or the social and political aggregates which, directly or indirectly, consciously or unconsciously, prompt the demand for science.

The second and third characteristics are *constructiveness* and *self-reference*. I group these two together because in this way they are easier to understand. Science does not reflect the world. Science creates worlds (Goodman, 1978). Research activity is intended to be an activity for the production of software, for the construction of fictitious worlds. This is constructiveness. Models, theories and analytical schemes provide knowledge, not because they reflect or describe reality but because they mimic it. On the other hand, postmodern approaches tend in different ways to highlight the fact that scientific discourse is wrapped up in itself. When a theory refers to something else it refers to another theory. This is *self-reference*. Even empirical data imply self-reference. In fact they are conceived as a product of scientific research: the result of selective perception guided by theory. Thus the explanation of a fact (or the solution to a problem) turns out to be none other than a reference to a fact that has already been explained (or a problem that has already been solved). Metaphor is the basic instrument of knowledge. A theoretical model is conceived as a semiotic construct which aims to direct the mind to another model whose capacity to *represent* reality is taken for granted from the scientific community. To represent and mimic the world (as in the theatre); not to photograph, nor even to mirror, nature (Rorty, 1979): this is what science does. Scientists need to recreate the world in order to understand it, which means that the cognitive function of science cannot be defined by moving out of the sphere of subjectivity, however concrete and collective this subjectivity may be. But if things go like that, what is the relationship that binds science to objective reality?

This is where the fourth characteristic comes into play: *pragmatism*. Science is an instrument of action. By creating models of the world, scientists build the instruments to modify it. So, while it is true that each theoretical model is always and in any case epistemically arbitrary, it is not true that one model is as good as another. The best models are those which provide better instruments for modifying the world. Not only are empirical research and laboratory activity not downgraded by this way of conceiving science but, on the contrary, they are exalted. The validity of a theory can indeed be assessed, and the best way of checking whether a theory works, before even trying it out in the world, is to test it in the laboratory. Of course, because of the complexity of the division of labour that exists in modern intellectual communities, a single cog in the machine may remain unaware of the final outcome of its work. Thus the individual scientist may be quite convinced that knowledge is cultivated for the sake of knowledge. The real subject of science is not, however, the individual scientist but the wider social community. Now, if theoretical activity as such is unable to escape from itself then the only real link existing between science and the objective world is pragmatic rather than epistemic. Postmodernists are not very impressed by the great ontological axiom (Benedetti and Solari, Chapter 3 in this volume). 'What is matter? never mind; what is mind? does not matter' – goes an English saying which postmodernists could well take to heart. But they cannot tolerate the methodological axiom and tend to substitute it with another, less ambitious and more down to earth: the proof of the pudding is in the eating.

It is a fact that the social world is made up of many different individuals, each with different aims and different ways of looking at the world, and consequently with different cognitive interests. This is how theoretical plurality is explained: humans have different tastes and make different puddings.

Methodological plurality is explained by the same token. In fact a method is none other than a theoretical construct itself and does not escape the law of scientific self-reference. Every theoretical system is associated with a suitable methodological apparatus. Obviously this need not be a one-to-one mapping. And it may happen that the same method is adopted by different theoretical systems. But there is no reason to expect that all theoretical systems submit to the same method. Numerous methods may exist simply because of the existence of a plurality of theories. In short, methodological plurality cannot be explained in terms of ontology nor on the ground of any property of the object. It is explained on the ground of some properties of the subjects. In particular it is accounted for in terms of two propositions. First, because of the constructiveness and self-reference of scientific practice, methodological discourse cannot be placed in a metascientific sphere. Second, because of the pragmatism and sociality of science, given the multiplicity of social subjects, there may be numerous methods associated with theoretical systems.

In this way radical uncertainty is also accounted for: people like different types of puddings and *de gustibus non est disputandum*. There is no way of ascertaining, of assessing with certainty, the truth of a theory. Every truth is theory-laden. Every method is theory-laden. Every theory is subjective. There is no escape from the circle of subjectivity.

Thus we can return to posing the main problem of this note. Can methodological pluralism be justified or founded somehow? In view of the impasse which realist philosophers come up against with this problem, can a postmodern way out be found? Alas! …

Postmodernists tend to recommend immediate abolition of the profession of Methodologist. Not, mind you, the methods: not the methodological discourses which scientists themselves are driven to make out of necessity to assess the various theories they work on. As already said, methods, like metaphysics, are constructs of local importance and heuristic value, products of the same constructive activity that produces science. The possibility of taking a point of view *outside* that activity, a point of view from which to assess all the specific theories and valid for all, is not admitted. A method that is not local cannot exist. No meta-method is granted. Scientists are entitled to construct methods or to choose those which are must suitable for appraising their theories. The Methodologist, i.e. the methodologist *super partes*, can be of no help to them. No researcher has a privileged supporting basis on the strength of which he can say which is the best method and what is truth. The normative or prescriptive function of Methodology must be abolished.

But if it is not possible, *from outside science*, to say that one method is better than another, that one theory is better than another, then nor is it possible to say that many methods are better than just a few. The advocacy of methodological pluralism cannot be a methodological precept.

## 4. CONCLUSIONS

Today methodological pluralism is the fashion. It was proposed as a temporary and stop-gap solution to problems arising on the death of Popperian thought (Caldwell, 1982, 1988). But a great number of philosophers immediately accepted it as a way out of the difficulties generated by the acknowledgement of epistemological uncertainty and the inescapable theory-ladenness of truths. Nevertheless as soon as an attempt is made to justify it rationally and find some kind of strong foundation, the difficulties return to the surface.

The position of modern realists is particularly uneasy. In an attempt to save what remains of the concept of truth as correspondence, and find new foundations for a non-relativist epistemology, they have had to resort to postulating a strong ontology and a strong methodology. And it is precisely methodological pluralism that brings the fundamental difficulties to light.

As shown in section 2, the great axioms of ontology and methodology do not admit methodological pluralism. Only if one gives up the latter axiom is a pluralist position acceptable. But by giving up the latter the former is condemned to irrelevance. What use is it to know that an objective reality exists as a field of scientific research if it is recognized that the latter cannot draw on it with any certainty? Or worse still, if the appeal to data 'reflecting' objective reality cannot serve decisively to settle a theoretical question and least of all to confirm a truth?

In other words: either recourse to some form of objective checking serves to resolve theoretical controversies – and in this case the existence of a plurality of methods must be judged as a consequence of human error, a blemish and a limit of science rather than as a virtue to recommend; or methodological pluralism is to be encouraged as a weapon for the defence from the limitations of human reason – but in this case the appeal to data inferred from objective reality must be recognized as fairly irrelevant for epistemological aims.

This debâcle re-opens those doors to postmodern 'relativism' which realists intend to bar. But postmodernists are less able than realists to profess a pluralist faith, if pluralism is intended as a methodological canon. They, in fact, were the ones who buried Methodology, together with Popper – Methodology intended as a form of meta-criticism of scientific discourse. Postmodernists can no longer prescribe anything.

Rather a disappointing conclusion, it is admitted; but certainly not a meaningless one. We set out by demonstrating that it is impossible to found methodological pluralism from a realist point of view, and reached the conclusion that it is also impossible to do so from a postmodern point of view. So where does the validity of methodological pluralism lie? Why should we recommend it to our colleagues and students?

The answer is simple and perhaps no less disconcerting than the question. Methodological pluralism is not a methodological canon; it is only an ethical precept. Methodological pluralism is none other than the application of the principle of tolerance to scientific activity. It serves to liberate the flow of discourses in the contest of truths.

## ACKNOWLEDGEMENTS

Without bearing any responsibility, Bruce Caldwell, Daniel M. Hausman, Warren Samuels and D. Wade Hands deserve my warmest thanks for their comments on an earlier draft of this chapter.

## NOTES

1. Outside positivism, Bhaskar (1987) is one of the most important realist epistemologists of the present time. As far as economics is concerned, different forms of realist approaches to Methodology are cultivated by various students of institutionalist orientation. Lawson (1994, Chapter 1 in this volume), Mäki (1989, Chapter 2 in this volume) and Caldwell (1982) are three outstanding examples.
2. The postmodern attitude is perhaps even more diffused than the realist among institutionalist economists, and this is possibly ascribable to the pragmatist heritage of institutionalist thought. The present revival of this heritage is mainly due to Rorty (1979). The views of McCloskey (1986), Samuels (1991, Chapter 4 in this volume) and Weintraub (1989) are illustrative of the postmodern attitude in economics. On the other hand, the hermeneutic heritage contributed to the penetration of postmodernism among the neo-Austrians, for which see Lavoie (1990).
3. A similar view was put forward by the early Feyerabend (1962, 1970). Caldwell (1988) acutely observed that Feyerabend was driven to his postmodern turn by the logical difficulties of that view.

## REFERENCES

Bhaskar, R. (1987), *A Realist Theory of Science*, 2nd edition, Brighton: Harvester Press.

Caldwell, B.J. (1982), *Beyond Positivism: Economic Methodology in the Twentieth Century*, London: Allen & Unwin.

Caldwell, B.J. (1988), 'The Case for Pluralism', in N. De Marchi (ed.), *The Popperian Legacy in Economics*, Cambridge: Cambridge University Press, pp. 231–44.

Feyerabend, P.K. (1962), 'Explanation, Reduction and Empiricism', in H. Feigl, G.

Maxwell and M. Scriven (eds), *Minnesota Studies in the Philosophy of Science*, vol. III, Minneapolis: University of Minnesota Press, pp. 28–97.
Feyerabend, P.K. (1970), 'How to Be a Good Empiricist: A Plea for Tolerance in Matters Epistemological', in B. Brody (ed.), *Readings in the Philosophy of Science*, Englewood Cliffs, NJ: Prentice-Hall, pp. 312–42.
Goodman, N. (1978), *Ways of Worldmaking*, Cambridge, MA: Hackett.
Lavoie, D. (ed.) (1990), *Economics and Hermeneutics*, London: Routledge.
Lawson, T. (1994), 'Why Are so Many Economists so Opposed to Methodology?', *Journal of Economic Methodology*, **1**, pp. 105–33.
McCloskey, D. (1986), *The Rhetoric of Economics*, Brighton: Wheatsheaf.
Mäki, U. (1989), 'On the Problem of Realism in Economics', *Ricerche Economiche*, **43**, pp. 176–98.
Rorty, R. (1979), *Philosophy and the Mirror of Nature*, Princeton: Princeton University Press.
Samuels, W.J. (1991), '"Truth" and "Discourse" in the Social Construction of Economic Reality: An Essay in the Relation of Knowledge to Socioeconomic Policy', *Journal of Post Keynesian Economics*, **13**, pp. 511–24.
Weintraub, E.R. (1989), 'Methodology doesn't Matter, but the History of Thought Might', *Scandinavian Journal of Economics*, **91**, pp. 477–93.

## METHODOLOGICAL PLURALISM: THE DISCUSSION IN RETROSPECT

**Warren J. Samuels**

Ernesto Screpanti's Afterword reaches sensible conclusions which I believe are entirely or substantially congruent with the position of methodological pluralism. These conclusions can be reached only if one avoids extreme or indefensible positions on all sides of the issues, whether they involve ontology or epistemology.

Let me make the following points on matters as I, for one, see them.

It is indeed impossible to found methodological pluralism on a realist point of view. Methodological pluralism is a principle of tolerance in both ontological and epistemological matters. Even if we were all philosophical (or scientific) realists we still would likely disagree as to the substantive content of, as well as the means of studying, reality. Yes, there is an economy, an object of study, but that does not get us very far in dealing with whether the economy is a system of harmony or of conflict or whether Adam Smith's, Karl Marx's, Alfred Marshall's, Thorstein Veblen's, John R. Commons's, John Maynard Keynes's, Joseph A. Schumpeter's, Friedrich von Hayek's, John Kenneth Galbraith's or Robert Lucas's picture of it is correct. Philosophical or scientific realism should not be used to legitimize a particular view of reality. This is particularly important because, at least arguably, the economy continues to undergo a process of social construction, in part on the basis of our conception of it.

Similarly, methodological pluralism – an epistemological position – should not be approached and interpreted solely from a realist ontological position, one which would require of methodological pluralism an ontology and a methodology based thereon. Methodological pluralists are agnostic with regard to ontology in general and to realism in particular. From the point of view of methodological pluralism, realism, through its axioms, assumes the point at issue, and analysing methodological pluralism from a realist perspective necessarily assumes its position on that point.

The realist argument requiring one and only one true theory is not acceptable even when methodological pluralism accepts the existence of more or less objective reality. For one thing, that objectivity is only more or less. Second, the reality is arguably in the process of social construction. And third, there is no conclusive *a priori* reason to assume that the reality, such as it is, is homogeneous and universally so. The object of study may be heterogeneous, subject to many theories, such that no one true theory can be correct.

Methodological pluralism does not reject the concept of truth, meaning thereby descriptive accuracy and/or correct explanation. Methodological pluralism cautions against jumping to conclusions as to what is true, based on ontological, epistemological or substantive preconceptions. Methodological pluralism also claims that much of what is taken to be economic knowledge (and therefore deemed to be within the ambit of the category of 'truth') is not truth at all but tools. Thus it is that John R. Hicks, for example, considered that concepts, models, theories, etc. are tools of analysis, not necessarily definitions of reality themselves. A cautious practice of ontology or of epistemology would not jump to premature conclusions in these matters.

Apropos of truth, I would also insist that pragmatism is *not* a theory of truth, though it has often been treated as such. Pragmatism is an approach to human meaning in terms of instrumental usefulness. It is not a theory of truth in the sense of accurate description and/or correct explanation, though in its approach to human meaning and instrumental usefulness pragmatism, too, must be concerned with truth in those senses.

Methodological pluralism not only does not reject the category of truth, it does not call for the abolition of methodology (epistemology). The objection is to absolutist presciptivist epistemological positions. Methodological pluralism calls for the identification of a variety of epistemological approaches and credentials, leaving it to the researcher to evaluate and accept/reject them as he or she will. Whereas the prescriptivist role would be abolished, the methodological pluralist would continue to insist on the establishment of epistemological credentials, and the correlative identification of the credentials of particular propositions as claims to knowledge.

The bottom line may be encapsulated in the question: is there only one correct theory of what capitalism is all about? Capital? Interest? Macroeconomics? Competition? Etc. From the Hicksian point of view, these concepts are tools; from the pragmatist point of view, they are useful as tools in comprehending – and, yes, evaluating – what 'works', which is a subjective category.

# Index